The Dream of Civilized Warfare

The Dream of Civilized Warfare

World War I Flying Aces and the American Imagination

Linda R. Robertson

University of Minnesota Press
Minneapolis • London

To Paul T. Povinelli, Ph.D.

The publication of this book was assisted by a bequest from Josiah H. Chase to honor his parents, Ellen Rankin Chase and Josiah Hook Chase, Minnesota territorial pioneers.

Published by the University of Minnesota Press
111 Third Avenue South, Suite 290
Minneapolis, MN 55401–2520
http://www.upress.umn.edu

Library of Congress Cataloging-in-Publication Data

Robertson, Linda R. (Linda Raine), 1946–
    The dream of civilized warfare : World War I flying aces and the
American imagination / Linda R. Robertson.
        p. cm.
Includes bibliographical references and index.
    ISBN 0-8166-4270-2 (hard. : alk. paper)
    1. World War, 1914–1918—Aerial operations, American. 2. World War,
1914–1918—Campaigns—Western Front. 3. Heroes. 4. Fighter pilots.
5. World War, 1914–1918—Social aspects—United States. 6. War and
society—United States. I. Title.
D606 .R63 2003
940.4′4973—dc21
                                                    2003013284

Printed in the United States of America on acid-free paper

The University of Minnesota is an equal-opportunity educator and employer.

12 11 10 09 08 07 06 05 04 03   10 9 8 7 6 5 4 3 2 1

Contents

Acknowledgments

I wish to express my gratitude to the helpful archivists at the manuscript reading room of the British Imperial War Museum, where they and the scholars they so ably assist sweltered in the heat of the rotunda reading room in late summer 1995. Equally helpful there were the curators for the posters and art collections and for the photographic archives.

I was assisted in my research on Theodore Roosevelt by the librarians of the rare book and manuscript collections in the Carl A. Kroch Library at Cornell University, Ithaca, New York.

Helpful and productive guidance in locating records and correspondence relevant to the recruitment drive of the U.S. Air Service came from the archivists at the National Archives who specialize in the military history of World War I.

Valuable insights were inspired by exhibits at two museums in the region of the Somme, Historiale de la Grande Guerre (Peronne) and Musée des abris (Albert), and by visits to the memorials, gravesites, and preserved battlefield sites in the region of the Somme, many of which are under the supervision of the Commonwealth War Graves Commission.

This study was supported in part by research grants from Hobart and William Smith Colleges, Geneva, New York, which also contributed funding for borrowing privileges from the libraries of Cornell University. The Hobart and William Smith library also contained useful holdings for this study, and the reference librarians offered support and valuable information.

Professor Iva Deutchman in the political science department of Hobart and William Smith Colleges provided valuable support and encouragement throughout the period I worked on this study.

Gary Robertson was a valuable research assistant at the British Imperial War Museum and the battlefields of the Somme. Andy Robertshaw, education director at the British Museum of the Army, contributed highly useful historical information during a second tour of the battlefields of the Somme in 2001. Sharon Sutley provided valuable assistance in preparing the final draft of this manuscript.

I have reserved for last the individual to whom I owe my deepest debt of gratitude. Michael C. C. Adams is a rare brand of scholar, one who not only has chosen to investigate the social history of modern warfare, but who also manages to write at once with objective detachment, moral grounding, clarity, and skill with the English language. I had already learned much from reading his books, *The Best War Ever: America and World War II* and *The Great Adventure: Male Desire and the Coming of World War I.* My debt especially to the latter should be apparent in what follows. I regarded myself as fortunate to have had him as an early reader for this manuscript. In the subsequent iterations, I found him an extraordinarily fine guide and advisor, all the more exceptional given that it was entirely disinterested on his part. By that I mean that we have met only briefly and have neither school ties that link us nor a professional history. Whatever is meritorious in what follows owes more to him than possibly even he will recognize, and the weaknesses are entirely mine.

Introduction

This is the story of an air force that did not exist, except in the American imagination.

This is the story of how war-as-imagined gave birth to the dream that America could design, build, and fly the largest aerial armada in the world and use it to become the arbiter of war and peace.

This is the story of how a war-as-imagined was shaped by the forces of the mass media and state-sponsored propaganda, offering a promise that has shaped the American vision of air power as the foundation for America's emergence as the premier military force into the twenty-first century.

Telling the story of the seductive vision of American air power requires a different kind of attention than is usual for telling the story of the actual development of American air power, which came during World War II. As a cultural and political force, this vision took shape at the time the United States entered World War I. This study is an argument for the significance of that vision, although it was intangible and the American participation in World War I was too short to allow for the dream to be realized.[1]

When the United States entered World War I, two things were true. It did not have an air force, and there was a deep aversion to the prospect of sacrificing American lives to the slaughter of the ground war in Europe. Within four months of the declaration of war, the Wilson administration, key corporate interests, high-ranking members of the military, and the overwhelming majority of members of both houses of Congress were proclaiming that the United States would break the stalemate on the ground and turn the tide of war with a vast aerial armada of American-built planes—exceeding in number the total of all combatant air forces along the Western Front—flown by American pilots.

The United States did not have suitable planes, the designs to build them, or men trained to fly them. The absence of an air force was coupled with a nearly complete ignorance of the various uses of aircraft in combat developed by the European combatants during the war, and an overweening confidence in American technological know-how and production capacity. In other words, it was a plan unencumbered by facts and fueled by both fear of the potential losses in the trenches and hope that they could be averted by waging war from the air. By the end of the war, America was relying upon planes built by our allies, and Congress began conducting hearings into the failure of the vision.

The fantasy of a vast American aerial armada was fed in the public's imagination not only by the vague and exaggerated claims of elected officials and military leaders, but also by the images of the "knights of the air," the celebrated heroes of the sunlit skies flying for Great Britain and the Commonwealth nations, Germany, France, and Americans flying for the Lafayette Escadrille.

The influence of this publicity cannot be overestimated. Whatever Americans knew about air combat at the time the United States entered the war derived entirely from the mass media. An airplane was still a rare sight in the United States before the war, something one was more likely to see in the pictorial sections of the newspapers than actually flying through the skies. Air combat was invented during World War I, and the public's understanding of it derived from controlled sources of information, both in the form of overt propaganda and in the less obviously controlled accounts in the press, in newsreel footage, in ephemera bearing photographs of the great aces, and in their biographies and autobiographies.

To study the appeal of air combat takes us to the heart of the mechanisms for influencing the imagination, for shaping desire according the wishes of the state, and for the lasting impact these influences had not only on how war is recalled, but on how the expectations about future warfare reflected the engineered vision of warfare in the sky. My tracing the emergence of the dream of American air power during World War I follows two major lines of inquiry. The first considers how political and military leaders persuaded themselves and the American public that the United States could quickly build the largest aerial armada in the world and train the men to fly them, and that this would break the stalemate along the Western Front. The second considers how the cultural values assigned to the European aces were translated into an American idiom, resulting by the end of the war in a vision of the American ace as especially symbolic of American national values and character.

Part I. America Looks to the Skies

The declaration of war in April 1917 was quickly followed by the passage of the aviation appropriation bill of July 1917. It was the largest single appropriation bill passed to that date in the history of Congress, and it was passed without significant debate. Indeed, the press pilloried as near traitors those few congressmen who wished to raise what turned out to be very important questions about how the appropriations were to be spent. Its quick passage was accomplished by a combination of political hoopla about an American air force winning the war coupled with a nearly complete obfuscation of how the money would be spent. This celerity was justified as essential to saving American lives on the ground, making a virtue not only of necessity, but of the complete lack of information about the kinds of planes the United States would build, and who would profit from those decisions.

Rep. James R. Mann (R.-Ill.) gave one of the most significant speeches relevant to the war effort when he urged his colleagues to pass the bill quickly, comparing it favorably (and one must say, rather oddly) to "buying a pig in a poke." The *Washington Post* enthusiastically seconded the appeal to ignorance: "The American people don't care a rap about the defects of the airplane bill, if there are any defects."

Defects there were, and in such abundance that within a year the press was calling for hearings into the question of why the United States had failed to produce the promised armada. The sorry history of that initiative is summed up by a historian writing in 1940. The chapter title "196 Planes for 1 Billion Dollars" states the case succinctly. The chicanery, greed, and arrogance born of ignorance associated especially with the automotive industry is so patently a factor in the failure of the United States to live up to its promise that this moment in American history might be categorized as merely one in a string of scandals involving the government and monied interests on the way to constructing the military-industrial complex. But to do so would perpetuate the misperception that America's rise to the greatest air power the world has ever seen should be traced from the advent of American air power in World War II. This understanding misses the larger point, which is that the dream of dominance through air power, of exerting American will throughout the world without having to risk the lives of ground soldiers, and of relying on bombing to achieve that end, began at the time of America's entry into World War I.

In 1917 the United States did not have an air force and had no idea how to build one. This vacuum was filled by dreams and fantasy, or by what Secretary of War Newton Baker termed the belief in a "miracle." It was precisely because the vacuum was so complete that the dream could take on the dimensions that it did.

What filled the vacuum were promises that married the vision of air combat with the most powerful symbols of American exceptionalism, a message that stressed how ideally air combat suited the American character and inventive ingenuity. America would rescue Europe, mired in the mud, from the skies. All that was necessary, the military leader most responsible for promoting air power argued to the public and Congress, was to put the "Yankee punch into the air."

The search for inspiring symbolism for American warfare came at a time of profound changes in how the nation went to war. Two changes especially undermined the vision of the officer as charismatic leader and the soldier as individualist. The first was the advent of Selective Service; the second was the decision to no longer accept voluntary officers who had traditionally received an automatic commission. These shifts and what they portended were particularly evident in the dispute that arose between Theodore Roosevelt, who wanted to lead a voluntary militia to Europe, and Woodrow Wilson, who had no intention of allowing his political archrival to steal the symbolism of the war. Ultimately, the romance formerly associated with the volunteer and the officer—and epitomized in Roosevelt's leading an all-voluntary force in the charge up San Juan Hill—was transferred to the combat pilot, and along with it came an idealized image of both American values and masculinity.

Massive forces were brought into play to achieve this tectonic shift in the idealized American war-as-imagined. How America first dreamed the dream of air superiority fascinates as a study of historical forces because the image was fashioned from such flimsy threads of reality. This makes the ephemeral influences so obviously substantial. A synergy of state-sponsored propaganda, press reports, industrial public relations hoopla, political speeches, and political rivalry wove for the American public a magical vision of wars won from above, on the wings of eagles, without the need to shed American blood on foreign soil—or at least not as much of it as the public had reason to fear from the reports of the war along the Western Front.

The triumph of image over reality is made more obviously the greater achievement when considered in light of the yawning gap that existed between the vision and the reality of America's knowledge of and capacity for producing the largest aerial armada in the world. To tell the story in all its richness required excursions into various cubbyholes of history, far from the Western Front.

The first mise-en-scène is set in the inner sanctum of the military and the hushed offices of the secretary of war. It was in these corridors of power that the request from the French for the largest air armada in the world electrified American military, industrial, and political leaders into committing themselves to a vision that would ultimately shape the future of the United States as the world's dominant air power.

The scene then shifts to the floor of Congress, and to the influence of the press and the Committee for Public Information—the propaganda ministry established by Wilson—on its deliberations, as first the House and then the Senate were subjected to arguments for the quick passage of the largest military appropriation bill in the nation's history without the information necessary for an informed opinion.

The final scene seems at first consideration far removed from the examination of how Americans became mesmerized with air power. It reveals the fight between the traditional elites and the growing power of organized labor to claim the potent imagery associated with the voluntary commissioned officer. This struggle for control over the symbols of leadership was made all the more imperative by the resort to Selective Service, which some congressmen had reacted violently against as a breach of the most fundamental principles of American individualism, a breach that in their minds reduced American men to little more than slaves. The struggle over who would lead and whether there would be voluntary forces was played out most visibly in the clash of the two titans of the era, Roosevelt and Wilson. But the struggle also involved organized labor, who demanded that the officer class not be given over to an American aristocracy and members of the eastern seaboard elite, who prior to America's entry into World War I had organized summer businessman's training camps as a kind of propaganda of the deed in favor of the traditional elite assuming leadership over any army assembled to confront the Germans.

Ultimately, World War I brought with it the end to both the direct commission and all-voluntary, privately funded units. The symbolic potency of the volunteer warrior, and the individualism he embodied, was transferred to the pilot who flew alone into the skies.

Part II. The Images of the Ace

The desire to make America the supreme rescuer from the skies was fueled by the images of the European aces, which were well known to the American public by the time the United States entered the war. Georges Guynemer of France, Billy Bishop of Canada, and Manfred von Richthofen, known as the Red Baron, and Victor Chapman, who flew for the Lafayette Escadrille, were the idols of many Americans, especially young men far from the battlefield who dreamed of the glory of single-handed duels in the sky. If the stalemated war on the ground meant, as Wilson declared, that "war had lost all of its glory," the war in the air, the newest form of combat, was a powerful alternative. When the U.S. Air Service called for volunteers, the recruitment offices were so overwhelmed by the number of young men who presented themselves that many were turned away.

The glorious image of the ace originated in the dismal realities of the ground war. The Germans, French, and ultimately the British all found that concentrating attention on what many regarded as the least important aspect of the war—the role of the combat pilot—satisfied the public's longing for heroes and heroism in a way impossible to sustain by recounting experiences in the trenches, especially as the war dragged on.

What aspects of national aspirations the flyers were taken to represent varied from country to country. The French and the British linked the role of the ace to the *casus belli*, the defense of civilization against the barbarian at the gate. Crucial to this explanation were the atrocity stories laid at the feet of the German invaders. These accounts were told and retold, and investigated by both French and British authorities. These accounts were also used to engage the sympathy of the United States. When the United States entered the war the role of the Allies as Europe's rescuers from the barbarian was played out in the American idiom through lurid posters depicting the raping German beast, and in feature-length films that heightened the sense of melodrama and threat.

It was a small imaginative step from representing the Allies as defending civilization in a new crusade to representing the aces as a new order of knighthood. The appealing image of the new Galahads, of the boy-knights motivated solely by love of family and of country, gave birth to what remains the dominant trope for describing those who flew in World War I—the "knights of the sky."

This trope supported an array of culturally conservative meanings associated with the ruling class. But another image emerged which stood in sharp contrast with the image of the selfless knight. Billy Bishop, the great Canadian ace, and Bert Hall, who made a living from his image as a hero of the Lafayette Escadrille, both represented the self-made man, the individual who flew for personal aggrandizement, and whose identity was formed from competitive aggression. Billy Bishop toured the United States to promote his autobiography in which he bragged about his single-handed attack on a German aerodrome, an account that inspired skepticism from his squadron mates. Bert Hall became a vaudeville star, recounting his exploits while wearing both medals he had earned and some he had not.

The representation of the British and French aces as popularized in the United States before America entered the war embraced without acknowledgment these contradictions, which points toward the larger contest of the era between the feudal elites and the emerging parvenu classes, between an identity based upon duty and one based upon skill and celebrity. Whether presented as a selfless knight or as a man in search of personal glory, the ace emphasized individualism, the capacity of the individual to motivate himself to seek the enemy in a duel to the death, and the ability to control his destiny by bending the newest weapon of mechanized warfare to his will.

The German fighter emerged as skilled, pitiless, and efficient, a man who subordinated his will to both the machine and the discipline of the unit. Outnumbered in terms of both planes and the men to fly them, the Germans inflicted devastating casualties on the Allies time after time. The Germans were the first to perfect squadron flying, which depended upon defensive combat and unit discipline rather than upon taking the war to the enemy in the desire to gain sufficient individual victories to be named an ace. Initially, the Germans were sneered at as "cowards" by the Allies; ultimately, the superiority of their approach became obvious.

By the end of the war, a specifically American version of the ace had been formed from these various elements. The American ace, epitomized in the top-scorer from the top unit, Eddie Rickenbacker, borrowed some elements from the British imagery of both the chivalric hero and the ambitious self-made man, and some from the German image of the "new man," motivated by a machine-like efficiency and subordination to the unit.

The initial recruiting drives for American pilots were aimed at college men, and the dominant comparative imagery to their own experience was that of a football team. The imagery associated with squadron life also compared the life of a flyer to that of gentlemen game hunters gathered at an especially grand lodge, who flew out to the hunt twice a day. Sometimes the call to a patrol interrupted a tennis match, so the pilots flew in their tennis whites. But always, they returned to a three-course meal at a linen-covered table. And women were theirs for the asking. It was an especially civilized way for a gentleman to fight a war in defense of civilization.

Part III. Death and Transfiguration

The image of the aces was constructed initially by intelligence officers in their offices far from the front, who fed their accounts directly to reporters. Later in the war, the flyers themselves contributed to the publicity surrounding the imagery of the aces through the books and articles they wrote and even through the films in which they were the featured leads.

The problem with war heroes, obviously, is the danger that they will die, and indeed, the casualty rates among flyers, especially among the Allies, was very high. It is with regard to how death was configured, how it was used to represent the ultimate sacrifice of the hero, that the clearest index to the cultural values of the aces is found. The nature of the ground war gave rise to a number of what in retrospect can be regarded only as rather bizarre positive assertions about masculinity. Some argued that war had a genuinely therapeutic effect, rather like a high colonic, in purging the male spirit of the effeminacy, weakness, and lack of a sense of adventure brought about by a life made altogether too easy by the realities of middle-class life in the industrial age. Both the British and the American authorities found a benefit in the requirement that men revert to the "primitive," casting off the veneer of civilization, confronting head-on the overmastering passions of fear and the desire to kill or be killed.

This argument, as it turned out, was rather more determined by the nature of the ground war than by the nature of the air war. The air war came to symbolize the older, chivalric conception of the warrior as the embodiment of all that was best in civilization—constraint under pressure, fairness to one's enemies, skilled combat, and a willingness to sacrifice one's life on behalf of king and country. While the war-as-purgative argument placed the blame for both physical and moral degeneracy on civilization itself, the alternative version mated warfare with civilization. As a consequence, the role of the combat pilot wedded air wars with the image of civilized violence undertaken in the name of civilization, a connection between the mode of warfare and its purpose which was lost with the advent of brutal, mechanized warfare on the ground.

This meant, oddly enough, that how a pilot met his fate came to be invested with very significant meaning. An ace was supposed to be the master of his fate; if he was shot down, it was because by some momentary weakness or lapse he was defeated by an equally skilled enemy—rather the same mentality that is brought to Olympic sports events. For an ace to be shot down by ground fire, therefore, sent significant consternation through the ranks. This seems improbable to the uninitiated, but just how much it matters is revealed by the very serious competition between ground units and the Royal Air Force to claim credit for shooting down Baron von Richthofen. The dispute continues to this day and is the source of lively controversy.

The idea that an ace would be shot down only through his own recklessness emerged as a paramount principle for the American representation of the ace by the end of the war. The image of the ace is one of hypermasculinity, an individual who both embodies the highest national ideals and who cannot be defeated by death—an impossible image, yet one that captures the reason for the long-lived romance associated with the aces of World War I. They were men who rose to the skies to answer the seductive siren call, the tune of the dance of death. It is not the reality of the very high death rates and the toll on the human spirit, but the image of them engaged in that deadly dance that endures.

Epilogue: Democratizing War

At the end of World War I the elements of America's emergence as the most powerful nation relying on the most powerful air force were in place, awaiting realization in the subsequent wars of the century. The death of the flower of manhood along the Western Front gave the theorists of air war the idea that in the future the war should be carried directly to the civilians at home, what America's strongest advocate for a postwar air force, Billy Mitchell, called democratizing warfare. Certainly, Americans had a revulsion against bombing cities, but the plans for an American air force had from the outset of America's involvement in World War I included the concept of strategic bombing as the way to break the stalemate on the ground. The average American could not be fully aware of this intention because the hoopla and bravura surrounding the passage of the military aviation bill was strong on the glory of air power and vague to obscure on the subject of exactly what kind of air power was envisioned. This, coupled with the heavy emphasis on single air-to-air combat, naturally led to imagining a vast cavalry of American combat planes piloted by the men who epitomized American strength and values, a hyperbolized masculinity defined as a rich mix of individualism, team spirit, and celebrity.

From the perspective of the most recent use of America's air power—in the post-9/11 period—the realization of the original dream is complete. The use of American forces was persistently characterized as a defense of civilization; the use of precision weapons signals the restraint required for civilized violence. The reliance on nonprecision weapons is simply regrettable and not much discussed; the civilian casualties are equally to be lamented and are both unfortunate and unintended. What is absent is the glory assigned to the pilot who delivers the bombs, a product ultimately of the reality that America's air wars are inevitably disproportionate, the launching of American advanced technology against those who cannot muster any defense. What legitimates it is the relief that because America can strike with impunity from the air, the nation is spared ground casualties.

The questions that motivate this book are uncomplicated: What is it we have ignored in a moral sense in how we have imagined not the worst kind of combat, but the kind we admire? What has shaped our tolerance—if not admiration—for war we conduct from the air? How have the romantic images of air wars influenced the way we define for our boys what it means to be a man?

These questions are subsumed under the centrality of the focus on how a nation's imagination was influenced from 1914 to 1918, how America came to project itself ideally in terms of how it ought to conduct warfare. This self-image was shaped initially and primarily by messages composed for the purposes of state-sponsored propaganda, or to forward industrial interests, or for political ends. The failure to produce the imagined air force during World War I was far less significant to the growth of American air power than the lingering and seductive power of the original image of an American armada darkening the skies over Europe.

PART I
AMERICA LOOKS
TO THE SKIES

There is no doubt . . . that democratic governments must assume
the task, regardless of all complicating difficulties, of mobilizing minds
as well as men and money in war.

—Harold Lasswell, *Propaganda Techniques in the World War* (1927)

CHAPTER 1

"We Were Dealing with a Miracle"

The Fantasy of Air Power

The outcome of World War I was determined by the mobilization of vast resources of soldiers, material, manufacture, and transportation. It was also determined by information—who had it, who did not, and who controlled its distribution. The fantasy of winning the war from the air was born of both the absence of information and the control over it—a costly and lethal combination of innocent and willful ignorance—coupled with fear, hope, and greed: the fear of potentially high American casualties in the ground war; hope that an air force might turn the tide and that the news of an American air armada would bolster the flagging morale of the French; and greed especially on the part of those in the automotive industry who positioned themselves in remarkably porous relations with government officials to profit heavily from government contracts.

The Wilson administration joined forces within the military and private industry to persuade the American public to invest $1 billion in building from scratch an air force larger than the combined forces of the European combatants, while avoiding any precise mention of how exactly this force would be used, particularly when it came to plans to develop a strategic bombing force. Ultimately, the allocation yielded very few American-built planes utilized in combat (between 200 and 400 according to various estimates), a congressional hearing and a Justice Department investigation into corrupt practices, and a recommendation to court-martial one of the leading captains of industry who not only had received a commission as colonel but was also most involved in using airplane contracts to pursue patriotism for profit.

Since brought to light in 1918 as a consequence of both the Justice Department and congressional hearings, the corrupt practices and poor judgment of those in top decision-making roles have been recognized as key factors in the failure to develop an air force during World War I. The importance of the gap between what was promised and what was delivered, however, has not been considered for the influence it had on the public's imagination of the potential of air power. The public, press, and Congress were angered by the realization that the United States—lacking knowledge, experience, and airplanes—could not in a matter of months produce more planes than Germany and the European Allies combined. The bitterness of the reaction to this rather obvious reality indicates how powerful the heroic vision of Americans winning the war with airplanes was. It also indicates how limited the general understanding of air combat and how high the faith in it were—an almost magical vision of a little-understood but marvelous technology for securing peace through warfare.

The distance between what was promised and the underlying realities needed to be obscured with glittering, unsubstantial, and vague promises of the winning potency of air power. The hyperbole combined with an absence of information glorified and romanticized air war. The disillusionment was ultimately not with the promise itself, but with the failure to deliver on it. To understand how that positive image was conjured requires first understanding what the public did not know about the progress of the war in Europe, what motivated those in government, industry, and the military to promote the dream of building the largest air force in the world in a matter of months, and the factors that made it impossible. Only then can it become apparent just how much effort went into creating a mesmerizing vision for the public based on scant information, and how potent that vision became.

The full extent of the potential consequences of committing American forces in support of the Allies was not shared with the public. When the

United States entered World War I in April 1917, the public was told the war was stalemated. It was much worse than that. Britain was essentially bankrupt, a factor worrisome both to the U.S. Treasury and the private banks holding British bonds. The French faced an even worse potential collapse. On April 15 Gen. Robert Nivelle gave the order for 1,200,000 soldiers to assault the German lines along a forty-mile front from Soissons to Reims. By May 5, 120,000 men had been lost, a tenth of the attacking force. The French *poilus* mutinied, joining their Russian counterparts in finally breaking under the strain of harsh discipline and a seemingly unending slaughter. Between May and June, upwards of half the French army was refusing orders. By mid-June order was restored. The French made sure the Germans did not learn of the mutiny, which meant Americans did not know about it either. April 1917 was also the period of the highest casualty rates to that date for Allied pilots.

Help from America was needed desperately, but in 1917 the Signal Corps, which was the branch of the Army where the Air Service was located, totaled only 1,200 people, including officers, students, and enlisted men. Of the 65 flying officers, most were in training; only a handful were qualified to fly in combat. There were no combat-ready planes. Yet within three months, the U.S. Congress had passed the largest single appropriation bill in its history, allocating $640 million for what it promised the public would be a vast American armada capable of defeating Germany from the skies.

The French Request an Air Force: The Ribot Cable

Planners in the United States had to learn in a hurry—and while trying to wage war—how far air combat had developed since 1914. Matters were so muddled that decisions about doctrine, type of force, and manufacturing were made—and changed—simultaneously with little effective coordination. Each delay and each blunder necessitated a compensatory hyperbolic enthusiasm to cover with vague, glittering promises the difficulties the nation would have in meeting the dream of winning the war from the air with American-manufactured airplanes.

Initially, the military assumed a rather modest role for the airplane, confined essentially to aerial observation in support of the ground forces. Between early February 1917, when Wilson severed diplomatic relations with Germany, and the end of March, the small group of flight officers in the U.S. Signal Corps prepared an appropriation request of $54 million. They envisioned airplanes as useful, but not for offensive purposes. The role of the airplane was to provide tactical support: observation planes were to be used as air reconnaissance units for Army infantry and artillery. The aim of any contact with the enemy would be defensive—to protect the planes from enemy interference with observation and artillery spotting and to deny enemy surveillance planes the opportunity to photograph Allied trenches.

The request reflected the uses of the airplane in combat as the "eyes of the Army," their sole use in 1914 when the war broke out in Europe. But by the spring of 1917, French and British air commanders had evolved the doctrine of offensive air warfare, or carrying the war to the enemy, and as a result some specialized planes were being used and others tested. Pursuit planes were being massed in squadron formations to attack enemy aircraft, protect bombers, or to strafe columns, trenches, and trains. Bombers were being designed and deployed for strategic purposes: to attack military supplies behind the lines in the theater of war and to bomb industrial sites in cities. So promising did the use of strategic bombing seem as a way to tip the balance of the war that all of the Allies wanted to enlarge their bomber forces, and the British were developing an independent bombing service.

Initially planners in the United States were oblivious to these developments. Estimates called for 1,850 aviators, 300 balloonists, and sixteen reconnaissance squadrons. The plan anticipated 3,000 planes for both training and combat to be built in 1918 and 4,000 in 1919. The Congress apparently felt no urgency in addressing this request. The bill was sent to the Hill about the first of April and passed into law as an appropriation of $45,450,000 on June 15.[1]

But by the time the bill passed, the military had been hit with the equivalent of a conceptual bombshell. A cable from the French premier Alexandre Ribot to the White House on May 23 stated:

It is desired that in order to co-operate with the French Aeronautics, the American Government should adopt the following program: the formation of a flying corps of 4,500 airplanes—personnel and material included—to be sent to the French front during the campaign of 1918. The total number of pilots, including reserve, should be 5,000 and 50,000 mechanicians.

Two thousand planes should be constructed each month, as well as 4,000 engines, by the American factories. That is to say that during the first six months of 1918, 16,500 planes (of the latest type) and 30,000 engines will have to be built.

The French Government is desirous to know whether the American Government accepts this proposal, which would allow the Allies to win the supremacy of the air.[2]

The request was staggering: at the time, the French had 1,700 planes in combat and 3,000 training planes. In requesting an air force in excess of 20,000 planes, the cable literally asked the United States to exceed the production of airplanes and engines of all combatant nations in Europe. Frederick Palmer, in his official biography of Secretary of War Newton Baker, comments on the magnitude of the request. The French "seemed to have accepted the extreme estimate of American sky-blue optimism that America's industrial capacities were unlimited."[3]

The electrifying effect of the cablegram can be judged from the rapid response to it. The White House received it on May 23 and sent it to the Joint Army and Navy Technical Board the next day. On May 27 both the board and the secretary of war approved the request. On May 29 the resulting requested allocation for $707 million was sent to the General Staff, where it stalled.

Gen. Joseph E. Kuhn, head of the Army War College, in a memorandum dated June 23, 1917, gave the proposal only lukewarm support. He said that he was "not entirely satisfied that the plans of the Signal Corps can be fully realized in the time indicated," but that he felt nevertheless they should be approved: "Even if the plans should not be fully realized, they constitute a project worthy of the United States and will inevitably contribute to the establishment and maintenance of air supremacy."[4]

Despite that tepid endorsement, the awareness that the goal could not be met, and the unwillingness of the General Staff to support it, the proposed allocation was sent to Congress. In his autobiography Gen. H. H. "Hap" Arnold recalls the effect of the appropriation request he helped develop. As a thirty-one-year-old colonel, Arnold was the second-ranking officer in the War Department's air division, the youngest colonel in the Army, and the senior ranking officer who knew how to fly. "In the Aviation Section of the War Department," recalls Arnold, "we came out of our huddle over the appropriations . . . and they almost staggered us."[5] The top brass were unprepared for the development, to say the least: "Our immediate superiors were aghast; the War Department General Staff could not understand it. But the Allies were awaiting an answer."

Arnold stresses the urgency to justify what happened next. In early July, Brig. Gen. George O. Squier, the commanding officer of the Signal Corps, went over the heads of the General Staff directly to Secretary Baker, who authorized submitting a request pared down to $640 million to the House Military Affairs Committee. It was introduced on July 6, reported unanimously by the committee on July 13, and debated and passed by the full House on July 14. Two days later, it was introduced in the Senate, where it passed on July 21 and was signed by President Wilson three days later. "As far as I know," says Arnold slyly, "it has never, up to the date of this writing [1949] had the approval of the General Staff of the Army."[6]

It is difficult to disagree with those who have concluded that those involved in developing the plan lacked a clear sense of what they were proposing to do. While the Ribot cablegram asks for tens of thousands of planes, it does not mention what kinds of planes or offer a doctrine to suggest how planes will be used; that is, was the aim a primarily tactical force, or a strategic force, or a combination of both, and would the force be used primarily for offensive or defensive purposes? Nonetheless, the cable was understood both then by those involved in military planning and now by military historians as "the foundation of the nation's program for aviation."[7] More than any other factor, it precipitated the chain of events that led very quickly from assigning a relatively insignificant role to the airplane to the belief that American air power would turn the tide of the war. "Until the Ribot cablegram came in May," Arnold reports, "our Army superiors were not especially interested in the airplane as a shooting weapon." Similarly, Col. Edgar S. Gorrell, the official historian of the American Expeditionary Force Air Service, concluded: "From that cablegram grew America's world war aeronautical program."[8]

The Ribot cable was a request to develop the largest air force in the world in terms of number of planes. The key justification was that it would allow the Allies to "win the supremacy of the air." It was a phrase essentially devoid of meaning, a semantic vacuum waiting to be filled by a number of different interpretations. It would be difficult to imagine who would argue against gaining "supremacy of the air," but it was equally difficult to discover what it ought to be taken to mean. For those in the ground command, "supremacy of the air" would most likely suggest tactical superiority. This would retain the originally conceived mission for airplanes as essentially of service to the Army, but on a much vaster scale, in which case many more observation planes would be needed.

While Army officers were most intent on how the plane could provide immediate support for ground forces, those in the Army Air Service became increasingly intrigued—once they learned about it—with the other roles an air force could play. Key among them was Maj. William "Billy" Mitchell, who as head of the Army's aviation section was sent to Europe in April 1917 to gather information about the air war. Mitchell would emerge from the war as the dominant spokesperson for air power until his court-martial in 1925. Within a few weeks of arriving in Europe, he became, to use Arnold's words, "one of the most popular American heroes of the war." Mitchell was the first American in the American Army to fly over enemy lines. He received the Croix de Guerre. And he sent a steady stream of reports reflecting what he learned.[9]

Between April and June, when Pershing arrived in France, Mitchell was the sole representative for the U.S. Army Air Service in Europe. For ten days he observed at the front the Nivelle Offensive. The cost of this failed attempt drove home to Mitchell the futility of massed trench warfare, of the carnage that came with an all-out effort to gain a few yards of mud. This impression made him highly receptive to what he learned from meeting French air force commanders and, in May, Hugh Trenchard, the commander of the Royal Flying Corps. Both the French and British air commanders argued against the demands of ground commanders that planes be used only defensively, hovering over ground positions. They introduced Mitchell to the concept of the combat offensive, of carrying the war in the sky across the lines to the enemy. Trenchard argued not only for strategic bombing of industrial sites, he also advocated "morale" bombing, or the use of bombing to terrorize civilian populations. Mitchell learned from Trenchard, for instance, of the desire to bomb Berlin.[10]

Mitchell was soon sending messages advocating a reliance on heavy bombardment as the key to winning the war: "The bombardment people are sure that if they are given enough planes and explosives, there would be nothing left of Germany in a short while." Especially impressive was the use of air power as an alternative to the stalemate on the ground: "we could cross the lines of these contending armies in a few minutes in our airplanes, whereas the armies have been locked in the struggle, immovable, powerless to advance for three years."[11] Because of these and similar messages, Arnold was convinced that Mitchell was behind the Ribot cablegram.

Arnold's guess was correct. But the implications of Mitchell's involvement were lost, if not in the translation, then in the transmission. Mitchell met on May 6 with French staff officers to prepare a letter for the French minister of war outlining the contributions the United States should make to the spring offensive of 1918. The thrust of the request was to urge the development of bombers and offensive fighters—or the kinds of planes not included in the original $54-million request sent to Congress. The Mitchell request as worked out with the French asked for

4,300 bombers and fighters, replaceable at the rate of 2,000 per month. The Ribot cable, which arrived in Washington on May 23, requested a combat-ready force of 4,500 planes (requiring a total production of over 20,000 planes for reserves and replacements), but neglected to mention what kinds. On May 17 Mitchell sent a clarifying message to Washington, explaining the need for a bomber and offensive fighter force in addition to the Army observation force already envisioned. His cable, however, did not reach its destination until June 4—five days after the $640-million appropriation request was sent to the Hill. One more effort at clarification arrived in July from the American ambassador to France, W. G. Sharp, who cabled the secretary of state to say the 4,500 planes mentioned in Ribot's message meant "half bombers and half fighters," and these were to be in addition to "other necessary types."[12]

The emerging interest in strategic bombing made for one of the more significant gaps between what the public was asked to imagine would be the uses of aircraft and what military planners had in mind. The Zeppelin bombing of cities in England was regarded as morally reprehensible, a sign of the barbaric degeneracy of the Germans. It also points to a significant disagreement between the military and civilian command. Secretary of War Newton Baker was a pacifist and opposed the use of weapons against civilian populations. There was no public debate about the potential for strategic bombing, and the desire to avoid one was arguably a factor in presenting the imagined air force to the public in vague language that failed to distinguish among the various uses of the airplane in combat.

What Kind of Air Force? The Bolling Commission

In May 1917 U.S. concern over the lack of knowledge and expertise about plane design led the Signal Corps to send a technical mission to meet with the Allies for advice on what kinds of planes would be needed. The commission, headed by Col. R. C. Bolling, included two military aeronautical engineers, two Navy aviation officers, and two civilians from the automotive industry. Departure for the commission was delayed until the middle of June, when it sailed with about 100 technical experts and vague orders to inform the Signal Corps of the types, numbers, and kinds of aircraft that would be needed over the coming year.

Military advisors on the Bolling Commission came to share Mitchell's acceptance of the Allied belief that the stalemate on the ground could be broken by bombing attacks. Lt. Col. V. C. Clark agreed with the commission's finding that bombing was a highly important part of the effort to win the war. He concluded that night bombing inside Germany would "put an end to the war far more quickly than sending one or two million men to line the trenches." Maj. E. S. Gorrell, who was also a member of the Bolling Commission, urged building up to 3,000 bombers because he agreed to their importance in winning the war:

> This is not a phantom nor a dream, but is a huge reality capable of being carried out with success if the United States will only carry on a suffi-ciently large campaign for next year, and manufacture the types of air-planes that lend themselves to this campaign, instead of building pursuit planes already out of date here in Europe.[13]

Ultimately, the Bolling Commission did not make a recommendation to place primary reliance on bombing, but it did urge development of a bombing capability.

The Lure of Mass Production: The Aircraft Production Board

The Bolling Commission selected certain Allied planes to ship to the United States as models for American manufacturers at about the same time that Congress passed the enormous aviation appropriation bill. To say the least, the cart had been placed before the horse. But lack of coordination was not the only problem. The plan to export models to the United States revealed an additional obstacle to manufacturing warplanes in the United States. The planes used during World War I, especially pursuit planes, rapidly became obsolete. The Bolling Com-mission, for example, selected the French Spad as the best available fighter and was preparing to ship one to the United States at the end of July. The Battle of Verdun in August showed that the Spad model had been rendered obsolete by German design advances. Such rapid technological development was typical throughout the war.[14]

An additional hindrance was that the responsibility for letting the contracts and overseeing the manufacture of planes resided with the private sector. Automobile manufacturers had positioned themselves to gain control over the manufacture of America's air armada, which meant that the building of airplanes was given over to those who knew nothing about their design, manufacture, or use, and who shouldered aside those who did. Seven weeks after war was declared, the Advisory Commission of the Council of National Defense authorized the formation of the Aircraft Production Board, which soon became independent of the Council of National Defense. The Aircraft Production Board was supposed to coordinate efforts with the newly created Joint Army-Navy Board on Design and Specifications. This organization proved unwieldy. Later efforts at reorganization never resolved the problem; questions of aircraft production remained in the hands of civilians, while the problems of efficiency, training, and military requirements were the responsibility of the military.[15]

The caliber and motives of the individuals appointed to the Aircraft Production Board also caused problems, even granting that they faced hydra-headed difficulties.[16] The board was headed by Howard E. Coffin, one of the "dollar-a-year-men," a group of influential financiers and industrialists appointed to production boards and paid a dollar to meet the federal requirement that those providing civil service be employees of the government. Coffin was widely acknowledged for his role in fostering the standardization of automobile construction. He was a cofounder of the Hudson Motor Car Company, president of the Society of Automotive Engineers, and had before the war recognized and advocated the benefits of patriotism for profit, or private industry building armaments for the government. Keen to break down the barriers between public expenditure and private ownership, Coffin had called World War I "the greatest business proposition since time began."[17]

The other civilian members who accepted military commissions and were appointed to the Aircraft Production Board were S. D. Waldon, who had been vice-president of Packard Motors, E. A. Deeds of the Dayton Engineering Laboratory, and financial and business advisor R. L. Montgomery. The military members were Brigadier General Squier and Rear Adm. D. W. Taylor. The civilian appointments reflected the incursions made by major automotive interests into the realm of airplane manufacture during 1915 and 1916, when it became evident that there was government money to be made from aircraft production if—or when—America entered the war.

In 1915 Wright-Martin was formed from the merger of two companies started by aviation pioneers Orville Wright and Glen L. Martin, but neither Wright nor Martin was involved in the company for very long after its formation. The syndicate included directors who served on the boards of other aviation companies, and the same group held interests in both the Simplex Automobile Company and the American rights to the reliable and respected Hispano-Suiza airplane engine. Curtiss Aeroplane and Motor Corporation was formed in 1916 to consolidate the various Curtiss companies, which had pioneered aircraft design. Shortly after its incorporation, Willys Car company interests acquired a sizable minority holding in the Curtiss Aeroplane and Motor Corporation.

But the real muscle behind the effort to funnel lucrative government contracts for aircraft into the automotive industry came from two interrelated groups, one centered in Dayton, one in Detroit, neither with any prior connection with aviation. In 1911 Edward A. Deeds— who had formerly headed the National Cash Register Company—and three other directors formed the Dayton Engineering Laboratories Company (Delco), which produced ignitions for the automotive industry. Deeds had additional interests with General Motors and represented the Dayton interest in the Detroit Group, which was headed by Coffin, and included Jesse G. Vincent of the Packard Company and Henry Leland from Cadillac, among others.[18]

The military depended on the civilians on the Aircraft Production Board to provide the estimates the military needed to decide on the feasibility of the request from France. At the time the Ribot cable arrived, the military had no way to estimate what kind of air force would be needed, what the production capacity for planes might be, or how much of the nation's resources might be siphoned off to develop an air force of 20,000 planes. This latter was a matter of great concern to the General Staff because of the focus on quickly mustering and provisioning a million-man army and sending it to Europe. There were serious reservations about the availability of enough spruce, linen, castor oil, and other supplies needed to build as many planes as quickly as proposed in the military aviation appropriation act.[19] These were compounded by worries that the need for all the resources to build a sizable air force would hinder the efforts to provision the Army and Navy.

Even though it was realized by all concerned that Howard Coffin and the other civilians on the Aircraft Production Board were essentially staggering around in the dark and had considerable private interests at stake, their positive recommendation was ultimately decisive. In a letter to Coffin from General Kuhn dated June 13—ten days prior to Kuhn's report giving qualified support to the plan to meet the request in the Ribot cable—Kuhn asked whether the plan was feasible. Coffin responded the same day that the automobile industry was certainly capable of meeting the demand and that "We firmly believe the airplane program can be met."[20]

Coffin, a close friend of Brigadier General Squier, simply used his influence on the Aircraft Production Board to convince the military that aircraft should be mass-produced in factories designed—and yet to be built—along the lines of automobile factories. He had no apparent basis except optimism and the vision of profits upon which to make such a claim. As no such factories existed in the airplane industry, and since the American airplane manufacturers had legitimate reservations that airplanes could be mass-produced along standardized designs, the consequence was to deny contracts to smaller companies, even though they actually built airplanes, unlike any of the factories of car manufacturers. The automobile manufacturers were represented on the board; the aviation manufacturers were not. When Wright-Martin's Dayton factory closed as a direct consequence of these policies, which had starved the company of resources, Deeds and his partners moved in on the company. They formed a new company by luring Orville Wright and a number of Wright-Martin department heads. The Dayton Wright Airplane Company incorporated three days after Wilson declared war. Deeds was well practiced in driving out the competition. About four years before the war, he had come under federal prosecution and was convicted for alleged bribery and using other criminal methods to force his competitors out of the cash register business; he appealed and the federal government elected not to pursue the case.

Having benefited from Coffin's influence in driving Wright-Martin out of the market, Dayton Wright Airplane Company built a new factory capable of mass production on land Deeds owned. Charles Evans Hughes, who led the 1918 Justice Department investigation into Deeds's conduct during the war, not surprisingly concluded that Deeds and his partners entered into this corporation "manifestly with the expectation of obtaining Government contracts."

Not long after the formation of the Dayton Wright Airplane Company, Howard Coffin appointed Deeds to be the procurement chief of the Aircraft Production Board. Subsequently, Deeds received a commission of colonel in the Signal Corps as head of its Equipment Division. This gave him control of the Army production of combat planes, and he proceeded to steer lucrative contracts to his Ohio partners.

Along with the civilian members of the Aircraft Production Board, Deeds advocated producing planes and especially engines—including their ignitions—of standardized American design, rather than copying the Allied engines and planes chosen by the Bolling Commission. The dominant initial mentality among the civilians on the production side mixed visions of profit with an ignorant optimism about the ease with which mass production and standardization could be applied to the building of aircraft. This illusion was reinforced by the military's failure to understand either that models rapidly became obsolete in combat or that diverse models with different specializations would be required. During the first six months of 1918, the military leadership placed greatest faith in sheer quantity. The policy of those in command of the

Air Service was stated succinctly in a cable from the front: "Improvements are good but production is better."[21]

Deeds, who was an engineer, was particularly keen on the implausible idea that the United States should concentrate on manufacturing one type of engine to be used in all types of aircraft. It was assumed that it would normally take two years to design a new aircraft engine, but Deeds convinced two well-known automotive engineers to sequester themselves in the Willard Hotel in Washington, D.C., until the engine was designed. Jesse Vincent and J. G. Hall worked for five days on what would become the Liberty engine. On June 4 their plans were presented to the Aircraft Production Board, members of the Bolling Commission, and the Joint Army and Navy Technical Board. In less than a month from the time Vincent and Hall locked the door of their hotel room, a model of their engine was ready for testing. The first Liberty—rigged with a Delco ignition, never before used on an aircraft engine—was a 300-horsepower, eight-cylinder engine. But combat conditions rendered it immediately obsolete, and it had to be redesigned.

In fact, the Liberty engine never lived up to expectations for the simple reasons that it is impossible either to design an engine separately from the aircraft it is supposed to power, or to use the same engine in aircraft designed for very different purposes.[22] The decision to use untested American engines and to rely on standardization and mass-production techniques to manufacture aircraft proved a dismal failure. By January 18, for example, a British Bristol scout—a model selected by the Bolling Commission and fitted with the Liberty engine—was ready for flight testing. Production plans were already in place for 2,000 of these planes, but the problem of the additional weight added to the Bristol proved insurmountable. Twenty-six Bristols crashed during test flights; the program was abandoned at the cost of more than $6 million. The Senate Military Affairs Committee, which investigated the failed promise to produce an American aerial armada, came to the same conclusion in August 1918 as did a number of other investigative bodies. Primary blame was placed on the decision to adapt all airplanes to the Liberty engine rather than to copy Allied designs for both engine and aircraft. "Standardization may be the birth of production," comments I. B. Holley in summarizing his study of the role of the Liberty engine, "but it is at the same time the death of development."[23]

A similar and related consequence of obtuse confidence in sheer mass production is illustrated in a conversation Hap Arnold recalled with Howard Coffin, who was ecstatic because contracts had been let for 40,000 planes. Arnold asked how many spare parts Coffin had ordered and was met with the startled question, "What do you need spare parts for?" As a consequence, according to Arnold, "production figures meant nothing, because so many aircraft had to be cannibalized for spare parts to keep others flying."[24]

Ultimately, it was the bomber rather than the pursuit plane which became the centerpiece for American production. The British reconnaissance bomber, the De Havilland DH-4, mounted with a Liberty engine, suited the American methods of mass production and utilized an American-made motor. The early models arriving at the front proved deadly. They were poorly made by unskilled workers, utilized inferior materials, had significant design problems, and had unreliable Liberty engines. Particularly murderous was the design for the gasoline tank and feed system, both of which were unprotected. The French models were protected by an asbestos-rubber coating that sealed holes when penetrated by bullets. The unprotected American model meant that if a bullet penetrated the gas tank, gas was forced through the pressure system and sprayed the fuselage. A single spark from a tracer bullet would ignite the entire plane. It was not long before American pilots gave the DH-4 the nickname "Flaming Coffin"—whether wittingly or not offering a grim pun on the name of the man most responsible for choosing not the best models and manufacturing methods, but the models that could be produced using American automotive manufacturing methods.[25]

While the failure to fulfill the promise of an American air armada reflects the understandable reality that neither the military leadership nor those in the civilian sector responsible for planning the manufacture of airplanes fully appreciated the realities of design, engineering, and production of combat planes, there is very real culpability in the efforts by those with interests in the automotive industry to prevent those with actual knowledge of the design and building of airplanes to get anywhere near the flow of money and information from the Airplane Production Board to private contractors. Donald Douglas, who was then a young aircraft designer with a degree from MIT, was appointed to the engineering department of the Signal Corps after leaving Wright-Martin when both its Dayton and California plants were closed. The engineering division was headed by Col. Virginius E. Clark, who was regarded as the brightest of the aeronautical engineers in the Army. Douglas was assigned to study the planes sent from Europe by the Bolling Commission where they were housed in one of the Smithsonian buildings. He recalls one day when "one of the top members of the [Aircraft Production] Board came in, called on Colonel Clark and said within my hearing: 'Don't let any of these American aircraft people in here to see these airplanes.'" Fully aware of the implications of this order, Douglas decided upon a course of industrial espionage, taking the documents with the airplanes' technical specifications home each evening, copying them, and sending them to his friends in different aviation companies.[26]

Pershing's Air Force: Call on Britain and France

After Pershing's arrival in France in June, his sense of what would be needed from the Air Service evolved—and frequently changed—as a result of his consultations with Mitchell, the members of the Bolling Commission, and the British and French. Pershing's original plan of July 1917 included 59 squadrons of only tactical planes—or those providing support for the ground forces. By October Pershing had adopted Mitchell's plan for 260 additional squadrons, including both tactical and strategic aircraft. By June 1918 Pershing sought 120 additional squadrons, including an additional 101 for bombardment, to complement the 60 bomber squadrons approved the previous year. The growing interest of the American military command in strategic bombing is further indicated by the agreement in August 1918 to the formation of an Inter-Allied Bombing Force to bomb German industrial centers, a plan that was not brought to fruition before the war ended.[27]

Chief of Staff of the Army Peyton C. March complained bitterly that the "confusion existing was largely increased and accentuated by the fact that General Pershing was constantly altering his requests for airplanes. We never knew from day to day where he stood. . . . He did not seem to have the faintest conception of the effect on production of all this vacillation."[28] Pershing realized early on that it made little sense to rely upon American manufacturers to produce the planes needed for either combat or training. He agreed with the Bolling Commission that "our manufacturers could not begin to furnish airplanes before the summer of 1918" and that it seemed unlikely the Army would "have even sufficient airplanes for training." Pershing approached the French Air Ministry in August 1917 and committed $60 million to purchasing 5,000 planes and 8,500 engines. Reflecting on the general confusion, Pershing says of his decision: "to make a contract to pay such an amount appeared somewhat bold, but under the circumstances some one had to take the initiative in providing planes needed at once for the development of our air force." Pershing also diverted Liberty engines from the American Navy to England, where they were used in British-made scouts and observers to release British production capacity to produce more bombers.[29]

The Dream Unravels

Pershing's decisions in France make it obvious that at the time America entered the war some recognized both the impossibility of quickly building a vast fleet of standardized combat planes and motors to fly them. As early as December 1917 the *New York Times* began to draw attention to the problems production delays posed for America's French ally, at the same time that Secretary of War Baker blamed "seditionists and spies" for skepticism about America's ability to keep its promises. The next month the Committee on Public Information (CPI), the ministry of propaganda formed when the United States entered the war, added fuel to the fire when it related information that it later said had originated with Colonel Deeds. Deeds gave the CPI four photographs of DH-4 bodies and engines. They were printed in the *Official Bulletin*, a six-day daily published by the CPI and widely disseminated, with the caption incorrectly claiming that hundreds of planes had been shipped to France and thousands more were to follow. Sen. James Wadsworth (D.-N.Y.) of the Military Affairs Committee called the CPI's attention to the error, and there was a failed effort to recall the pictures and caption before the article ran. The incident served to draw unwelcome attention to the production problems, and at about the same time Deeds was ousted as Equipment Division chief.

By March 1918 it was apparent that a great deal of government money had been spent and very few planes produced. The Senate launched a number of investigations and President Wilson approved the appointment of his former rival Charles Evans Hughes to conduct a Justice Department inquiry into what seemed by then to be blatantly obvious corruption. A month later Coffin resigned as chairman of the Aircraft Production Board.

Oddly, the government's misrepresentation of American aviation production continued. In July 1918 Sen. James Reed (D.-Mo.) complained that Secretary Baker had said on an inspection trip to France that he had seen "one thousand American airplanes in the sky," a report that had appeared in the *Official Bulletin*. The lame excuse that the source for the story had been the *Paris Herald* did little to quell the resentment or suspicion, nor did it help when in the next month George Creel, the head of the CPI, advised his subordinates to respond to questions about airplane production by referring to newspapers articles that said that over one thousand planes had been sent and more were on the way. Even so, Gen. William L. Kenly was quoted in a popular magazine in September 1918 as reporting that to the best of his knowledge not one American-made plane was flying in combat as of July 1918. Kenly headed the Division of Military Aeronautics formed when Congress separated the Air Service from the Signal Corps in May 1918.[30]

The congressional Thomas Committee investigating the failure of the aircraft manufacturers released its report the same month that Baker was reported to have sighted "thousands" of American planes in the sky over France. The report concluded that the failure to produce an American air force was because "the airplane program was placed in control of great automobile and other manufacturers, who were ignorant of aeronautical problems." In October the U.S. Justice Department's Hughes Report brought light to bear on the lack of personal integrity and violations of the criminal code involving those most closely associated with both the Aircraft Production Board and the automobile industry. While Deeds could not be prosecuted under the criminal code, the Hughes Report recommended that he be investigated for a court-martial, given his rank as colonel, a recommendation supported by the Attorney General. Baker blocked the court-martial.[31]

In her succinct and sharply critical account of these events written in 1940 Elspeth E. Freudenthal summarizes the matter in the conclusion to her chapter titled, "196 Planes for 1 Billion Dollars":

> Most important for the subsequent development of the aviation industry was the fact that Army aviation was really a school run by the government for a whole group of businessmen. . . . They were given key positions through which they learned how to develop holding companies and patents pools, what criminal statutes to avoid, and the intricacies of cost-plus and fixed-price contracts. The government entrusted them with over one billion dollars for Army aircraft to fight the war. As their part of the bargain, they spent this money, and the Army forces on the battle front received 196 defective observation planes.

Most of the men involved in this debacle went on to play key roles in the development of the aviation industry.[32]

Jacob Vander Meulen is inclined to agree with later historians and view more sympathetically the problems faced by industrialists struggling to invent economic structures suited to modern industrial capitalism while also provisioning a war. He argues for the merit of "organized private elites directing positive but limited state intervention to regulate change and foster growth."[33] Ultimately, however, Freudenthal's conclusions seem to come closest to the mark. In contrast with the Army, the U.S. Navy, working with aviation manufacturers and building its own aviation factory, was able to contract for and take delivery of naval aircraft, although admittedly their needs were more modest than the gargantuan vision of an American air armada sent to rescue Europe.[34]

Beneath the economist's detached language justifying the early experiment with private industrial contracting for weapons is the reality—rarely acknowledged—that modern capitalism has emerged not because of unfettered markets and open competition, but because of government-subsidized support for design, development, and manufacture. Wartime provided particularly fertile and unregulated grounds for this relationship between the public and private sector.

The crucial conclusions to be drawn from the effort to build an air force in 1917–18 are: (1) it was impossible to achieve the stated goal in so short a time, but no one in a position of responsibility was prepared to say so; (2) there was a lack of clarity about the military uses of aircraft in combat; (3) those in the private sector given greatest responsibility for realizing the plan had no experience in aviation manufacture and every reason to make sure that those with the experience were not made central players in the endeavor; (4) the relationship between private enterprise and the government was essentially unregulated and resulted in criminal conduct; and (5) the failure to meet the expectations of the public led well-placed government officials to betray the public's trust, to rely upon propaganda to assuage a watchful public and Congress, and in general to undermine confidence in government.

There might be a way to legitimize these facts as illustrative of the benefits of corporatism on the American model, but the best that can be said in that case is that the sorry history illustrates very clearly how not to build a military-industrial complex if the aim is to spend government funds to acquire airplanes that are not death traps for pilots. The dismal litany of lessons points to the additional consequence that there was a lot to cover up, much that those in positions of authority would not want to share with the public or Congress. If the first effort to build the largest air force in the world provided fertile soil for inventing the military-industrial model of capitalism, it also provided the seedbed for learning how to manipulate image and message in order to secure public support for the funds necessary to underwrite the enterprise.

Dream Along with Me

One of the more obvious questions to ask is why, given the impossibility of the goal, the United States said "yes" to the French request to build such a large air force in so short a period of time. The military leadership in the United States, as well as their counterparts in France apparently, realized that the predictions of planes produced in the tens of thousands exceeded the production capability of the United States. Baker's biographer suggests that the French General Staff "might be dropping an eyelid when it asked for more flying power. . . than all Europe could produce."[35]

It was highly useful propaganda for the French to tell their war-weary public that the Americans were providing such an extraordinary number of airplanes, pilots, and mechanics. For the U.S. government to have officially declined the request would have undermined that morale boost and embarrassed the French.[36] This was a matter of special concern for two reasons: the revolution in Russia of March 1917, and the mutiny of French infantry in April. Some showed the influence of the revolt in Russia by electing "Soldier Councils." Entire regiments marched on Paris demanding that peace be negotiated.[37]

It is not difficult to imagine the concern over how the American public would respond to such reports at a time when many thought that U.S. participation could be limited to sending supplies and material and only a small force for a symbolic showing of the flag. Of Secretary Baker's hopes, his official biographer says pointedly: "Our youth might be saved from death, wounds, and misery in the trenches by our aviators in a war which, after all was not of the defense of our own soil." Nor is it difficult to understand why the United States would be reluctant to refuse the French request for thousands of airplanes and the men to fly them. According to Palmer, Secretary Baker felt "[w]ord that we were to send an armada of airplanes would stir the French imagination and stiffen French endurance."[38]

But while censorship and propaganda were factors in encouraging the belief that an air armada would save France and spare American lives, the decision-making procedures used to respond to the Ribot cable were crucial in making it possible for men like Secretary Baker to believe in the fantasy themselves. Baker's decision to accept the challenge of the Ribot cable was based on the assurances he received from confident industrialists and from both the War College and the General Staff. He carefully weighed the advantages of a reliance on air power: it would compensate for the unpreparedness of the ground forces, solve the problem of trying to ship a vast army to Europe with an insufficient number of available ships, and reduce ground casualties. And while the administration was very concerned about potentially adverse reaction to conscription for ground forces, the aviation corps had a surplus of volunteers.[39]

The Ribot cable seems quite simply to have captivated the imaginations of political leaders who knew more about the real conditions in the trenches than they were willing to share with the American public. Even before Baker received the tepid approval of the War College, he told Wilson that he "was thoroughly fascinated by the possibilities of the thing." And Wilson's closest advisor, Col. Edward House, advised the president two days later: "If you give the word, and will stand for an appropriation of one billion dollars, the thing is done."[40]

Secretary Baker said after the war, "The airplane itself was too wonderful and too new, too positive a denial of previous experience, to brook the application of any prudential restraints which wise people know how to apply to ordinary and military developments." In other words, he seems to say, he along with others simply lost their heads. To use his words, "We were dealing with a miracle." But it seems more accurate to say that he and his advisors were hoping for one. And, as illustrated in what follows, they had at their disposal the communications technology and the authority for controlling, coordinating, and deploying information from both domestic and foreign sources in ways that made it possible to give a vivid reality to the miraculous vision while steamrolling over any dissent.[41]

CHAPTER 2

"Did You Ever Buy a Pig in a Poke?"

Promoting the Military Aviation Appropriation Bill

While the decision to attempt to build an American air armada is significant for understanding the origins of the American military-industrial complex, the act of getting congressional approval to pay for the scheme is equally significant as an example of the new techniques used to manufacture consent. The skilled use of information and image, first practiced on such a large scale during World War I, was to become as important to America's economic and political future as was the channeling of government funds to private industry. The campaign to pass the Military Aviation Appropriation Bill depended upon conjuring an allegory of American military, technological, and moral superiority—embodied in the largest air force in the world—rescuing the Allies in their darkest hour of need. America's idealization of air power as emblematic of American exceptionalism was born from this publicity campaign, which necessarily relied upon symbols and hyperbole.

The Military Aviation Appropriation Bill, passed in the summer of 1917, was the largest single appropriation to that point in the history of the United States Congress. The $640-million appropriation followed two others, one for $12 million and one for $43,450,000. In all, about $1 billion was allocated to military aviation in 1917. The largest passed quickly through both houses of Congress with little or no debate. The marshaling of support for it illustrates the effectiveness of the new model for shaping public opinion. The campaign involved the efficient

mobilization of private interests, the American military, the Wilson administration, the French, and the press in pressuring Congress.

Once the United States declared war, the American press was
essentially enlisted as a fifth branch of government through the combination of control over information about the preparations for war
coupled with legislation imposing harsh penalties for publishing news
or information unwelcome to the government. Government agencies
and the CPI disseminated positive information about the ability of the
United States to produce planes and train pilots; this information was
favorably reported by the press or reprinted verbatim. Because packaged information about the plans for an American aerial armada was
printed as news reports, the public was not aware that the newspapers
they were reading were simply reprinting the views of the government. This indirect propaganda was most useful to the government
because the source was effectively obscured. On the basis of this packaged publicity, leading newspapers took editorial positions supporting quick passage of the bill. Several such editorials were read into the
Congressional Record as proof of support by a responsible, informed public; in other words, packaged news disseminated by the government in
ways that ultimately disguised its source became an integral part of the
news cycle.

Government sources relied on a combination of informational and
inspirational propaganda, along with scare tactics and a sense of crisis,
to influence the passage of the legislation. The need for quick action
was used to override any concerns over the obvious lack of clarity
about how the funds would be used. As a consequence of what was said,
glossed over, and kept secret, the various potential uses of air power
condensed into a glittering image of thousands of planes flying across
the skies—and the enemy capitulating. In posters and illustrations,
Americans were presented with images of echelon upon echelon of airplanes allied with national symbols, that is, formed into the shape of
the American flag or following Columbia to France. All of the planes
in these illustrations were crudely drawn and they all look exactly the
same. This vision of a vaguely realized, undifferentiated, but mighty

force existing at the symbolic level but nowhere else was ironically more truthful than the public realized at the time.

The advent of World War I is generally recognized as the moment when industrialized nations began using organized propaganda campaigns as a necessary adjunct to warfare. It is also widely recognized that governments in democratic nations face a distinctly different challenge in mounting successful propaganda campaigns compared with authoritarian or totalitarian regimes. Democratic governments are obligated to sustain public confidence in the democratic process while at the same time manufacturing consent for decisions already taken. For this reason, maintaining the semblance of debate and objective reporting were essential to the successful campaign; the key was to legitimize the suppression of effective debate as a sign of the health of the political process.

It was from this effort to get the Military Aviation Appropriation Bill passed without offering any clear information about where the money was going to go that the lasting image of American air supremacy was born. To understand how the desire for the largest air force in the world was forged, and why it took such a firm hold over the imagination as an essentially American undertaking, requires attention not simply to the substance of what was said, but to how it was offered: the tropes and metaphors, the appeals to fear and hope, the invocation of famous poets, the weaving of memory with desire, and the manipulation of symbols to arouse support for a glorious vision that could not be painted with any precise detail.

Howard Coffin: "The Eagle Must End This War"

Howard Coffin was the most vocal advocate for the military appropriation bill on the civilian side, while Brigadier General Squier led the charge for the military. Coffin opened the campaign on June 8 with a speech at a luncheon in New York to editors and the heads of press associations. In what was to become typically vague but highly inspirational rhetoric, he encouraged them to publicize the tremendous advantages of air power. "The future history of the world's nations may be influenced by your action," he declared.

Mere numbers of men count little in this great struggle. The land may be trenched and mined; guns and bayonets form an impossible barrier. The sea may be mined and netted, and the submarine may lurk in its depths. But the highways of the air are free lanes, unconquered as yet by any nation. America's great opportunity lies before her. The road to Berlin lies through the air. The eagle must end this war.[1]

Depending on how the metaphor of the "road to Berlin" is understood, it could suggest either a willingness to rely upon carrying the war over the lines to the German military, or bombing German industrial sites or cities, or both. To say "The eagle must end this war" conveys a vague, undifferentiated conception of the plane in battle while attaching to air combat a symbolism that is both heroic and nationalistic (see Figure 1).

When Coffin gave his luncheon address, Congress was considering the original appropriation requested by the Signal Corps, which asked for a modest number of aircraft to serve as trainers and observation planes, and which did not envisage either offensive pursuit planes or strategic bombers. But by May 29 the Aircraft Production Board had already agreed that the demands of the Ribot cable could be met. Coffin used the luncheon to prepare the pacesetter press for the colossal appropriation request that would soon be announced. He was subsequently quoted in both the *Official Bulletin* and the *New York Times* claiming that America can "surpass both our enemies and our allies" in the development of an air force.[2]

The veil was lifted on the new proposal ten days later. On June 14 the *New York Times* carried three related stories. One was an account of Pershing arriving in France. The second was a report of the German Zeppelin raid on London which killed 97 and injured 437. The third was an advanced release of Coffin's announcement of a new proposal to spend "hundreds of millions" to gain air supremacy. The plan, according to the report, "greatly enlarged" the aircraft program previously planned and promised to "give America and her allies a permanent supremacy of the air." Coffin is quoted as saying that "domination of the

FORWARD AMERICA !

Figure 1. In "Forward America!" (1917), Carroll Kelly seems to capture Howard
Coffin's declaration that "The eagle must end this war," as well as his vague,
undifferentiated conception of the plane in battle. From the Bowman Gay Collection,
University of North Carolina.

air will in all probability prove the deciding factor in the present war." America, Coffin reportedly argued, could not send enough men to the front to make a difference during the coming year, but it would be possible to "overwhelm the Germans in the air."[3]

The news of the war that accompanied this announcement makes it hard to imagine how the argument in favor of relying on air power could have been easily resisted. The reports of Pershing's landing brought home the realization that American blood would soon be shed on the Western Front, possibly to little avail. The reports of the German raids made it clear that the enemy was immoral. As Coffin used the term, "air supremacy" meant "blinding" the enemy through offensive air-to-air combat. This, he said, "is America's one chance for turning the scale within a year"; otherwise, "the war probably will drag on for years in a constantly increasing toll of lives."[4] Defining "air supremacy" as the use of offensive air-to-air combat at the same time that the Zeppelin raids were outraging the public sensibility offered the implicit reassurance that the United States and its Allies fought their wars honorably and did not terrorize civilian populations or bomb industrial sites in cities. The implication was unavoidable that America would be building a fleet of pursuit planes, even though the quantities sought in the Ribot cable included bombers as well.

America's superior moral character in the conduct of war was a useful distraction from explaining why it was not feasible for American manufacturers to try to build combat planes especially by utilizing the mass-production approach of American automotive factories. The *New York Times* of June 15 reported Coffin's testimony before the Senate subcommittee hearing testimony on the Sheppard-Hulbert bill to form a separate air force. Coffin invoked stereotypes of national character which were already typical of British propaganda, and which reinforced the image of single-pilot pursuit planes engaging in single-handed combat in the skies. While the Germans may have had superior machines, the Allied pilots were superior because the "German is a more methodical type of airman, who acts under orders, while the British, French, and American airmen use their own initiative," and it is "initiative"—coupled with more planes—which will determine the question of air superiority. When asked if he thought the original appropriation request of $54 million would suffice, Coffin replied, "Decidedly not."[5]

A cautionary note was sounded in an editorial in the June 15 *New York Globe*, which argued that building combat planes in the United States would be counterproductive because the designs would have to be changed rapidly in response to combat conditions, the United States was far away from the theater of war, and it would take a long time to ship models to the United States to be copied, as well as the time consumed shipping manufactured planes back to the front. Instead, the editorial advocated training 100,000 pilots and manufacturing trainers, "reconnoiterers and bomb carriers" because these could be standardized. The editorial called for developing the air force as a matter of urgency on the grounds that a delay will prolong the war, and "for every day of prolongation there will be a sacrifice of 5000 Americans."[6]

The inclination on the part of the private sector promoting aviation was to sweep such doubts aside in favor of hyperbolic promises. The Sunday *New York Times* of June 17, 1917, criticized the delays in Congress in passing the initial appropriation request of March 1917 and reflected the perspective of the Aircraft Manufacturers Association. Even though the United States had at that time only 17 percent of the production capacity of Great Britain, Benjamin Williams, secretary of the association, was confident that the "possibility for expansion is practically limitless, or rather limited only by the size and number of the orders which the Government will place."[7] This optimism can be contextualized by the events in July, when the Aircraft Manufacturers Association was transformed into the Manufacturers Aircraft Association, a patent pool for the aviation industry, which through cross-licensing agreements applying to all members brought particular profit to two companies: Curtiss Aeroplane and Motor and Wright-Martin Aircraft, whose patents had passed to the new owners. The patent fees were charged to the government at the initial rate of $200 per plane. The arrangement quickly became a source of controversy as establishing what critics condemned as an "Airplane Trust."[8]

Brigadier General Squier:
"Put the Yankee Punch into the War!"

The airplane trust was formed after the passage of the Military Aviation Appropriation Act. In the period leading up to its passage, no clouds were allowed to darken the horizon. A widely quoted statement by Brigadier General Squier appeared on June 15 in the *Official Bulletin*, in which he informed Congress that the $640-million appropriation was needed to "put the Yankee punch into the war!" Squier, like Coffin, defined "air supremacy" as the use of overwhelming offensive air combat to "blind the eyes of Germany until her gunners, absolutely deprived of range finders, would be put out of business by the allied artillery." This advantage would be coupled with raids behind the German lines to bomb their camps and ammunition dumps and to strafe German troops."[9]

Squier joined Coffin in conjuring the image of an aerial armada built from the unlimited resources available to the nation: "With the wealth we can devote and our unqualified facilities for manufacturing there is no reason in the world why we should not be able to produce, in a comparatively short space of time, an absolutely overwhelming aerial fleet."

The appeal to the "Yankee punch" elaborated the importance of American character and temperament to the success of an air campaign. Squier contended that Americans could fight a ground war well, but that kind of fighting was ill-suited to the national temper:

> Airplanes are the logical fighting machines for Americans because we are an imaginative people, and when our imaginations strike fire nothing can stop us. We are impatient of plodding methods, a Nation of individualists. We are willing to send our hundreds of thousands to the front if needs be to dig holes and burrow in the soil for interminable months; but we don't enthuse over the idea. We want something that appeals to our knack for inventing things, for getting over obstacles. . . . And the air way is our way.

Air combat, as a symbol of the national temperament and therefore as a superior way to conduct warfare, not only made for a flattering appeal, it also obscured the reality that America lagged far behind both enemy and Allies alike in developing an air force. Squier made it sound as if the United States was going to win the war not simply by building more planes, but by inventing air combat.

Squier noted that inventions of warfare so far had been credited to the Europeans and especially the Germans: Zeppelins, massive artillery, and submarines. The airplane was, after all, an American invention to begin with, and it is how the "American punch must be given." The implication was not only that Americans are especially good at inventing and manufacturing, but that certain kinds of technologies reflect national character. The "German spirit" went "wild with patriotism" when "Zeppelin's monsters went after England with bombs while 'big Berthas' began dropping unbelievably gigantic shells into Belgium." The thrust of Squier's analysis was that the American character would, on the other hand, produce and rely upon an altogether more admirable and morally justifiable weapon, one used only in the theater of war against the enemy. In other words, Squier enlisted the public imagination to envision the American moral superiority as exemplified by air-to-air combat and tactical support, not bombing industrial sites or cities.

Squier—perhaps cognizant of the General Staff whom he had circumvented in gaining approval for the plans—acknowledged that his vision of winning the war with a vast aerial armada might seem exaggerated or fantastic. But he adroitly converted the skepticism as a positive sign of the American spirit: "The idea is so vast that it would read like the dream of an old-fashioned fiction writer." But that sense of inspiring "adventure" appealed to the American imagination, while the "Prussians have never dreamed of an expedition so mighty or so sensational." The Prussians were implicitly plodding; the Americans adventurous, risk-taking dreamers. It is easy to forget in this rosy fog that the outnumbered Germans nevertheless had air superiority at that time on the Western Front and were responsible for many of the major innovations in air combat during the war, while the Americans had the dream of an air force and little else beyond the request for $640 million.

Newton Baker Pledges America to Air Supremacy

The stage had been set for an announcement from the secretary of war, which came almost a week before Baker received the tepid approval of the plan from the head of the War College. On June 18, 1917, the *Official Bulletin* released a statement: "Great U.S. Air Fleet Urged by Secretary Baker; May Turn Tide of War for Her Allies." Baker threw his support fully behind the proposal: "The War Department is behind the aircraft plans with every ounce of energy and enthusiasm at its command."[10] His statement is vague on the subject of how many planes will be built or how they will be used. He confines himself to assuring the public that "we can train thousands of aviators and build thousands of machines without interfering in the slightest with the plans for building up our armies."

Much of his message is intended to inspire confidence rather than impart information. He makes the predictable appeal to pride in national character: the plans for an air force "live up to all America's traditions of doing things on a splendid scale: it will put us on our mettle from the point of view both of mechanical ingenuity and of individual daring and initiative." In addition, reliance on the air force provides a welcome alternative to the ground war. Adding American forces to the trenches may do little to tip the balance while a "few thousand trained aviators . . . with the machines for their use, may spell the whole difference between victory and defeat. The supremacy of the air, in modern warfare, is essential to a successful Army." He concludes with the by-now predictable cliché about using air power to "turn the tide" of the war.

On June 23 the *Official Bulletin* printed a letter from Wilson to Baker endorsing the plans for aviation production and the training of pilots. "I am entirely willing to back up such a program," the letter said, and "I hope that you will present it in the strongest possible way to the proper committees of the Congress."[11]

Baker chose the elaborate and highly emotional Fourth of July celebrations in New York City as his moment to open the campaign to win over the public and pressure Congress. The article about his speech before an audience of 25,000 in City College Stadium was headlined "America Pledged to Air Supremacy." The opening sentence emphasized Baker's pledge to "contribute to the Allies the unquestioned supremacy of the air." Speaking on the day after the first American troops had landed in France, Baker appealed to the idealized American character in promoting the dream of winning the war by air supremacy:

> The program is that American skill and ingenuity, American scientific knowledge and the skill of handicraftsman, of inexhaustible resources of supplies, shall all be drawn upon and we shall contribute, with those with whom we associated in this war abroad, to the unquestionable supremacy of the air. So that our army will have eyes that can see and be able to ferret out our adversary and enemy and save the military operations for those who depend upon the airmen for their knowledge of the enemy's disposition.

The term "air supremacy" had such a wonderful ring to it, coming as it did in tribute to the ingenuity of the American people, the unbounded resources of the nation, and with the promise that it—whatever "it" was—would end the war quickly.

The promise must have sounded all the more wonderful in the context of the gargantuan patriotic spectacle that surrounded Baker's speech. Earlier in the day, 3,000 people paraded down Fifth Avenue, as divisions of Civil War and Spanish-American War veterans marched with men soon to embark for France and women in the American Women's League for Self-Defense; former president Theodore Roosevelt gave a patriotic speech to a crowd of 2,000 at Forest Hills, Long Island; Secretary of the Navy Franklin Delano Roosevelt spoke at Tammany Hall; in Prospect Park, Brooklyn, Sarah Bernhardt delivered a message from France and was serenaded by an audience estimated at 50,000 singing the "Marseillaise." The celebration that evening addressed by Secretary

Baker included not only the thousands in the stands, but 10,000 people on the field, representing patriotic groups, the Red Cross, the Boy Scouts, and the U.S. Army.[12]

Baker chose the emotionally laden day and patriotic spectacle as the vehicle to promote the military aviation bill on the eve of its being presented for consideration to Congress. Little more needs to be said about the shrewdness of the choice beyond the observation that it would be very easy in such a context to forget that whether or not one votes in favor of a bill in Congress is not usually a test of patriotic loyalty. It was a point that could be—and was—lost sight of given the highly charged atmosphere in which the military appropriation bill was presented and considered.

Congressional Action: The Press Weighs In

The bill was considered first by the House, whose members came under considerable pressure to act quickly. Coffin issued a statement on July 10 stressing the urgent need for congressional approval and became an unwitting prophet of the scandal the haste ultimately yielded: "Whatever we do must be done quickly. All world's records for industrial development in a new art must be broken. Whatever of crimes there may be later laid at the door of the aircraft production board, that of inaction must not be one of them."[13]

As the time approached for the full House to vote on the appropriation request, editorials in pacesetter newspapers urged swift action without debate as an act of patriotism. Representatives intending to ask question, offer amendments, or raise objections were characterized in advance as either indulging in self-interested grandstanding or close to treasonous. The Military Affairs committee reported the bill out of committee with unanimous support on July 13. On July 14, the day the House was to begin its consideration of the report from the Committee on Military Affairs, the *Washington Post* included an editorial—which was read into the *Congressional Record*—applauding the committee for acting "with an Americanism that commands admiration" in quickly and unanimously supporting the request. The editorial is exemplary of both the pressures exerted on Congress and the tone of leading editorials:

> This is courageous; it is magnificent; it is war.
>
> Now, gentleman of Congress, do your duty! Set aside everything but the victory of the United States over Germany! If any personal or factional suggestion occurs to you, smother it. If you see an amendment which by considerable debate might get you a little credit, forget it.
>
> Any slacker can suggest a way to delay and amend and fail. It takes Americans to join hands and hearts, stifle their individual preferences and rush forward to victory.
>
> The American people don't care a rap about the defects of the airplane bill, if there are any defects. It is its splendid assurance of victory that they are interested in. . . .
>
> Here is a way to win. Seize upon it, men of Congress! Don't postpone for a day the mighty preparations that this bill will put into action. The manhood of the Nation is eager to assemble and direct the forces that will annihilate the enemy. Go to it, Congress![14]

The implication is scarcely subtle: Airplanes will win the war; to delay passage of the bill or to vote against it will hinder victory and cost lives; therefore, no true American would do anything except vote in favor of the bill quickly.

The French, who after all had been responsible for inspiring American interest in building an air force, became active allies in the publicity campaign, exploiting the publicity value of having Americans enlisted in French escadrilles. In June a dozen American foreign correspondents in Paris were invited by the French Inter-Allies Aviation Service to visit the aviation school at Avord. In an article appearing in the *Nation* on July 12, two days before the House approved the aviation bill, Stoddard Dewey reported that seventy Americans were currently being trained there. "By the time this is printed," comments Dewey, "enough will have been said in America of the need and the use, the moral comfort and physical certitudes bound up with the aircraft of this war," and "time will tell" whether America will offer the "advantage of countless aeroplanes in the offensive which shall terminate the war." Dewey made it clear that the French saw the contribution as essential: "The fact that the American correspondents of Paris were taken to visit the greatest French school of military aviation . . . is a sign of the hopes which are placed in Americans." Dewey concludes with an account of returning to Paris in the early morning to learn "a Zeppelin had been brought down in England." The closing line was obviously intended both to reinforce the urgent need for American air power and to offer a pointed contrast between the honorable way the Allies conducted air wars and the outrages of the Germans.[15]

Three interviews by Captain de la Grange of the French air force appeared in the *Official Bulletin* during the time the bill was under consideration in the House and Senate. The articles echoed the American sense of urgency and the lack of clarity about doctrine, development, and feasibility. While his first article argued for a diversified air force, the second and third placed primary emphasis on the need for a vast number of combat planes to tip the tide of war. Despite his acknowledgment of the frequent need to alter pursuit designs, de la Grange ultimately advocated not development but sheer numbers: "The United States, with their great industrial capacity, will be able finally to overcome these difficulties." The articles are oddly self-contradictory because de la Grange set aside the lessons about rapid obsolescence he himself described in favor of faith in mass production—even though the lessons learned along the Western Front had been that at those times when Germany achieved superiority over the Allies, they had fewer planes. Instead, he urged that many fighter planes be built quickly in the United States for a quick and decisive victory. The alternative, warned de la Grange, was that the conflict between democracy and autocracy "would be brought up again in 10 years, and would then probably be fought out not in Europe but on American soil."[16]

His message was reinforced by a letter on the editorial page of the Sunday *New York Times* of July 22—the day the Military Aviation Appropriation Bill passed in the Senate. Dated July 3 from Dieppe, the letter, whose author was identified only as "B.," included a clipping from the newspaper *L'Eclaireur* (Dieppe) "which is the very expression of my own opinion."

The *L'Eclaireur* report was reprinted almost in its entirety. It reported that by spring 1918 the Germans intended to have 3,500 planes on the battlefront along with sufficient reserves to replace the losses, which amounted to 50 percent per month for scouting planes and 20 percent for bombers.

> Our enemy seeks to become mistress of the air. . . . We must not await the Spring of 1918 with folded arms to find out with our own eyes whether this aviation program be realized. . . . We must have, not two thousand or four thousand airplanes, but twenty, thirty, or fifty thousand. If we were to possess this number the war would be over in three months.[17]

The number 3,500 for the combat-ready planes as well as the anticipated number of needed reserve planes reflects the numbers requested in the Ribot cable, and indicates the need for a diversified air force, including strategic bombers as well as fighter planes. The French editorial did little to help the American public understand the military doctrine behind the percentages of planes sought for specialized uses, nor did it recognize the vast gulf between the realities of the American aircraft industry and the actual demands for design, development, and manufacture. Ultimately, the French editorial reinforced the messages coming from Congress, the American press, and the government: more planes rapidly built will quickly end the war; to delay will give an advantage to the Germans that might not be possible to overcome.

Congressional Debate: The House

Considering the pressure placed on Congress to pass the military aviation bill quickly, it is less surprising that it passed the House the same day it was reported out of committee than that some representatives nevertheless managed to raise objections to certain provisions when it was brought forward. Several were openly skeptical about the claim that the need for secrecy precluded any questions about how the money would be spent; others wanted assurances that the General Staff had approved the plans; and some complained because the House Appropriations Committee had been circumvented. On the whole, those with questions were not necessarily opposed to the appropriation but were reluctant to pass it without more information or open debate.

The proponents of quick passage came from both sides of the aisle. Congressman Stanley H. Dent (D.-Ala.), as chair of the Military Affairs Committee, led the debate. He and his supporters offered assurances that the General Staff had approved the plan, that details of the appropriation could not be discussed without revealing secrets to the Germans, and that action was urgently required. Aware that they were asking Congress to vote in the dark, they embraced that liability as a virtue, arguing that ignorance should never be allowed to stand in the way of progress. Representative Kahn of California, the ranking Republican on the Military Affairs Committee, was applauded when he said that it was necessary to "prevent the enemy from getting any knowledge" about the Army Air Service.

Rep. John J. Fitzgerald (D.-N.Y.) argued that the bill violated the Constitution because it had not been submitted to the Appropriation Committee, which he chaired. He said that he refused to abdicate the responsibility of Congress to monitor the use of taxpayer monies even when faced with the arguments that secrecy was necessary: "When it was desired to create public sentiment for the program provided in this bill there was no suggestion that information be suppressed; but when legitimate discussion of the bill is proposed here, there is alarm lest the Members mention matters that are as stale as news matter."[18] Fitzgerald mounted a valiant if futile campaign against relinquishing the powers of Congress to the White House.

The balance tipped in favor of the "don't ask, don't tell" contingent when Minority Leader Rep. James R. Mann (R.-Ill.) rose to his feet. He appealed to the ignorance of the House members with regard to the details of the appropriation. His speech has been described as "possibly the most influential speech in Congress during the War—at any rate the most dramatic."[19]

I can see to-day no way in the near future of [Germany] starving out the allies—England or France. I can see no way for the German Army breaking through the line into France on the west front. I can see no way for the allied army breaking through the German Army on the west front under any existing standards of warfare. But here is an unknown quantity—the use of flying machines. No one knows what can be accomplished by it. No one knows its limitations. Did you ever buy a pig in a poke and take chances on it? Sometimes it turns out very fortunately; sometimes with the loss of the money invested. And I believe that the time has arrived with our country when we can afford to spend an immense sum of money in trying out the control of the air [*applause*] and see, first, whether that will give us control of the battle front; second, whether it will strike demoralization and produce revolution in Germany itself. [*Applause*]. If I had my way about it, I would pass this bill without saying a word. [*Loud applause and cries of "Vote!" "Vote"*].[20]

Mann drew upon all the available doctrines about the potential uses of air power, both tactical and strategic, and surprisingly hinted at the "morale" bombing of cities. It is difficult to recall when reading the speech that the European combatants had been engaged in air combat for three years, the United States essentially lacked an air service at the time, the doctrines of strategic bombing were in their infancy, Americans found the German Zeppelin raids on cities morally reprehensible, and Pershing's plans for how to use airplanes in battle were changing from day to day. The speech is on the one hand laughable and on the other a sobering index of the prevailing mentality because it elevates "buying a pig in a poke"—usually synonymous with being a fool—to the highest form of patriotism and duty.

Mann's rousing speech led immediately to a motion for the House to rise from the committee of the whole to convene itself as a voting body. As the moment for the vote neared, Dent yielded fifteen minutes of time to Rep. George M. Hulbert (D.-N.Y.). It was the longest period yielded during the discussion, undoubtedly in recognition of Hulbert's sponsorship of the Sheppard-Hulbert bill to create a separate air service, which he essentially withdrew from consideration so as not to delay consideration of the appropriations bill.

Hulbert was one of the few in Congress who knew anything about aviation. He was a member of the influential Aero Club, a private organization founded in France to establish the qualifications for becoming a pilot. While he could have brought considerable knowledge and experience to bear, his prepared speech instead elaborates the appeal to ignorance. It is an extended conceit to the point that it is wrong to stand in the way of a new technology whose potential cannot be understood. Hulbert provided his colleagues a mind-numbing account of important discoveries and inventions that were initially hindered by skepticism, doubt, or ridicule. For page after page, he gave brief "they-all-laughed, but . . ." anecdotes about technological innovations, including the spinning jenny, power loom, locomotive, cotton gin, steamboat, McCormick reaper, telegraph, sewing machine, submarine, telephone, and airship. For good measure he threw in discoveries that were initially regarded as hare-brained (the voyage of Columbus to the New World, William Harvey's theory of circulation of the blood), projects that were seen initially as impossible (building the Erie Canal), and even the ideas of shared political power that sparked the Revolutionary War. The point was obviously to suggest not only that Ignorance is always prepared to stand in the way of Progress, but also that it is impossible to imagine the consequences of a new invention: "in the case of each of these great discoveries and inventions, even those who had their eyes wide open knew the least about them."

Not until the closing paragraphs of his speech did Hulbert actually mention the bill that was before Congress. His arguments in support of its passage were that delay would cost American lives ("every 24 hours' delay upon our part in putting a substantial force of American aviators in the field on the Western Front will mean the loss of 5,000 lives of American soldiers"); and that it offered an opportunity to pursue patriotism for profit ("those who only now are beginning to realize that the mastery of the air will be the determining factor in this war

[will] begin to appreciate what its commercial utility will be when peace is established"). Invoking Tennyson, he said, "we will live to see"

> the fair white-wing'd peacemaker fly
> To happy haven under all the sky,
> And mix the seasons and the golden hours,
> Till each man find his own in all men's good,
> And all men work in noble brotherhood,
> Breaking their mailed fists and armed towers
> And ruling by obeying nature's powers.

Having offered both the Orwellian sentiment of the warplane as a "wing'd peacemaker" and the promise of profit from aviation after the war, Representative Hulbert ended his speech to general applause.[21]

The speeches by Mann and Hulbert are indicative of what kind of oratory is necessary when the speaker has little information to offer but has to say something, preferably inspirational, especially when the aim is to legitimize spending millions of tax dollars on a bill that is not debated. The resort to empty oratory is made all the clearer as a ploy when it is contrasted with the few examples of informed congressmen who endeavored to raise important issues with regard to the bill. One of the more informed comments on the bill came from Rep. Fiorello H. LaGuardia, another of the few men in Congress who knew how to fly, and who would soon command flyers in Italy. He disagreed with the arguments that the bill could not be discussed without revealing secrets to the enemy. He rightly argued that the only information legitimately withheld was the type and number of machines and the type of motor. He also argued that the plane would not be the determining factor in the war, but that it would be determined in a "much more cruel and less spectacular manner" by the control over food supplies; that is, the embargo of Germany. He also disagreed with those who said that little could be known about the appropriation because aviation was in its infancy, and therefore had to be voted on as a kind of ignorant risk-taking:

the uses of the plane were well known and essential to the functioning of a modern army.[22] One can only speculate how much more realistic the expectations for the use and development of aircraft might have been during World War I if more members of Congress had been as informed as LaGuardia—and how differently the appropriations might have been distributed.

Rep. James L. Slayden (D.-Tex.) also took a realistic and informed approach when he questioned Dent closely to be sure the secretary of war was authorized to spend all or part of the appropriation in England, France, or Italy to purchase planes there. "I believe," he said, "we can get more machines for a given amount of money in Europe than in this country." He argued that the United States could procure more planes more quickly by purchasing them overseas, while at the same time avoiding the hazards of submarine attack on trans-Atlantic shipment.[23] As matters eventuated, Slayden's vision was more accurate than the vague prophecies about an American-built armada.

What carried the day ultimately was the belief that the airplane—however it might be used—would win the war and spare the lives of the ground soldiers, along with the faith that American industrial capacity and ingenuity were up to the challenge of developing an air force of unprecedented size in one year despite evidence and common sense to the contrary. In other words, the Congress agreed to purchase the "pig in the poke." The bill passed after four hours of debate.

Congressional Debate: The Senate

After the House acted on July 14, attention turned to the Senate and the Military Affairs Committee, headed by Sen. George E. Chamberlain (D.-Ore.), who indicated initially that he anticipated reporting the bill to the Senate in time for action by August 1. Proponents pushed for quicker action. The July 16 *Washington Post* carried an editorial objecting to any delays in passage and opposing any discussion of the plan on the grounds that it would give away information to the Germans. Insisting that an American air fleet would "change the course of the world and confer a blessing upon all mankind," the *Post* urged quick and unanimous passage as a "gloriously patriotic feat, worthy of the traditions of this imperishable free nation." There was no hint that the money might best be used to buy planes overseas. This was to be an example of American enterprise: the millions appropriated by the act, the editorial concluded, will be "translated into victory by American genius and American valor."[24]

In a July 18 editorial, the *Post* advocated moving the bill ahead of other pending war legislation and passing it without debate, urging quick action because of reports that the Germans had stopped producing Zeppelins in favor of building more planes. The editorial argued: "Time is the essence of the problem," and delay "may give Germany an advantage which she will be quick to seize." This suggestion obscures for the reader the realization that the Germans already had air superiority over the Western Front while the United States had not yet begun to build combat-ready planes; rather, a "race" is suggested between equally matched opponents, which will be won by the runner who is first off the mark.[25]

Those who wanted the bill introduced without hearings or amendment prevailed. The bill was reported from committee and introduced to the full Senate on July 18. Senator Chamberlain, who chaired the Senate Committee on Military Affairs, introduced the bill saying, "it does not seem to me to be necessary nor advisable in the crisis which confronts our country to undertake to analyze the several sections of it or to discuss the bill at any length. It speaks for itself." Chamberlain acknowledged the members of the committee found flaws in the bill but felt it was more urgent to pass it than to spend time addressing them.[26] Sen. Robert L. Owen (D.-Okla.) unwittingly invited calumny when he introduced an amendment to create an oversight committee to prevent graft in the awarding of contracts, citing the astronomical leaps in the costs of planes since the plan was announced.[27]

Because amendments had been introduced, action on the bill was postponed soon after it was entered. It was scheduled for further discussion on July 21. The press declared open season on the senators who had introduced amendments. The *New York Times* headlined its report

"Senate Insurgents Block Aviation Bill." Reporting on the response in the House, the report said representatives expressed fear that "winning the war may be lessened by an appreciable delay." Representative Kahn referred to the secret, "startling information" made available by the War Department to the House Military Affairs Committee, and said it made very clear that "any one who attempts to stop the progress of the Aviation bill cannot know what the results may be." Kahn praised the House members for voting in favor of the bill without discussing its military aspects.[28]

Owen's measure to prevent graft was branded in a *New York Times* editorial as another example of the same kind of shameful delaying tactic being used to slow passage of the food bill. All these senators—those proposing amendments to the aviation bill as well as to the food bill—were harshly condemned as treasonous without using the word: "The names of these men will be remembered in the dark days to come. They have struggled to prevent measures for national safety. They have hampered the government in a dangerous crisis. They have earned the cordial approval of the enemies of this country."[29]

On July 20 Owen called a point of privilege to protest the editorial in the *New York Times* "in effect charging me with being a public enemy." The *Times* carried the report on page 3 and misquoted Owen. Surrounding the headline "Senator Owen Replies" were others that read, "American Pilot Hurt," "Flying Course in France," "100 Fliers Train in Canada," "Air Fighting Hotter on the British Front," and "Germans Building Bigger Air Fleet." The latter repeated earlier reports that the Germans had stopped building Zeppelins to build more planes in anticipation of the American challenge. In short, the *Times* buried Owen without saying a word in response to his protest.[30]

It would not be long before its editorial pages were protesting against exactly what Owen had sought to prevent: mismanagement and corruption in the production of military aircraft. But that was in the future. At the time the bill passed, the sense of urgency and promise made any hesitation seem tantamount to willfully losing the war. The bill passed unanimously and without amendment on July 21.

The *New York Times* editorial of July 23, headlined "At Last the Planes," praised the quick passage of the military aviation bill and took one last swipe at those who had voiced some reservations about it: "The obstructionists were on hand, but they were powerless." The passage of the bill made it possible for the United States to build "such an air fleet as the world has never known." The *Times* was confident that the machinery needed to build the fleet was in place and the men needed to fly them were being trained. "It is no longer doubtful that the United States will do its share to end the war through its air service. We have begun. What we begin we carry through."[31]

CHAPTER 3

A Matter of Class

World War I was fought along a symbolic front, a contest for public opinion, which proved no less significant in terms of the outcome of the war than the massing of men and the weapons of warfare. The requirement that the entire nation be mobilized to support a war of that scope and level of mechanization placed significant importance upon the ability to shape the war-as-imagined in the public mind's eye and to hold it as a point of fascination. The importance of the image of the war to winning the real one on the ground was well recognized by the European combatants, particularly the British and French. When the United States entered the war, the talents and capacities of official sources for major and sustained control over information and image were demonstrated, as was a keen awareness on the part of those in the public eye for the significance of their own images. This necessity, along with shifts in the cultural iconography of the warrior, including the officer and the volunteer, created conditions in the United States that would shift the traditional idealism of the warrior to the combat pilot.

The nature of the ground war and the necessity of mustering a million men to fight it challenged a number of traditional assumptions about the qualities that best suited men to lead others into combat. The older, romantic conceptions of the officer as a charismatic leader were pitted against the newer vision of war conducted efficiently and along scientific principles. Assumptions about the natural leadership role of the elite classes were pitted against democratizing demands that officers be drawn from other classes, particularly labor.

There was no doubt in the minds of those in key leadership positions that what was at issue was the symbolism of the war—who would control it, and what it would be understood to symbolize not only in a cultural sense, but in a political sense as well. As the realities of the new form of warfare and the need to provision it bore in on and undermined traditional conceptions of warfare, there was a transfer of the traditional symbolism and value from the ground war to the air war. In the combat pilot, it was anticipated, would be preserved the symbolism of caste and gender that legitimized the leadership role of the elites both in war and in peace.

In searching out how this transfer of meaning occurred, it is not difficult to find examples of political leaders who overtly laid the mantle of an elite corps upon those who volunteered as flyers. But to understand fully how a particular kind of idealism was transferred to the combat pilot, it is necessary also to trace the effects on the more traditional conceptions of the warrior which were a consequence both of the advent of conscription and the decisions about preparing the officers to lead draftees. The most publicized example illustrating the consequences of these changes was the dispute between President Woodrow Wilson and Theodore Roosevelt over Roosevelt's desire to lead a volunteer regiment to France.

It was the question of class that had greatest salience in distinguishing the combat pilot. Men without high school diplomas or college training were assumed to lack the necessary self-discipline, intelligence, and—though this was implied—breeding to be flyers. Matters of class were therefore added to other exclusions by sex and race. Although a few women flew as combat pilots in Russia, they were not allowed to by any of the other combatants along the Western Front. Only white Americans were allowed to fly into combat for the United States; the one American of African descent who flew in World War I flew for the French.

The exclusions from the Air Service based on race and sex maintained inequities fully naturalized in the minds of the majority of Americans and certainly in the minds of those making the important decisions about how human life would be both used and symbolized during the war. Those based on class were a different matter; they were contested at the time with regard to the qualifications for both Army officers and combat pilots.

The flashpoint reflected the deeper cultural rifts that opened over the question of how men were to be allowed to serve the nation. The contrasts between the conscript and the volunteer, and between enlisted and officer, were made particularly apparent in the feverish days when America entered the war. By the time Wilson had foreclosed upon Roosevelt's request to lead a volunteer, privately financed regiment to France, the rhetoric of the ground war as romantic adventure had been replaced with a grimmer rhetoric of efficiency and science. Given these cultural shifts and tremors, it was inevitable that the combat pilot flying solo into the sky would be heavily invested with the romantic symbolism of the volunteer officer. To him devolved the image of the self-motivated man of courage, intelligence, and skill who willingly offered himself, un-constrained and uncoerced, as the defender of his nation.

Qualifications of the Pilot in the
Military Aviation Appropriation Bill Debate

The exchange on the floor of Congress over the qualifications for flyers revealed a struggle between those who would democratize the enlist-ment rules and those who favored drawing upon college men to fill the requirements for combat pilots. During debate over the draft provision, congressmen complained that candidates from their districts who had tried to volunteer for the Air Service were turned away because they did not have three years' college education. Rep. John L. Burnett (D.-Ala.) asked caustically "how men can be drafted into the service, when a lit-tle bureau autocracy is going to make a college autocracy of it and pre-vent men from going in unless they are college men?" Rep. William R. Wood (R.-Ind.) entered an amendment, the effect of which was to say there were no fixed academic requirements:

> There are many . . . young men in this country to-day who are not gradu-ates of colleges or not graduates of high schools who have all the ambition

and all the enthusiasm of the Wright brothers, and who are just as anxious for an opportunity as they were in the days of their struggles for recognition of their genius. The Wright brothers, or Orville, the senior, could not qualify to fly one of his own machines under the present regulations of the War Department.[1]

Wood was, he said, motivated partly by the complaint from one of his constituents who was a qualified flyer that he had been turned down when he tried to volunteer because he lacked sufficient education; other representatives offered the information that their districts had only recently made public high school education available to their constituents. The amendment as well as the debate about manpower requirements in general reflected the knowledge that there were four or five times the numbers of men attempting to volunteer for the Air Service as there were positions; the implicit conflict around issues of class lay just below the surface of the debate.

Representative LaGuardia addressed the issue of qualifications head on. Men who fly, he argued, must necessarily be both more intelligent than average and capable of both study and discipline:

I have had some experience in flying. I assure you, gentlemen, that it will be dangerous to limit the department in any way in prescribing regulations to establish qualifications for student aviators. A man may have a mechanical knack, may be bright and intelligent, and yet unable to acquire all that he must know about the theory of flying in a short time. . . . Unless his mind is disciplined, is trained to study, and accustomed to acquiring facts and details and retaining them, he will be unable to grasp all this information in the short time available to take the course.

LaGuardia said that the military would not insist upon a college education but would require a demonstration of mental aptitude by offering a mental test or accepting equivalent studies to a college education. He reminded his colleagues that an aviator needed a long list of special skills: familiarity with the motor and the terminology associated with it, an ability to communicate well and intelligently, read maps, navigate, and repair an airplane shot down behind enemy lines, an understanding of weather conditions, and "quick judgment."[2]

The failure of the amendment by a vote of twenty-one ayes to sixty nays validated the intention to recruit college men for flight training. The assumption that they were better suited in terms of character and intelligence to serve as combat pilots was made even more explicit in the debate over the draft provision in the same bill. The draft provision was intended to provide for mechanics and other ground crew, not for pilots. Representative Hulbert proposed an amendment to clarify the apparent intention, to the point that "no person so drafted shall be assigned to serve as an aviator without his consent." He noted that over 20,000 men had volunteered for the service, and that it was his understanding that the British only allowed volunteers for flight training. While he agreed with those who suggested the provision was included to allow for the drafting of mechanics and other ground support, he also noted that unless his amendment was passed, men could nevertheless be ordered to fly.

Rep. Julius Kahn (R.-Calif.) expressed resentment that combat pilots should be given a level of control over their destinies not allowed to the ground soldier: "Suppose a general commanding a force orders a lot of drafted men to take a certain position, knowing that it means certain death to go there and face it, would the gentleman have a provision inserted in the law that the general could not do that?" Hulbert found this beside the point because under the circumstances a general would presumably call for volunteers: "The fires of true American patriotism never extinguish . . . but our service of that character has been predicated upon volunteer service." The larger point taken up by Hulbert and others was that combat flying was not an occasionally dangerous kind of mission; it was extraordinarily dangerous by its very nature, and the kind of man required to meet extreme danger differed in temperament and spirit from the conscript, who had his will taken from him and was conditioned to follow orders.[3]

Rep. Robert B. Gordon (D.-Ohio) went even further in expressing his support for the amendment: "Any man of common sense knows that for so highly technical and hazardous a service as that you do not want any drafted men. You only want men who volunteer for the service, because they are subjected to the most critical physical and mental examination of any branch of the military service."[4] He was supported in this assessment of the special character required to be a flyer by Rep. Irvine L. Lenroot (R.-Wis.), who had supported conscription, but opposed the conscription of aviators:

> An aviator is very different from a man in the Infantry or a man in the Cavalry. To fly requires altogether different qualifications. It requires nerve, bravery, and those things that cannot be acquired because each man has got to be his own boss and must act on his own initiative, and as one Member I do not want to say, by voting against the amendment, that I am willing to have the War Department go and take a clerk out of a store who has no qualifications for this very dangerous service and say, "We are going to make you fly whether you will or not."[5]

For Hulbert and Lenroot, flying required a particular kind of courage, one that depended upon initiative and individual will to such an extent that the usual training methods used to prepare men to act effectively in warfare would be futile if the effort were made to apply them to preparing combat pilots.

The Hulbert amendment was defeated twenty-nine ayes to fifty-six nays, but clearly the point had been made that no man was to be coerced into flying; to be a pilot was to be a volunteer. The House also passed provisions establishing grade and rank for flyers with a 25 percent increase in pay for anyone who flew regular and frequent combat missions, a provision that was amended to apply to any enlisted men who flew into combat as well.

The substance of the personnel provisions of the Military Aviation Appropriation Act envisioned the need for combat pilots as one that would be met by men qualified to receive commissions, who had a college education, and who by reason of their character would be generally more qualified than enlisted men to act upon their own initiative. While the mass of young Americans would be best fitted for warfare through conscription, the combat pilot could avoid the draft by volunteering for the Air Service, a route also available for entering the Navy. But as the comments made in the debate indicate, the operative presumption was not that volunteering for the air force was a way to avoid conscription; rather it was that only a man who volunteered would have the individual drive and courage necessary to being a combat pilot. The prevailing supposition was that such a man would be of that class, background, and breeding that suited him for a commission, particularly as he had to be of such character that in a very real sense he could give himself orders to fly alone into battle. For those exceptional men with the abilities who lacked the requisite background to qualify for a commission, provisions were made for enlisted men to fly; but again, the representatives wanted to assure that this was a voluntary commitment and not one that even an enlisted man could be ordered to undertake.

When the Military Aviation Appropriation Bill moved to the Senate, the debate over the draft provision was both more heated and more obviously about the larger issue of conscription. When it was introduced on July 18, Sen. Charles Curtis (R.-Kan.) questioned why the provision for raising men for the Air Service included the phrase "or by draft." He was assured by Senator Chamberlain that the provision was intended only for those who provided ground support and that no one would be ordered to fly. Sen. Thomas W. Hardwick (D.-Ga.) nevertheless entered an amendment to strike the phrase. He argued that the provision would allow the president to draft additional men over and above those approved by the Conscription Act, which he opposed because he was against drafting anyone to serve in World War I. Drawing a distinction between defense of homeland and fighting on foreign soil, Hardwick maintained "to draft a freeman for military service on foreign soil is utterly incompatible with freedom." While he had to accept that conscription was now the law of the land, he could not, he said, in good conscience vote for a bill that allowed even more men to be drafted.[6]

Hardwick's objections went to the heart of the debate over conscription as a violation of the bedrock values of American democracy, and by implication, the voluntary service of the flyers came to stand for those more conservative, traditional values. Hardwick questioned how the Air Service could be designated as a voluntary service when the argument made to support conscription was that it would have been "folly" to rely upon men to volunteer for this war: "Starting out to destroy Prussianism, it is asserted that we must Prussianize this country in order to accomplish it." Hardwick's condemnation made the traditional connection between national values and aspirations and the kind of individual the nation therefore depended upon for its strength: "Personal liberty, individual freedom, competition, are among the sources that have made this Nation among the greatest and most powerful factors in all this world's affairs." He questioned how senators can hope to

> reverse the processes of American thought, the habits of American life, abandon the traditions of the American people, and fight a war more successfully, more gloriously, more effectively, than we could if we fought it naturally, and as free men, who are willing, yea, anxious, to give their blood to its last drop to uphold the national honor and to provide for the national safety.[7]

Hardwick was joined by two other senators opposed to conscription. Sen. James A. Reed (D.-Mo.) was sympathetic to Hardwick's amendment, but felt it was a futile gesture because the Conscription Act allowed for the drafting of over a million men—which meant that men for ground support could be mustered by draft with or without the provision in the aviation bill, and that the provision could not possibly apply to flyers because it would be "inconceivable" for the War Department to "take a man who was unwilling or not qualified to take charge of a machine and by force compel him to get into one of these aeroplanes and undertake to navigate in the air." A far more virulent attack on conscription itself was mounted by Senator Vardaman, who agreed that there ought to be no additional allowances for drafting men: "I think we have had enough conscription in this country for the time. . . . The men of America have suffered the treatment usually accorded subjects rather than citizens quite enough."[8]

Between the first reading of the military aviation bill on July 18 and the vote on July 21, those senators who had proposed amendments were subjected to scathing attack in leading editorials. The *Times* editorial for July 18 had the headline, "Hampering the Government." It attacked both Hardwick and Vardaman for their antidraft amendment in the same article that attacked Owen's proposed oversight committee to monitor defense contracts to aircraft and engine manufacturers: "The mischief these comparatively few ill-disposed men have been able to accomplish thus far is serious." The condemnation of Hardwick and Vardaman was particularly harsh: "Does the Mississippi Senator hope to incite draft riots in this country?"[9]

When the Senate convened on July 21 to consider the bill, senators were quick to defend themselves against the attacks in the press by offering assurances that they did not intend to delay the bill. Senator Hardwick said of himself and his supporters: "We have been grossly slandered. . . . If the Senators who are for the bill are ready to vote on the amendment, I think we can dispose of it in a very few minutes."[10] But not every senator was cowed by the attacks. Sen. Robert M. LaFollette (R.-Wis.) spoke in support of the Hardwick amendment in order to make an anticonscription speech: "Any war a democracy prosecutes ought to be prosecuted without a resort to draft. A democracy should not enter upon any undertaking that has not the support of the people." He argued that there was no authority in the Constitution to raise an army by draft to send overseas for foreign service:

> Furthermore, . . . this particular service [aviation] is a service to which men ought always to volunteer, or they ought never to be employed in it. It is a service which calls for special and particular qualifications, a service that depends for its efficiency upon temperamental qualities. Men for the aviation service . . . ought to be secured by voluntary offering.

This was the case especially because there were "five to ten times as many applicants as there are positions to fill whenever there is a call for flying students." LaFollette used this as a sign of the willingness of all men to volunteer themselves, and called for a repeal of conscription.[11]

LaFollette drew upon the exceptional nature of air combat to frame the argument against conscription as a violation of traditional American values and to argue that conscription as a practical matter was therefore not necessary. Sen. George W. Norris (R.-Neb), who also favored the Hardwick amendment, also framed his argument with the supposition that air warfare was an exceptional form of combat. Noting that if there was no intention to order men to fly, then Congress should not allow a provision for it:

> even if we did draft a man and put him on a machine when he flies out over the enemy or anywhere else he must necessarily in a sense be his own commander. He is really supreme. If he did not want to do any good, he could not be compelled to do any good. If he did not want to hit anybody, he could not be compelled to do it. There will be plenty of men who are peculiarly fitted by disposition and otherwise to do this flying and they are anxious to do it. They will volunteer. We can not make a success of aviation any other way, in my judgment.[12]

The Hardwick amendment was defeated twelve ayes, sixty-six nays, eighteen not voting.

The Tradition Breached: "The Slur of Conscription"

The combat pilot was assigned cultural significance as much by what kind of warrior he was imagined to be as by what he was imagined not to be—that is, as a warrior at the extreme opposite of the conscripted ground soldier. A more subtle distinction between the image of the combat pilot and the conscript becomes apparent when considered in the context not simply of conscription itself, but of how conscription was represented to the American public by the Wilson administration. Wilson was well aware that conscription violated the most fundamental of American values, and he had opposed it consistently until the declaration of war made it necessary in his estimation. On May 18, 1917, just over a month after Congress declared war, Wilson signed into law the Selective Service Act. When he announced that June 5, 1917, was the day set for all eligible males to register for the draft, he proclaimed it was a "selection from a nation which has volunteered in mass."[13]

Wilson's efforts to redefine the conscript involved his own keen understanding of both the political realities he faced when the nation went to war and the breach with tradition which not only conscription but conscription for a foreign war would constitute. When Congress granted Wilson's request for a declaration of war on April 2, the question was not simply how to muster an army, but whether to. Some members of Congress advocated sending arms and supplies to the Allies, but not soldiers; most held the traditional aversion to conscription. Members of the administration and Congress knew that the draft laws enacted in the latter years of the Civil War had touched off civilian riots in Northern cities and the marshals sent to New York City to enforce the draft had been killed by angry mobs. In the event, draftees accounted for only a very small percentage of the total men under arms for the Union during the Civil War.

The warrior most idealized as representing the spirit of individualism and freedom of choice was the Revolutionary militiaman. The challenge facing Wilson when he proposed the draft was how to appropriate the values associated with the Revolution to the form of military organization at the furthest remove from it. His success at achieving this political legerdemain reflects the skillful use of the government's powers of organization and coercion, but especially the effective use for the first time of a carefully orchestrated propaganda campaign intended to convince the American public to embrace decisions that had already been made for them.

Wilson could look to the British for an example. Early in the war, the English believed that fighting the war to prove the superior values of democracy called for a reliance on volunteers. In 1914 H. G. Wells had written:

I find myself enthusiastic for this war against Prussian militarism. We are, I believe, assisting at the end of a vast, intolerable oppression upon civilisation. We are fighting to release Germany and all the world from the superstition that brutality and cynicism are the methods of success, that Imperialism is better than free citizenship and conscripts better soldiers than free men.[14]

By 1916 the easy equation that made volunteer soldiers the symbol of a free, democratic, and civilized nation had to be reconfigured as Britain passed the first conscription act in its history, with the justification that everyone must play an equal role.

Wilson would have reason to resort to this same line of argument. When the Selective Service Act was introduced, Democratic Speaker of the House Champ Clark said, "I protest with all my heart and mind and soul against having the slur of being a conscript placed upon the men of Missouri; in the estimation of Missourians there is precious little difference between a conscript and a convict,"[15] while one antiwar senator articulated the connection between the values for which the war was presumably fought and the need to conduct the war in a way which reflected them:

I have thought that in a Republic like ours where the public sentiment was supposed to control, a cause for war must be so plain and so just and so necessary that the people would rise as one man and volunteer their lives to support the cause. Do you find any such proposition suggested in the United States Senate or in this Congress today? No! We must, in order to raise and arm troops, adopt this same militarism that we have denounced and decried. In order to raise an army we must make compulsory universal military service.[16]

Wilson astutely appropriated the arguments against conscription. He argued that able-bodied men would of course wish to volunteer for military service—which was precisely why conscription was required. By registering men for service, the government had an efficient way to organize and direct the available manpower; for example, retaining those working in essential sectors of the economy, such as agriculture, while also directing those who were drafted into the branches of the military where they were most needed. The use of the term "Selective Service" was intended to reflect this reasoning: all men would wish to serve the nation in its hour of need and it was the responsibility of the government to select from them those who ought to fight the war on the battlegrounds of Europe while leaving in America those who could best contribute on the homefront.

Understood in this way, military service represented the equalizing force of democracy, a way of mobilizing the will of the nation. While conscription might appear to bear an uncomfortable similarity to the militarism of the declared enemy, the similarity was rationalized as merely superficial; hence, the United States could resort to conscription while at the same time maintaining that to do so illustrated the distinction between American democracy and German autocracy.[17]

When Wilson issued his proclamation on May 18 declaring that draft-eligible men had to register, the plans, publicity, and propaganda campaign were smoothly implemented. Registration forms were mailed to local sheriffs, the polling places were prepared, celebrations were planned, the proclamation was published:

> In the sense in which we have been wont to think of armies, there are no armies in this struggle, there are entire nations armed. . . . The nation needs all men: but it needs each man not in the field that will most pleasure him, but in the endeavor that will best serve the common good. . . . The whole nation must be a team, in which each man shall play the part for which he is best fitted. . . . It is in no sense a conscription of the unwilling: it is, rather, selection from a nation which has volunteered in mass . . .

The predicted antidraft demonstrations and riots failed to materialize or were thwarted and 9,660,000 men registered for the draft between 7 A.M. and 7 P.M. on June 5, 1917.

This new significance attached to conscription was congruent with the views held by some Progressives that American participation in the war would forward their social agenda. John Dewey, for example, thought it would accelerate the aim of utilizing "the more conscious and extensive use of science for communal purposes," create "instrumentalities for enforcing the public interest in all the agencies of production and exchange," and temper "the individualistic tradition" by emphasizing the "supremacy of public need over private possessions."[18] Viewed from this perspective, conscription, far from being a sign of autocratic Prussianism, could be taken to represent a highly progressive instrumentality for social change.

The significance assigned to conscription made it inevitable that the newest form of combat would take on the value formerly assigned to the officer and volunteer. The combat pilot was a volunteer in the traditional sense, and he volunteered for a form of combat so dangerous that a man could not be ordered to undertake it. While conscription emphasized the value of commonality of purpose and subordination to a greater social necessity, the combat pilot represented the will of the individual whose exceptional courage, judgment, and skill were willingly offered to the nation. While conscription was made to represent the equal responsibilities born by the common man as a duty, the combat pilot was set apart as the member of a new military elite who carried forward the oldest traditions of service.

The Plattsburg Idea: "A Citizenry Trained in Arms"

It was not only as a member of a new military elite that the combat pilot was idealized; it was also as representative of that class that had traditionally filled the ranks of those who received a direct commission during times of national emergency. It was a tradition obviated by decisions taken at the beginning of the war about the qualifications for officers.

While midwestern Democratic congressmen bridled at the very idea of conscription, members of the ruling elites, particularly those along the eastern seaboard, had for some time supported those in the military establishment promoting both the idea of universal military

service and that men of their class and distinction should be the officers who would lead a large, Regular national army. The deeply rooted
assumption that proper breeding provided the quality of character naturally suited to military leadership gained new celebrity in the years prior
to America's entry into World War I. Socialites, luminaries, and professional men garnered themselves a good deal of publicity by attending
summer military training camps as a way of publicizing both the desirability of universal military service and their natural abilities as leaders.

Prewar advocates for a strong navy and universal military service
were concentrated along the eastern seaboard. They saw the protection of overseas trade as a necessary underpinning for an expansionist
economic policy and their sympathies (and investments) were with the
Allies, especially the British. The so-called preparedness movement—
less an organized movement than a class consensus—had long argued
that a strong navy and universal military training were the best preparations for defending America's interests. Key members of the chiefs
of staff in the years just prior to the war agreed with the vision of an
expanding American role supported by military clout. Among them was
Gen. Leonard Wood, commander of the Eastern Division. He had led
the campaign against Geronimo, was a friend of Theodore Roosevelt,
and had been Roosevelt's commanding officer in the Spanish-American
War. In 1913, in pursuit of a larger Regular Army and obligatory universal service, Wood interested the presidents of the prestigious eastern
colleges in his plan to establish summer training camps for college men.
The training was conducted by Regular Army officers. The intent was
overtly propagandistic: no one supposed that men could be properly
trained in a few weeks and participating in the camps did not require
any further military obligation. Both the training and the lectures were
intended to drive home the lesson that an effective military could not be
quickly mustered and trained, hence the need for universal military training and a large reserve. An additional purpose was to alert the nation's
elite youth to the role they should play in creating the large officer class
that would be needed for an increased military force. Wood's efforts
included expanding the Reserve Officer Training Corps (ROTC). He

wanted to see the ROTC not only on state land-grant colleges (where they were already required), but also on the campuses of private colleges and universities.

The civilian advocates of preparedness and their allies in the military felt their mission was given new urgency when the war in Europe erupted in 1914. The conventional wisdom in the United States was that the arms race in Europe had been the cause of the war, which gave added weight to the antipreparedness arguments that had preceded the war. Further encouragement to this prevailing mood came from Secretary of State William Jennings Bryan, who declared in December 1914: "The President knows that if this country needed a million men, and needed them in a day, the call would go out at sunrise and the sun would go down on a million men in arms."[19]

This was just the combination of bombast, idealism, and ignorance about the realities of mustering a modern army that sent waves of consternation rolling through the ranks of the preparedness movement. The prewar summer training camps had enjoyed a modest success: about 112 primarily college students had enrolled in the summer months immediately preceding the guns of August 1914. After the sinking of the *Lusitania* in May 1915, the idea of summer military training camps suddenly captivated the imagination of many young men of the upper or professional classes. What was to become the Plattsburg Movement began with a summer Businessmen's Training Camp for 1,200 professionals, politicians, financiers, attorneys, and other blue-stockings held in the summer of 1915 in Plattsburg, New York.

Grenville Clark, a partner in a small Manhattan law firm, spearheaded what was to become a national movement organizing summer training camps across the country and ultimately becoming an important lobby for universal military service. He seized upon the idea of expanding the summer camps for college men to train a military reserve corps of men in their twenties and thirties. Some idea of the collective clout of those drawn to the Businessmen's Camp he organized is given by Clark's quip that his efforts had emptied the tables at Delmonico's. Organizers included DeLancey K. Jay, a descendant of John Jay and

John Jacob Astor, and Robert L. Bacon, the son of the former secretary of state and ambassador to France. His father, Robert Bacon, spoke at the camp and told the press his presence was "a protest . . . against the state of unpreparedness in this country."[20] Others who attended the camp included professors from Harvard and Princeton, a congressman, the mayor of New York, New York Police Commissioner Arthur Woods and forty policemen, the son of the ambassador to England, the editor of *Vanity Fair,* the collector of the Port of New York, the former chargé d'affaires to Mexico, a New York City alderman, several former Rough Riders, three of Theodore Roosevelt's sons, and Willard Straight, a highly influential young diplomat in the Taft administration who had become a senior partner in J. P. Morgan and Company, and along with his wife had provided the money for the *New Republic* when it was founded in 1914. Straight had considerable influence at this important Progressivist organ; at least one anonymous article praising the Plattsburg camp is attributed to him.

The eastern press especially had a field day covering the camps, printing photographs of New York's mayor struggling to put up his cot, or relishing tales of eastern brahmins being ordered to KP. Enthusiasm swept the watering holes of the upper classes throughout the country. By the end of the summer, a second Businessmen's Camp was held at Plattsburg and several were held at other sites in the Midwest and West. The Military Training Camp Association (MTCA) was formed, with an advisory board of college presidents to foster military training on elite campuses and a committee to focus both on planning other camps and on lobbying Congress.

By the summer of 1916, 16,000 men had been trained under a provision in the Defense Act for "public-spirited citizens who . . . have manifested their willingness to serve the nation by participation in the so-called students' camps and business men's camps." Both those who opposed any move toward a national army and military planners like Wood who favored it understood that the crucial element this provision represented was the precedent of reserve units under direct federal control—the camel's nose for a federalized military based on obligatory service. In November—five months before war was declared with Germany—the governing committee of the MTCA resolved "to bring about a system of universal obligatory military training and equal service for the young men of the United States under exclusive federal control."

The lobbying efforts of the MCTA played an important role in the passage of the Selective Service Act in May 1917. The MCTA joined Theodore Roosevelt in making the argument, which was ultimately embodied in Wilson's proclamation of universal registration, that in a democracy serving the nation is a duty, required as much as paying taxes. Books written by Plattsburgers included propaganda about Boston bluebloods sharing a tent with a butcher from Elmira. Theodore Roosevelt also maintained that the dog-tent was the "cradle of democracy."[21]

Ironically, the argument offered by the MCTA in favor of universal conscription was used to frustrate their desire to preserve the direct commission. At first, all went as the MCTA wished. When war was declared, the War Department needed 100,000 officers. Five thousand noncommissioned officers of the Regular Army were given commissions, doubling the number of professional officers.[22] The MCTA offered to recruit the remaining tens of thousands of officers under the provision for summer training camps passed the year before. The key to this provision was that it permitted qualified men to volunteer for officer training without first enlisting in the ranks of the Regular Army. This offer was accepted. Incredibly, the MCTA was able to recruit volunteers for the sixteen proposed training camps (and the doctors to give them their medical exams) by May 15—or about six weeks after war was declared and three days before the passage of the Selective Service Act. To achieve this the MCTA spent $350,000 in private funds.

The three-month officer training camps held that summer were attended by 43,000 men; 27,341 eventually earned commissions. The volunteers were drawn from the same social strata as were those who had attended the earlier camps. The press called them "The First Ten Thousand," with "first" suggesting not only the initial number but an elite as well. The camps were seen as successfully training volunteer officers who neither waited for the draft nor sought direct commissions the old-fashioned way—through political wire-pulling.[23] This was the essential novelty of the officers training camps: that men drawn from the privileged classes actually received military training before being given a commission. The MCTA repeatedly stated that it would be "criminal" to send men to Europe under the command of untrained officers.

The assumption underlying the MCTA's efforts was that the elite would participate in the war not as regular enlisted but as members of the officer class, and would retain as well the symbolism of service voluntarily given even in a conscripted military. The professional military decided against this plan, for one thing because of the accusation against the summer camps that they were only for aristocrats. The decision was made that beginning in September 1917, all officers' training camps would draw recruits only from those men already in the ranks. This approach—which was used during both world wars—appropriated the arguments that a conscripted army ought to be democratic and base awards on competitive merit. In effect, the professional military snatched these arguments away from the Plattsburgers and foreclosed the possibility that anyone could volunteer as temporary officers for the duration and avoid enlistment in the Regular Army.

Objections to favoring men of privilege for officer training were voiced by labor leaders. Samuel Gompers, president of the A.F. of L., supported President Wilson's move in the direction of preparedness following the sinking of the *Lusitania*, a change in position attributed to the dependence of labor on the orders from the Allied powers, an economic advantage threatened by the German submarine embargo.[24] A week after the draft registration date, Gompers sent a letter to Secretary Baker pointing to the bias toward college students and "moneyed men" who were admitted to the summer officer training camps. Gompers objected to the system that "perpetuated a forbidden form of aristocracy." He proposed that draftees be formed into units led by foremen and trade-union leaders.

Baker greeted this proposal with arrogant contempt. He turned the matter over to General Bliss who condescended to instruct Gompers on the "false analogy" he had made. Bliss agreed that workers may have come to have confidence in a foreman possessed of "quickness of wit," "ready resource," and "forceful character." But that did not mean such men were qualified to lead others into battle, any more than a highly respected gang boss of a coal mine was qualified to run a locomotive.[25]

The leadership of the MCTA did not join in dismissing the demands of the labor unions for access to the officer ranks. In his October 25, 1917, letter to Secretary Baker opposing this plan to draw officers only from those already enlisted in the Army, Langdon Marvin, the executive secretary of the MCTA, embraced the demands of the labor unions:

> The college graduate has no better right to be an officer than the labor-ing man, unless his training and character better fit him for the position; and the laboring man of higher efficiency than the college graduate or business man should, of course, be given prior consideration. But educa-tion, business experience and leadership in civilian life must not be over-looked. We believe that all questions of class should be eliminated and that the only question is one of efficiency.[26]

From the perspective of the post-Vietnam era, it would conceivably be easier to understand if both Gompers and Marvin had argued that the groups they represented ought to be exempted from service. The effort to assure their people could volunteer directly for officer training aimed at securing the symbolism of the nonprofessional officer who volunteers for commission during the time of need and serves only for the dura-tion. He was understood to symbolize both for himself and for his class a kind of natural selection, one that fostered the ability to lead others into the jaws of death. To serve as a volunteer officer legitimated claims to privilege and leadership not only during the war but in time of peace, and not only for the individual but for the class or group that had nur-tured such talents and ability. A related issue was a latent anxiety over members of the upper-middle class moving into a position to domi-nate the ranks. An officer caste made up of the "cultured bourgeoisie" with authority over conscripts seemed to forebode Prussianism, a way of consolidating the power of the social and economic elites.[27]

Volunteering for the Air Service

Given the lobbying efforts by the MCTA and the interests it represented, it is perhaps not surprising that as early as March and certainly after war was declared in April, many male college students were keen to volunteer not just for aviation, but for officer training, an enthusiasm that was typical throughout the country but particularly at the Ivy League schools. Little of such enthusiasm had been anticipated. For one thing, the war had been underway in Europe for almost three years, draining it of romanticism. "By 1917 the glory had passed from war," comments Frederick Parker. "Young men saw soldiering as a cruel duty rather than as a sport."[28]

Some of the accounts of the alacrity with which privileged youth reported for war have to be tempered by an awareness of the complaints from within the War Department of how easy it was to find volunteers to become officers for "bomb-proof" jobs and how difficult it was to fill the line-officer ranks of the infantry and artillery. Each potential opening in the newly forming Air Service had five times the number of applicants, and, as the congressional debate indicates, the image of the man who flew in the Air Service had condensed to the pilot, particularly the combat pilot—the man who flew alone. It was a form of service that was not "bomb-proof"; quite the contrary, it was regarded as so exceptionally dangerous that a man could not be ordered to do it or even to train for it. While it carried extra pay, this would scarcely have counted as an inducement to the class of men drawn to it or sought out as recruits.

There were very practical reasons to volunteer for the Air Service. Given the alternative potential represented by the draft and serving in the ground war, becoming a fighter pilot gave a man an imagined control over his own destiny because he assumed he determined the terms of combat. Moreover, flying alone was assumed to make a man responsible for himself alone, while being a line officer made a man responsible for the lives—and deaths—of those in his command in a war where the ground casualties were notably high.

The cultural significance attached to the combat pilot as the warrior who would turn the tide of the war has to be factored into a consideration of what motivated a young college man to volunteer himself for particularly dangerous service. While Palmer may have spoken for all those who contemplated the ground war when he said "the glory had passed from war," the qualities of warfare that made it "glorious" had passed to the combat pilot. It was not only especially dangerous, it required demonstrations of particular skill, intelligence, and judgment; it required above all the will necessary to volunteer not simply for the kind of service, but for the particular kind of battle each time the engagement loomed.

While traditional frameworks for defining the roles of the elites in the national defense were dismantled at the outset of World War I, the image of the combat pilot made a new opportunity available, one that preserved much of the older tradition. In addition, air combat was widely supposed to save civilization from barbarism. For reasons both practical and symbolic, the role of a combat pilot had particular allure for young men of privilege attending the Ivy League schools of the eastern seaboard.

Roosevelt as Image: "Send Them Roosevelt. . . . It Will Gladden Their Hearts"

The combat pilot gained an additional significance from an unexpected quarter: the political struggle between Woodrow Wilson and Theodore Roosevelt over the control of the symbolism of the war, a struggle that led Wilson to emphasize repeatedly that Roosevelt's brand of Rough Rider warfare was obsolete, and that scientific efficiency was needed to replace the older approach to the ground war, which had relied upon charisma and the sense that warfare was a personal adventure. By the time Wilson had finished with Roosevelt, Roosevelt's plan to lead a volunteer regiment had been squelched, as had the possibility of any voluntary regiments being formed and sent. The public nature of their dispute thus heightened the contrast between the kind of war awaiting the man who would fight on the ground and the man who would fly into combat.

On February 3, 1917, President Wilson formally severed diplomatic relations with Germany. That same day, Theodore Roosevelt—

Wilson's predecessor in the White House by eight years and his political archrival—sent Secretary of War Baker a hurried telegram: "I and my four sons waited the call for volunteers and wanted to raise a division." On March 19 he sent Baker his plans for assembling a division of 25,000 men at Fort Sill. Roosevelt asked the War Department to provide arms and supplies, but said he would pay the remaining expenses himself. He also requested that the officers be drawn from the Regular Army. The former leader of the Rough Riders wanted back in the saddle, and he wanted his four sons at his side.

Both men recognized the potent symbolism that would attach to the leader of a privately funded, volunteer division as the first American troops to land in France. Wilson had no intention of paving the way for his rival. The intensity of the dispute that arose between them illustrated their keen awareness that charismatic leaders were crucial to assuring public support for the war and lifting morale in Great Britain and France.

The terms of the conflict between Wilson and Roosevelt reveal a cultural quandary caused by modern warfare. On the one hand, there was a need to inspire public identification with the war and sustain support for it. On the other hand, there was an equally compelling need to prepare both soldiers and civilians for the brutal realities of the war in the trenches. The rhetoric employed against Roosevelt sought to hammer home the point that the traditional and romantic values associated with the ground soldier—and especially volunteer units—were obviated in the trenches. But the dispute and its resolution indicate that the traditional imagery could not be easily—or for political reasons—abandoned. The president, secretary of war, and the Joint Chiefs drummed the point that the war required a "professional," "scientific," and "efficient" approach. This was a war, they argued, that precluded the romantic sentimentalism attached to the amateurism of volunteer regiments in general and certainly one led by a man whom Baker regarded as essentially an overgrown adolescent—Theodore Roosevelt.

But the Great War made the imagination desperate for war heroes of the old kind—charismatic, energetic, inspirational—and Roosevelt was well aware not only of the power of the Roosevelt image, but that the image itself could have an effect on material reality by bolstering the resolve of the Allies at a time of mutinies in the French trenches, and inspiring young American men to answer the call to arms. Much of the ferocity of the dispute between Roosevelt and Wilson has to do with precisely this contradiction between the brutal realities of modern warfare and the need to conjure a more inspiring vision. Because it required mobilizing the entire nation and its resources, and massing tens of thousands of men, warfare now required—as it had at no other previous time—that leaders sustain the assent to and enthusiasm for war in both citizen and soldier.

The dispute between Wilson and Roosevelt is significant for the illustration it provides of the importance assigned to publicity, propaganda, and the control of public opinion. The terms in which the dispute was couched demonstrate that both men were very much aware of the shifting conceptions of masculinity and warfare that the realities of trench war would bring in its train, and of the heightened importance attached to how the soldier was symbolized. At the same time that warfare was being scrubbed clean of any lingering romanticism by the rhetoric of the Wilson administration, the vision did not leave the arena of the American imagination quietly. Roosevelt saw to it that it went out like an old lion—with a roar.

When Secretary Baker said no the first time—March 20—to Roosevelt's request to lead a volunteer division, he sounded the theme that would inform much of the Wilson administration's rationalization not only for turning Roosevelt down, but disallowing any volunteer units at all: the need for military professionalism. Baker advised Roosevelt that plans called for conscription to raise a "very much larger army than the force suggested in your telegram" and that officers for all volunteer forces would be drawn from the Regular Army.[29] In his reply, Roosevelt included a sharply worded reminder that he had not only been a colonel in combat but was a former commander-in-chief and therefore qualified to command "American troops." Baker undiplomatically responded on March 26: "The military record to which you call my attention is, of course, a part of the permanent records of this Department, and is available, in detail, for consideration." This remark scarcely veiled Baker's assessment of Roosevelt's competence in leading his men in Cuba. In private conversation Baker said, "We could not risk a repetition of the San Juan Hill affair, with the commander rushing his men into a situation from which only luck extricated them."[30]

By the end of March Baker was convinced that Roosevelt did not intend to go away quietly. He sent Roosevelt's plans for assembling a division at Fort Sill to President Wilson. Wilson's reply to Baker indicated clearly how the matter would end: "This is one of the most extraordinary documents I ever read! Thank you for letting me undergo the discipline of temper involved in reading it in silence."[31]

Historian Daniel R. Beaver concludes that Baker's concerns about Roosevelt's persistence affected his decision to raise the army exclusively by drafted conscription without any provisions for volunteer units. It is difficult to assess how much of a factor Roosevelt's demand was. Initially, before war was officially declared, Wilson considered a plan that suggested there was no need to send troops immediately; it called for waiting until an army of over a million men was trained, which would have required up to two years to achieve. He also seems to have held out some hope that troops could be committed only toward the end of the war (when the worst of it was over) to reduce casualties while assuring the United States played a role in shaping the peace. And he seems to have thought that perhaps troops could be sent to conduct flanking attacks from Italy or the Balkans—thus avoiding the Western Front altogether.

But after the United States entered the war, the real exigencies of the Allies were revealed to Wilson. Both the British and the French pressed him hard to commit troops as soon as possible. What they wanted was for American soldiers to be seconded to their armies; this was ultimately rejected as wholly unacceptable to the American public—which meant an army had to be organized and sent under the American flag.

All of these considerations certainly were important factors in the decision to propose a conscription bill to Congress shortly after war was declared. Still, there is some evidence that Baker's decision was influenced by concerns over the political implications of Roosevelt's energetic campaign to lead one or more volunteer divisions to France. In February 1917 Baker had advised President Wilson that the War College had prepared a plan "for the training of a large volunteer force" of 500,000, to be followed by conscription of 500,000 when volunteering had dwindled.[32] On March 24 Baker asked the Council of National Defense to consider how to raise an army and received essentially unanimous advice to ask Congress for immediate authorization for conscription. Baker did not indicate his preference at that meeting, but the following week—at about the same time that he forwarded Roosevelt's memo outlining his plans to organize a volunteer division—Baker advised President Wilson against relying first upon volunteer units and advocated that instead the army should be "raised and maintained exclusively by selective draft."[33] Beaver concludes: "Thus it would appear that the Roosevelt affair was to some extent instrumental in bringing the administration to take immediate steps toward conscription."[34] While it is not possible to judge whether purely political concerns constituted the decisive factor in Baker's recommendation at the end of March that Wilson send Congress a bill calling for conscripts and excluding volunteer units, the decision-making process points to the role played by essentially symbolic concerns in making substantial military decisions.

A War of Symbols: The Dispute Goes Public

The dispute became a political spectacle on April 10 when a well-publicized and highly charged meeting took place between Wilson and Roosevelt—who had rarely met before and would never meet again. Only four days had passed since the congressional proclamation of a state of war. The war in Europe had been waged for over three years at a cost of millions of lives and Wilson had run successfully for reelection on the slogan that he had kept America out of the war. Now he faced strong opposition from his own party to conscription. At that moment, Theodore Roosevelt—former president, outspoken critic of Wilson's reluctance to prepare for war, and a hero of the Spanish-American War—visited the White House to offer to raise a volunteer army and lead it to France.

Both men were keenly aware of the role public opinion would play in the outcome of this confrontation. Wilson, who had already made up his mind, seemed to be deliberating carefully before he said no in public. Both men understood well how to utilize the mass media to shape public opinion. Wilson broke with his usual rule and allowed the press and motion-picture cameramen to assemble at the north entrance to the White House, so the press had interviews and the newsreels had footage. That same day Roosevelt met at the Washington, D.C., home of his daughter, Alice Roosevelt Longworth, with Secretary Baker and later with Senator Chamberlain and Congressmen Dent to discuss the draft bill. The occasion was used to garner publicity as well as political support. In her account of it, Roosevelt's daughter said that her "house was overrun with politicians, personal friends, and representatives of the press, at breakfast, lunch, and dinner."[35]

Two days after meeting with Wilson, Roosevelt wrote to Senator Chamberlain, who was leading the prodraft element in the Senate, and sent a copy to Baker. While Roosevelt reiterated his support for permanent universal obligatory service, he argued that it would take a good deal of time for an army to be mustered using conscription, but a volunteer force could be quickly assembled and sent. He lobbied for a provision in the Selective Service Act authorizing the president to "raise a force of not more than 100,000 (or 200,00 or better still 500,000) volunteers"—or up to half of those needed for a million-man army.[36]

It is not difficult to imagine how unwelcome the suggestion was to the White House, Baker, and the General Staff that up to half the army could be raised by volunteer divisions. It was, of course, the plan they had themselves adopted prior to the change in policy at the end of March. Obviously, if Roosevelt had been allowed to raise a division, and if he had managed to do so as quickly as he claimed he could, it would have lent credibility to claims such as this that half of the entire army could be quickly mustered without relying on conscripts. This was not what Wilson needed if he was to convince Congress to pass the Selective Service Act.

On April 13, the day after Roosevelt wrote to both Baker and Chamberlain, Baker wrote to Roosevelt, again denying his request.[37] This time he made a point of saying he was supported by the War College. Baker argued that a professional army and efficient approach were needed, as opposed to the outmoded, sentimentalized, and romantic approach of amateurs. He informed Roosevelt that all available experienced officers in the Regular Army and National Guard would be needed to train the new conscripts and therefore could not be spared for Roosevelt's division. He also said that no decision had been made about whether to send an expeditionary force in the near future, but if one were sent, it would be led by professional officers because the nature of the war demanded that it be fought according to sound scientific principles:

> any such expedition will be made up of young Americans who will be sent to expose their lives in the bloodiest war yet fought in the world, and under conditions of warfare involving applications of science to the art, of such a character that the very highest degree of skill and training and the largest experience are needed for their guidance and protection.

He hammered home the point that Roosevelt was superannuated from a military point of view:

> It is, of course, a purely military policy, and does not undertake to estimate what, if any, sentimental value would attach to a representation of the United States in France by a former President of the United States, but there are doubtless other ways in which that value could be contributed apart from a military expedition.

Cutting though the remark was, it was also astute. Roosevelt was well aware of his propaganda value to the British and French and actively sought their support. On April 23 Roosevelt sent Baker a long response to his letter of April 13.[38] He sent a copy to British Ambassador Cecil Spring Rice, to the French ambassador, and to *Metropolitan* magazine.

Roosevelt took a no-holds-barred approach in pressing his case. He argued that a conscripted army offered a sound approach, but that it would take two years to muster a sufficient fighting force and that his plan would draw upon men otherwise exempted from the draft. He accepted combat on the terms laid down by Baker. Rather than deny that his personal reputation would serve as a powerful symbol for the French or British—what Baker had called his "sentimental value"— Roosevelt energetically embraced the point, but turned it upon Baker as a way of demonstrating how benighted were the members of the General Staff: "I have not asked you to consider any 'sentimental value' in this matter. I am speaking of moral effect, not of sentimental value. Sentimentality is as different from morality as Rousseau's life from Abraham Lincoln's."[39] He quoted a telegram from James Bryce—who had been the British ambassador and was very highly respected by Wilson—in which he urged sending American troops immediately: "'The moral effect of the appearance on the war line of an American force would be immense.'" Roosevelt put it to Baker that the Canadian, British, and French governments had all pressed for an American presence at the front and that he had also heard them express "earnest hopes that I myself should be in the force."

Roosevelt condemned Baker for listening to military advisors who did not recognize that morale would be a crucial factor in winning the war. He quoted Napoleon, "who stated that in war the moral was to the material as two to one." Baker's advisors, said Roosevelt, are like the "pedantic militarists" who became the "helpless victims of Napoleon" because they thought "military policy" had nothing to do with morale. Roosevelt's assessment of the importance of "morale"—and hence the central role of propaganda, publicity, and the manipulation of symbols— was by this time essentially the conventional wisdom of the British and French.

Roosevelt turned the tables on Baker, who in his reply had suggested that Roosevelt's understanding of warfare was outmoded, unscientific, and romanticized. He mocked Baker for his failure to recognize that the realities of total and mechanized warfare gave material significance to symbolic realities: in other words, the boost to morale that would result if Roosevelt led volunteer American forces to France had to be calculated as having a potentially important impact on the willingness of the French and especially their infantry to continue fighting.

Roosevelt was relentless in making the point that Baker was listening to military advisers who were behind the times; they were "well-meaning military men, of the red-tape and pipe-clay school, who are hidebound in the pedantry of . . . wooden militarism." He said that he feared Baker was listening to officers in a service "where a large number of the men who rise high owe more to the possession of a sound stomach than to the possession of the highest qualities of head and heart."

Baker waited until May 5, 1917, to reply—and again deny Roosevelt's request. Baker seemed to think it was very important to demonstrate that he grasped the central importance of "morale" to winning a modern war:

> The war in Europe is confessedly stern, steady and relentless. It is a contest between the morale of two great contending forces. Any force sent by the United States into this context should be so chosen as, first, to depress as far as may be the morale of the enemy; second, to stimulate as far as may be the morale of our associates in arms; third, in itself to be as efficient from a military point of view as possible, and fourth, so organized and led as to reduce its own losses and sacrifices to the minimum.[40]

Baker once again told Roosevelt that it was on points three and four that they disagreed; Baker thought only a professional army would do.

The public importance of this quarrel—and the skill applied to controlling public opinion—can be gauged by the front page of the *New York*

Times of May 19.[41] Only a few days earlier, General Petain had pressed hard and in public for a volunteer force to be sent to France immediately and urged that Roosevelt be granted his request to form a division. Now Americans were confronted with headlines announcing that for the first time in the nation's history, a conscripted army would be mustered and sent to fight on foreign soil: "President Calls Nation to Arms; Draft Bill Signed; Registration on July 5; Regulars under Pershing to Go to France." Dominating the center above the fold is Wilson's proclamation—printed with Gothic capitals—telling men between the ages of twenty-one and thirty to register for the draft or face imprisonment.

Antidraft senators had made prophesies that blood would flow in the streets if conscription was enacted. Certainly, the Wilson administration would have preferred at that moment to have ignored the problem Roosevelt posed. Yet there, to the left of the proclamation, was a headline for the lead story that makes it obvious just how much a thorn he was in the side of the Wilson administration: "[Wilson] Will Not Send Roosevelt; Wilson Not to Avail Himself of Volunteer Authority at Present; Commends the Colonel [Roosevelt], But Declares the Business at Hand Is Scientific and for Trained Men Only." The last headline indicates how Wilson chose to finesse Roosevelt's offer that he lead a division to France within a few months: "Sending of Pershing Division Believed to Be in Direct Response to France's Call."

There must have been many draft-eligible men, their parents, siblings, and lovers—not to mention congressional leaders—who read with great interest why Wilson had decided it was better to invoke conscription immediately while at the same deciding to (1) deplete the ranks of the Regular Army and National Guard, who were needed to train draftees, to form a division for immediate transport to France, (2) turn down the offer of a privately financed volunteer division led by Theodore Roosevelt, and (3) disallow the formation of any volunteer units.

The rationales Wilson offered were by this point predictable: the modern, professional army could not rely on zealous, over-the-hill veterans who were out of touch with the demands of modern warfare. Wilson's statement read in part:

It would be very agreeable to me to pay Mr. Roosevelt this compliment and the Allies the compliment of sending to their aid one of our most distinguished public men, an ex-President who has rendered many conspicuous public services and proved his gallantry in many striking ways. Politically, too, it would no doubt have a very fine effect and make a profound impression. But this is not the time or the occasion for compliment or for any action not calculated to contribute to the immediate success of the war. The business now in hand is undramatic, practical, and of scientific definiteness and precision. I shall act with regard to it at every step and in every particular under expert and professional advice from both sides of the water.

The press recognized the suggestion that Roosevelt's offer was essentially a politically motivated publicity stunt. The report noted unnamed sources had expressed the opinion that "friends of Colonel Roosevelt might take umbrage at some of the comments of the President in his statement on the grounds that he was ironical at the Colonel's expense." Especially noted were the implications of the phrases "very fine effect," "fine impression," and "the business now at hand is undramatic."

The report also suggests that the decision to send a division was itself essentially a symbolic show of force important for propaganda reasons. Referring to the high-level British delegation, which had arrived in the United States in late April, the report notes that the British:

stressed that the presence of American troops in the trenches would have a marked psychological effect upon the French and British forces in the field and would cause a corresponding lowering of the morale of the German armies. There is also reason to believe that the British observers here reached the conclusion that America needed something to awaken it to a realization that it was actually engaged in the bloody European conflict, and that nothing would better accomplish this than sending an expeditionary force to France.

Americans anxious and fearful about what conscription would mean for them and their loved ones had good reason to wonder at the political infighting and attention to image over substance surrounding the announcement of the draft. Roosevelt himself declined comment, except to say that earlier in the day he had again wired Wilson to confirm his willingness to raise one or even two divisions "at once." But the matter did not end there.

Ten days later, the *New York Times* published the translation of an open letter to Wilson from Georges Clemenceau, who would become head of the French government in November. The headlines for the letter read: "Clemenceau Pleads for Col. Roosevelt: Addresses President Wilson Advising Him to Use Ex-President's 'Vital Idealism'; His Mere Name is Magic." Clemenceau explained to Wilson that "there is in France one name which sums up the beauty of American intervention. It is the name Roosevelt." All of Clemenceau's plea was addressed to Roosevelt's symbolic value, to his utility as a boost to morale. He referred admiringly to Roosevelt's "vital idealism," "his influence on the crowd," and his "prestige." He asked Wilson to consider "the vital hold which personalities like Roosevelt have on popular imagination": "you are too much of a philosopher to ignore that the influence on the people of great leaders of men often exceeded their personal merits, thanks to the legendary halo surrounding them. The name Roosevelt has this legendary force in our country." He concluded this paean with the request that Wilson grant Roosevelt a commission to lead a volunteer division. He granted that the *poilus* (French infantry) were heartened that an American force was coming, but, he concluded, whenever they see the Stars and Stripes, they nonetheless ask, "'But where is Roosevelt?'" Clemenceau concluded with the plea: "Send them Roosevelt . . . it will gladden their hearts."[42]

The appeal did not change Wilson's mind.

By this time Roosevelt had decided the war would have to do with one less hero. He explained to a friend his decision not to apply to the president for a line position in the Regular Army. Roosevelt wrote that he had requested permission to form a volunteer division because "there was a really great service which I was competent to render and which no one else could render nearly as well. I could have raised four divisions (or eight divisions—200,000 men) of the finest fighting men . . . and could have got them into the fighting at the earliest moment."

Other men could have drilled and trained the troops, but it required Roosevelt himself to muster that number of volunteers. In other words, Roosevelt's utility in making a material contribution to the war resided in his symbolic identity—in his image—because it would serve as a magnet, inspiring men to volunteer for war. Anything less than that was, for Roosevelt, essentially lacking in true utility, a waste of his value to the nation: "To ask to do a big job, a hazardous job, which I could do especially well was one thing; to ask to do a much smaller job, which many other men can do at least as well as I can do, is another thing. . . . I bitterly hate not to be in the war; but I don't see that I would be of much use in drilling troops at home."[43]

The dispute between Roosevelt and Wilson provides a focus for the attention of those who look back upon the Great War from the perspective provided by more than eight decades. It reveals how conscious both the political and military leadership were of the need to shape and control the public's consciousness of warfare: how important the figure of the warrior was to morale—and how contrary the realities of the ground war were to that expectation. Ground war could no longer easily satisfy the belief that violence could be civilized, fair, even heroic—a cultural vacuum ultimately filled by the symbolism of another kind of warfare.

PART II
THE IMAGES OF
THE ACE

He seemed so certain "all was going well,"
As he discussed the glorious time he'd had
While visiting the trenches. . . .
"By Jove, those flying chaps of ours are fine!
I watched one daring beggar looping loops,
Soaring and diving like some bird of prey.
And through it all I felt that splendour shine
Which makes us win."
The soldier sipped his wine,
"Ah, yes, but it's the Press that leads the way!"

—Siegfried Sassoon, "Editorial Impressions"

CHAPTER 4

"They Made Grand Copy"

Origins of the Images of the Ace

Air warfare entered the arena of combat as a "war-as-imagined," and it is in that capacity that it was most useful during World War I. The combat pilot made his greatest contribution to the war as a tool for propaganda. The iconic qualities of those who flew into single-handed combat during World War I were invested with the symbolism of air power as the embodiment of idealized national values, ambitions, and desires, a symbolism that was the foundation for the emergence of the United States as the world's chief military power in the remaining years of the century.

The feverish enthusiasm for winning the war from the air which led to the passage of the Military Aviation Appropriation Bill did not spring full-blown from the American mind as Athena from the skull of Zeus. The idealized conception of the combat pilot as an elite warrior reflected the influence of the publicity about the combat pilots coming to the United States from Great Britain, France, and Germany, beginning in 1915 and taking on increasing significance from 1916 forward. These publicity campaigns made international heroes of pilots such as the French Charles Nungesser and Georges Guynemer, the British Albert Ball and James McCudden, and the Canadian Billy Bishop.

The concern in part II is to examine the air war from the unique perspective provided by the utility of the combat pilot for the purposes of war propaganda. While the ultimate aim is to examine how the image of the combat pilot was shaped to suit the particularities of American idealized aspirations, the history necessarily traces the emergence of the combat pilot as a symbol in the European theater of war, with particular but not exclusive attention to the French and British. In this chapter, which introduces those that follow, the brushstrokes are necessarily broader than in subsequent chapters. The aim is an overview of the factors that affected the emergence of the combat pilot as a symbol, including the nature of the ground war, the technological advances that made air-to-air combat possible, the high casualty rates among combat pilots, and the use of the imagery of the combat pilot as part of broader propaganda campaigns.

The nature of the ground war was a factor because the tremendous gap between the conduct of the war and wars as conventionally imagined created the need for heroic images to manage the perception of the war, a way of inducing the public to substitute the emotional responses to the images for authentic or genuine understanding or emotional entailment.

The development of the technologies of air combat was important not only for the obvious reason that without them the elevation of the combat pilot in the public's imagination would have been impossible. The combination of actual success in defeating the enemy in the skies coupled with publicity campaigns could exaggerate the military advantage and undermine morale and confidence in the enemy.

The high casualty rates among combat pilots (which was not made public) are an important factor in considering the propaganda value of the glamour attached to the image of the combat pilot, because high casualty rate necessitated vigorous recruitment, which the heroism of the combat pilots aided.

Underlying all of the uses of the combat pilot as image is the carnage and stalemate of the ground war. The iconography of the combat pilot reflects the failed iconography of the ground war, that is, the failure of the ground war to match the prior expectations of how a war ought to be fought, of the qualities and virtues that a war ought to invoke, and of the disappointed hopes for an early victory. To understand the significance attached to the symbolism of combat in the air requires beginning with the war in the trenches.

The Ground War: Never Such a Fierce Absurdity

The Thiepval Memorial rises abruptly and incongruously from the quiet, gently rolling hillsides and pastures of the Somme Valley. It is a bitterly ironic structure, integrating elements of a Roman or Napoleonic triumphal arch with the cruciform barrel vaults of a Romanesque church or mausoleum. Designed by Sir Edward Lutyens, it rises 141 feet above the otherwise unobstructed Picardy landscape. It is the largest British war memorial in the world. Just behind it is an Anglo-French cemetery, containing the graves of 300 soldiers from each nation, which commemorates those who fell in the First Battle of the Somme in 1916. The cemetery is dwarfed by the looming memorial, as is another, smaller cemetery tucked in the quiet corner of a hayfield, just beyond the country road leading to the memorial, and which can be seen from its grounds.

Thiepval is a memorial to the missing. Into its sixteen massive piers are cut the names of 73,000 British and Commonwealth men who have no known graves, and who fell along the Somme Valley between July 1916 and March 20, 1918. For Lutyens, the monument memorialized his impression of the battlefield of the Somme: "What humanity can endure, suffer is beyond belief." For others, the stairs up the monument lead to "nothing at all," an emptiness, while for others, the impression while facing the monument is of a "silent scream."[1]

If one climbs the steps to the War Stone at the center of the cruciform and stands with one's back to it and the cemetery beyond, the view straight ahead carries the eyes through a double row of planted trees, set in two perpendicular lines, forming an angle of perspective, as if set in place by a Renaissance painter to guide the eye. The horizon intersects the rows, connecting them, making the letter "H." No trees rise in the middle distance beyond or dot the horizon.

Nothing can prepare the innocent observer for the stark realization that the horizon bracketed by the trees—a gap no wider from this perspective than a thumbnail held before the eyes—is the battlefield of the Somme. It was only about fourteen miles long, and perhaps two miles wide, counting the reserve, communication, and frontline trenches of the opposing forces, and no-man's land separating them. That narrow corridor of death bears the remains of the 73,000 missing. Within its confines died or were mortally wounded the tens of thousands of others who are buried in numerous tiny cemeteries that appear as regularly as wheat and barley fields every few miles throughout the area.

On September 15, 1916, tanks were used on that little strip for the first time in battle, lumbering from what is now the right toward the left as the observer stands at the Thiepval Memorial looking through the grove of trees. They traversed no-man's land, terrifying the German soldiers who looked upon this new and monstrous weapon for the first time. The tank assault was General Sir Douglas Haig's effort to retrieve the catastrophe of the opening day of the Battle of the Somme, July 1, 1916. On that day alone, the British suffered an estimated 58,000 casualties, the worst single day in the history of the British Army. By comparison, the French had 4,000 casualties, and the Germans 8,000. At the time of the final attack in November, the total casualties are estimated at 420,000 for the British and 195,000 for the French. The Germans have never issued official figures. Their casualties are estimated to range from about 420,000 to 650,000.[2]

To say the attack started on July 1 and ended in November is to distort the picture if the image is of armies advancing, gaining ground, or retreating over long distances. Certainly some ground was gained, but it could be measured in yards or half-mile increments.

To imagine the Western Front, one has to think of the narrow strip of land viewed between the trees at Thiepval as extending, like a slowly meandering river, a total of 400 miles. The number of trenches amounted to 25,000 miles, or the equivalent of a single trench that would encircle the earth. When the war ended in November 1918, 30 million men on all sides had been killed or wounded, the significant proportion of them along the Western Front, an intimate killing ground extending from the North Sea to the Swiss Alps.[3]

The opening day of the Battle of the Somme was an unprecedented catastrophe. But so was the carnage that preceded it. During the third week of the war—which began in August 1914—the French had 140,000 casualties in four days along the Lorraine to Mons front; by the end of the month, their casualties totaled half a million. In September the British and French succeeded in halting the German advance on Paris at the Marne, with half a million casualties on each side. In October the British had 30,000 casualties in an action given the sanitized name "The Race to the Sea," and by November the original British force had essentially been wiped out as the armies stopped moving and settled into the trenches.[4]

Throughout 1915, trench warfare was marked by stalemates punctuated by attacks and counterattacks that would cost one side alone casualties in the tens of thousands. In 1916 Germany began an offensive at Verdun. It was to last seven months, from February 21, 1916, to December 15, 1916. French and German casualties amounted to three-quarters of a million dead, wounded, or missing.[5] The battle so weakened the French that the initiative was thrown to the English, who planned a major offensive for the spring, the Battle of the Somme.

That battle was witnessed from the air by pilot Sholto Douglas, who remembered it clearly in his autobiography, which he wrote in the 1960s:

Figures alone can never tell the story of the way in which a whole generation of men was crippled. On that first day alone [July 1, 1916] our casualties on the Somme numbered fifty-seven thousand, of which twenty thousand men were killed or died of wounds. That slaughter went on until the Battle of the Somme ended in the mud of the winter. To those concerned it cost, all told, over one million casualties, with three hundred thousand British, French, and German dead. What was achieved? Although they have tried, no historian has really been able to say.[6]

Never had there been such a fierce absurdity as the trench warfare along the Western Front.

Pilots as Celebrities: The Origins of the Ace System

The Germans were the first to organize a massive publicity campaign around combat pilots. It must have seemed a useful tonic to offer the public after the German command had failed to achieve the promised victory in three weeks as envisioned in their Schlieffen Plan. By the end of 1915 it was obvious to the German command that Germany would not soon prevail. That year the Germans began celebrating the exploits of their combat pilots, and in January 1916, just a few weeks prior to the German assault at Verdun, Kaiser Wilhelm personally bestowed Prussia's highest military honor on two pilots. The Pour le Mérite or "Blue Max" had been awarded to German warriors for almost two hundred years, but never to combat flyers. The medals were given to Max Immelmann and Oswald Boelcke, who had scored a total of eight victories each. This was followed by a massive publicity campaign. Postcards, trading cards, press accounts, photographs, and newsreels brought their pictures and news of their exploits into every German home and schoolroom (see Figures 2 and 3).

At first, this singling out of individuals and promoting them as celebrities seemed to the Allies an appalling breach of military decorum. But six months later, the French, who lost 542,000 men at Verdun, apparently perceived the positive propaganda value to the publicity for pilots. The French decided to name in the dispatches any pilot who had shot down five planes. This was the beginning of the "ace" system, an organized effort to gain publicity for pilots which replaced the previous and far less systematic practice of giving attention only to pilots of extraordinary achievements. The Germans soon followed suit, setting ten verified victories as their threshold score. While the British were more reticent, and never adopted the practice of always mentioning in military dispatches pilots who had shot down a set number of planes, they also began to give extensive public attention to their outstanding pilots when the calamity of the Battle of the Somme became apparent.

It may seem obvious in retrospect that the combat pilot was well suited to filling the void left by the usual candidates for war heroes, but it does not appear to have been so immediately obvious at the time.

Oberleutnant Immelmann

Figure 2. German postcard of Max Immelmann wearing the Pour le Mérite ("Blue Max"), 1916. The attention given to combat pilots for shooting down fewer than a dozen enemy planes stands in stark contrast to the casualty figures of the ground war. The Germans were the first to celebrate their flyers as both celebrities and heroes. From National Air and Space Museum, Smithsonian Institution.

Figure 3. German postcard of Oswald Boelcke, 1916. Boelcke received the Pour le
Mérite at the same time as Max Immelmann; they were the first pilots to receive the
medal. From National Air and Space Museum, Smithsonian Institution.

Douglas made this observation about the German publicity campaigns of the summer of 1915:

> the Germans started indulging in the most astonishing adulation of their fighter pilots, and it was then that we began to hear more and more about men like Oswald Boelcke and Max Immelmann. . . . It was not until later in the war that our people came to understand the value of some form of hero-worship and to give more attention to the names of our outstandingly successful pilots; but we never at any time reached the hysteria indulged in by the Germans.[7]

The considerable resistance on the part of the Royal Flying Corps (RFC) command to publicity for individual combat pilots irritated some members of Parliament, who were quite possibly eager to offer the public some good news from the front during the opening days of the Battle of the Somme. On July 19, 1916—or just over two weeks after the disastrous opening attack of July 1—Sir A. Markham, M.P., put the question to the government of "why the name of the young aviator who shot down Immelmann (June, 1916) . . . had been suppressed by the Press Bureau, and why the names of airmen who had distinguished themselves were not allowed to appear in the press." The government replied that the British aviators themselves did not want their names to appear in the papers. This would have been an expected reply from any aviator, because of the standing orders disallowing publicity for flyers.[8]

In October 1916 the issue came to a head when British pilot Albert Ball had accumulated thirty-one victories. Neither the information nor the details were made available; however, journalists pressed for information when Ball received both the Military Cross and the Distinguished Service Order. As a consequence, Ball and other British combat pilots began to receive the same kind of attention as their counterparts in Germany and France. Members of Parliament would mention the names of noteworthy pilots in debate, or news would be leaked to the press, and ultimately the top British combat pilots were awarded medals by the king at court ceremonies. During the Battle of the Somme, for example, the British heard of the exploits of not only Albert Ball but James McCudden as well.

The Emergence of Aerial Combat

An essential factor for lionizing the combat pilot was the development of forward-firing combat planes. Air-to-air combat in single-seater combat planes emerged at the same time that the war entered the bloody attrition campaigns of Verdun and the Somme. At the beginning of the war, airplanes, which were relatively new to the battlefield, were used exclusively for observation, either flying unarmed over enemy lines to take photographs or helping to correct the aim of their own artillery units. Pilots and observers flying to photograph positions and troop movements, if they met their enemy counterparts, would be as likely to wave at them as anything else, although there were occasional and ineffective efforts to demonstrate hostility by firing carbines or tossing bricks or flechettes.

In October 1914, two months after World War I began, a French observer flying in a two-seater plane used a machine gun to shoot down a German plane, the first air-to-air kill with a machine gun. Over time, all the combatants turned to arming two-seater observation planes with machine guns; subsequent developments saw the appearance of scout or pursuit planes—single-pilot airplanes which, unlike the two-seater observers or the later multicrew bombers, had air-to-air combat as their primary mission. Most earlier models were armed with a machine gun usually mounted above the pilot on the upper wing of the biplane.

It took a bit more time for the development of the combination of man and machine most closely identified with the image of the combat pilot, that is, the single-seat plane armed with a fixed, forward-firing machine gun aimed directly at the opponent, making the pilot, his plane, and the machine gun a synchronized and synergistic weapon. This development dates essentially from April 1915 when the French pilot Roland Garros took off in a Morane monoplane with a device he had invented, which permitted him to fire his machine gun through the rotating propeller without blasting the blades to smithereens. When he shot down a German plane that day, he was the first to have aimed his entire plane as if it were a weapon. Several days later, he was shot down behind German lines and was unable to set his plane afire—the normal expectation—so that it fell into German hands.[9] It was not long before the Germans developed an improved version, the Fokker, named for Anthony Fokker, who had modified the design of the captured plane to allow synchronized firing: the bullets went through the gaps in the rotating propeller blades rather than simply being deflected when they hit a blade. The modification clearly opened a new phase in air combat: both Immelmann and Boelcke flew Fokkers. But it was not long before all the combatants had forward-firing, synchronized planes, which were increasingly maneuverable and could fly at higher altitudes and faster speeds.

Engagements by single-pilot pursuit planes—rather than the defensive combat characteristic of two-seater observation planes—were seized upon to draw public attention to the air war. This tendency, in fact, explains in part why the British were slower to make celebrities of their fighter pilots. The commander of their air services, Hugh Trenchard, felt that privileging their status tended by implication to diminish the courage and importance of other aspects of the air war, particularly the work of the observers and pilots in the two-seater planes, who had to fly in a straight line up and down the enemy trenches to obtain clear photographs and who were therefore highly vulnerable to artillery shelling and enemy pursuit planes.

The Need for Propaganda Heroes

The second factor making it possible to celebrate the combat pilots as heroes was the advent of mass communication coupled with the control over its content. The ability to shape for the public at home an image of the war that gratified their expectations and their desire to identify with the men fighting it was a significant development in modern warfare, as governments and military leaders discovered that control over the content or substance created images of warfare with the force of reality.

The aim of constructing a symbolic hero out of the combat pilots certainly outweighed any intent to explain the real significance of the air war to the public. Selected for attention was the individual who sought combat in the skies rather than the team that persevered in gathering information vital to the ground war. The emphasis was placed on single-handed combat and individual victories instead of on the teamwork, cooperation, and interdependence characteristic of observers and spotters. Moreover, the military command at the time, and military historians since then, concluded that of the contributions made to the outcome of World War I by the various uses of the airplane, air-to-air combat was the least significant, especially compared with the support to the ground forces provided by artillery spotting, aerial photography, and other functions.

The reason for this emphasis resides fundamentally in the human need for heroes. Considerable attention has been paid to chronicling the propaganda ministries formed in Great Britain and the United States when those two nations entered the war. Both nations attached considerable importance to controlling the public's understanding of the war, and both showed an advanced grasp on how to use publicity campaigns to promulgate desired messages. The aim here is not to revisit that history, except to notice that it is readily available; rather, the interest is in focusing on one aspect of the propagandists' aims as they themselves perceived it, which was to provide an image of the hero during the war in order to galvanize the public.

In his seminal essay *Public Opinion* (1922), Walter Lippmann, who served in the overseas branch of the Committee on Public Information, explained the general principles used to construct a hero during the war. All public figures have what Lippmann called a "constructed" or "symbolic" personality—what is termed now an "image." During times of war, Lippmann observed, the image of a hero has a potentially galvanizing effect simply because one can imagine or visualize him in the war. A hero who symbolizes the war promotes a positive emotional identification with him and, by implication, with the war. The aim is to induce the public to imagine the hero as representing the war—as standing for it or symbolizing it—so that neither the imagination nor the understanding dwells upon the material realities of war. The image of the hero substitutes for either the knowledge of war or a genuine emotional engagement with it.[10]

Military publicists were well aware of the need to manage the image of military leaders, a point Lippmann illustrated with an anecdote included in the memoirs of Jean de Pierrefeu, an officer on General Joseph Joffre's staff for three years. One day a photographer came to take pictures in Joffre's office: "'Suddenly it was noticed that there were no maps on the walls. But since according to popular ideas it is not possible to think of a general without maps, a few were placed in position for the picture, and removed soon afterwards'" (9). Lippmann made it clear that those working in the propaganda ministries were highly conscious of the need to arouse the desired emotions by representing war as the public believed it ought to be: "The only feeling that anyone can have about an event he does not experience is the feeling aroused by the mental image of the event." Therefore, the need is to manage the "mental image" (8).

During a war, Lippmann argued, the public is most susceptible to the emotional appeal of symbolic personalities. This is the case for a number of reasons. For one thing, the public is far removed from the battlefield, and can gain understanding or awareness of the war only through mediated sources. In addition, constructed personalities more easily become heroic, in the sense of having the capacity to galvanize a population, during a war—the "one human activity left in which whole populations accomplish the union sacrée." Unanimity of purpose drowns out (or represses) the diversity of desire and opinion that prevails in times of peace (8). Lippmann might more accurately have noticed that during World War I public opinion was controlled in part through rigorous censorship and harsh penalties for public dissent.

The full implication of Lippmann's analysis of how image is managed is often overlooked. The successful image is one that resonates with the already-imagined, or how the public expects a war ought to be conducted or how a hero ought to appear. That insight is the force behind the anecdote about the stage-setting for Joffre's photograph. Managing the "mental image" of war means constructing images to match what war is already imagined to be.

To illustrate this point, Lippman borrows a character from Sinclair Lewis's *Main Street*, Miss Sherwin of Gopher Prairie. He asks the reader to imagine Miss Sherwin reading about World War I from the comfort of her home in the Midwest. She reads about three million men clashing upon the battlefield, and she cannot imagine it—in fact, it exceeds the capacity of anyone's imagination. As a consequence, Miss Sherwin "fastens upon the Joffre and the Kaiser as if they were engaged in a personal duel." If we could see into her mind's eye,

> the image in its composition might be not unlike an Eighteenth Century engraving of a great soldier. He stands there boldly unruffled and more than life size, with a shadowy army of tiny little figures winding off into the landscape behind. Nor it seems are great men oblivious to these expectations.

Lippman follows this with his example from the photography session with Joffre (8–9). The lessons drawn here are clear: first, the images-in-the-mind of the public about warfare are derived from the mediating images of previous wars, from the artistic rendering of them in prose, poetry, painting, or engravings. Second, the very scale of World War I—never mind the differences made by mechanization and stalemate—made it impossible to imagine, not simply because of the numbers of soldiers involved, but also because it did not live up to the romantic image of warfare conducted along Napoleonic example—no armies under the guidance of an inspiring Caesar sweeping across the landscape, conquering all that stood before.

It is in this context that the significance can be most fully realized of the opportunity provided to propagandists by the emergence of air combat during the stalemated and highly mechanized trench warfare on the Western Front. The combat pilots offered a way to compensate for the problem the ground war presented to the construction of heroes, especially because air-to-air combat was a new form of warfare about which the public knew little. Glamorizing the pilots offered a substitute for understanding the war's complexities or comprehending its horrors. Such symbols domesticated the scale of war, making it more manageable in the psychological sense: they distracted attention from the reality of war, enforced the impression that it could be understood, and elicited the emotional identification needed to sustain public unity and support for the war.

Lippman's example concentrates on the "homefront" audience, but there were other target audiences in addition to the civilians at home. It was also desirable, for instance, to undermine the confidence or morale of the opposing forces and the faith of the enemy's civilians in their military or political leadership. An additional objective of the Allies was to bring the neutral United States into the war. And recruitment was yet another aim: young men in the Commonwealth nations and the United States were badly needed to replace the pilots and observers who were casualties of the air war.

Perhaps the clearest example of an air-war propaganda campaign is provided by the German publicity centered on Boelcke and Immelmann. It was the first propaganda campaign to appropriate air-to-air combat specifically for the purpose of demoralizing the enemy and undermining the opposing public's confidence in its leadership. The campaign is now referred to as the "Fokker Scare," but the Allied pilots at the time called it the "Fokker Scourge." An understanding of the campaign reinforces the important role played not simply by publicity but also by technological advances in promoting the combat pilot. Both Boelcke and Immelmann flew the new Fokker Eindecker (monoplane), with its forward-firing synchronized capability. There were never very many Eindeckers on the front and they were actually less maneuverable than Allied fighters. But their psychological impact was tremendous, in part because the Allies had to that point held considerable advantage in the air war with the Germans. Before the advent of the Fokker Eindecker, the Germans had been overmatched by the Morane monoplane—the model armed and flown by Garros—and often had to return machine-gun fire with side-arm weapons. The Germans were simply unable to respond effectively; for example, the RFC reported only sixteen aerial combats during the entire month of August 1915. At about the same time, however, the Allied military had some disquieting hints about what was coming when Fokker Eindeckers were used successfully to attack French bombers. By the fall of 1916, the Fokkers were beginning to take their toll in aerial combat at the front. Between November 7 and January 12, the RFC reported the loss of twenty aircraft, figures in sharp contrast with those of the previous spring and summer.[11]

The Germans deployed their air force, including the Fokker Eindeckers, to provide air support to the Battle of Verdun (February 1916) in a way that gained them what previously had only been conceived as a theoretical potential: air supremacy. The French, who bore the brunt of the assault at Verdun, were caught unawares and had to reorganize their air force and quickly reconceive its use. They were soon copying the new tactics of the Germans, first conceived by Boelcke, of flying combat planes in organized patrols or small formations of two or three planes. In the skies over Verdun for the first time separate organized fighter forces engaged in air-to-air combat using formation flying. It was also in the skies over Verdun that the Lafayette Escadrille saw its first real battle action. By August the Germans had begun forming *Jagdstafflen* (or separate "hunting squadrons" consisting of fourteen planes). But they also lost the advantage to the French, who were able to produce and commit a larger number of fighter planes to the battle.[12]

The appearance of the Fokker Eindeckers on the front demoralized the Allied flyers to such an extent that in April 1916 Trenchard reported he had found it necessary to reduce aerial operations "enormously." Flyers had the perception that the Fokker Eindecker was superior to any Allied aircraft not only because it could fire along an axis directly through the propeller, but also because it was faster, more maneuverable, and in greater numbers. Cecil Lewis, in his autobiography *Sagittarius Rising*, says that the pilots believed, "You were as good as dead if you so much as saw one."[13]

Historians subsequently adopted the official story of the time, which is that the pilots simply panicked unnecessarily. There were, for example, no more than an estimated fifty Fokker Eindeckers operating along the front at any one time, and in January 1916, when reactions to the Eindecker were strongest, the British air losses were in fact only ten planes. Moreover, when an Eindecker was finally captured in April 1916, it proved less maneuverable than available Allied aircraft.[14]

This information, while true, seems an overly eager attempt to dismiss the impact of the Eindecker on the front. The presence of fifty Eindeckers may seem a small number compared to a 400-mile-long front, but they made their important debut concentrated for an attack and utilized new offensive formation tactics against an enemy who was disorganized and lacked the firing capabilities of the Eindecker. And while the British may have lost "only" ten planes in January 1916, the French rather than the British bore the brunt of the Battle of Verdun, which magnifies the significance of the losses to the British, who had previously enjoyed such air superiority over the Germans.

Due consideration should be given, therefore, not simply to the purely psychological impact of the Eindecker on the pilots, but the material difference its appearance—coupled with new tactics that gave birth to air-to-air combat—made to those young pilots who had to encounter it. Equally important is the consideration rightly given to the effect of the publicity and attention that accompanied the appearance of the Fokkers at the front. The press in both Britain and the United States sensationalized the "Fokker Scare." While the reports were attacked as "fatuous sensationalism" in some quarters, the attendant public outcries were reflected in debates heard in both the British Parliament and the French Chamber of Deputies in the winter of 1916. This furor occurred at just the time that the Kaiser awarded both Immelmann and Boelcke the Blue Max, and German propagandists launched the extraordinary publicity campaign celebrating their achievements.[15]

The "Fokker Scare" illustrates how many factors coalesced to assure what for the Germans had to be regarded as a successful effort to demoralize the enemy: new technological advances, new tactics, profound losses to the French because of the attack at Verdun, and the exploitation of the mass media not only for the purpose of inspiring confidence on the homefront, but to demoralize the opposing forces and undermine public confidence in the enemy's military and political leadership (see Figure 4).

By July 1916 the French had developed the "ace" system to recoup the loss of public confidence, especially as the Allies had by that time regained control of the skies. By October 1916 questions were being raised in Parliament contesting the British air command's silence about its combat pilots. The ground offensive had shifted from Verdun to the Somme (July 1916), and while the disastrous ground offensive was borne by the British in particular, they had overcome the effects of the "Fokker Scourge," which had kept them on the ground in April, and had achieved sufficient air supremacy to demoralize the German ground troops in the Somme sector. Allied pilots kept a constant presence over the German lines, while German planes were absent, so that by August it was common to see signs posted in the German trenches, "Gott strafe England und unsere Flieger" ("May God punish England and our flyers").[16] Quite obviously, one of the lessons learned by the British and French at the hands of the Germans at Verdun was the potential use of the combat pilot both as a warrior and as a symbol; the lesson learned was applied by the following summer not only to inspire confidence at home (especially when the news was bad about the ground war), but to demoralize the enemy's troops.

Recruiting Aviators

The celebrity of the combat pilot was useful for an additional propaganda purpose: to recruit new volunteers into the flying service as the ranks of pilots and observers were depleted by significant casualty rates. It is one thing for history to agree that the combat pilot played the least significant role in the air war. But it would be a mistake to take that as meaning that flying was not both arduous and dangerous.

The tolls among trainees were high. Flying daily patrols required men to fly at high altitudes without oxygen masks, often in freezing temperatures, and with the fumes of castor oil burning off their engines.

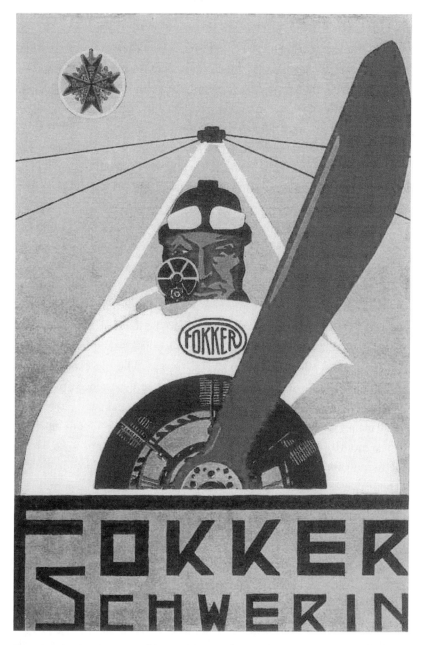

Figure 4. This German poster from 1916 gives sinister expression to the new synergy between man and machine. The appearance of the forward-firing, synchronized Fokkers opened a new phase in air combat, and the picture of the Pour le Mérite refers to the medals awarded Immelmann and Boelcke, who flew the new Fokkers to deadly effect. From U.S. Library of Congress.

The canvas covering wings on early models had a tendency to shred during sharp descents. Directional equipment was crude—it required considerable skill and experience simply to know when one was flying toward or away from enemy territory. Spotting aircraft depended upon not only keen eyesight, but the experience to actually spot aircraft at some distance and identify it as friendly or enemy. Maneuvering the plane during combat while firing at the enemy or avoiding the bullets spitting from an opposing plane required skill and nerve. And the pilots did not have parachutes.

The highest mortality rates in the air service occurred among the combat pilots. Between 1914 and 1918 6,000 RFC aviators were killed in combat with the German Air Force—or about one out of three—and 8,000 died while training to fly in England. During "quiet periods" at the front, life expectancy of pilots was eight weeks, and during heavy fighting less than three. At the time that the United States entered the war, March 1917, the Germans had regained air supremacy. They defeated Allied pilots at a ratio of five to one. The life expectancy of an RFC pilot was reduced to three weeks for an experienced pilot, and a mere eleven days for a rookie. In March, April, and May, more than 1,200 planes were shot down; in what became known as "Bloody April"— or the month before Billy Mitchell assisted the French in formulating the request for the massive American aviation program included in the Ribot cable—one-third of the total RFC was destroyed. The period witnessed the heaviest British casualties and losses to aircraft of the war; some squadrons suffered casualties of over 100 percent.[17]

The casualty rates associated with air-to-air combat have led one historian to call it a form of ritualized suicide. In terms of casualties and losses, flying was a very dangerous form of mechanized combat that exacted a high toll. Certainly, a life expectancy of eleven days in combat, or the realization that more men died training to fly than died in combat, does not make air combat seem quite so obviously a romantic and preferable alternative to the trenches.

The need to replace the losses was an especially challenging objective because the air service was a volunteer force. These realities underscore the important role to recruitment played by the efforts to glamorize air combat and make celebrities out of the aces. One British editorial written at the time of the debate over whether to mention aces in the military dispatches argued for the change in policy because of the need to recruit new pilots:

> If we expect young men to volunteer to fly with the R.F.C., we must offer them the chance to become heroes, like Captain Ball. Here in Britain we are playing down our airmen and are having to go into the trenches to beg young infantrymen to volunteer for flying. What a chance! They see war in the air every day—in all its grisly action. But over in Canada and America every young kid who can read wants to learn to fly. Why? Because all they know of war flying comes from the stories of French and German aces and how they are winning all the medals.[18]

The editorial is remarkably candid. The commentator was angry because the government had not permitted the press to lie with greater regularity to the public, and particularly, to the Canadians and Americans needed to fill the depleted ranks of the British air service.

The editor is obviously familiar with the principle Lippmann explains, that propaganda is most persuasive to those who are far removed from the battle. During the war—because of the tight controls over information—this meant, in effect, that civilians would understand it only in the terms framed by writers who had placed their skills in the service of their government or whose words were approved by the government. The angry editor was very willing to be of such service, if only the authorities would grant him the permission and access to the necessary information.

They soon did give that permission, and as Dan McCaffrey—a recent biographer of Canadian ace Billy Bishop—wryly observes, "To the propagandists, the swaggering aces were a godsend. They could do nothing to break the stalemate in France, but tales of their deeds were instrumental in the recruitment drive." Nor were they proven wrong in their estimates of the persuasive power of the aces as war heroes. The losses suffered in April 1917 forced the RFC to expand its number of squadrons to 106, which required increased recruitment. The campaign resulted in hundreds of Americans crossing the border into Canada to enlist rather than waiting for the air branch of the U.S. Signal Corps to sort itself out sufficiently to handle the tens of thousands of men who wanted to volunteer but were turned away because the military was unprepared for such a large number.[19]

The Value of the Lafayette Escadrille

The French developed a keen interest in attracting potential recruits from overseas, particularly the Americans, but they (and, for that matter, the British) had other objectives as well. When initially approached by young Americans from prestigious families with the plan of creating an all-volunteer American pursuit squadron in the French air services, the French had been decidedly uninterested. But eventually some members of the French ministry recognized that such a squadron could be a valuable propaganda tool for encouraging the United States to enter the war on the side of the Allies—something the French were, by 1916, very eager to have happen—and they gave their support to the formation in April of what was to become known as the Lafayette Escadrille.

The Escadrille carried all the traditional romanticism of voluntary soldiering. It was privately funded and membership in the Escadrille was small, amounting to thirty-eight Americans from its inception until it was absorbed into the American service.[20] Those who served, many of whom had seen earlier service on the front as volunteers in the French Foreign Legion or in the ambulance corps, understood that the French government felt they had an important propaganda or "publicity" role to play. In his account of the squadron, Escadrille member Edwin C. Parson says candidly of the French motives: "The French are smart diplomats. They wanted American support desperately, and . . . saw the possibilities offered by the publicity attendant on the spectacular efforts of prominent young Americans flying as a unit in French uniform."[21]

Just how high the stakes were felt to be in the propaganda war over the celebrity of combat pilots is illustrated by the international controversy ignited at the highest government levels when the news of the French intentions became known at the end of 1915. At about that time, three of the pilots, who were to be among the first members of the squadron when it formed and who were already flying in French squadrons, were granted leave to the United States. They were William Thaw, Norman Prince, and Elliott Cowdin. Prince is credited with having the idea for the all-American unit, and Thaw with using family influence very effectively in persuading the French to pursue the idea. When these three arrived home, they discovered that the publicity that had already been generated about them had made them, in Parson's words, "demigods . . . to the American public": "Much against their wills, from the moment of their arrival they were lionized and kept constantly in the public eye. They made grand copy for a nation athirst for first-hand news of the war."[22]

In response, the Germans demanded that they be interned for violating the neutrality treaty because they were active servicemen from a neutral nation in the uniform of a combatant nation. The three managed to sneak out of the country on a French liner, aided by American officials on the quiet, but they had served the intended purpose of creating "a tremendous enthusiasm and a real sympathy for France."[23]

When the squadron was finally formed (Spring 1916), it was called the Escadrille Americaine, a designation that the Germans protested for constituting a violation of neutrality, which is why it came to be known instead as the Lafayette Escadrille. The name indicated the historical military ties between France and the United States but avoided a label that declared that it was an all-American unit. The Germans' strident protests over what amounted to a handful of Americans in one privately financed squadron indicates how potent the symbolism of combat pilots was understood to be, especially when the neutrality of the United States was at stake.

The Americans who helped organize and those who financed the American squadron also understood the symbolism and its implications. The guiding force in making the arrangements for an American squadron was Dr. Edmond Gros, a successful American physician with a practice in Paris who moved in highly influential French social and political circles. At the start of the war, he played an important role in organizing the American Ambulance Field Service and used his influence to put Norman Prince and his friend Frazier Curtis in touch with French officers who supported the idea of an American squadron especially for its symbolic value in engaging American sympathy for the Allied cause. He also contacted influential Americans living in Paris to solicit funding, including Mr. and Mrs. William K. Vanderbilt, who advocated American intervention in the war. They gave an initial $20,000 to the fund and continued to make sizable contributions through the time that the Lafayette Escadrille flew for France.[24]

The French were careful initially not to assign unduly dangerous missions because of the squadron's recognized political and propaganda value and made sure the squadron was very well billeted and fed. They also gave the press access to the base. The squadron was first assigned to an old inn at Luxeuil, the site of an opulent health spa built for Louis XV. According to Capt. Georges Thenault, the squadron's French commander, they dined on "delicious trout from a neighboring stream, fat chickens, game hens, wild fowl . . . carefully cooked and washed down with generous burgundy" while outside "cars adorned with brass headlamps awaited the pilots personal use; inside, servants appeared at a clap of the hands."[25]

In twenty months of combat, the Lafayette Escadrille scored fifty-seven victories. The French proclaimed widely all the achievements of the squadron, especially to the Americans.[26] The French efforts did not abate even after America entered the war. They sent a military mission to lobby Congress for passage of the aviation appropriation bill, which the French themselves had initiated, and to recruit American college men for the air services. In the January 1918 issue of *National Geographic*, which published a number of articles written by members of the mission, the recruiting assignment fell to Capt. Jacques de Sieyes, who in his article, "Aces of the Air," was quite candid about his purpose: "I would like to think that I have not wasted my time here, and if I have been able to persuade some of my comrades in arms to become aviators my work will not have been in vain."[27] Captain de Sieyes not surprisingly holds up the Lafayette Escadrille for particular attention, even though he knew its members would soon be transferred into the U.S. Air Service:

> Americans have already proved their valor in the Lafayette Escadrille, some of whose members have fallen, but which has continued to increase in numbers until now it is the richest in pilots of any squadron in France. . . . The Lafayette Squadron is a squadron of pursuit, equipped with one-seater machines—swift, light, fast climbing, well armed, made to battle against enemy machines.[28]

That Americans were very familiar with the prestige of the Lafayette Escadrille is obvious from the economy of de Sieyes's prose. He clearly understood that he need not provide details. By 1918 publicity had been promoting the Lafayette Escadrille in particular and the combat pilot in general for over two years—the case had already been made that to be in the air services was to be a combat pilot, and to be an "ace" was to be a hero.

Pilots, Propaganda, and the Press

It was not simply the case that military publicists or the press reported the exploits of combat pilots; the pilots themselves were very much involved in promoting the role of air combat. The efforts by the Americans Thaw, Prince, and Cowdin to promote in the United States both the Lafayette Escadrille and the French cause is an early example, but participating in publicity campaigns became a customary facet of the life of a successful combat pilot.

There is, in fact, something of a cyclical nature to the propaganda campaigns promoting the aces of World War I. The initial publicity campaigns influenced young men to volunteer; they then also became involved in contributing to the publicity and propaganda about air combat. Some wrote memoirs of themselves as pilots which were published during the war, notably in terms of influence in the United States, the top ace flying for the RFC, the Canadian Billy Bishop, and the Americans James R. McConnell and James Norman Hall, both of whom flew with the Lafayette Escadrille. Eddie Rickenbacker, who became America's top ace, recalled in his memoir that his unit was instructed for a time by two flyers from the Lafayette Escadrille—Captains David Peterson and James Norman Hall, "the author of Kitchener's Mob and High Adventure." "We had all," says Rickenbacker, "idolized them before we had seen them."[29]

As a member of the Lafayette Escadrille, Hall recognized the public-relations role he and his fellow pilots were expected to play. He had already gained a reputation as a writer because of his novel *Kitchener's Mob: The Adventures of an American in the British Army* (1916), which is an account of his service as a volunteer in the British army until he was wounded and discharged. In 1916 he sailed from the United States for France with a commission from the *Atlantic Monthly* to complete a series of articles on the Lafayette Escadrille, which he planned to do before reenlisting in the British army; however, he soon found himself volunteering for the famous squadron. His articles were published in the *Atlantic Monthly* in 1917 and 1918, and as the book *High Adventure* in 1918.

By the time Rickenbacker arrived at the front with Pershing's first forces, the "aces" had become a self-constructed image, and the boundaries between their symbolic and actual identities blurred. Rickenbacker's own memoir reflects the influence of the earlier accounts; the self-constructed image of the pilots became a generative paradigm for subsequent accounts.

It was not, of course, only or primarily autobiographical accounts that invested the pilots with celebrity. By the time the United States entered the war, the press coverage of combat aviators had become a matter of routine, a kind of "beat" that bore some resemblance to celebrity coverage. Reporters awaited pilots returning from freshly confirmed victories, and the top aviators were standard fare for publicity campaigns, newsreel footage, and newspaper copy. The level of coverage was made possible only by the close working relationship between the press and the military, which had already become routine for the Allies before America entered the war.

An indication of how the celebrity of the combat pilots of World War I impressed their young readers in the United States is provided by a passage in *Falcons of France: A Tale of Youth and the Air*, a fictionalized autobiographical account published in 1929 by Hall and another flyer for the Lafayette Escadrille, Charles Nordhoff, a partnership later made famous by their coauthorship of a number of books, most notably *Mutiny on the Bounty*. The first-person reflection by the central character in *Falcons of France* undoubtedly echoes the seductive power exerted by the exploits of the World War I aviators on the imaginations of American and Canadian boys during the war:

> Like thousands of other young Americans, I thought of the war by day and dreamed of it by night; all the everyday interests of life had gone flat and stale, and their places in my mind were filled with daydreams. . . . Particularly [of] aeroplanes—small hornetlike ships manned by a single pilot, swooping down to spit machine-gun fire into the enemy's ranks, or maenoeuvring high above the battlefield in duels to the death. . . . And when I read accounts of the American volunteers flying for France in the Escadrille Lafayette, I read them twice or three times over, fascinated in a mood of despairing envy.[30]

The "despairing envy"—despairing because of the sense that the young adolescent reading of these exploits would never have the chance to be an aviator in war—was an envy aroused because of the successful condensation of national aspirations and values into the image of the combat pilot.

Once the air-war-as-imagined took hold, it became the truth of the air war for millions of Americans. As a tool for propaganda, the image of the combat pilot was the most significant contribution to the war effort, a potent and seductive image for structuring male desire and the aspirations of the nation.

CHAPTER 5

Casus Belli

War as Melodrama

In the American popular imagination, the combat pilots of World War I were and typically still are the "knights of the air." This consistency of both the image and its positive connotation is a remarkable history for a trope of warfare in the twentieth century; indeed, the motives and conduct of the combat aces are still held out as beacons to a world made cynical by the realities of warfare. Three examples will give the flavor of these postwar characterizations. Arch Whitehouse, a veteran of the first air war and the author of numerous popular histories of the aces, introduces his account of the Lafayette Escadrille, published in 1962, with the lament, "The words 'volunteer' and 'patriot' have all but vanished from our vocabulary. . . . To the many pacifists, patriotism is the unrealistic gesture of a deluded individual." By contrast, the story of the volunteers of the Lafayette Escadrille is exemplary of a different spirit: "No chapter in the story of the professional soldier can be more stirring than the experiences of this handful of winged Galahads," men who were "spiritually attuned for the defense of their civilization."[1]

A view from the same perspective is offered by Edward Jablonski in his introduction to *Warriors with Wings: The Story of the Lafayette Escadrille* (1966):

following the terrible waste of life, the hypocrisies, the blunderings and betrayals of trust of the First World War, causes, altruism and even patriotism became almost passe. Still, this did not affect the motivations of the men who gave or were willing to give their lives because they believed that civilization itself was facing extinction.[2]

In a more recent account of the Lafayette Escadrille published in 1991, Dennis Gordon attributes the motives of the American volunteers to a "curiousity" about the Great Adventure, coupled with "a genuine desire to serve the French Republic in its time of peril," and he quotes one pilot who said, "'there was no man there who was not ready and willing to give his life, if necessary, for the Allied cause, because he believed in it.'"[3]

Volunteers who wanted to serve the "cause" and defend civilization, young men motivated by an idealism about the necessary defense of threatened values—these are the attributes most consistently assigned to the Americans who flew for the Lafayette Escadrille, and in general to those who flew over the Western Front. The imagery of the "knights of the air" has had its strongest connection with those who flew for France and Great Britain and has influenced how the great German flyers were characterized by the British and Americans (most notably, how they attached the designation the "Red Baron" to Manfred von Richthofen).

An obvious though often overlooked question implicitly raised by successful propaganda is how it works as a convincing message. The word "propaganda" as often as not denotes "lie" or "untruth" and little more. Sometimes, in an effort to inoculate citizens against the effects of propaganda, the answer to the question of how it works is reduced to listing a set of techniques that once taught to an otherwise innocent member of the public will enable him or her to see through the repetition, or the big lie, or the demonizing of the enemy.

A deeper understanding of propaganda, however, depends upon its similarity to cultural discourses because it draws upon cultural myths, values, and beliefs as validating, interpretive frameworks. The example examined in this chapter is the framework of the Great War as a crusade. Once a framework is chosen, facts or images are deployed as signs that refer to it. "Knights of the air" was a trope that acquired its cultural meaning from the use of the medieval Crusades as an interpretive framework for justifying the war as a defense of civilization. The Crusades resonated with precursor assumptions about moral values and national destiny particularly important to how Great Britain and France idealized themselves. It is because such precursor beliefs, values, or myths are already naturalized within the society—that is, are already not only understood, but taken as foundational, or inevitable, or as historically true or as an unchanging aspect of human nature—that the effective propaganda message is convincing.

The most interesting question to ask about a propaganda message that is an outright fabrication is why it was believed in the first place. It is also the most interesting question to ask about those propaganda messages that convey accurate information. The answer to both resides in the connection between the message itself and the cultural framework upon which its meaning is made to depend. In other words, the issues most germane to grasping the persuasive power of propaganda messages cannot be addressed only by trying to decide the degree to which the message varied from an accurate report. Rather, what must be excavated is the power of the precursor beliefs that the message is said to signify, and the credibility of the link forged between the image, message, or information and that interpretive framework.

The representation of the combat pilot, for instance, admittedly involved suppressing certain unappealing information—especially the high mortality rates, poor pilot training, and inferior equipment. On the other hand, government inquiries were held in Great Britain about combat-pilot mortality rates, with some members of Parliament referring to them as the equivalent of "murder." In the United States, it could hardly have been lost on the public that many of the accolades heaped upon the Americans who flew for the Lafayette Escadrille and the European aces were posthumous. In other words, the evidence suggests that even had the press accounts of the combat in skies over western Europe included more accurate accounts of the mortality rates, the result may not have been a reduction in the romance attached to them, or a lessening of the belief in their heroism. Coming at the question of the effectiveness of propaganda with the idea that it works only because it is a "lie," and would not work if the truth were told, does not really explain the persuasive power of a particular message.

In addition, propaganda is not always untrue or fabricated. During World War I the press reported conduct that, though true, seems extraordinary to the jaundiced eyes of those looking back upon the wars of the twentieth century. Pilots, especially in the early days of air-to-air combat, sometimes really did land next to a plane they had just shot down and offer a cigarette and a handshake to the person they had just a few moments earlier wanted to kill, or, as a courtesy fly over opposing aerodromes to drop messages telling the name of someone whom they had shot down and whether they were dead or wounded, or treated prisoners with courtesy, or toasted the fallen enemy by name.

Such courtesies were observed with increasing rarity as air-to-air combat became more organized and more deadly, and they were never universally observed. But dwelling only on the contrast between what was reported as typical and what the "facts" were, while interesting, will inevitably miss the more important point to be made about the persuasive power of the trope "knights of the air."

The most striking feature of the figure of speech is that in the United States it continues to be the most often invoked image of the World War I aces in popular culture. The representation of the ground war as a crusade has since then lost its luster, resounds as an irony or a sarcasm or the Big Lie when put up against the loss of human life, the futility of trench warfare, the reality that the world was soon enough again at war following the Armistice, the failed peace. But the imagery, when applied to the combat aces of World War I, has been untarnished in terms of the popular histories of the air war, free of the postwar irony that otherwise characterizes the references to the romantic veil drawn over the grim realities of modern warfare by the propagandist's pen.

To understand how this image of warfare has survived for the better part of a century even its ironic treatment by William Faulkner or John Dos Passos requires attention to the necessary connection—in terms of how war is effectively characterized as reflecting favorably upon the nation—between the way the war was justified (the *casus belli*) and the way it was fought. The transfer of the trope of the crusade to the "knight of the air" reflected both the unsuitability of the ground war for credibly representing the war-imagined-as-crusade, and the corollary desirability and feasibility of fastening the imagery of the crusade onto the combat pilot.

The cultural potency of the "knights of the air" has its source in how the *casus belli* was represented by the Allies to audiences in the United States and how, once the United States entered the war, those themes were adapted to the American experience to arouse public support and fervor. Representing the *casus belli* as a crusade relied heavily upon characterizing the Germans as barbarians who threatened civilization itself. The threat to civilization was framed as a melodramatic rescue of the damsel/madonna from the fiend. Civilization was rendered as "female," and her rescuer as not only "masculine" but also exemplary of a particular kind of masculinity, one refined by the influences of civilization, an aristocratic, chivalrous masculinity pitted against an atavistic masculine barbarism intent upon rape and pillage.

The "knights of the air" image is rooted in the values ascribed to civilization defined as an artifact of aristocratic breeding, morality, and paternalism. To understand the resilience of the trope requires an apparent digression from the story of blue bullets blazing in the sky to the images used to justify the Allied cause and how that framework was adopted to American tastes when the United States entered the war. It is also possible to infer something of the impact of these messages on the imaginations of young, well-bred scions of the rich and established families in America who volunteered as airmen.

Civilization and Barbarism

By the middle of the war, and certainly by the time the United States intervened, Germany was easily and regularly represented as barbarous, militaristic, and autocratic, its people mere automatons incapable of independent thought. Prior to the war, Germany had epitomized high culture and advanced learning to both Europe and the United States, and its crowned head was related to the king of England. But soon after the war began, Germany became "uncivilized," held in the firm grip of "Prussian militarism," and the Allies were engaged in defending civilized values against the clear and present danger of encroachment by a barbarian horde—the Huns.

Essential to this narrative was the idea that Germany had caused the war by pursuing expansionist, imperialistic aims at the expense of the weak and defenseless. Their selfish and barbarous motives were revealed in Europe by the atrocities their military committed against civilians in occupied territories, especially women and children, and in the rest of the world by their deplorable colonial methods that did not bear comparison with the sound and enlightened policies of the British. The Germans' barbarism was also reflected in the use of advanced weapons technology against not only combatants, but also civilians—siege cannons directed against the towns of Belgium, Gotha bombers attacking cities, submarines sinking passenger liners—as well as the introduction of poison gas to the battlefield.

The Allies, for their part, were fighting for unselfish reasons to defend the principles of civilization. They had entered the war only for self-protection (in the instance of France) and to protect the weak and defenseless, Belgium being the most obvious nation. One corollary of this narrative was that war conducted against such a barbarous nation obviated the possibility for a negotiated end (which meant that German efforts toward that goal were rejected); the war had to be fought to achieve total victory, which meant that ultimately the United States would have to be convinced to join the Allied efforts.

The characterization of Germany as barbaric hinged upon the accounts of German military atrocities, especially in Belgium, but also in occupied France. Using the invasion of Belgium as the justification for Great Britain's entry into the war was easier than explaining the failure to address the international frictions that precipitated the war as well as their deeper sources, which were the competing desires of all the belligerent nations for control over the resources and markets of colonies and concessions in other parts of the world. To probe too deeply into the primary causes of the war would call into question not only the probity of England's leaders but the underpinnings of British prosperity and the values it represented. Moreover, by defining the war as a conflict between civilized and uncivilized nations, there was no need to consider that modern, mechanized warfare reflected the application of the most advanced and hence civilized capabilities to the most reptilian of ends, or that far from meliorating violent and dehumanizing tendencies, the advantages of both modern technology and the highly organized modern state made it possible to conduct warfare at a level of destruction previously unimaginable.[4]

Atrocities: Crimes against Civilization

The British indictment of German atrocities against civilians used a discourse of civilized constraint to condemn Prussianism as barbaric. The indictment invoked the concept of crimes against humanity as a universal moral and legal principle, and was made against the officers who commanded the troops and, ultimately, against the government of Germany.

When the Germans invaded Belgium, one of the concerns that plagued both officer and enlisted alike was the fear of the *franc-tireur*, snipers and terrorists who were not in uniform, and who could slip into the anonymity of the civilian population after an attack. The German army had experienced their effects during the Franco-Prussian War (1870–71), and as a consequence their invasion of Belgium included planned *Schrecklichkeit*, a campaign of terrorizing the civilian populations to assure their submission. The Germans felt they were acting within the bounds of the Hague Convention in seeking to protect themselves from unidentified civilian terrorists and snipers. In the German *White Book*, published in the spring of 1915 to respond to the charges that the German military engaged in a policy of systematic atrocities, the German government acknowledged, for instance, that they had rounded up male hostages and executed them in Dinant (Belgium), but made no apologies for this, arguing it was a legitimate retaliation for unorganized resistance to the German invasion. In a similar vein, the report of a commission ordered by the German Reichstag in 1924 to investigate violations of international law during World War I justified the *Schrecklichkeit* campaign with the observation: "In war everyone is a sacrificial lamb. The humane thing is, in a higher sense, often the most inhumane."[5] The intended point was that by quickly subduing the civilian population, the terror campaign saved lives in the long run.

The Allies did not regard the atrocities as examples of conduct permitted under the Hague Convention, but as exemplary of a nation that had reverted to barbarism. From the time the Germans invaded Belgium, American newspapers carried accounts of systematic terror conducted against civilian populations. The prime mover behind the dissemination of the accounts in a manner that supported the British cause was Wellington House, the British Ministry of Information, which disseminated favorable propaganda and information about the war to neutral nations—including, most important, the United States. It published a number of pamphlets concentrating on the German invasion of a neutral nation and war atrocities both in Belgium and elsewhere. *Belgium and Germany: Texts and Documents* (1915) was written by Henri Davignon, the Belgian foreign minister, and included an address by Cardinal Mercier, Primate of All Belgium. It reported terror campaigns at Aerschot and the destruction of cultural centers, including the library at Louvain. That same year, L. H. Grondys compiled a pamphlet entitled *The Germans in Belgium*. Even detractors of the Wellington House publications agree that the pamphlet is even-handed; for example, it reports the case of a sixteen-year-old girl who had been bayoneted to death for resisting rape but includes the information that the soldiers were punished by their officers. In reporting the devastation at Aerschot, Grondys also included the German explanation, which is that it was done in retaliation against *franc-tireurs* (snipers) who fired on German soldiers.[6]

Wellington House also published the anonymous pamphlet *The Death of Edith Cavell* (1915), which reported the execution by firing squad of a Red Cross nurse who was accused by the Germans of permitting the wounded to escape. The Germans made no apologies for their actions, justifying it as legitimate under the rules of warfare. The incident aroused international outrage and was to assume iconic significance well after the war ended. It was retold by American journalist James Beck the following year in *The Case of Edith Cavell* (1916). In *The Last Phase in Belgium* (1917) Lord Bryce attacked the Germans for deporting Belgian workers. This condemnation was reinforced by pamphlets written by Belgian journalist Jules Destree and Brand Whitlock, the head of the American Delegation in Belgium.

As the atrocity stories about Belgium waned with the occupation, other pamphlets on the subject of German barbarism were written by members of Wellington House to report outrages in other parts of the world. These include Thomas Masaryk's accusations against the Hapsburg government, *Austrian Terrorism in Bohemia* (1916), and anonymous pamphlets accusing the Germans of mistreating colonial natives (*Black Slaves of Prussia*) and of using bacteriological warfare in Romania (*Microbe Culture at Bukarest*). Perhaps the most notorious pamphlet was a *Corpse-Conversion Factory* (1917), a four-page report alleging that the Germans were shipping the corpses of their dead soldiers to Liège to be boiled down for soap. In 1925 the story was exposed on the floor of the House of Commons as a fabrication. This was the spark for the volley of criticism leveled against British propaganda of World War I, notably with the publication in 1928 of Arthur Ponsonby's *Falsehood in Wartime*, and followed soon thereafter by critical attacks in the United States.[7]

The most important British report of German atrocities was the widely disseminated Report of the Commission to Investigate German Outrages (1915), often called simply the Bryce Report.[8] In December 1914 Sir James Bryce accepted appointment by the prime minister to head what was called the "German Outrages Inquiry Committee." Bryce was widely respected in both England and the United States, where he had served as British ambassador from 1907 to 1913. He was a friend of President Wilson and was highly regarded as a scholar, having received not only several honorary German doctorates, but also the Pour le Mérite. For the committee, Bryce was joined by a distinguished panel: Sir Edward Pollack, both a jurist and a legal historian, H. A. L. Fisher, both a historian and vice chancellor of Sheffield University, Harold Cox, the editor of the *Edinburgh Review*, and several distinguished lawyers.

The committee examined 1,200 witnesses; 500 of their statements were included in the report, as were excerpts from thirty-seven diaries taken from dead German soldiers, some of them officers. Many of the accounts included in the final report repeated those published previously in newspaper accounts, or in official accounts released by the Belgian government before the final fall of Belgium to the Germans. But they were lent renewed credibility by the status of the British committee. The report included accounts of the German soldiers' gratuitous killing of women and children, committing rape, executing men taken as hostages, burning villages, using women and children as human screens, burning people alive in their homes, widespread looting, mutilating the dead, and wantonly destroying entire villages.

The general condemnation of British propaganda in the postwar years has certainly tainted the Bryce Report, which was criticized among other reasons for relying solely upon the accounts of Belgian refugees, although why that should be taken as an altogether disqualifying factor is difficult to understand. The Germans for their part did not deny some of the more serious allegations, such as targeting women and children. In the example cited above from the *White Book*, the report acknowledges that not only were male hostages executed in Dinant (Belgium), but some women and children were also killed, though this was unintended. The male hostages, the report states, were grouped together and some women and their children "contrary to the arrangements made, had left their station which was apart from the male hostages, and had crowded together with the latter." How this account supports the conclusion that killing the women and children was unintentional remains a mystery. Similarly, even those American scholars who in the postwar years were most avid in their condemnation of British propaganda in general and the Bryce Report in particular concede the factual basis for some of the reports. The sacking of Louvain, which was the subject of numerous accounts, is described by one such apologist as having occurred because the Germans thought the population supported the attacking Belgian army (hardly a surprise), and in retaliation the "Germans executed some of the civilians and destroyed about one-eighth of the city." The burning of the Louvain library—which became a singular icon for the cultural barbarism of the Germans—was, according to a postwar report by a highly placed American official, not an example of a deliberate order having been given by an officer but the act of a soldier's "wantonness."[9]

From these accounts and debates, three conclusions seem reasonable. First, the treatment of civilians at the hands of the Germans in August 1914 was by the Germans' own admission brutal and intentionally so; second, the atrocity accounts as reported by the British were undoubtedly exaggerated and told in a way that favored a particular political end. And finally, it would be a mistake, as some have done or attempted to do, to write off all the accounts of what occurred in Belgium as mere fabrications.

The propaganda value of the Bryce Report to the British is beyond doubt. The English, French, and American publics had been skeptical initially about the reported atrocities. Lord Bryce's reputation made the report especially credible in the United States. In addition, the final report was filed near the time of the sinking of the *Lusitania*, May 7, 1915, a timeliness not lost on Sir Gilbert Parker, who was the member of Wellington House charged with information and propaganda aimed at the United States. Parker rushed the Bryce Report into print, so that it appeared just five days after the news of the *Lusitania*. In the same week that Britains, Canadians, and Americans read the names of civilians killed in the attack on the *Lusitania*, they could read lurid, personal accounts of German brutalities during the initial occupation of Belgium. Similar findings were published that year by the French Ministry of Foreign Affairs about the French-occupied territories, and then translated into English and published under the title *Germany's Violations of the Laws of War*, with the British aiding in its distribution in the United States.[10]

The Bryce Report was widely available and inexpensive. It gained additional potency when it was printed with accounts of other outrages, such as the sinking of the *Lusitania*. For that reason, the Bryce Report will be examined in what follows as it appeared in Logan Marshall's *Thrilling Stories of the Great War* (1915), a commercial, mass-market publication that framed the war in the terms set out by the British propaganda ministry. *Thrilling Stories* included accounts of the sinking of the *Lusitania* and the German destruction of cultural sites in Belgium and occupied France, as well as excerpts from the Bryce Report and the official French report. Notably, one of the contributors was Sir Gilbert Parker, identified only as a member of Parliament and British novelist and not identified for his role at Wellington House.

The theme used to tie together all of the accounts was that the Germans were guilty of crimes against civilization or crimes against humanity; for example, the title of one of several accounts of the sinking of the *Lusitania* was "A Crime Against Civilization: The Tragic Destruction of the *Lusitania*—An Unprecedented Crime Against Humanity." In his account of the submarine attack on the *Lusitania*, Marshall declares, "It may be war, but it is something incalculably more sobering than merely that. It is the difference between assassination and massacre. It is war's supreme crime against civilization." The attack is condemned as "an outrage unknown heretofore in the warfare of civilized nations," because previously it had been impossible to believe that "any civilized nation would be so wanton in its lust and passion of war as to count a thousand non-combatant lives a mere unfortunate incidental of the carnage."

A similar note is sounded in Parker's appeal for American relief for Belgian refugees written at least six months earlier and reprinted from the *New York Times*. The refugee camps in Holland were "a sight repugnant to civilization" and tens of thousands of refugees were left destitute. "Will the American nation rise to the chance given to it to prove that its civilization is a real thing and that its acts measure up with its inherent and professed Christianity?"[11]

The accounts of German conduct in Belgium and occupied France reiterated the accusation of crimes against civilization. The summary of the French report on German atrocities is titled "The Unspeakable

Atrocities of 'Civilized' Warfare" and the account of the sacking of Louvain is titled "Destroying the Priceless Monuments of Civilization." The language used to frame these reports—presumably written by Marshall—is sometimes strained, excessive, or melodramatic; for example, "such horror that the whole civilized world stood aghast." But such locutions are relatively rare. The style used in the excerpts from the official reports is objective, almost detached, and eyewitness accounts are offered without comment, primarily because of the skepticism about the atrocity accounts coming from French and British sources.

This strategy is characteristic of the excerpt from the French official report, which includes accounts reportedly taken from the diaries found on the bodies of German soldiers. The entries include stark references to what a soldier witnessed, sometimes without comment: "Langeviller, Aug. 22—Village destroyed by the eleventh battalion of Pioneers. Three women hanged to trees; the first dead I have seen." Others include expressions of revulsion at the conduct of other soldiers: "we bayoneted two men, with their wives and a young girl eighteen years old. . . . we could not master the excited troops, for at such times they are no longer men—they are beasts" (144–45).

The French commission report also summarizes the accounts by French civilians of German looting, rape, beatings, and arson. These are written for the most part in an objective style:

> At Auve nearly the whole town has been destroyed. At Etrepy sixty-three families out of seventy are homeless. At Huiron, all the houses, with the exception of five, have been burned. At Sermaize-les-Bains only about forty houses out of nine hundred remain. At Bignicourt-sur-Saultz thirty houses out of thirty-three are in ruins. (155)

The tight-lipped reticence heightens the representation of the Germans as outside the bounds of civilization. The style conveys moral umbrage, based not on mere passion, but on a detached rationality and a careful weighing of the evidence. The effectiveness of letting the facts speak for themselves as mediated through the responses of an eyewitness is seen again in another account included in *Thrilling Stories*, the sacking of Louvain. This time, the witness is not a German soldier, but the treasurer of Louvain who managed to escape deportation to Germany. The account is reprinted from the *London Times* of late August 1914. The report emphasizes the premeditated nature of the assault, a reprisal for what the Germans claimed was sniper fire:

> The cavalry charged through the streets sabering fugitives, while the infantry, posted on the foot-paths, had their fingers on the triggers of their guns waiting for the unfortunate people to rush from the houses or appear at the windows, the soldiers praising and complimenting each other on their marksmanship as they fired at the unhappy fugitives. Those whose houses were not yet destroyed were ordered to quit and follow the soldiers to the railway station. There the men were separated from mothers, wives, and children and thrown, some bound, into trains leaving in the direction of Germany. (164)

Soldiers used bombs to raze the town, destroying the Church at St. Pierre, the university buildings, and the library. The destruction was described by one eyewitness, a professor of the University of Louvain as "a smoking heap of ruins. . . . It is a veritable Pompeii." The razing of sacred, cultural, and intellectual sites aroused a sense of outrage perhaps equal to that expressed over the suffering of civilians, not only with regard to Louvain, but with the irreparable damage to the Cathedral at Rheims as well.

The accounts of the sinking of the *Lusitania*, rape, looting, pillaging, arson, and the destruction of culturally important sites and artifacts are seen to form a pattern of "crimes against civilization," while the use of eyewitness narration vividly invokes the scene and evokes sympathy for its victims.

This is the approach taken as well with the summaries and excerpts from the Bryce Report. The excerpts included in *Thrilling Stories* do not dwell on the eyewitness accounts taken as depositions and included as an appendix in the original report. What is included are excerpts from the body of the report, which summarize the evidence from both Belgian witnesses and the diaries of German soldiers. The style of the report is to list examples of different kinds of brutalities: for example,

> [the] indiscriminate shooting of civilians of both sexes and . . . the organized military execution of batches of selected males. Thus some fifty men escaping from burning houses were seized, taken outside the town [Herve] and shot. At Melen, in one household alone the father and mother (names given) were shot, the daughter died after being repeatedly attacked and the son was wounded. In Soumagne and Micheroux very many civilians were summarily shot. In a field belonging to a man named E——, fifty-six or fifty-seven were put to death. (122)

The point to collecting and cataloging these acts and classifying them was to show that the actions of the Germans against civilians had a pattern to them, and to make the evidence for the pattern overwhelmingly convincing. This was not simply to overcome skepticism, but to make the case that the acts were not the random results of individual soldiers who temporarily lost all military discipline. The aim was to demonstrate the actions were repeated and therefore represented either military policy or a consistent and inexcusable failure to maintain order and discipline in the ranks. The indictment was against the German military command, not individual soldiers or war itself.

There was, for instance, the recognition that some individual soldiers would revert to barbarism—the "war is hell" equivalent of "boys will be boys." For this reason, the military leadership was held especially responsible for anticipating that some men in their command would lose control and for taking the necessary measures not to encourage it and to punish it when it occurred:

> In all wars occur many shocking and outrageous acts of men of criminal instincts whose worst passions are unloosed by the immunity which the conditions of warfare afford. Drunkenness, moreover, may turn even a soldier who has no criminal habits into a brute, and there is evidence that

intoxication was extremely prevalent among the German army, both in Belgium and in France. Unfortunately little seems to have been done to repress this source of danger. (131)

A similar distinction was drawn with regard to rape. The report acknowledges, for instance, evidence of a public rape at Liège that included five officers. The conclusion reached is that while rape was not obviously a military policy, the unleashing of soldiers on the civilian population—which was military policy—led inevitably to savagery against women, and the military command ought to have recognized this reality:

> In the evidence before us there are cases tending to show that aggravated crimes against women were sometimes severely punished. These instances are sufficient to show that the maltreatment of women was not part of the military scheme of the invaders, however much it may appear to have been the inevitable result of the system of terror deliberately adopted in certain regions. (128)

The gravest indictment laid against the Germans, therefore, was not that the military command failed to control the ranks; rather, it was that the command violated the rules of civilized warfare by undertaking a systematic policy of waging war against civilians, including noncombatant men, women, and children. In making this indictment, the Bryce Report is very clear on the point of "civilized" and "uncivilized" nations. Those that are "civilized" are western, European, and Christian; those that are not are eastern, Asiatic, and non-Christian:

> In the present war . . .—and this is the gravest charge against the German army—the evidence shows that the killing of non-combatants was carried out to an extent for which no previous war between nations claiming to be civilized (for such cases as the atrocities perpetrated by the Turks on the Bulgarian Christians in 1876, and on the Armenian Christians in 1895 and 1896, do not belong to that category) furnishes any precedent. (131)

The indictment is clear on the point that the Germans were especially blameworthy because, unlike the Turks, the Germans claimed to be civilized, were bound by the same conventions as the rest of Europe, and ought to have recognized the limits of civilized conduct during war. Instead, they violated those boundaries by undertaking systematic warfare against noncombatants and destroying nonmilitary sites.

The report hammered home the point that the evidence taken from the diaries of soldiers as well as Belgian citizens made it clear that the conduct of German soldiers represented a deliberate plan: the killing of civilians, destruction of property, and razing of cities was done in response to orders, and "some of the officers who carried out the work did it reluctantly and said they were obeying instructions from their chiefs." The report firmly rejects the German explanation that the military acted in response to the atrocities and attacks against German soldiers committed by snipers. The assault on the civilian population, it says, was part of a deliberate military plan intended to "strike terror into the civil population and dishearten the Belgian troops": "The pretext that civilians had fired upon the invading troops was used to justify not merely the shooting of individual franc-tireurs, but the murder of large numbers of innocent civilians, an act absolutely forbidden by the rules of civilized warfare" (131, 133).

In summarizing the indictment, the Bryce Report laid full blame at the feet of the Germany military caste for conducting war against civilians as a matter of policy, thereby degrading as well the morality of their own forces:

> In the minds of Prussian officers war seems to have become a sort of sacred mission, one of the highest functions of the omnipotent state. . . . Ordinary morality and the ordinary sentiment of pity vanish in its presence, superseded by a new standard which justifies to the soldier every means that can conduce to success, however shocking to a natural sense of justice and humanity, however revolting to his own feelings. . . . Cruelty becomes legitimate when it promises victory. Proclaimed by the heads of the army, this doctrine would seem to have permeated the officers

and affected even the private soldiers, leading them to justify the killing of non-combatants as an act of war, and so accustoming them to
slaughter that even women and children become at last the victims.
(133–34)

The influence of the report resides in the final analysis with this indictment, rather than in the sensationalism of the accounts. Similar har-
rowing stories had been repeatedly published in newspapers and other
publications. The clarity of the indictment leveled against the Prussianism, the framework, is what gives meaning to the cataloging of
atrocities.

The summary of the French report included in *Thrilling Tales* also
makes the point that the German acts against civilians have a systematic pattern: "[N]ever," it says, "has a war carried on between civilized
nations assumed [such a] savage and ferocious character." The Germans
used pillage, rape, arson, and murder as a "common practice." They
engaged in "definite crimes against common rights, punished by the
codes of every country with the most severe and the most dishonoring
penalties, and which prove an astonishing degeneration in German
habits of thought since 1870." The frequency of assaults against women
were treated in a manner similar to the conclusions found in the Bryce
Report. While "strictly speaking" they could be understood as "the
individual and spontaneous acts of uncaged beasts," it is also the case
that "fewer would have been committed if the leaders of an army whose
discipline is the most rigorous had taken any trouble to prevent them."
The report concludes that as a matter of common practice, the German
military engaged in arson, theft, murder, killing of the wounded, and
that "they kill without pity the inoffensive inhabitants of the territories
which they have invaded, and they do not spare in their murderous rage
women, old men or children" (153).

While the terms of the French accusations as included in *Thrilling
Tales* were similar to those used by the British, it was the Bryce Report
that gave the clearest and fully developed indictment. It declared that
the conduct of the German military reflected coolly calculated policy,

an intentional terror campaign aimed against noncombatants intended to force the capitulation of the enemy. German soldiers were interpreted not as yielding to baser instincts otherwise controlled by civilized restraint; rather, it was understood that while some may have had criminal natures, most were following orders to commit acts that were otherwise repugnant to them, ignoring their better impulses because of an autocratic culture of militarism and obedience.

The Bryce Report takes aim at Prussianism, that is, at the power elite in control of the government. It was careful to draw a distinction between the German people per se, or German culture in general, and those who were directing the war:

> [Waging war against civilians as a matter of policy] cannot be supposed to be a national doctrine, for it neither springs from nor reflects the mind and feelings of the German people as they have heretofore been known to other nations. It is specifically military doctrine, the outcome of a theory held by a ruling caste who have brooded and thought, written and talked and dreamed about war until they have fallen under its obsession and been hypnotized by its spirit. (134)

For this reason the Prussian agenda, if victorious, threatened the civilized way of life: "This is not the only case that history records in which a false theory, disguising itself as loyalty to a state or to a church, has perverted the conception of duty and become a source of danger to the world" (134).

The Bryce Report resonated with other accounts of German conduct, making a collection such as *Thrilling Tales of the War* useful for the insight it provides into the many ways that the message of German barbarism was conveyed and reiterated to the public, especially in the United States, by the spring of 1915. The public would already have been familiar with accounts of the Belgium refugees in Holland, the recent sinking of the *Lusitania*, the razing of Louvain, the damage to Notre Dame at Rheim, and the eyewitness accounts of looting, arson, rape, and summary execution in the occupied lands. Collecting these accounts between two covers in a popular and inexpensive publication such as *Thrilling Stories* reinforced the impression of a consistent pattern.

This narrative not only reinforced and substantiated the impression of German atrocities, it made it apparent to Americans, who had a stake in the civilized world, that American interests were also entailed in the war. This motive was clearly articulated in the introduction to the English translation of the French report included in *Thrilling Tales.* The translator, J. O. P. Bland, wrote the introduction to overcome the central liability of the French report, which consisted of a very sparse introduction, followed by the collection of documentary evidence. The report thus lacked the interpretive framework of the Bryce Report. Bland, speaking on behalf of the French intentions, reiterated the primary point of the Bryce Report, that the actions of the Germans came about "[n]ot by the independent acts of undisciplined individuals, not as the result of misunderstandings or in the heat of fierce passions evoked in battle, but by the cold-blooded premeditation of general orders, prepared for the army in time of peace, by the deliberate adoption of methods of barbarism which civilization has denounced." The French decision to present the documentary evidence without comment and "devoid of sensationalism" was explained as a way of "framing the indictment of civilization against Germany" which seemed "best calculated to create an intelligent force of dispassionate opinion abroad, and hereafter to convince even the disillusioned German people of the heinousness of the crimes committed in their name."[12] The method was used, Bland explains, especially because the French realized the public skepticism in neutral nations about reported war atrocities.

The larger purpose was to gain the support of the United States by making it clear that American interests were obviously at stake:

> so long as Germany remains undefeated, there can be no effective redress for these outrages, nor any means of compelling her to respect the principles of justice and humanity. Until she is utterly broken and repentant, there can be no safety for the lives and property of non-combatants by land

or by sea. Unchecked by any of the humane considerations which have been embodied in the laws of civilized States, she will continue to apply all her murderous inventions to purposes of indiscriminate destruction.[13]

Such a statement illustrates the appropriation of atrocity accounts to particular political purposes. It was in the interest of both Great Britain and France to make of the United States at the very least a friendly neutral nation and, most desirably, to get America into the war on their side.

The Bryce Report was an example of direct or overt state-sponsored propaganda: the message served a particular political purpose, but the source of the message was clear, as was the purpose behind it. In all of those ways, it functioned as a form of persuasive political discourse. The framing of the information to arouse American fears as a way to induce American involvement in the war and to legitimize British involvement as entirely unselfish and disinterested moved it into the category of propaganda; it was a message intended to serve a particular political interest by the manipulation of both information and emotion.

The inclusion of portions of the Bryce Report in an anthology— *Thrilling Tales*—aimed at the mass market is an example of indirect propaganda. The original source is clear—the government of Great Britain—but the report gains credibility by being included in a non-governmental publication. The reprint of the newspaper article written by Sir Gilbert Parker, whose role at Wellington House was not attributed, is also an example of indirect propaganda, but of a more invidious form because of the failure to provide full attribution. All of the selections in *Thrilling Tales* illustrate how a particular discourse about the war originated in official sources and, once put into circulation, gained currency—both in the sense of value and in the sense of seeming fresh and newsworthy—from repetition and an increasing distance from the originating source.

The British message was that war could not be used as an excuse for a reversion to mere barbarism. But a certain point can be lost sight of in dismissing the Bryce Report and other examples of the efforts of

British propagandists as merely manipulative, exaggerated, or fabricated. Granted, the British themselves had much to answer for in their conduct of their imperial wars, and the disillusioning effects of their conduct during the Boer War; granted, the Germans learned something about the lessons of warfare conducted against civilians from consulting with the American general Tecumseh Sherman after the Civil War. Granted, too, public opinion was manipulated by sensationalized accounts during World War I, and the accounts of violence directed against civilians were sometimes exaggerated or lacked verification. All of these are examples of both hypocrisy and manipulation by public officials.

But what is also clear and which can be overlooked is that the British addressed a public, in England, the Commonwealth nations, and the United States, which readily responded to the principle that warfare, when engaged in by civilized nations, imposed limits on the conduct of soldiers and the policies of military commanders, included the expectation that officers are responsible for the discipline of the men they command, and assumed a duty to refuse orders for actions that violate the conventions for warfare.

These important constraints ought not be trivialized through their association with a propaganda campaign. They are principles for reasoning about warfare which draw upon the moral imagination and insist upon limits to organized violence; they turn out to resonate as much if not more with events at the end of the century as they did at the start. As the dimensions of total warfare began to unfold before the eyes of the watching world, the significance of public opinion as a constraint on military behavior was not only recognized, not only manipulated, but was reckoned from the first as a serious factor that had to be taken into account especially by the democracies. And public opinion responded to an account of warfare framed as violating basic principles that placed moral constraints on warfare on both sides. When the debris of the efforts to manipulate public opinion is cleared away from the Bryce Report, what remains is the reality that the public on both sides of the Atlantic readily related to the premise that wars—even modern, mechanized wars—ought to be subject to constraints, particularly against waging war against civilians, and that those who fail to observe those constraints should be held accountable to history. In a war that saw the birth of strategic bombing, it was a significant public morality, and one that should not be buried in the scorn and derision heaped upon the propagandists who appropriated it for a particular political end.

The Trope of War as Melodramatic Rescue

The heavy emphasis on the German atrocities not only had immediate consequences for how the German national character was symbolized, but also shaped the idealization of the national character of the Allies. If the Germans represented barbarism, the Allies represented civilization; if German barbarism led to the invasion of a neutral country and waging war against civilians, the Allies represented respect for law and rescuing the weak from the strong.

The often-repeated atrocity stories aided in condensing these ideas into a melodramatic structure that personalized the war in the imagination. The American public was invited to conceptualize the war in terms of the heroic rescue of the Maiden from the hands of the clutching Fiend. The symbolizing of young women as the victims of German barbarism represents a significant distillation of war conducted against both men and women civilians into a female iconography. The accounts of German attacks on Belgian towns, for example, included repeated accounts of Germans rounding up sizable numbers of unarmed men and killing them; similarly, a thousand men, women, and children lost their lives in the sinking of the *Lusitania*. But the propaganda represents the atrocities in Belgium primarily with images of women, and often mothers and their children, while the most famous American poster about the *Lusitania* depicts a drowned woman and her baby. The "outrages" are not visualized as having been committed against human beings (men, women, and children), or even against the weak (the elderly, for example, are not depicted). The imagery is of young women, either virginal or with babes clutched to their breasts. This imagery rendered the commonplace reference to nations as "she," and, in the case of the invasion of Belgium, reproduced definitions of "male" and "female" that placed primary emphasis on their differences. "Women" are represented as sexualized, weak, and defenseless victims, and male aggression is sexualized. In its natural or uncontrolled state, it becomes the motive for rape; submitted to "civilized" constraint, it becomes the motive for protecting women from the unleashed forces of masculine nature.

The elision of women being raped and the rape of a nation is found, for instance, in Logan Marshall's condemnation: "We have seen a nation despoiled and raped because it resisted an invader, and we have said that was war."[14] Sir Gilbert Parker uses the same metaphor in appealing for aid to assist the Belgian refugees:

> Whoever or whatever country is to blame for this war, Belgium is innocent. Her hands are free from stain. She has kept the faith. She saw it with the eyes of duty and honor. Her government is carried on in another land. Her king is in the trenches. Her army is decimated, but the last decimals fight on.[15]

In British poster propaganda, the "rape of Belgium" or the "innocence of Belgium" was represented with images of women, or of women and children. The distinction between "actual women" and an abstraction (a nation, Belgium) is easily blurred. As a consequence, the individual soldier is symbolized as well. He becomes the rescuing hero. A British recruitment poster from 1915 shows a village burning in the far distance, a woman leading a child away in the middle distance toward a British soldier standing erect in the foreground, holding a rifle, staring sternly at the viewer. The slogan for the poster is "Remember Belgium: Enlist To-day" (see Figure 5).[16] The poster implicitly defines the young man viewing it as capable of rescuing women and children and as failing in his obligation if he does not enlist. As a message it carries much more impact than the "Scrap of Paper" (1914) poster from early in the war. With no illustration, it urges British men to enlist by presenting the legal case against Germany: that the Germans had acknowledged the neutrality treaty with Belgium, but regarded it as a mere "scrap of paper," while Britain, on the other hand, regarded it as "Britain's bond"

Figure 5. "Remember Belgium: Enlist To-Day" (1915) depicts war as the melodramatic rescue of women and children. British Imperial War Museum poster 5075.

and makes the melodramatic appeal for rescue: "Can Britons stand by while Germany crushes an innocent people?"[17]

By 1915 the concept of "innocent people" was routinely condensed into the visual representation of the Virgin or the Madonna: young women or mothers with children. The most frequently recalled posters of this genre were produced in America. Perhaps the best known is Ellsworth Young's "Remember Belgium" (1918), produced for the fourth bond drive. Against a dark background, flames rise, illuminating a ruined cityscape. In the foreground the silhouette of a bloated Prussian is leading away a screaming young girl, also in silhouette, her hair flowing wildly behind her. H. R. Hopps, "Destroy This Mad Brute: Enlist/U.S. Army" (1917), appropriates the style and symbolism of a horror movie (see Figure 6). A grotesque ape gapes at the viewer. On his head is a Prussian helmet marked "militarism," on his upper lip the incongruous German military moustache. In his right hand he carries a bloody club bearing the word "Kultur"; in his left, a half-naked blonde woman ("Columbia"), swathed in flowing drapery, faints in horror. The land upon which the slavering ape stands is labeled "America," while in the background, across the "sea," Europe stands in ruins. A much more compelling image is found in Fred Spear's "Enlist" (1915), which evokes the outrage over the sinking of the *Lusitania* by depicting an underwater portrait of a woman, her hair flowing upward in the currents, cradling a baby, both of them seemingly peacefully asleep.[18]

By drawing upon clichéd dramatic plots, the justification of the war was effectively presented as a melodrama: Virtuous Hero saves Virgin/Madonna from Fate Worse than Death by taking violent action against Fiendish Villain. As a familiar narrative that rendered characters as symbols of absolute attributes, the structure permitted the shaping of a narrative that relied primarily upon images, requiring little textual emendation or explanation. This avenue for promulgating the war as a melodrama depended upon both the widespread circulation of atrocity stories and the technology for the mass production of images, including poster graphics, illustrations for newspapers and books, and the moving image.

Figure 6. H. R. Hopps, "Destroy This Mad Brute" (1917) imagines war as rape by brutes. Poster Collection, Hoover Institution Archives.

The commercial film industry in the United States saw the advantage of exploiting the atrocity stories, both because sensationalism would draw patrons to the box office and because of the anticipated benefit to an industry in its infancy of placing its resources in the service of the government. Between 1914 and March 1917 Americans could see both feature films and newsreels depicting the war. Some of these were produced in the combatant nations for distribution in the United States. Some were made in the United States. In *The Little American*, Mary Pickford is crossing the Atlantic to visit a sick aunt when her ship, the *Veritania*, is sunk by a German submarine torpedo. Surviving the ordeal, she arrives in France to discover her aunt is dead. Her aunt's home, which had been used as a hospital for wounded French soldiers, has been occupied by the Germans. Included among them is a prewar German boyfriend she knew in Washington, D.C., who attempts to attack her in the dark. When he recognizes her, he is ashamed and seeks to shield her from the fate of the other women kept at the chateau, who are used as camp prostitutes. Pickford witnesses the execution by firing squad of a number of French peasants and, neutral no longer, calls the French military on a secret phone line. She is captured and sentenced to death by firing squad; her reformed former boyfriend protests and is also sentenced to death. They are saved at the last minute when the French begin shelling the chateau and they escape to a ruined church. The boyfriend is sent to a prisoner-of-war camp but is later freed when Pickford intervenes with a French count who is also in love with her.

The film includes references to the most often repeated allegations of German atrocities: the sinking of the *Lusitania*, rape, and executions of noncombatants. The film heightens the effect by telling the story through the eyes of a woman as victim, near victim, heroine, and witness. The film also shows signs of what, in retrospect, might be called the restraint of the neutrality period. Karl (as symbolizing Germans) is not seen as inherently degenerate; rather, he has been corrupted by an evil system. He says this himself when he is sentenced to die: "I am done with you and your Emperor. I was blind to your system—now, thank God, I See!" The film was very popular and continued to play to large audiences nationwide eight months after its release. It serves as an index to the changing sentiments after America entered the war because from surviving script notes it seems likely that the ending was changed in subsequent releases, uniting Pickford with the French count rather than the reformed German boyfriend.[19]

A number of commercial films released in 1918 were hate films that appropriated the atrocity accounts to portray the Kaiser and all Germans as vicious degenerates. Mark M. Dintefass produced *My Four Years in Germany*, based on a memoir written by the former ambassador to Germany, James W. Gerard. The film, which assures the audience it is watching "Fact Not Fiction," portrays the Kaiser as riding a hobby-horse, Chancellor Bethmann-Hollweg as playing with toys, and Admiral Tirpitz as planning the naval war by playing with toy boats in a basin. The film includes scenes of the German deportation and execution of Belgian women, the mistreatment of prisoners of war, and the rape and murder of women. The Kaiser's taunt, "The Americans will not dare to fight," is answered by scenes of American regiments marching to the front; the assaults on women are answered by an American soldier bayoneting a German. The most often recalled subtitle in the film comes after an American has bayoneted five Germans in the trenches. He turns to stab another, saying, "I promised Dad I'd get half-a-dozen."[20]

The film opened in April to applauding and cheering audiences and enjoyed large national audiences in the months that followed. It was used to promote Liberty bond drives in some cities and was praised by organizations such as the Washington Chamber of Commerce and the National Convention of the General Federation of Women's Clubs. One reviewer at the time praised it for showing "the German emperor and his advisors in their true light—a lot of ruthless savages whose lust for conquest has made them lower than the beasts." Outside some theaters, the Kaiser was burned in effigy and in some cases the police had to be called to control spectators who turned into excited mobs.[21]

A number of local authorities objected to the sensationalism and prurience of the film. They were joined by President Wilson, who disapproved the use of films for arousing a mob mentality and felt Gerard, as a former ambassador, should not have contributed to making the film. Mrs. Wilson raised similar objections to D. W. Griffith's *Hearts of the World*, which was distributed nationally in May 1918, starring Lillian and Dorothy Gish and Robert Harron. The film played for many months to cheering audiences, inspiring one theater manager in Atlanta to say, "The people down here went wild. It was all we could do to keep many persons from standing in their seats."[22]

Subtitles to the film tell the audience that the war is "the struggle of Civilization." The story is framed to merge scenes of fighting the war in the trenches with the melodramatic plot of a woman rescued from the clutches of the Fiend. The focus is on young Americans living with their families in France when the war breaks out. There are scenes of the German destruction of villages and the flight of refugees. Two small orphans bury their mother, who is killed by a shell, in a cellar, and then hide out there. Lillian Gish is pressed into forced labor. When she becomes too weak to continue, a German guard beats her mercilessly until she bleeds. Later, a German officer attempts to rape her but is interrupted by the hero. In the ensuing fight, Gish kills her assailant—another example of the American films rendering the heroine, who embodies the Nation, or Columbia, as full of spirit and more to the point, capable of defending herself. The resolution occurs when the Allies bomb the trenches and America wins the war.

Hearts of the World is an excellent example of a joint venture between the government and private interests in promulgating a particular vision of the war. The British government commissioned Griffith to make a film supporting the Allied cause. When Griffith accepted, he was given access to the front, where he shot footage later used in the film and purchased German documentary film. The plot elements were shot at a studio in Hollywood, and versions of the film were released in America, Britain, and France. The documentary footage gave credibility to the melodramatic plot, as did the prologue, which includes footage of Griffith at the front and shaking hands with Prime Minister Lloyd George, who endorses Griffith's project and wishes him success.[23]

Obviously interested in adding to this mantle of official approval,

Griffith wrote President Wilson, urging him to see the film, which Griffith assured him was "the biggest propaganda to stir up patriotism yet put forth." When Griffith pressed a second time, the president and Mrs. Wilson agreed to attend a private screening in June, a month after the opening. Griffith did not receive the response he anticipated; instead, Mrs. Wilson sent him a note expressing her concerns about the exploitative rawness of several scenes. In his response, Griffith explained that the public is "a very very stolid hard animal to move or impress. We must hit hard to touch them." He admits that in his zeal to "bring home the truth of what they have suffered over there in an intimate human way," he lost sight of the need for restraint and "overshot the mark." He offered to eliminate two objectionable scenes so as not to "offend the refined and sensitive spirits such as yourself." He consulted with Mrs. Wilson, eliminated some scenes, and reshot the sequence in which Lillian Gish is brutally beaten.[24]

The advocacy of such restraint was overwhelmed by other films also released in 1918 that escalated the demonizing of the Kaiser and Germans in general. *The Kaiser, the Beast of Berlin* was released as a film, a novelette in newspapers, and a separate book.[25] The film was so extreme in its emotional arousal against Germans that the Committee on Public Information (CPI) voiced an objection to it. Right-wing anti-LaFollette (or anti-Progressive) elements in Wisconsin appropriated the film to promote their political agenda, printing posters advertising the film with the words "Anyone who resents the message of this picture IS NOT A LOYAL AMERICAN." Other advertisements showed marching German troops labeled "baby-killers." The film reviewed all the German atrocity stories, including the sinking of the *Lusitania* and the terror campaigns in Belgium. The Kaiser tells an officer, "I may ask you at any moment to strike down your own mother, sister, or sweetheart." In the tradition of the melodrama, audiences were encouraged to hiss every time they saw the Kaiser, which they evidently did. The film broke box-office records in some cities and inspired near-riots in Boston. Some measure of how patriotism, hate, and melodramatic films had merged in the public imagination is indicated by the prosecution in a California federal court of Rudolph Lahnemann for making anti-American remarks when the film was shown. He was found guilty and sentenced to five years in jail.[26]

My Four Years in Germany, Hearts of the World, and *The Kaiser, Beast of the World,* were released at the time America entered the war, as was *To Hell with the Kaiser,* in which the Kaiser literally goes to Hell, where Satan gives up his throne to one who has obviously outdone him. These four films each reviewed the catalog of atrocities laid at the feet of the Kaiser. Other films featuring women focused on specific outrages. The story of Edith Cavell, a Red Cross nurse tending the wounded in Belgium who was shot for allowing her patients to escape, had already been printed in pamphlet form. The news of her execution naturally horrified public sentiment around the world. The first film about her was produced by an Australian company under the title *Martyrdom of Nurse Cavell* (1916); it was retold in *The Woman the Germans Shot* (1918), released in the United States the month after the Armistice. And while the sinking of the *Lusitania* was invoked in a number of films, two releases devoted attention solely to it in 1918. Winsor McKay's one-reel animated film, *The Sinking of the Lusitania,* depicts a young mother holding a baby over her head as they both sink into the waves. The caption reads, "The Man who fired the shot was decorated by the Kaiser. AND THEY TELL US NOT TO HATE THE HUN." The feature film *Lest We Forget* starred Rita Jolivet, who was a survivor of the *Lusitania* and who in the film is given what was probably a personally gratifying role of a heroine who strangles to death a German diplomat villain.[27]

These films appropriated the British atrocity stories and rendered them as the *casus belli* to justify American intervention. They exploited the sensational aspects of atrocity stories, using them as signs of the degeneracy of the enemy and, by implication, the virtue of the Allies, while also often arousing the spectators to the point of riot. Little can be said in favor of films intent upon manufacturing hatred and the mob mentality, while legitimating the project as patriotic public service and raking in unprecedented profits at the box office. These films served a propaganda purpose, but most of them were not state-sponsored and the

exploitation of atrocity stories for commercial profit was at times sufficiently excessive to run counter to the desires of the government.
Nevertheless, they were in conversation with the dominant themes of
wartime propaganda emanating first from Britain and France, and then,
after America's entry into the war, the poster propaganda published by
the CPI. The themes the films developed had been sounded by official
sources and the atrocity stories had been reiterated in newspapers and
legitimated by official inquiries and reports.

The additional impact on the public imagination made by silent
films was both to provide the atrocity accounts a conventional coherence
within a melodramatic narrative and to deliver the unique emotional
impact that came from enacting the already familiar accounts on the
screen. The films also personalize the war. In some cases, scenes of combat in the trenches are presented as part of the larger melodrama, so
that face-to-face combat in the trenches is constructed as the same thing
as the rescue of the maiden or revenge for brutalizing women and children; sometimes the army functions as the cavalry in western movies,
showing up just in time to save the woman from catastrophe. The characters symbolize the forces caught up in the war, so that the Hero/
Soldier saves the Virgin/Madonna from the Degenerate Fiend/German,
and then the army shows up to save them both. In films depicting the
shooting of Nurse Cavell or the sinking of the *Lusitania*, where there is
no melodramatic rescue, the implicit urging is for the viewer to complete the drama by becoming the Hero who avenges the death or who
sees to it that those responsible are stopped.

War as Melodrama and the Individual Imagination

The justifications for the Allied cause and America's entry into the
war shed indirect light on the motives of the American males who either
volunteered to serve Great Britain or France before the United States
entered the war, or enrolled by the tens of thousands for flight school
after Congress declared war. What role did these justifications play in
motivating them to volunteer? This is, of course, a difficult question,
since ultimately the decision to volunteer for war reflects personality

and psychology as much as it does socially constructed images of masculinity and propaganda messages intended to justify war. But some insight can be gained nevertheless into how young aviators imagined their role in the war and the degree to which their motives reflected the discourses about saving civilization and humanity, or rescuing the Maiden from the Fiend, or preserving Christianity from the barbarian hordes.

Kiffin Yates Rockwell was a founding member of the Lafayette Escadrille. He was born into an established land-owning South Carolina family, and was raised on the plantation of his maternal grandfather, Maj. Enoch Shaw Ayres, who often told his grandson of his experiences as a Confederate officer. Rockwell was educated privately at Virginia Military Institute and secured an appointment to the Naval Academy, which he resigned in favor of attending Washington and Lee. Both Kiffin Rockwell and his older brother Paul volunteered to serve with the French Foreign Legion in August 1914. Wounded while fighting at the front, Kiffin Rockwell was sent to Paris, where he was reacquainted with William Thaw; the two had met while both were serving in the Foreign Legion. Thaw was flying with a French squadron while actively engaged in the arrangements for an all-American squadron. He urged Kiffin Rockwell to transfer to aviation. On April 20, 1915, Kiffin Rockwell and Victor Chapman became two of the first seven members of what was to be the Lafayette Escadrille. On September 23, 1916, Kiffin Rockwell was shot down and killed over Luxeuil. He was credited with downing four German planes and had received the Medaille Militaire and the Croix de Guerre with four palms. He was twenty-four years old when he died.

An insight into his motives is contained in a letter to his mother, dated February 17, 1916, "Now, I do not want you to worry about me. If I die, I want you to know I have died as every man ought to die fighting for what is right. I do not feel that I am fighting for France alone, but for the cause of all humanity, the greatest of all causes."[28] The motivation to fight "for the cause of all humanity" resonates with the *casus belli* as developed by the Allies; the Great War was not identified as a war of nationalism, or of imperial ambition, or over the balance of power, but a war to protect and defend Europe and the rest of the world from a lethal force, a force equated with all that is inhuman.

Kiffin Rockwell's letter to his mother reveals the private motives of an individual during the war and signifies something of how the larger themes and motives of the day influenced one young man who grew up in a military tradition; however, his way of characterizing his motives did not influence how others thought about the role of the combat pilot because his letter was not published until after the war. But there was a significant public dimension to Kiffin Rockwell's death because he was written about by those who served with him and in the press. How he was described reflects both how the deaths of American aviators were framed before America entered the war, and how the public was asked to imagine the significance of their achievements.

James Rogers McConnell, who flew with the Lafayette Escadrille, published an autobiographical account during the war. *Flying for France* went through two editions in 1916 and 1917. It was one of those works that influenced how the men who came after the first generation of flyers imagined themselves as aviators in the war. Of Rockwell's death, McConnell wrote:

> No greater blow could have befallen the escadrille. Kiffin was its soul. . . . Kiffin was imbued with the spirit of the cause for which he fought and he gave his heart and soul to the performance of his duty. He said: "I pay my part for Lafayette and Rochambeau," and he gave the fullest measure. The old flame of chivalry burned brightly in this boy's fine and sensitive being.[29]

Kiffin Rockwell is represented as literally embodying the link between knighthood, chivalry, and the larger idealism—"the spirit of the cause"— which gave the trope its meaning.

Kiffin Rockwell's death was the subject of very heavy press coverage in France and the United States. Paul Scot Mowrer's report, cabled to the *Chicago Daily News*, carried a Paris, September 29, 1916, dateline. He reported an earlier interview with Kiffin and concluded with the encomium: "he loved the cause—the cause of France which for him was the cause of all mankind."[30]

An unsigned editorial in the *Charleston News and Courier* sounded a similar note, linking the idealism for the cause with knight errantry, and with a second important image, the Great Adventure:

> Kiffin Rockwell . . . must have had in his veins the blood of some knight-errant of the age of chivalry. Why should this young Southerner have given his gallant life to France? Perhaps because this splendid France of to-day stirred his imagination so powerfully that he could do nothing less than offer her his sword as Lafayette offered us his in our fight for liberty. Perhaps because he was one of those restless spirits to which life without adventure is but a sad and monotonous pilgrimage.[31]

The suggestion here that death is a small price to pay for escaping a dull life would seem uniquely callous, as if the editor was going out of his way to express a kind of cynical skepticism, except when it is understood as a conventional trope. The invocation of the war as the Great Adventure was tied into the Peter Pan fantasy of eternal youth; dying while young, engaged in the Good Fight, was in this grisly metaphor understood as preferable to dying in bed of the infirmities of old age.

While Kiffin Rockwell's letters were not published until after the war ended, those of Edmond Genet, a brother-in-arms in the Lafayette Escadrille, were published in June 1918. Genet was born in Ossining, New York. His father was a lawyer, and Genet was privately educated. He, like Rockwell sought appointment to the Naval Academy; however, unlike Rockwell, Genet was a poor student and failed his entrance exam. On the advice of an influential family friend, Genet signed on with the Navy in the hopes that with a good record and a second try at the exam he might yet succeed. Genet was very hard on himself; he referred to himself in letters to his widowed mother as the "black sheep of the family" and repeatedly set himself the goal of making a name for himself. On December 14, 1914, while on leave, he heard a sermon in St. Paul's Church in Boston on the subject of the war in Europe and a Christian's duty. This seemed to have fixed his resolve. He deserted the Navy, requested a cross to wear around his neck from his mother, wrote her that he expected to die in the war, and embarked for France, where he joined the Foreign Legion. By March 25, 1916, he was being soaked in the trenches, fighting for France. After sixteen months of rain, mud, snow, and artillery bombardment, Genet sought transfer to the American squadron. He joined the Lafayette Escadrille in January 1917; on April 16, 1917, he was shot down and killed. He bears the distinction of having been the first American airman killed in battle following the American entry into the war. He was awarded posthumously the Croix de Guerre with two palms, and the Medaille Militaire. Shortly after the end of the war, the secretary of the Navy expunged Genet's name from the record of deserters from the U.S. Navy in recognition of his contribution to the war. Genet was twenty years old when he died.

Genet was motivated by the personal desire to achieve fame and success to compensate for his sense of being a failure; he volunteered, for instance, to fly for the French forces in Romania because he felt it would bring him faster promotion; he also adopted the mentality of war as the Great Adventure and often wrote of his imagining himself dying a glorious death. He identified with the *casus belli* as defined by the Allies. Discouraged by the news that Wilson was elected to a second term (which meant at the time that the United States would pursue a policy of neutrality), Genet wrote in November 1915 to a friend in the United States with great passion about the dishonor he felt neutrality brought to his nation. He lambasted Americans who were "making money hand over fist because their country is at peace—a peace at the price of its honor and respect in the whole civilized world—at peace while France and Belgium are being soaked in blood by a barbarous invasion—while the very citizens of the United State are being murdered." He urged, "Come over here and you'll be engulfed like the rest of us in the realization of the necessity of the whole civilized world arming itself against this intrusion of utter brutality and militaristic arrogance."[32]

Genet's letters were reproduced in popular magazines, and his achievements were recounted in the press even before his death. This was the case for all of those Americans who had volunteered for the French Foreign Legion and for those who entered the Lafayette Escadrille by transferring to it from the Foreign Legion. Genet received special recognition both because he was the first American airman to die after America entered the war and because he was the great-great-grandson of Edmond Charles Genet, the French Republic's first minister to the United States in 1792. While his indiscretions led to his recall, the elder Genet did not return to France but married Cornelia Tappan Clinton, the daughter of New York's governor DeWitt Clinton. Young Genet's ancestral connections with both the fledgling American Republic and France made him an outstanding candidate for promoting both the theme of the traditional ties connecting France and the United States and the idea of repayment of the debt to Lafayette that Rockwell sounded.

Both Kiffin Rockwell and Edmond Genet joined the Foreign Legion at the start of the war and were among the first Americans to fly for France. How did young volunteers who constituted the second wave of American flyers conceptualize their role at the time the United States entered the war? Some insight into the effect of the repetition of the justifications for the war and the representation of the American cause in terms of lurid melodrama can be gained from a letter written by Kenneth MacLeish, younger brother of the poet Archibald MacLeish. In March 1917, while an undergraduate at Yale, Kenneth asked for his parents' blessing on his plan to enlist in the newly formed Yale aviation corps:

> War is terrible, but there are two or three things that are worse. The brutality of Germany with respect to Belgium, the statement by Germany that international law and humanity are mere scraps of paper compared with her needs, the wanton murder of helpless American women and children, the open insults to the honor of the United States—they're all worse than war! There are many things worth giving up one's life for, and the greatest of these is humanity and the assurance of the laws of Christianity. Some people think that the only words Christ uttered were,

"Resist not evil." Do you think for a minute that if Christ had been alone on the Mount with Mary, and [a] desperate man had entered with criminal intent, He would have turned away when a crime against Mary was perpetrated? Never! He would have fought with all the God-given strength he had. Religion embraces the sword as well as the dove of peace.[33]

MacLeish's reasons include the conviction that war is a necessary response when international law has been violated (the indictment of Germany for calling the neutrality treaty with Belgium a "scrap of paper") and a personalized vision of what it means to be a soldier (saving women from danger and rape). Belgium and the sinking of the *Lusitania* here blend together so that protecting and revenging Belgium and women become very much the same things. To be that kind of soldier is to imitate Christ, identified as one who would have been militant on the subject of protecting women (notably his mother) from rape. The war becomes a requirement under international law, and an adolescent fantasy of sexual violence and rescue of the Virgin/Madonna. War is imagined as both a six-reeler melodrama, with MacLeish as the Hero/Soldier, and an *imitatio dei*, with MacLeish as the knight who will fight the crusade against barbarism.

MacLeish's conviction is expressed as a confused mixture of the messages constructed by Wellington House (and later by the Creel Committee) and repeated in films, posters, and print. For MacLeish these were not ideas planted in his head by others; they were his ideas, or ideas he believed were his own and which he held with a proud if not ferocious tenacity. This is the hallmark of effective propaganda, which is that individuals have to believe they have made up their own minds or come to their own conclusions even if it varies not a jot from the propaganda message. There remains something touching in both his fervor and the confusion of the public message with his personal psyche. It is something which after all these decades remains troubling because of the recognition that MacLeish's morality, deepest spiritual impulses, psychological needs, and sexual fantasies were appropriated to ideas that originated in other minds intent upon manipulating the sensibilities of young and untried men; yet, in the end, there is no denying the intensity of his fervor. His parents granted MacLeish the permission he sought; he was shot down and killed shortly before the war ended.

There is a coda to this story. Archibald MacLeish went on to become the head of the Congressional Library and to accept appointment from President Franklin Roosevelt to head the Writers' Bureau of the Office of War Information (OWI), which was charged with sustaining morale on the homefront during World War II. MacLeish, along with all the other writers, resigned when the leadership of the OWI was turned over to advertising specialists and publicists. MacLeish had been dedicated to the goal of providing Americans sufficient information to assure their understanding of and participation in the determination of domestic policies during the war. When it became apparent that the OWI would instead present war as advertised, he resigned. MacLeish may have been overly naive in assuming the OWI would differ in its aims and methods substantially from the propaganda ministries of World War I. But one cannot help speculating that his willingness to accept the appointment might have come at least partially from recalling the influences that had been at work on his brother.

CHAPTER 6

Civilized Warfare and the Gentleman-Knight

The Historial de la Grande Guerre is a museum devoted to World War I, located in Peronne (Picardy), site of what was the German headquarters in the Somme region. Established by the French in 1988, the museum's announced aim is to "surmount the clichés" about the war and to avoid "reducing the war to a battlefield phenomena." A chilling documentary of the First Battle of the Somme provides grim archival footage, narrated with eyewitness accounts recorded by veterans in their eighties, their voices shaking from both age and emotion. Uniforms and kits of those who fought against each other are laid out on the floor, as if one has entered a polished and sanitized morgue where the remains of the dead have been carefully arranged, awaiting identification by the surviving relatives.

A startling and obscene counterpoint to those silently accusatory displays are the reminders that there was another war, the constructed war-as-imagined, prepared for those on the homefront. Glass-encased exhibits along the walls represent the appropriation of the war for commercial purpose and entertainment—war toys and advertisements for consumer products linked to images of the war. Beside each display of kit and clothing laid out on the floor is a tall, slender stand surmounted by a video screen at eye level to the viewer. On each, newsreel or documentary film clips from the period play as continuous loops, their silent repetition a suitably fitting sign for the surreal pointlessness of the war itself: Secretary of War Lord Horatio Herbert Kitchener endlessly recruiting the British "million-man army," elderly women and young children forever being evacuated, tanks always traversing the same trenches to no apparent end, diplomats and statesmen in shiny top hats being trotted about in high carriages in an absurd political "no exit," men forever ravaged by shell-shock, so wounded in their minds that they are unable to walk or rise from the floor.

The Historial de la Grande Guerre gives very little attention to the air war. One floor exhibit lays out the gear used by pilots late in the war, along with a model of a biplane. Further indication of the judgment that the air war had very little to do with the outcome of the war is that the caption for the film clip is "the myth of the ace." It shows flyers from Great Britain, France, and Germany, including the Red Baron (Baron von Richthofen) and the French ace Georges Guynemer. The floor exhibit bears the comments: "It is intriguing that the most advanced kind of warfare struck the public imagination as the most feudal, marked by individual deeds by 'knights of the air.'"

The sparse exhibit, arranged neatly in a rectangular space set into the polished wood floor, includes a wooden propeller, a few flight instruments, a heated flight suit, and one or two other artifacts. These fail to resonate in any obvious way with the attributes of knighthood and the armored, mounted warrior. Nor do the silent newsreel clips of the aces talking to the men in their squadron, waving from the cockpit, or standing at attention to receive a medal.

The exhibit raises two implicit questions. The first is how the representation of the ground war has come to be so definitively associated with a surrealistic rendering of traumatic fragmentation, a repetition of images that are meaningless or have meaning primarily because they point toward no larger meaning other than futility and destruction. The second is how the imagery of "knighthood" and the sense of continuity with the past, of the just conduct of warfare, and of a brotherhood of warriors united in a chivalrous purpose has attached so firmly to the air war.

The salient imagery for answering both questions is the Crusade. The Allied *casus belli* as a defense of civilization against an atavistic barbarism was linked with the representation of the war as a crusade. It is no more immediately obvious why the Great War on the ground, which was a modern war in terms of weaponry, should have been called a "crusade" than the air war should have been. In other words, the framework of the "crusade" is an arbitrary one, not necessarily called forth by the claim that a war is fought in defense of civilization or civilized values.

The trope of the crusade appropriated to justifying the war had significant cultural, class, and political significance, particularly in Great Britain. The difficulty in sustaining the image was the nature of the ground war, which required a way of fighting very much at odds with the imagined warrior as "crusader." The image of "knighthood" was not so much extended to the air war as transferred to it when the capacity to utilize it for the ground war waned in terms of its effectiveness on the British homefront. The Great War provides a demonstration of the failure of an imagined war to sustain itself in the face of an actual one. It was the distance between the war-imagined-as-crusade and what fighting the war involved that accounts for the disillusionment characteristic of the postwar era, and with the representation in the Historial de la Grande Guerre of the ground war as a meaningless, unending, repetition of delusion, disruption, and death.

The year 1916 is usually understood as the year when the trope failed in Great Britain to continue providing inspiration for the ground war. It was the same year that the air war was used to evoke the era of knighthood. The failure of the trope as an image for the ground war carried significant cultural as well as political implications because it had served as a legitimizing framework for conservative and aristocratic values in the prewar era. The successful transfer of the image to the air war therefore carried a significance beyond the apparent capacity to glamorize the air war.

The prewar interest in the images and values of the age of chivalry was found in the United States as well. The lionizing of the aces as exemplary of the virtues of knighthood was a significant part of the literature about the British and French aces available in the United States prior to the U.S. entry into the war. Probably because Americans knew less about the ground war, the image of the crusade crossed the Atlantic in all its shining glory when the United States entered the war and found a receptive audience once it was appropriated by the Committee on Public Information to the American accent and stripped of its British imperial overtones.

The significance of the imagery of the combat pilot as a knight underscores the necessary link in the public's imagination between the *casus belli* and the conduct of the war. For the war to remain admirable and honorable in the public's imagination required that the belief in a just *cause* be sustained by the capacity to conceive the war as one of just *conduct*. The Great War was represented to the American and British public as a defense of civilization; the corollary was that the conduct of the war required a civilized violence. The conduct of the United States in the Philippines in the Spanish-American War or in the Indian Wars, the British conduct in Africa, or for that matter, Belgium—held out as a pitiable victim in World War I—in Africa, does not bear scrutiny as exemplary of civilized violence.

Those in charge of managing the public's perception or under-standing of the conduct of the war thought they needed to draw a con-nection between the conduct of war and the larger meaning or purpose attached to it. If Great Britain took it as a primary propaganda aim to demonstrate Prussian barbarism by classifying the atrocities committed in Belgium as signifying the dumb, obedient products of an autocracy, as a corollary, the conduct of British soldiers had to be represented as of an entirely heroic kind. The nature of the ground war made this increasingly insupportable, which is why the transfer of the imagery to the air war is significant: by the war's end, the use of air power emerged in the public's mind as the remaining symbol of civilized violence used in the defense of civilization, a connection especially important in the United States.

1916, Great Britain, the Chivalric Metaphor, and Air Combat

Although there is a general impression that all the combatant nations cultivated the chivalric imagery to promote their pilots, the provenance of the imagery resided with France and especially Great Britain. Henry

Newbolt's *Tales of the Great War* (1916) might be understood as the beginning of the official transfer of the imagery of chivalric warfare from the trenches to the sky:

> our airmen are singularly like the knights of the old romances; they go out day by day, singly or in twos and threes, to hold the field against all comers, and to do battle in defence of those who cannot defend themselves. There is something especially chivalrous about these champions of the air; even the Huns, whose military principles are against chivalry, have shown themselves affected by it.[1]

Newbolt was among the literati enlisted in 1914 by Wellington House, which is the usual term used for the British Ministry of Information formed one month after the war started. Samuel Hynes, in his account of the cultural history of Britain during the war, quips sarcastically that enlisting writers was a "mode of warfare without precedent" and notes that it reflected the government's awareness that both the public and the men who would fight the war were well educated, and that it was necessary to assure public assent to the war.[2]

It took a little time to find a suitable fit between the narrative conventions of the chivalric code as interpreted by the Victorians and air combat. In 1916 Jane Anderson, a correspondent for the jingoistic *Daily Mail*, was the first woman given permission to fly in a combat plane over London. The sensationalism of the stunt is difficult to appreciate now, because it is so easy to forget that at the time very few people had flown, and flying prior to the war was regarded as an extremely dangerous sport for men. The *Daily Mail* was owned by Alfred Harmsworth, Lord Northcliffe, who built the first newspaper empire in Great Britain. In addition to the *Daily Mail*, he owned the *Evening News*, the *Daily Mirror*, and the London *Times*. His editorial policies in the *Daily Mail* have been described as a "robust imperialism," and he used it to voice his early advocacy for war with Germany. He responded enthusiastically to government requests that he use his position to influence public opinion favorably to government policies during the war, and in May 1917 he accepted the assignment from Prime Minister Lloyd George to the British war mission in America. In February 1918 Northcliffe accepted an appointment to direct British propaganda campaigns against enemy nations, an undertaking that—one of his biographers unblushingly noted—Northcliffe "could combine with his newspaper work."[3]

Given the highly permeable boundaries between the press, propaganda, and the interests of the government, Anderson's stunt, and that it was printed in the *New York Tribune*, carries a significance beyond its mere sensationalism. Not surprisingly, Anderson takes a stab at framing the combat pilot in medieval terms:

> From the day of the medioeval archer, who notched his crossbow, to the day of the Western bad man, who notched his gun, men have always sought to preserve some mark of military prowess, some tally of their victims. This war has not changed human nature. The modern military aviator, the only soldier who still fights single-handed, does not notch his gun; he paints a death's head on the wing of his plane to show that he has vanquished his foe in combat.[4]

Anderson does not get it quite right because she focuses on counting coup without attention to the gallantry of the combat, and she mixes her metaphor in comparing the British flyer with the "Western bad man," perhaps out of a desire to appeal to the American reader. But the rest of what she has to say incorporates the attributes essential to making the combat pilot a chivalric hero: the connection with the Anglo-Saxon past, the soldier who "fights single-handed" to demonstrate his "military prowess" in order to "vanquish . . . his foe in combat." These attributes are, above all, natural, exemplary of "human nature"—by which is clearly meant the essence of masculinity: skill in aggression. Implicit in Anderson's hyperventilated prose is the sense that the mechanized warfare of the trenches inhibits the fullest expression of masculine prowess, but as the role of the combat pilot reassuringly demonstrates, "This war has not changed human nature." It was not the last time the image of the combat pilot would be used to offer that reassurance.

These early efforts to publicize the combat pilot and drape his exploits with the mantle of knighthood came at a time in England when it was increasingly difficult to maintain the same fiction about the ground war. In July 1916 questions were raised in Parliament asking why the names of distinguished British airmen could not appear in the press; in October Albert Ball received the Military Cross and the Distinguished Service Order, and from that point forward British pilots began to receive the level of publicity already usual for their French and German counterparts. During the same period, a number of the literate British officers who had volunteered for the war returned from the disastrous First Battle of the Somme to recover from their wounds, and some of them endeavored to counter the illusion of warfare that had been offered to the public. One of them, Siegfried Sassoon, served as a lieutenant in the Somme offensive, and received the Military Cross. In July 1916 he was sent to England with trench fever. By winter his poems began to appear in the *Cambridge Magazine*, the clearest voice for dissent in England. In December Sassoon published "The Poet As Hero" to explain the rawness of his depiction of the war:

> You are aware that once I sought the Grail,
> Riding in armour bright, serene and strong;
> And it was told that through my infant wail
> There rose immortal semblances of song.
>
> But now I've said good-bye to Galahad,
> And am no more knight of dreams and show:
> For lustless and senseless hatred make me glad,
> And my killed friends are with me where I go.
> Wound for red wound I burn to smite their wrongs;
> And there is absolution in my songs.[5]

What gives Sassoon his voice is the distance between the preferred vision of warfare as a crusade and the reality he encountered. It is a poetics that depends upon declaring not what the war is, but what it is not. The meaning of the war resides in both the rejection of the vision of soldiers as knights ("I've said good-bye to Galahad") and the ironic juxtaposition of the romantic diction of chivalry with the war experience through the appropriation to opposite meaning of the words "hero," "smite their wrongs," and "absolution."

In September 1916 Ford Madox Ford was on duty at the Battle of Ypres and was struggling to write an account of it for the Ministry of Information. His essay was not published for the reasons he later explained:

> in the territory beneath the eye, or hidden by folds in the ground, there must have been—on the two sides—a million men, moving one against the other and impelled by an invisible moral force into a Hell of fear that surely cannot have had a parallel in this world. . . . But there it stopped. As for explanation, I hadn't any: as for significant or valuable pronouncement of a psychological kind, I could not make any—nor any generalisation. There we were: those million men, forlorn, upon a raft in space.[6]

The Great War inspired either an inarticulateness in the face of the unimaginable, or the bitter expression of ironic distance between the war-as-imagined and -as-experienced, or the surrealism of nightmare.[7]

Faced with the need to give meaning to a million men forlorn, the trope of knighthood failed. Paul Fussell, in *The Great War in Modern Memory* (1975) traced the change in literary diction that signaled a profound cultural discontinuity. The distinction between prewar diction and T. S. Eliot's *Waste Land* was a breach in the representation of masculinity, a severing of the connections that linked warfare with romance, adventure, and medieval chivalry. Two generations of readers had been tutored by "the boys' books of George Alfred Henty; the male-romances of Rider Haggard; the poems of Robert Bridges; and especially the Arthurian poems of Tennyson and the pseudo-medieval romances of William Morris." Collectively, they offered a pseudomedieval or elevated diction that made a friend a "comrade," a horse a "steed," the enemy a "host," and danger "peril": to conquer was to "vanquish," and to attack was to "assail"; the various kinds of bravery were "gallant," "plucky," and "staunch." The failure of the language led to the cultural condition of irony, an expression of meaning essential to the modern temperament, a locution of dislocation.[8]

The diction went with a particular kind of moral imagination that in 1916 lost its voice after Kitchener's Army was decimated, the nation turned to conscription, and a war weariness set in. While the calamitous First Battle of the Somme was optimistically suggested to the British public as a positive turning point in the war, the year 1916 signaled, according to cultural historian Samuel Hynes, a "loss of momentum, a running down of feelings." The English who had entered the war with optimistic expectations were by 1916 feeling disappointed: "the war was not going to be short, and showed no signs of being heroic." As if reflecting this general dispiritedness, the major Edwardian writers had either fallen silent or written very little: Arnold Bennett, Robert Bridges, Rudyard Kipling, John Galsworthy, Joseph Conrad, Henry James, William Butler Yeats, John Masefield, and Thomas Hardy. As a sign of the change in national mood, Hynes points to the change of heart in the early and ardent true believer in the war, H. G. Wells, who published in the fall of 1916 his novel *Mr. Britling Sees it Through*. Speaking through his main character, Wells despairs not of the original idealism, but the failure of the war to live up to it: "it is a war without a point, a war that has lost its soul."[9]

More was at stake than preserving a metaphor; invoking the era of knights had not only cultural but political significance; the medievalism bore the weight of how the war should be understood, and had hanging over it like a dense cloud the unmistakable colorings of class and caste. Prior to conscription, between August 1914 and January 1916, 2,476,000 men in Great Britain volunteered for service. On the day war was declared, August 5, Lord Kitchener began a publicity campaign to appeal for "the First Hundred Thousand," and hundreds of thousands of young men responded immediately. Government recruitment posters appealed variously to the sense of duty and responsibility, the legitimacy of the war, hatred of the enemy, a sense of comradeship and adventure, intimidation, and public shame ("Daddy, What Did You Do in the War?"), and defense of homeland.[10]

Some of the recruitment poster imagery appealed overtly to the era of knighthood. "Britain Needs You at Once" depicts St. George slaying the dragon (see Figure 7), while "Take Up the Sword of Justice: Join Now" showed a sheathed sword lifted to the viewer's eyes.[11] The era of crusades and knighthood was invoked in a variety of other ways as well, ranging from postcards meant to be sent between soldiers and sweethearts to inspirational poetry. Such iconography may or may not have appealed to young men from all levels of society who volunteered. Chivalric imagery and values mattered most to young men from the class represented by Sassoon. They described their comrades as knights; they recited the poetry of Scott and Tennyson to themselves in their diaries and journals as they went off to war. It was they who felt betrayed in terms of the cult of chivalry when dreams of honor and the cavalry charge were dashed by the realities of modern, mechanized, and total warfare.[12]

The imagery of the crusades, knights in shining armor, and chivalry had by 1914 saturated upper- and professional class British culture. Elements of the neo-Gothic revival were seen in the architecture and furnishings of private manors, public buildings—such as the rebuilt Houses of Parliament—and royal apartments. Paintings reinvoked the knights errant of the Round Table, and commissioned portraits depicted contemporary lords and their families as if they were knights and ladies of the medieval or Elizabethan period. The literature of moral improvement used the imagery of the knights and their presumed code as the vehicle for instruction, while writers such as Alfred Lord Tennyson, Robert Browning, William Morris, and Sir Walter Scott invoked the idealized virtues of the Victorian ruling elite through the lens of the medieval period. Public school boys attended chapels hung with contemporary paintings reinvoking the chivalric era, read books holding forth the virtues of knighthood, and were told that organized sports derived from the medieval joust.[13]

The person credited with giving the "fullest expression of the chivalric myth as a framework for the war" is Henry Newbolt, one of

Figure 7. "Britain Needs You at Once," from Great Britain Parliamentary Recruiting Committee, 1915. The image of St. George slaying the dragon appealed to both patriotism and iconic representation of the age when knighthood was in flower. Poster Collection, Hoover Institution Archives.

the men of letters enlisted by Wellington House.[14] Newbolt was a close friend of the commander of the British Expeditionary Force, General Haig—which only begins to suggest his mentality toward the war. Newbolt has entered history as the epitome of the Old Men who callously sent the sons of England to die by the thousands in the trenches. He seems so perfectly to embody the assumptions of the breed that later historians have dubbed him and what he represented as "Newbolt Man," whose attributes are summarized by Paul Fussell as "honorable, stoic, brave, loyal, courteous—and unaesthetic, unironic, unintellectual and devoid of wit."[15] In a letter Newbolt wrote in 1924, his singular obtuseness was revealed in his comment, "I don't think these shell-shocked war poems [of Wilfred Owen] will move our grandchildren much."[16]

Newbolt is useful to a consideration of the meanings that attached to the image of the soldier for four reasons. The first is his breathtaking myopia, as just indicated. The second is that he offered the most complete explanation to the young male mind of how the government wished the role of the officer to be imagined as a kind of chivalric service. Third, he is also one of the earliest writers to transfer to the combat pilot the role of the chivalric knights. Finally, his private correspondence traces how a man who had completely internalized—to the point of an unhealthy vicariousness—the rhetoric of the chivalric warrior came to find that the Great War fell short of his expectations. He is a very useful example of a particular kind of disillusionment, of the sort Hynes criticizes in H. G. Wells; a disappointment not with war itself, but with the failure to the Great War to live up to an idealized vision of war-as-imagined. Even so ardent a true believer as Newbolt could not in the end continue to frame the Great War in chivalric terms.

Newbolt's *The Book of the Happy Warrior* was published in 1917 because of the need to recruit replacements for the officer class, drawn from the ruling elites, which had been decimated in the first two years of the war. His aim was overtly to enlist not only "lesser" public school boys in England who would not otherwise have been of sufficient social rank to suggest themselves as officers, but also boys in the Commonwealth nations, and undoubtedly in the United States as well, who could be prepared to become both officers and gentleman. Newbolt's book is one of the egregious examples, found on both sides of the Atlantic, of books and textbooks used as tools for propaganda directed at schoolboys and -girls.

The book retells the tales of Roland, Richard the Lionheart, St. Louis King of France, Robin Hood, the Black Prince, and Bayard. The closing two chapters hammer home the point—in case a particularly slow-witted boy might miss it—that the code of chivalry remains the ideal of all young men, and hence they should enlist in the war.

The book is particularly useful to understanding the various elements of the chivalric imagery because it so clearly articulates the conception of the gentleman-knight that permeated the propaganda messages emanating from Britain. Much of what Newbolt described as inherent to the conduct of a knight in warfare was transferred to what became the typical descriptions of the duels of "knights in the air."

In his "Preface to All Boys," Newbolt tells them:

> Chivalry was a plan of life, a conscious ideal, an ardent attempt to save Europe from barbarism, even when nations were at war with one another. . . . It still survives, and still gives the answer to both barbarians and pacifists.

He instructs his pupils on the main chivalric principles:

> First, Service, in peace and war, in love and in religion. Secondly, Brotherhood and Equality throughout the Order—whatever their rank or nationality, and whether they were hunting or dining together, or fighting against one another, all knights were brothers. Thirdly, a Right Pride . . . not in yourself but in your Order. Fourthly, the Consecration of Love; and Fifthly, the Help and Defence of the Weak, the Suffering and the Oppressed.

These rules alone, as handed down by "our ancestors," can "save the weaker from slavery and the stronger from universal hatred and moral ruin."[17]

In the concluding chapters, Newbolt drew a sharp distinction between the traditions and values of the Germans and the British. The latter is characterized by an innate or "natural" temperament of "kindliness and fair-mindedness" but it is the "order of chivalry" that has provided the legacy of "courtesy and self-restraint." For these reasons, Newbolt assured his readers, when history judges how the Commonwealth conducted the war, "It will be found that they have . . . kept faith with humanity; they have fought without hatred and conquered without cruelty, and when they could not conquer fairly and lawfully they have preferred death, and even defeat, to the deliberate use of foul means."

The enemy, on the other hand, had adopted the opposite values:

> they proclaim that victory is an end in itself, and justifies any method used to attain it. We cannot understand this; to us it seems clear that human welfare is the end in view for all communities of men, and that if victory for any one nation can only be achieved by ruining and corrupting human life, then we must do without victory.

The chivalric legacy is the sole means for maintaining this distinction:

> [I]n short, in public as in private life, we must see that the weak do not suffer injustice for the strong. . . . That was the danger that threatened Europe in the Dark Ages, and it was to meet it that chivalry arose. The same danger has threatened us in these days, and it is being met by the same method, a method handed down through the centuries.

Newbolt reiterated the basic principles of chivalry, which he enumerated in the preface, linking them in the conclusion with the stories the boys had presumably read. The principle of "service" is understood as "service of your King, or the service of your country," making the argument used to rationalize conscription in both the United States and Britain: "a soldier . . . finds the only perfect freedom in service, where all men find it if they would; and he is proud to serve, because the finest pride can only come from serving something greater than self."

The same doublethink that makes military "service" a sign of "freedom" makes the military hierarchy a sign of "equality"—which is the second principle of chivalry: "every man within the order was the equal of every other, and was bound to him as by brotherhood" even though "there must be commanders and subordinates."

This principle extends as well to an equality between enemies; all "knights" were (and therefore are) members of the same "Order," and therefore belong to a common fraternity, even if they find themselves fighting on opposite sides, an ideal that led Newbolt to draw (although he was oblivious to its implications) the particularly challenging conundrum: "this feeling [of spiritual fraternity] while it did not abolish war, went a long way towards taking the bitterness out of it."

When he discussed the role of women in this social order based upon warfare, he argued that the chivalric principles of equality also defined the status of women:

> [The feudal knights] set women in their right place, as the stars and counsellors of men, and it was only when chivalry declined for a time that the position of women was altered for the worse. Among the real knights there was never any talk of the inequality of the sexes: ladies ruled castles and armies in the absence of their husbands, and more than held their own in their presence.

The reassurances having been given—and the dependent status of women defined as a sign of their "equality" with men—Newbolt hurried past the subject of medieval "lovers" who while they did "dress extravagantly, and lie awake at nights, and do reckless things to gain the approval of their ladies," were only acting "as lovers will always be acting unto the end of time," and he advised his boy readers to demonstrate toward women "a gentleness of manner and a readiness to serve, based upon a real feeling of reverence."

Newbolt was far more comfortable—and spilled far more ink—extolling the connection between the chivalric code and sports—especially blood sports. He dismissed the critics of the British emphasis on sport by acknowledging that "these things can be overdone" and that they can "end in dulling the minds of the young," but that concern aside, detractors simply "fail to understand the real source of the prestige of the sport." Athletic competition or the hunt allows men to express their fellowship with each other, and this clearly was for Newbolt the most significant and fulfilling social bond:

> in games, as in war, and in all active life, there is something more than amusement. You cannot make a bond of brotherhood out of a companionship in amusements. That which bound the hunting men and jousters of old time together was their faithful observance of the rules. . . . If you give your opponent, man or animal, no fair chance, you will, in a minor department, be corrupting life for yourself as well as others. It is the sense of this, the sense that there is something better than success, something that must not be sacrificed even for the sake of winning, which bound men together and will always bind the best of them.

This is a shocking passage for the morality it teaches. On the one hand, killing another human being is placed on the same footing as killing an animal—both are defined as "opponents." One goes about it "fairly" because not to do so is self-corrupting. For that reason, there are rules of warfare that give opponents a "fair chance," because in that way, when one man kills another he need not relinquish those finer principles that define the masculine civilized human being.

The desire to remain civilized thus makes those who kill in warfare members of a common fraternity, assuring that the warrior achieves and sustains his identity as a man. In peacetime, sports and the hunt substitute for the common fraternity, but the principle remains that for a male to be fully self-realized—to become a man—he must pit himself against "opponents." To be a man requires the exercise of aggressive impulses. From aggression, the "brotherhood" of the sportsman or the soldier arises; said another way, civilization arises from the constraints men agree to place upon the necessary exercise of their violent aggression. Agreeing to observe those restraints constitutes the social ties that bind one man to another and thereby sustains civilization. The particular constraints are that a man should never take unfair advantage of another and should kill only from a sense of duty or obligation; above all, he is to observe the Christian virtue "not to hate his enemies."[18]

Michael Adams, who finds nothing favorable to say about Newbolt, rightly condemns him especially for *The Book of the Happy Warrior* because "Newbolt proposes youth as a time to prepare for war and death—he positively shoves youth into the cauldron."[19] Newbolt was writing at a time when the casualty rates of the war inspired the British to undertake energetic recruiting campaigns in the Commonwealth nations and the United States. Newbolt's book was obviously written in aid of that campaign. In his concluding exhortation, Newbolt challenged the boy reader to become a man by becoming a "happy warrior":

> Come and make yourself a man, with a man's life; not a narrow, shut-in life, selfish or idle or entirely specialised, but a useful, friendly, all-round life, with a wide outlook on the world you live in and the people you live among. . . . Take the full happiness of life, the happiness of serving, living, befriending, and defending—the happiness of fighting and conquering all that is difficult or dangerous or devilish, whether in man or circumstances. . . . [L]earn to be a man yourself, not a half developed or lop-sided creature, but a man full grown, full of all life that can be got from men and spent for men again.

The final line is perhaps the most chilling (if unconscious) confession of all; Newbolt clearly realized that his, the older male generation, was engaged in seducing boys to believe that they could realize themselves as men only by entering the brotherhood of war, that they get their life from men and therefore become men by spending their lives "for men again." It is this chilling meaning of "legacy" and "tradition" that he reiterates in his poem "Hic Jacet," which he uses to close the book. It is an epitaph to an imagined soldier who

Feared not the battle's thunder
Nor hoped that wars should cease. . . .
Nor feared he in his sleeping
To dream his work undone,
To hear the heathen sweeping
Over the lands he won;
For he has left in keeping
His sword unto his son.

To transmit the legacy based upon civilized violence requires that each succeeding generation be constructed as soldiers who will be sent to die in order both to realize the legacy and become men.

In the concluding chapter, "Chivalry of Today," Newbolt indicates exactly which "youth" he was most interested in seducing to spend their lives "for men again." The theme running as subtext throughout his review of the history of the British military services is the need for officers to lead men into battle:

> The plain fact is that among the few absolutely vital elements of success in modern war, one, and that, perhaps, the most vital of all, has been supplied by our schools and universities. . . . [That wealthier] class has not only made possible the winning of this war, it has proved to be almost the only trustworthy source of leadership.

Implicit in what follows is Newbolt's recognition that this class has been decimated by the war, hence, the need to draw from a different class, while assuring that these newcomers or upstarts were fully initiated into the values and heritage represented by the older, established elite:

> It follows that our hope for the future must lie in extending the tradition beyond the boundaries of class; and happily a great deal has already been done in this direction. . . . There must be no exclusiveness . . . not looking down upon comrades, no talk of "temporary gentlemen." Everyone knows and recognises with admiration that in that first black year of the war our

line was held by the men of birth—that is, by the great-grandsons of those who faced Napoleon a hundred years ago. They in their turn cannot fail to welcome to their fellowship the men from small schools and less known families who rushed in to take their places when they were decimated and exhausted.

From that need, Newbolt sought to build a new civilized order based upon military training:

> this school for Happy Warriors is open not only to English and Welsh, Scottish and Irish, not only to the nations of the Commonwealth, but to all nations whatever. . . . It offers to the whole world what the old chivalry offered to a single class. . . . [T]he time may come when fighting will be infrequent, but so long as there remain in the world wild beasts, savages, maniacs, autocrats and worshippers of Woden, there will always be the possibility of it, the necessity for the indignant heart and the ready hand.

Even if—and Newbolt presented this both as an impossibility and with the implication that it would be regrettable if it occurred—"the possibility of war were done away with," nonetheless, he assured the boys reading his closing words, "human life is still a warfare, in which there is no victory but by the soldier's virtues, and no security but in their faithful transmission."

In advocating this new order, Newbolt implicitly expressed the fear of the ruling class of the parvenu; while the casualty rates made it necessary to recruit officers from those lacking the usual breeding and social status, the wish was to assure that this elevation be accompanied by an indoctrination into the values and legacy of that class. The nostalgia, glamour, and glory associated with the chivalric knight and his legacy thus masked a desperation, a need to believe that despite the high casualty rates of World War I, despite the sacrifice of men of all classes, the traditional values and hence status of the aristocratic order could somehow be sustained.

Ultimately, the vision of war as a medieval crusade could not be sustained even by one as self-blinded as Newbolt. He had seen both his son Francis, and his son-in-law Ralph Furse off to the war. On August 12, 1915, he wrote to Lady Alice Hylton to describe the day that Ralph departed for war, leaving behind his wife and two small children, one only two months old. "We began today in the fashion of the Middle Ages," he wrote, describing how the family attended a mass outdoors offered by the bishop of St. Albans, who was related to Ralph Furse. Afterwards, the family said goodbye to Ralph as he left in his motor car, and "Celia [Newbolt's daughter] came out in front of the house with Jill [her daughter] in her arms, like a Chaucerian Andromache seeing Hector off to Battle." Writing again to Lady Hylton two days later, Newbolt observed, "however we suffer, we have seen the England of our dreams—The Black Prince . . . and Philip Sidney . . . and all the Company of the High Order of Knighthood." On Christmas day, 1915, he wrote of Christmas dinner with his son and son-in-law: "It was like sitting at meat with St. Michael and St. George!" To another correspondent, he wrote on March 28, 1918, of his son Francis: "he has the one thing I could have wished for him, and feared life hadn't given him—the resilience and the joy of courage, not merely in the fight but in the dark hour." Of the departure of Ralph by train after a leave, Newbolt wrote to Emma Coltman on March 31, 1918, "He was splendid—he irradiated the whole dingy platform and crowd with a kind of halo."[20]

Newbolt's writing gives every indication that he experienced what Alice Longworth Roosevelt called her father's "grim elation" at sending his sons off to war. There is something wholly unsettling in this insight into a mind so preoccupied with medievalism that it cannot take in directly the reality of a son and son-in-law off to war. Newbolt found meaning in the parting not with the potential loss, but in how much it went toward confirming his idea of what the age of chivalry must have been like. The cultural values associated with the age of chivalry as it had been constructed by the Victorian era provided Newbolt both the intellectual and spiritual context for understanding not only the Great War but his personal responses to it. But this hazy scrim over the face of war had become tattered and torn for Newbolt by the end of the war. Writing to Lady Alice Hylton on October 6, 1918, he admits to a fatigue and numbness even to the fear that his own son might die:

> I don't even feel the joy of victory as wildly as I should have done three years ago. I am very happy about it at times, but I have come to believe that the best thing we can do is to kill the accursed and that isn't a job to rejoice over. To win a game makes the pulse leap; but not to massacre—that only chokes and disgusts.[21]

This is a disillusionment not with War but with how the Great War was conducted, with the nature of trench warfare. Newbolt was recanting his earlier glorification of war as the manifestation of civilized manhood; he noticed that the nature of the Great War reduced a vision of civilized violence undertaken to defend civilization to mere massacre and left not only the world but his own sensibilities the lesser for it. For him the war perverted masculine nature, preventing the manifestation of aggression restrained in the service of civilized values. It no longer served as the symbol of national character embodied in the gentleman knight.

The "Great Crusade" Crosses the Atlantic

When America entered the war, the justification of it as a crusade against barbarism was exported from Great Britain and taken up by the Wilson administration. Naturally, there were problems linking British aristocratic and imperial values with those of the United States. It would have been overwhelmingly distasteful to American sensibilities to import the justification that Allied colonial imperialism was morally superior to the Germans; instead, the thrust of this argument was translated into an American idiom by reinvoking the Civil War: just as that war had freed the slaves, so would World War I free those enslaved by German autocracy, and just as Lincoln had demanded total victory, so must the Allies.[22]

Pershing's Crusaders was a feature-length documentary produced by the Committee on Public Information and distributed to American theaters in the spring of 1918. It was advertised as the first film "to show the true conditions now prevailing where Americans are on the firing line" and used footage shot by the Signal Corps and the Navy. The opening scene was of a crusader in the Middle Ages flanked by two American soldiers. The subtitle told the audience:

> the world conflict takes upon itself the nature of a Crusade. . . . We go forth in the same spirit in which the knights of old went forth to do battle with the Saracens. . . . The young men of America are going out to rescue Civilization. They are going to fight for one definite thing, to save Democracy from death. . . . The mighty exodus of America's manhood to the plains of Europe may well be called "The Eighth Crusade."[23]

The desire to link participation in the Great War with European history and Christianity in general, and Great Britain in particular, led to some jarring stylistic anachronisms, especially when it came to figuring out how to get around the glaring problem of the Revolution. The July 1917 issue of *Ladies Home Journal* offered a singular example of an interesting if ultimately absurd effort when it reproduced George D. Sproul's illuminated panels of the Declaration of Independence decorated in the manner of a medieval or Tudor manuscript. Although the Declaration is decidedly Enlightenment in spirit and tone, and although it was written in the eighteenth century, Sproul uses an obviously neo-Gothic design, one worthy of an acolyte of Pugin or the arts and crafts school. The calligraphic style echoes an Elizabethan hand, and the decorations for the frames would do well in a room papered with a William Morris motif. The borders are illuminated with the royal crests of the thirteen colonies, and with Tudor-style portraits of important colonial figures as well as small, stylized scenes from colonial life.

One could hardly guess from the decorative style that the Declaration presented the legal case for revolution against the British crown. Nor can the choice of Sproul's illuminated panels to represent the Declaration have been merely accidental. On the page preceding the first panel is a color portrait of Woodrow Wilson, with a reproduction of his handwritten message: "The day has come when America is privileged to spend her blood and her might for the principles that gave her birth and happiness and the peace that she has treasured. God helping her, she can do no other." The *Ladies Home Journal* was highly conscious of conveying national resolve about participation in World War I by linking the past with the present. The past suggested by Sproul's designs for the Declaration of Independence tied the legacy directly—if incongruously—to the Victorian neo-Gothic revival and, therefore, to the symbolism of the British throne and the aristocracy, as well as to the romantic nostalgia for the chivalric code of honor, essentially undermining the historical point of the Declaration itself.

While this revisionism looks strained and foolish—although pleasing from a purely decorative point-of-view—the imagery of the chivalric age was a compelling one. American soldiers echoed the propaganda messages about chivalry and holy wars to explain in letters or diaries their personal or private reactions; for instance, this description of an infantry action: "The men had decorated their helmets with red poppies from the fields and they swept by like plumed knights, cheering and singing."[24] Or this comment by Heywood Hale Broun, who was then a correspondent for the *New York Tribune*:

> Verdun and Joffre, and "they shall not pass," and Napoleon's tomb, and war bread, and all the men with medals and everything. Great stuff! They'll never be anything like it in the world again. I tell you it's better than "Ivanhoe." Everything's happening and I'm in it.[25]

The pervasiveness of the imagery is noteworthy because of how often it arises as a spontaneous description rather than from an official source. "It is not especially surprising," comments social historian David M. Kennedy, "to find Stars and Stripes assuring a soldier reader that he was the 'spiritual successor' to the 'Knights of King Arthur's Round Table'":

> But it is to be remarked when countless common soldiers wrote privately of themselves in the same vein. American war narratives with unembarrassed boldness, speak frequently of "feats of valor," of "the cause" and the

"crusade." The memoirs and missives penned in France are shot through with images of knight-errantry and grails thrillingly pursued.[26]

The unthinking comparison of Ivanhoe to the battles of World War I as well as the use of what strikes the modern ear as a fatuous diction of knighthood can distract attention from the depth of feeling with which young men embraced the concept of a "holy war."

The Conventions of "Knights of the Sky"

When America entered the war, American popularizers of air combat employed the metaphor of chivalry with an ease borne of frequent use, while at the same time using the metaphor to reinforce Anglo-American cultural connections. The following is from an article by Laurence LaTourette Driggs, an American, which appeared in a popular American periodical in April 1918:

> Rivaling in romance the exploits of the knights of King Arthur, the daily flying sorties into the countless perils of a hostile and watchful enemy sky bring us to frequent revelations of human endurance, human adroitness and superhuman mystery that pale by comparison the wildest fiction of fancy.[27]

Between 1916 and 1918, framing air-to-air combat with images of knights and crusades had become commonplace. The evolution of both the diction and the conceptual framework is illustrated by three accounts available in the United States from 1916 to just before the war ended. Each is an account of one ace: Max Immelmann, Manfred Von Richthofen, and Georges Guynemer.

Max Immelmann was one of the earliest pilots of the Fokker Eindeckers and one of the first to receive unprecedented accolades and public attention following his being awarded the Pour la Mérite. Immelmann, who was nicknamed the Eagle of Lille, flew over the Western Front for just over a year. He was shot down and killed over Verdun on June 18, 1916. An article titled "A Courteous Ambush in the Air," appearing in the May 14, 1916, issue of the American magazine the *Literary Digest*, finds apt "proof that human nature is about as it always was" in the account of an encounter between Immelmann and RFC Capt. B. J. Slade:

> The code of honor in combat is not jealously observed in Europe, save by the aviation corps. Freed from much of the ruck and reek of war by their easy poise far above it, they can take time and pains to be gentlemen warriors. It is not strange to find them observing amenities scrupulously, and yet in obedience of a law that has never been spoken or written between two adversaries.

The account provides further evidence that by 1916 the realities of the ground war had made it impossible to sustain the vision of the ground soldier as a "knight" and was distorting the traditional defining characteristics of masculinity. By contrast, the air war breathed renewed life into what that image represented. The article anticipated Newbolt's praise in *The Happy Warrior* of the code that binds warriors together in a "spiritual fraternity" that takes the "bitterness" out of war. The reader was told that when an enemy aircraft was shot down, the victorious pilot would fly over the enemy base to drop a notice as a courtesy and homage, and that British pilots so respected Immelmann's skills that they would say, "It's no disgrace to be caught and shot down by him!"

Captain Slade was flying as the observer-gunner when Immelmann attacked from the rear, peppering their fuel tank with bullets. Out of gas, the pilot "tipped the nose of the plane downward and plunged toward the earth" with Immelmann "spitting bullets through their machine": "The pilot's thumb was mangled by a bullet, and while the pursued and pursuing machines were cleaving the atmosphere at high speed, and while the machine gun kept at its work, Captain Slade amputated Captain Darley's thumb with a penknife." Darley managed to land, and Immelmann came to earth beside them to offer his assistance. "He behaved in a kindly manner," writes Captain Slade. "He is a gentleman, and I hope that if we capture him he will be treated as one." The moral is drawn that the story illustrates "a bit of the romance of war."

The article also made much of the convention that those who fight in the air are not motivated by hatred. It reports an account in the *Berliner Tageblatt* that included an interview with two captured pilots in a German prison camp. Asked if they hated Immelmann, they regarded the reporter "with astonishment": "Hate! . . . Not a bit of it! He flies, fights and shoots hard; he's a soldier. We have no hatred for soldiers."

The features of the Immelmann-Slade/Darley account became conventional: the personalized nature of the war, in which the combatants knew each other by name and reputation; a code of honor and courtesy that was invariably followed; the respect of enemies for one another's skill; extraordinary initiative (exemplified here by Slade in amputating his pilot's thumb); stoic courage (shown in this account by Darley who endured the amputation while continuing to fly), the solicitous concern of the victorious pilot for enemies when the battle was over; the slightly archaic, elevated diction used to establish chivalry as the interpretive context for the combat; and the highly visual, concise language used to recreate the thrill of combat.

To say it was described in conventional terms should not be mistaken as meaning that the Immelmann-Slade/Darley battle was not extraordinary. The point here lies in the style of telling, that the story is framed—and made comprehensible—by the romanticized, public schoolboy version of the gentleman-knight and his code of honor. Both accounts—of a man who severs a pilot's thumb while their plane plunges in a nose dive, raked by machine-gun bullets, and who then shakes hands with the man who had pursued them, and the comment that British pilots so respected Immelmann they would not mind being killed by him—were potentially as stunning to the moral imagination as accounts of men in the trenches walking or crawling over the detached arms or legs of their fallen comrades, or even the image—as presented by Ford Madox Ford—of a million men confronting each other adrift on a barren island of their own creating. But the reports are framed by a familiar style that assures the reader that this is the "stuff from which legends are made"—that they are just like the tales from the epics and romances they read as schoolchildren, a rather queasy-making use of the fantasies of one's youth.

Another characteristic that became conventional was the admiration for those who followed the extraordinary code of honor because they were not under orders to do so; it was a code of their own devising, and there was no utility to it as far as winning the war was concerned. The implication that might have been drawn, viewed from another perspective, that gallantry was therefore essentially useless, a zany, deadly form of empty heroics, was prevented by another convention. Typically, an account was presented out of context; there was no effort to establish how it related to the progress of the war, how it fit into that larger picture; telling stories about the war in the air was useful for distracting attention from the ground war, boosting morale deflated by the news from the front, and, as here, giving the public in a neutral nation heroes with whom they could identify.

When Immelmann attacked Slade and Darley, he was flying one of the new Fokker Eindeckers. No hint of the "Fokker Scourge" is given in the account, not surprisingly given the outcries in both the French and British parliaments following their appearance over the Western Front. The impression given in this account is instead that the kind of plane flown is essentially irrelevant to the outcome, which depends upon the skill and temperament of the flyer. The context for the anecdote is clearly not the conduct of the air war; the frame that provides the story its continuity is the recollected imagery of romanticized chivalric warfare. The reader is invited to project onto the account a "war-as-imagined" because the report withholds information that would make it clear just how much the encounter in the sky actually differed from it.

The air war gained its storybook quality from this stylistic convention of lifting reports of encounters from the context of the war and placing them within the anachronistic frame of the chivalric code. It was easy to conclude that the code was universally followed—that the true heroes of the air war habitually landed to offer a cigarette and inquire as to the health of the fallen foe, or always flew over the site of their victories to drop flowers for the dead. In the earlier days of the war, such incidents did occur: opponents challenged each other to duels in the sky, and pilots flew over enemy airbases to drop information about killed or captured pilots. As the war intensified, however, these gestures became less and less possible. But they continued to be essential for how the combat pilots were imagined. The narrative convention converted the war to a fantasy, distracting attention from the actual air war while making the reader feel informed, which meant the public did not notice the silence about those matters that really count when it comes to understanding how an air war is progressing, or even the point of air power as a factor in supporting the larger aims of the ground war.

C. G. Grey wrote the preface to the English translation of Manfred von Richthofen's autobiography, *The Red Air Fighter* (1918).[28] It provides a good illustration of how accomplished writers had become by the end of the war at incorporating the air war—even a personal account written by an enemy flyer who was a hero in his own nation—into the framework of the chivalric legend as shaped by Newbolt in the *Happy Warrior*. The editor of the British periodical *The Aeroplane*, Grey explains that the decision was made to publish the translation in order to provide Allied combat pilots an insight into the German flying methods they were encountering along the Western Front. This may certainly have been part of the motivation, but the publication of the autobiography for popular consumption signifies as well an effort to place a dignified face on the British gloating that von Richthofen had been brought down in the vicinity of Vaux along the Somme Valley on April 21, 1918.

Von Richthofen was credited with eighty victories during the eighteen months he flew into combat over the Western Front. There are many who dispute this number and regard von Richthofen as arrogant and self-serving, just as many admire him for the legend he became. Both attitudes were also prevalent during the war, certainly among those who flew against him. There is no question, however, that von Richthofen's squadron used effectively a formidable German strategy: a chase squadron of handpicked flyers, utilized as a highly mobile unit that could be brought to bear quickly where needed, which flew in formations that centered upon a single leader. Von Richthofen painted his plane bright red so his men could know where he was as leader in the confusion of battle, while other planes in the squadron were also painted with bright, identifying designs. As the RFC pilots became aware both of the colorful planes and that they appeared one day at one position and another day somewhere else, they coined the description "Von Richthofen's Traveling Circus." From that date forward, von Richthofen has been known as the Red Baron and his squadron as the Flying Circus.

In his preface, Grey takes the reader back to the French chronicler Jean Froissart (1337–1410), who noted that it was "'impossible to inculcate into the German knights the true spirit of knightliness.'" The medieval German knight, according to Froissart, could never learn to follow the chivalric rule that applied when one knight broke his lance against the shield of another. The knight with this advantage was supposed to step out of the combat until his opponent could unsheath his sword and reengage on equal terms. "Probably," observed Grey, "the Hun of the period proceeded to stick his opponent in the midriff . . . and so finished the fight." This is quite unlike the "true spirit of knightliness" shown by the average modern Englishman who, having knocked a man down, stands back to give his opponent another chance (10).

Moving from this edifying account of the perfect English gentleman, Grey acknowledged that von Richthofen showed "surprisingly little Hunnishness." Nor is this surprising: "It is one of the accepted facts of the war that the German aviators have displayed greater chivalry than any other branch of the German services." Grey praised the German pilots for their earlier habit of dropping packets over British bases which contained letters from captured pilots or the personal belongings of the dead. This practice abated as the war in the air intensified, but nevertheless, the German squadrons treat captured and wounded British flyers very well (10–11).

Grey regarded von Richthofen as a slightly unevolved British schoolboy. He noted the egotism, pride, and sense of superiority von Richthofen regularly expressed, and noted that it was similar to what one might have expected in an earlier period from the British:

Happily that type of Englishman has been dead for some years, and his descendants have lost much of his point of view by contact with our gallant Allies of today, but he was a common type in his time, even among those commonly known in that period as "the gentry." Who then can blame one of the Teuton race, which by reason of its being so many degrees further East is just so many degrees further removed from the current idea of knightliness, for not possessing precisely the humility which is the pride of good form in these days? (11)

Undoubtedly it need not be pointed out that Grey demonstrated precisely the arrogance of racial superiority he condemned in the Germans, but the terms are interesting because of the echo of the condemnation of the Germans in the Bryce Report. Although part of Europe and therefore part of the civilized nations, the Germans as an occupying army resembled the uncivilized nations of the east—especially the barbarian cruelty of the non-Christians, such as the Turks.

Despite this unavoidable limitation on his character development, von Richthofen "fulfils all the requirements for the making of a first-class pilot" because of his "birth and education." He came from a family that included neither "politicians" nor "professional soldiers," but were "horsemen and game-shots." At school von Richthofen was a poor student but a good athlete, "all of which is very like the son of an English country gentleman" (12).

What all this has to do with fighting an air war is hard to tell. It is as if Grey was writing with Newbolt's volume at his elbow, so closely does it seem to invoke a similar image of the public schoolboy as the modern manifestation of the chivalric knight. His account indicates quite clearly that the original image of the young line officer had been fully translated into the iconography of the combat pilot. While Newbolt was at least sufficiently in touch with the implications for his class of the high casualty rates in the ground war, Grey, writing when the Allies were confident they would win very soon, seems not to acknowledge it as a factor. Newbolt recognized the need to enlist young boys into the code of chivalry even if they did not come from the stock of the landed aristocracy, because that traditional source for officer material had been decimated in the early years of the war. But for Grey, when it comes to combat pilots, the original symbolism remains intact: the inheritor of the guerdon of the aristocratic code of chivalry comes of the right stock, whether he is a Teuton or born to the British elite. Moreover, he may not be a terribly bright lad, but he is a good athlete and knows how to ride and hunt. It goes without saying that Grey presented the combat pilot as emblematic of national character. His preface therefore carries a not terribly subtle implication about the desirability of continuing the pre-war British social order as well. The chivalric symbolism is culturally and politically coded to offer proof that not only are the men who fight the same as their earlier medieval counterparts, but the world they are defending and the one that will emerge from the war should be, too.

The French also used chivalric imagery to describe their pilots, and they also exported the accounts to the United States. Georges Marie Ludovic Jules Guynemer was the most renowned of the French aces, achieving an international reputation while he was alive and legendary status after his death in 1917. Readers of the September 1918 *Ladies Home Journal*, for example, found the reproduction of a painting by Lt. Henre Farre depicting "The Forty-Fifth Victory of Guynemer, Knight of the Air" (see Figure 8). Using pastels of blue, yellow, and green, and in an impressionist style, the painting shows two indefinite shadowy figures—a German pilot and observer—falling to their deaths from a smoking plane, while a second French plane flies off into the middle distance. The reader is offered this thrilling account:

> Leaping from the silver heart of a cloud, he opened fire. The enemy plane's gas tank exploded while the aviator was attempting a nose dive, causing the machine to spin violently. The aviator lost control of the plane and, with his observer, was flung out at an altitude of three miles. Turning, then, the intrepid Guynemer drove back into the heart of that protecting cloud to await his next chance.[29]

Flying with the famous French escadrille Les Cigognes (the Storks) between June 1915 and his disappearance on September 11, 1917, Guynemer led all other French aces with fifty-three victories to his credit. On two occasions he downed three planes in one day; on one occasion he downed four. He was wounded eight times and continued to fly even though he was ill and ordered to rest.[30]

Henry Bordeux's *Georges Guynemer: Knight of the Air*, written after Guynemer's death, applies the imagery of the age of chivalry to an extreme, writing what is ultimately a hagiography. It was translated by Louise Morgan Sill and published in 1918 by Yale University Press with funds given in memory of Ens. Curtis Seaman Read (USNRF). Read was another Yale student who, like Kenneth MacLeish, joined the naval aviation service and was killed in France in February 1918. The introduction to the American edition was written by Theodore Roosevelt, who said of Guynemer, "He was the foremost among all the extraordinary fighters of all the nations who in this war have made the skies their battle field."[31] The book provides a very useful insight into how the imagery, diction, and quality of imagination usually reserved for fairy tales or romantic tales of knights in shining armor were used to frame the exploits of the aces.

Bordeaux achieved what Newbolt did not. Newbolt contented himself with retelling the tales of knights such as Bayard and abstracting from them a code of chivalrous conduct that was imagined as applicable to all gentleman warriors. But he did not describe any modern-day warriors as if they were chivalric knights. Bordeaux managed to elide Guynemer with the knights of old in a number of ways: he traced Guynemer's family genealogy to the days of Charlemagne, he compared him to earlier knights such as Roland or to medieval epics and romances, and he framed the descriptions of Guynemer's aerial combats in terms that evoke the pictorial canon of the painters of neo-Gothic themes.

Bordeaux's prologue included a theme written by an eleven-year-old French schoolboy, Paul Bailly, whose teacher, the schoolmistress at Bouclans, had assigned the exercise and forwarded the essay to Bordeaux.

Figure 8. Lt. Henri Farre, *The Forty-fifth Victory of Guynemer, Knight of the Air* (1917). The publication of this work in the September 1918 issue of *Ladies Home Journal* contributed to Americans' familiarity with the heroic feats of Georges Guynemer.

> Guynemer is the Roland of our epoch: like Roland he was very brave, and like Roland he died for France. But his exploits are not a legend like those of Roland, and in telling them just as they happened we find them more beautiful than any we could imagine. . . . Roland was the example for all the knights in history. Guynemer should be the example for Frenchmen now. . . . I, especially, I shall never forget him, for I shall remember that he died for France, like my dear Papa. (14–15)

The blurring of the imagined and the real is compellingly clear in this simple theme, indicating perhaps more clearly than any other example how constructed images of war appropriate the deepest private emotions—here, the loss of a father—to the symbolism suited to the needs of the state.

Bordeaux was utterly charmed by the sentiments of little Paul Bailly and wholly approved of them: "Guynemer is the modern Roland, with the same redoubtable youth and fiery soul. He is the last of the knights-errant, the first of the new knights of the air." As for the style of the telling, it too is suited to the imaginative range of a children's storybook: "Guynemer's life falls naturally into the legendary rhythm, and the simple and exact truth resembles a fairy tale" (15–16).

Guynemer came from a thoroughly middle-class background. His father was a retired Army officer turned historian. Bordeaux traced Guynemer's line to Charlemagne, and as if this were insufficient, he included an appendix that traced the family name through genealogies and fables and legends, paying particular attention to the accounts of the Crusades, enforcing both a natural nobility of deed coupled with nobility of descent:

> Guynemer is the flower of an old French family. Like so many other heroes, like so many peasants who, in this Great War, have been the wheat of the nation, his own acts have proved his nobility. But the fairy sent to preside at his birth laid in his cradle certain gilded pages of the finest history in the world: Roland, the Crusades, Brittany and Duguesclin, the Empire, and Alsace. (27)

Bordeaux raised class issues similar to those in Newbolt's *Happy Warrior*, although with less delicacy than his British counterpart. Acknowledging on the one hand the egalitarian nature of a war that draws on all classes, Bordeaux insisted upon retaining the traditional feudal distinctions between "peasant" and "aristocracy."

Bordeaux's approach shares much with Newbolt. Both linked the present with the past, trying to assure an association in the mind of the reader between the happy hours he might have spent as a child reading about Richard the Lionheart or Roland and the role of the modern-day warrior. Bordeaux took it a step further than Newbolt because Bordeaux was constructing a modern-day hero. His approach, which appropriated Guynemer to the framework of a storybook legend about knights, illustrated the conventional propaganda technique that divorced Guynemer the individual from Guynemer as "image."

Bordeaux also used language that would invoke the pictorial canons of illustrated storybooks in order to evoke in the mind's eye an image of the hero, as in this description of a group of planes returning from battle:

> One after another, the victorious birds came back to cover from every part of the violet and rosy sky. But joy over their success must show itself, and they indulged in all the fanciful caprioles of acrobatic aviation, spinning down in quick spirals, turning somersaults, looping or plunging in a glorious sky-dance. Last of these young gods, Guynemer landed after one final circle, and took off his helmet, offering to the setting sun his illuminated face, still full of the spirit of battle. (162)

Each of the descriptive techniques depends upon the reader recalling a familiar tale from the past, one that is already invested not only with high cultural valuing—as the connection between knighthood, class, and nationalism—but also with a romantic and nostalgic attachment, the intimacy and sense of identification that comes from reading quietly on a rainy day or lingering over a story on a hazy, summer afternoon, the pleasure of adventures vicariously experienced through the pages of a legend or romance. It depends above all on excluding a sense of familiarity with Guynemer as individual in favor of identifying with Guynemer as epitome of knighthood.

As with Newbolt, Bordeaux had in mind especially the young male reader. At the end of this biography, he said that the "ballades of olden times used to conclude with an envoi addressed to some powerful person and invariably beginning with King, Queen, Prince, or Princess." Bordeaux decides to dedicate his envoi to his "Prince," little Paul Bailly, and to those little French schoolboys who are like him. He reminds his "Prince" that Germany has not only waged war, but waged it in a wholly uncivilized manner:

> The enthusiasm and patience, the efforts and sacrifices, of the generations which came before you, little boy, were necessary to save you, to save your country, to save the world, born of light and born unto light, from the darkness of dread oppression. Germany has chosen to rob war of all that, slowly and tentatively, the nations had given to it of respect for treaties, pity for the weak and defenseless, and of honor generally. She has poisoned it as she poisons her gasses. . . . Parisian boys of your own age will tell you that during their sleep German squadrons used to fly over their city dropping bombs at random upon it. And to what purpose? None, beyond useless murder. (246–47)

This sounds as if Bordeaux is making the same argument as Newbolt: that all young men must prepare themselves for warfare fought as gentlemen fight. There is no doubt that Bordeaux aimed at stimulating the imagination for warfare in his young reader. But his final point takes a different direction from Newbolt's vision of an eternal "passing of the sword from father to son."

The problem with Germany's conduct of the war, Bordeaux tells his "little boy," is that it has forced "her opponents to adopt the same methods." The danger is that the lowering of morality brought about by the conduct of the war will infect French society after it ends, causing internal division and strain. It is to this challenge that Bordeaux calls the young reader, invoking the image of the Rescue of the Maiden not to urge the "little boy" to war, but to consider the needs of the nation when France is once again at peace:

> Little boy, do not forget that this war, blending all classes, has also blended in a new crucible all the capacities of our country. They are now turned against the aggressor, but they will have to be used in time for union, love, and peace. . . . The house, the city, the nation ought not to be divided. The enemy would have done us too much evil if he had not brought about the reconciliation of all Frenchmen. You, little boy, will have to wipe away the blood from the bleeding face of France, to heal her wounds, and secure for her the revival she will urgently need. (246)

The insistent urging undoubtedly reflects among other things the impression made upon France by the revolt among the *poilus* only nine or ten months before Bordeaux began Guynemer's biography.

The significance of Guynemer to Bordeaux's anxious plea lies in the sharp contrast Bordeaux made between Germans who bombed cities at random and the role of the French combat pilot. While the German bombers were intent upon "their loathesome work," says Bordeaux, "our airplanes, piloted by soldiers not much older than you, cruised like moving stars above the city of Genevieve, threatened now with unheard-of invasion from on high" (246). Air-to-air combat represented the one form of mortal combat that could still follow the civilizing codes of chivalry and the crusades. When Bordeaux urges his reader "let the life of Guynemer inspire you," he does not mean simply that schoolboys should prepare themselves to become combat pilots; rather, he means that in the combat pilot, youth can still find embodied the chivalric virtues that can be used to redeem the nation after the war: individual acts of honor, strength, and courage; the willingness to defend the weak against the strong against all odds. The other forms of warfare, on the other hand, teach soldiers and civilians alike to abandon civilized restraint, because of a reliance upon waging war against civilians (bombing) and upon weapons of mass destruction (gas).

Bordeaux's final plea reveals a war weariness similar to what New-bolt expressed in his private correspondence. For Bordeaux, Guynemer is significant as a symbol of the last remnant of continuity with the past, an emblem of national character and civilized values otherwise lost because of how the Great War was conducted. While the style is of a child's storybook and the ostensible reader is the French schoolboy, it is unmistakable that Bordeaux spoke to the adult audience as well. This was certainly true in the United States, where his book was published by the prestigious Yale University Press using a fund established to memorialize an aviator killed in the war. The dedication by Roosevelt also points unambiguously toward an adult audience.

The receptivity to Bordeaux's style of telling is an index to the seriousness with which the chivalric age was viewed, at least among certain influential quarters in France, Great Britain, and the United States. This is also evident in Newbolt's private correspondence. His frequent use of images and themes from the chivalric era to describe his feelings as relatives left for war indicates that the *Book of the Happy Warrior*, while written with a propagandistic purpose, was not an example of hypocrisy or deceit. It represented what Newbolt and his class and generation on both sides of the Channel and on both sides of the Atlantic hoped the war would preserve and that their class and status would emerge as a result intact and legitimated.

The disillusioning reality of the ground war coupled with the reiteration of the combat pilot as literally a modern knight made him the vessel for an entire way of life, a use of the image of the combat pilot to legitimate variously class privilege, cultural continuity, historical legacy, and the definitions of masculinity itself. The image of the combat pilot preserved the idealized conception of civilized violence directed toward the preservation of civilization, an application of skill, restraint, and breeding to the deadly business of warfare.

In the hands of the French writer Bordeaux, the image of the combat pilot as knight was used to invoke a new kind of future for France, reshaping the chivalric ideal to heal a country that because of the war had seen a "blending of all classes," and that would need to find ways to reconcile peacefully their inherent divisions. In the hands of C. G. Grey, the same metaphor became a way of legitimizing a society that he hoped would continue to be based on class, breeding, and caste. When America entered the war, the fantasy that it could be won by a vast fleet of American planes was built on the received vision from Europe of the air war as single combat, imagined duels promising a worthy test of the American character, especially America's gilded youth.

CHAPTER 7

Mechanized Warfare
and the Man

The appeal of air combat to the American imagination owed much to the development of the combat plane as a specialized weapon of warfare that resolved the tension between the machine and the man. This tension existed prior to the war as the industrial age made its increasing encroachments into civilian society, but it was brought firmly into the forefront with the advent of trench warfare.

The introduction of the "ironclad" warships during the Civil War impressed thoughtful Americans as the moment when romance and human agency in warfare gave way to utility, science, and mechanization; when men at war became cogs in a wheel rather than determiners of their own glory. These anxieties were realized in more deadly, material terms along the Western Front. With the combat plane, it was an entirely different matter. The rendering of the man and machine as chevalier and horse, and ultimately the combat plane as designed for the skills of the exceptional man, resolved the dissonance between man and machine and made it possible to imagine mechanized warfare in traditional terms: the decisive factor was not the weapon but the individual's skill in mastering it and bending it to his will.

War Deprived of Glory: American Visions of Mechanized War

Nathaniel Hawthorne's long essay "Chiefly about War Matters by a Peaceable Man" appeared in the July 1862 *Atlantic Monthly*.[1] Writing one

year into the Civil War, Hawthorne recorded his impressions while touring military camps and battlefields. Never evading his often-conflicting
ideas and emotions, Hawthorne voiced both contemporary sentiments
or conventional wisdom in the North and an ironic distance from them,
or a skepticism about them. While he never entirely disavowed the
optimistic sentiments of his countrymen, he often also reflected unambiguously upon the destructive implications of modern warfare for the
human spirit.

Hawthorne felt the impact of mechanization on traditional and
romantic visions of warfare most sharply when he visited the harbor
where four warships were moored: the flagship *Minnesota*, the *Monitor*,
and the ruined hulks of the *Congress* and the *Cumberland*. The *Monitor*
was the Union's answer to the *Virginia*, devised by the Confederacy to
break the Union embargo on foreign ships heading for the former
Southern states. For Hawthorne, the *Monitor* had rendered the *Minnesota* "as much a thing of the past as any of the Ships of Queen Elizabeth's
time, which grappled with the galleons of the Spanish Armada." The
passing of the flagship made the traditional naval officer obsolete as
well. The slightly gouty flag officer strutting on the deck of the *Minnesota* seemed to Hawthorne "a gallant gentlemen, but of the old, slow,
and pompous school of naval worthies," who, like their counterparts in
the British navy, were tied to "rules, forms, and etiquette" which made
them "too cumbrous for the quick spirit of to-day." Such officers would
"probably go down, along with the ships in which they fought valor-
ously, and strutted most intolerably."

With exquisite ambiguity, Hawthorne explained how the ironclads
rendered both the *Minnesota* and its officers obsolete:

How can an Admiral condescend to go to sea in an iron pot? What space
and elbow-room can be found for quarter-deck dignity in the cramped
look-out of the *Monitor*, or even in the twenty feet diameter of her cheese-
box. All the pomp and dignity of naval warfare are gone by. Henceforth,
there must come up a race of engine-men and smoke-blackened can-
noniers, who will hammer away at their enemies under the direction of a

single pair of eyes; and even heroism—so deadly a grip is science laying on our noble possibilities—will become a quality of very minor importance, when its possessor cannot break through the iron crust of his own armament and give the world a glimpse of it. (434)

The *Monitor*, which was moored close to the *Minnesota*, provided such a contrast that "it could not be called a vessel at all; it was a machine" looking "like a gigantic rat-trap." It appeared "ugly, questionable, suspicious, evidently mischievous . . . devilish." It was the "new war-fiend, destined, along with others of the same breed, to annihilate whole navies and batter down old supremacies. The wooden walls of Old England cease to exist, and a whole history of naval renown reaches its period." Going aboard for a tour, Hawthorne imagined the men inside being "sent to the bottom of the sea" and stifling in the impenetrable iron box. But such visions seemed not to touch the officers: "It was pleasant to see their benign exultation in her powers of mischief." Soon, even the advances of the *Monitor* would be exceeded by further improvements in the "science of war," when submarines attack unseen, until the ship that is its prey goes down in "a sucking whirlpool" (435–36).

As he viewed from the shore the wrecks of the *Congress* and the *Cumberland*, Hawthorne drew his reflections together. With the sinking of the *Cumberland* an era ended; the navies of Europe, Old Ironsides, and Trafalgar "became only a memory, never to be acted over again":

There will be other battles, but no more such tests of seamanship and manhood as the battles of the past; and moreover, the millennium is certainly approaching, because human strife is to be transferred from the heart and personality of man into cunning contrivances of machinery, which, by-and-by, will fight out our wars with only the clank and smash of iron, strewing the field with broken engines, but damaging nobody's little finger except by accident. Such is obviously the tendency of modern improvement. (437–38)

Hawthorne was divided by shifting emotions. He had little patience for the peacetime pomp and vanity of naval officers, while acknowledging their extraordinary skill and courage when leading men in battle; he recognized the superior efficiency of mechanized warfare, but remained skeptical that such a scientific approach meant men would not die. They will die in a different way, and for Hawthorne as for others who shared his views, that was the crux of the matter. A man would no longer look his enemy in the eye. The crew of the *Monitor* would never see the ship they sunk, and they themselves would stifle in their iron coffin at the bottom of the sea rather than in mortal combat with an enemy; the submarine would not even be seen by its opponent. Men would be replaced by machine; the "heart and personality" of the warrior would be supplanted, and with it the "pristine values" of manhood, courage, and skill. The machine ironically would be as dehumanizing and alienating on the battlefield as in the industrialized urban centers during times of peace.

Herman Melville also perceived in the ironclads the ascendancy of scientific rationalism over the traditional values of valor and courage, a conflict he presented in two poems: "The *Temeraire*" and "A Utilitarian View of the *Monitor*'s Fight." "The *Temeraire*," which sailed with Nelson's fleet and defended the flagship, is written in the voice of "an Englishman of the Old Order," who, recalling Trafalgar, compares the decisive sea battle with the stalemated encounter between the *Monitor* and the *Merrimack* on March 9, 1862. Their battle was one in which

> Splendors wane. The sea-fight yields
> No front of old display;
> The garniture, emblazonment,
> And heraldry all decay.

By contrast, the "fighting *Temeraire*" was "built of a thousand trees," and sailed

> impulsive on the van
> when down upon leagued France and Spain
> We English ran—the freshet at your bowsprit.

But the era was past when the sailing battleships "shone in the globe of the battle glow" because the

> rivets clinch the iron-clads,
> Men learn a deadlier lore.

The "ghost" of the *Temeraire* sails on, but the era of the sailing fleets is over:

> O, the navies old and oaken
> O, the *Temeraire* no more!

To the Utilitarian, the loss of "splendor" lamented in "*Temeraire*" is mere sentimentality compared with the greater efficiency of mechanized warfare:

> Hail to victory without the gaud
> Of glory; zeal that needs no fans
> Of banners; plain mechanic power
> Plied cogently in War now placed—
> Where War belongs—
> Among the trades and artisans.

The battle between the *Monitor* and the *Merrimack* entailed

> No passion; all went on by crank,
> Pivot, and screw,
> and calculations of caloric.

There will still be wars, acknowledges the Utilitarian, but it is now properly placed and its utility more properly assigned:

> War yet shall be, but warriors
> Are now but operatives; War's made
> Less grand than Peace.[2]

Melville's concluding irony offers the playful insight that a mechanized war violates an aesthetic that undergirds the moral imagination: a war reduced to mechanical throw power might be a deterrent to warfare because it made war duller than the alternative.

Some military planners expressed concerns that highly mechanized warfare could lead to what military historian Michael S. Sherry calls "passionless strife" which might, oddly enough, prolong wars because it could make men "more savage" by removing both fear and guilt as an element of warfare. But others argued on the contrary that the new, advanced weaponry available to the ground soldier would release him from the rigid and deadly confines of close formation, making it possible for him to fight "like an Indian"—or show more virility, prowess, freedom, and initiative. The opinions on both sides arose from the perceived need prior to World War I to defend the role of the individual in an increasingly mechanized society. "In an age nursing both great hopes and substantial fears about the fate of the individual," comments Sherry, "war was still seen as the foremost arena for the demonstration of heroic potential; the chief danger of the dreadnought or the machine gun or the airplane was that they might make men superfluous or anonymous in war."[3]

Prior to the advent of World War I, warfare could be imagined as an allegory not so much of Good versus Evil as of the Individual Male Proving His Virtue Even Unto Death. In April 1914 Wilson used a minor border incident with Mexico as a pretext for ordering American troops to occupy Veracruz, which proved a serious mistake both as a military operation and in terms of foreign policy. At a memorial service in May for the nineteen American servicemen killed in the operation, Wilson obviously did not expect his audience to interpret him as callous when he construed "war" as significant primarily as a symbol. Wilson said war was "only a sort of dramatic representation, a dramatic symbol, of a thousand forms of duty. . . . I fancy that there are some things just as hard to do as men are sneering at you as when they are shooting at you."[4] One cannot help but wonder if the surviving relatives of those who died or were wounded at Veracruz would not have preferred their young men had only been "sneered at." The oddity of the comment, its inappropriateness to the occasion, is a precursor to the Newbolt brand of denial. Wilson could not face squarely his responsibility for the pointless deaths he caused; instead, he constructed war as significant primarily because it provides support for the dramatic imagining of war as the extreme test and demonstration of idealized masculinity.

Wilson's sentiment that war was significant primarily as a symbol of the virtue of the men who fought was consistent with earlier statements to his closest adviser, Colonel House, who reported that Wilson observed in February 1913 that he did not share the views of those who thought war was "so much to be deprecated." While Wilson thought war was "as an economic proposition ruinous . . . he thought there was no more glorious way to die than in battle." To consider the conduct of war as primarily emblematic of something else averts the eyes from the material reality of war. Wilson was not alone in this tendency. Echoes of it can be found not only in the observations offered by Hawthorne and Melville, but also in William James's quest for a "moral equivalent" to war, or the belief in the "chastening and purifying effects of armed conflict" expressed by Princeton president John Grier Hibben, and in novelist Robert Herrick's praise for war's "resurrection of nobility."[5]

The vision of war as an allegory for manhood fully realized—this particular "war-as-imagined"—could best be sustained during peace, for instance, while reading the latest novel by Walter Scott and sipping sherry in front of a blazing fire in a private library done up in the Arts and Crafts style. It was an image of modern warfare difficult to sustain once the shooting started; moreover, it required at any rate suppressing the essential element of the moral imagination, which is that a dead man is a dead man who knows not of his own glory; it is assigned to him by others posthumously. The traditional "glory" of death in battle had to do with volunteering to put one's life on the line. But men ordered into battle, even the professional regulars sent to Veracruz, had little choice except to follow orders.

Wilson's reaction to the Great War illustrates just how contingent the appetite for war was upon the ability to render it as emblematic of a desired ideal of masculine character. By 1916, his biographer

John Milton Cooper observes, Wilson's "distaste for the World War had turned to repugnance" in large part because of how it was waged. Wilson wrote as a "prolegomenon" to a peace note in November 1916:

> Deprived of glory, war loses all its charm. . . . The mechanical slaughter of today has not the same fascination as the zest of intimate combat of former days; and trench warfare and poisonous gases are elements which detract alike from the excitement and the tolerance of modern conflict. With maneuver almost a thing of the past, any given point can admittedly be carried by the sacrifice of enough men and ammunition. Where is any longer the glory commensurate with the sacrifice of the millions of men required in modern warfare to carry and defend Verdun?[6]

The problem with World War I was that it was not so very charming—an odd choice of word, lacking presumably the irony of Melville's, "War's made/Less grand than peace." What made war glorious was the "fascination, and zest" of "intimate combat." The question is, glorious for whom? On the one hand, Wilson seems to be speaking on behalf of those who do the fighting, defending their right to die either gloriously or not at all. On the other hand, he is articulating a kind of voyeurism, the vicariousness Newbolt also expressed when he took pleasure in imagining his son as if he were Sir Philip Sidney off to the Lowland Wars (where, not incidentally, Sidney was mortally wounded). The Great War, judged peculiarly as a "dramatic representation"—to use Wilson's phrase in his eulogy for the Veracruz dead—naturally disappoints.

For Wilson as for Hawthorne, any potential for heroism or glory is lost when the combatants do not actually confront each other, a factor related to Wilson's reference to the "tolerance" of traditional warfare. Wilson reflects the conventional understanding that there is some restraint or limitation to warfare when a warrior sees the opponent and has to contend with the emotions of fear and guilt. Mechanized warfare threatened to render a man little more than the extension of a machine, making him into a mindless killer, divorced from the tempering reality enforced upon the warrior either by his own exposure to danger or by his having to look the man he is going to kill in the eye.[7] Nor is any skill required in a war that depends upon weapons of mass destruction or warfare that relies upon mechanized weapons. The combination of passion, restraint, and skill required for combat as a satisfying drama are lost when war becomes "mechanical slaughter," eliminating millions of men who are, like dumb sheep, simply submitted to sacrifice. Above all, there is no movement. The lack of maneuver in the ground war troubled Wilson as much as it did Hawthorne and Melville about the new kind of naval encounters—and especially Melville because he was on intimate terms with sailing as the collaboration of human knowledge, skill, and muscle with the natural elements of currents, waves, and winds.

When Wilson vigorously rejected Theodore Roosevelt's insistent requests to lead a volunteer division to France, he couched his disapproval in the terms of the Utilitarian who rejected the traditional forms of warfare embraced by the romantic "Englishman of the Old Order" in Melville's "*Temeraire.*" His decision to deny Roosevelt's request served a political purpose, reflected serious military thinking, and helped to prepare the public for the casualties that would result from trench warfare. Nevertheless, Wilson felt a nostalgia similar to Roosevelt's for war waged as a glorious demonstration of manhood. His insistence when he denied Roosevelt's request that the era of romantic warfare had passed and that modern warfare was "scientific" and unheroic spoke to deep cultural cross-currents because the realities of trench warfare seemed to offer little to sustain the definitions of manhood traditionally ascribed to warfare, especially as these appealed to the class represented by Woodrow Wilson, Theodore Roosevelt, William James, John Grier Hibben, and the readers of Hawthorne and Melville.

There was a compelling need to conceptualize fighting as conforming to a certain sense of style, making it possible to project upon the soldier the idealized version of oneself, imagining the warrior as an individual, as someone who would win the war because of his superior initiative, skill, and courage. The corollary need was to conceptualize the warrior as using mechanized weaponry to extend his skill, rather than as being either the mere extension of the machine or its helpless victim.

1916–17: British "Tommy" and *Our Flying Men*

Two British propaganda publications distributed in the United States illustrate how the British attempted to encode the realities of mechanized warfare as representative of the traditional values of the soldier. One paid particular attention to the ground war and the advent of the tank in the Battle of the Somme; the other celebrated the advent of air-to-air combat. Hilda Beatrice Hewlett's 1917 account of her visits to bases along the Western Front was published as *Our Flying Men*, which offered air combat as the manifestation of the British spirit of the mounted chevalier, a war that depended upon individual skill, where a man was in charge of his own destiny. Her account, placed against *Lord Northcliffe's War Book* (1916), which essentially ignored the air war, makes it pretty clear why the air war was given increasingly greater prominence; it offered better material for dramatizing what the war was supposed to represent. The comparison of the two is additionally useful because both were trying to candy coat catastrophe—Northcliffe wrote at the time of the failed Somme offensive and Hewlett at the time of very high losses in the British air forces.

The comparison serves as a reminder that the propagandist's job is not necessarily an easy or obvious one. Effective propaganda requires a resonance with what the home audience wishes to believe about what they know; it is a seduction into a particular kind of denial. Both Northcliffe and Hewlett aimed to make the advent of mechanized warfare resonate with the core beliefs about virility and courage; it is worthwhile to notice that, judged from this side of the twentieth century, Hewlett succeeded in making her case stick where Northcliffe did not.

In 1916, Lord Northcliffe visited the Western Front and published his account of the experience in *Lord Northcliffe's War Book*, which was distributed in both Britain and the United States, with a second edition in 1917. Given his role in supporting the views of the government through his newspapers, as well as his role later in the war as an official propagandist, his *War Book* was, to say the least, something other than the reflections of a private man upon the ruin of war. Much of it could have been written at his desk in London.

Lord Northcliffe paid scant attention to the air war, devoting very little to describing the airplane and considerably more to the tank. He represented British ground soldiers in general, and the tank crew in particular, as plucky, adventurous lads, full of initiative, who will inevitably defeat the German soldier because he is an obedient, unthinking, automaton, the product of Prussian autocracy:

> Our soldiers are individual. They embark on little individual enterprises. The German, though a good soldier when advancing with numbers under strict discipline, is not so clever at these devices. He was never taught them before the war, and his whole training from childhood upwards has been to obey and to obey in numbers.[8]

The Canadians, volunteer Americans, and Englishmen fighting for Britain, on the other hand, demonstrated the benefits of an upbringing in a liberal society: "'You will find the Canadians and Americans a thinking, independent army,' remarked the distinguished British general who had given me permission to spend this very interesting day, and so I found them."[9] The Germans, by contrast, were capable of nothing except "mass fighting" and "machine like discipline."

Given the idealized contrast between individualistic British, Commonwealth, and American soldiers and the machine-like qualities of the Germans, some human ingenuity had to be contrived for the weapons of mechanized warfare if the general picture Northcliffe was trying to convey was to be at all successful. He turned his attention to the newest weapon in the ground war, the tank, which was developed to offer advancing soldiers better cover from enemy machine-gun fire than the often ineffective protection provided by machine guns or artillery barrage. Originally called a "landship," it added armor plating to heavy tractors on caterpillar treads already in use to pull large guns. Haig introduced them at the Battle of the Somme on July 14. Of the forty-seven tanks making their debut, only about a dozen made it into the actual battle; they were cumbersome, slow, and unreliable. The dozen had some usefulness, but much of it was later attributed to their shocking effect on the German troops, many of whom must have frozen at the sight of these enormous armored beetles lumbering toward them, a child's nightmare made real.[10] By the end of the day, all twelve of the remaining tanks had also broken down.

Not surprisingly, none of these liabilities are shared with the reader in Northcliffe's account. He was fascinated with the tank when given a ride in one. Northcliffe was careful to make the point that the tank was not "invented" in the sense of being a new kind of weapon; rather it "grew" from the Roman battering-ram; hence, it represents a "traditional" kind of warfare and the genius of British ingenuity in adapting the past to the present, not, by implication, at all similar to the fiendish use of scientific knowledge by the Prussians to develop poison gas.

The tank crews were stereotypically British "Tommies": "In the light-hearted way in which we Britons go to war, our soldiers name the Tanks with a frivolity which is intensely annoying to the thick-headed Prussian." The crew of the "Creme de Menthe" were described as "young daredevils" who "enter upon their task in a sporting spirit with the same cheery enthusiasm as they would show for football"; they were as "nimble as cats" and had "no sense of danger."

This image of the ground soldier had entered the British imagination through the works of Rudyard Kipling, who dedicated *Soldiers Three* (1888) to "That Very Strong Man, T. Atkins, Soldier of the Line." Tommy Atkins became the archetype for the British soldier, the Tommy—lighthearted, brave, and devoted. Because the earliest novels of the war placed Kipling's Tommy in the Great War by fashioning the account of the soldiers who fought the earliest battles after Kipling's model, Samuel Hynes concludes that the image of the Tommy seems likely to have influenced both those on the homefront and the soldiers themselves: "It may be that Kipling, by writing about British soldiers in this mode, made them like that." Major-General Sir George Younghusband, writing in 1917, recalled that at the beginning of the war the soldiers in his command did not use the expressions used by Kipling's characters; however, a few years into the war, Kipling's words and phrases were part of the ordinary discourse of the soldier. Younghusband was convinced that Kipling and those who wrote in his style had "manufactured the cheery, devil-may-care, lovable person enshrined in our hearts as Thomas Atkins," and that the ground soldier had learned to emulate the literary character: "To Rudyard Kipling and his fellow-writers the army owes a great debt of gratitude for having produced the splendid type of soldier who now stands as the English type."[11]

Northcliffe was also an obvious contributor to this appropriation of fiction. He masked the reality of the war experience with the romantic vision of Kipling's Tommy, which is a small indication of what makes *War Book* obscene. The Americans who volunteered for service in the British Army were all versions of Theodore Roosevelt and his Rough Riders: though "caked with mud," the Americans Northcliffe met declared themselves to be having "a perfectly corking time," refused to "grouch" about any discomforts, and made such comments as "If any one asks you what sort of a time the Americans are having just hand them out one good home-word—'Bully.'"[12] The realities of trench warfare were either suppressed—as with being killed or seriously wounded—or assigned to the enemy, as with the feelings of fear and demoralization.

Despite Northcliffe's efforts to glamorize the tank as the desirable weapon for showing off the pluckiness of the British Tommy, or the Rough Rider spirit of American volunteers, the tank did not capture the public imagination as a romantic weapon. It was not until the tank gained the mobility that made it the obvious successor to the cavalry in World War II that those who commanded tank units were celebrated in the public's imagination: Rommel, Patton, and Montgomery.

Yet the tank, like the combat airplane, was a new form of mechanized warfare invented during World War I, and so it is worthwhile to consider why the attempt to symbolize it as an extension of the British character in the end did not stick. Ultimately, the tank, in addition to its poor mobility, bore perhaps too much resemblance to the "ironclads" of the Civil War, went too much by "crank and screw," and was too obviously not a weapon of the old school, but of the modern, mechanized and efficient variety, although the latter bit had yet to be shown. Fundamentally, there was neither glory nor glamour in it.

Hilda Beatrice Hewlett's *Our Flying Men* illustrates how much more useful the combat plane was to representing the war as dependent upon a certain breed of men and their character, rather than upon the efficiency of a machine. Hewlett visited British air bases in France and described her impressions in a pamphlet published in 1917. She was the wife of Maurice Hewlett, one of the notable men of letters enlisted by the Ministry of Information in 1914. Her pamphlet was undoubtedly regarded as useful to encourage enlistments in the Commonwealth nations and the United States, and to promote the interest of the United States in developing a large—very large—air force.

A number of the anecdotes Hewlett included are from 1916 and the period of the Fokker Scourge. These are used to demonstrate that it is the "man" and not the "machine" that determines the outcome in an air war, a convenient explanation for the British. Hewlett told a fanciful story—which she may well have taken as true—of how the Allies captured their first Fokker. She observed the British convention of not naming outstanding pilots and refers only to "A king amongst French aces" who was testing a new plane that was not yet armed with guns, when he spotted the Fokker and drove it to the ground: "he flew round and round the Fokker, just pushing him where he wanted him to go, like a dog driving sheep." The Fokker ran out of fuel and landed. The French pilot shook hands with the German pilot and said:

> he was glad he had carried no weapon, as he might have used it in the heat of the moment, and he would have regretted killing such a sportsman. When the German heard the name of this king of pilots he bowed very low and said he was not so ashamed of his poor performance now he knew who was the victor.[13]

This story seems to combine two different anecdotes. The first was told of Georges Guynemer. He was reportedly engaged in a fight with a two-seater when his gun jammed, but he boldly continued, outmaneuvering the Germans until they were so intimidated they landed and surrendered. The capture of the first Fokker occurred in April 1916—a year after Boelcke and Immelmann had flown the first models—when a young German pilot flying an early model became lost in the fog and landed in French territory, providing the Allies a Fokker to study.[14]

The apparent moral to be drawn from Hewlett's story is that what really counts, obviously, is not the kind of plane but the kind of person who flies it. Victory goes to the man of extraordinary skill, courage, and courtesy; because of such a man, the Allies found a way to discover the secret of the Fokker, which—contrary to the theme she was developing to this point—was important, even though the kind of machine one has to fly matters less than the kind of man one is. The sense of nervously dancing around the central issue—the Germans had Fokkers and the British did not—is scarcely concealed by Hewlett's insistent, overbearing cheeriness.

While Hewlett and Northcliffe both attempted to gloss over the seriousness of mechanized warfare, their pleasing fictions differ in noteworthy essentials. Northcliffe drew upon the Kiplingesque stereotype of the Tommy, while Hewlett's account is based upon the chivalric idealism that Newbolt synthesized in the *Happy Warrior*. Northcliffe presented the tank crew as taking a boyish pleasure driving a tank, but no special skill was evidently required for the joyride. Hewlett represented the pilot as having mastery over the plane; in fact, the quality of the pilot—his skill and character—predominated. While the tank crushed all who stood in its way, the French and German pilots confronted each other as human beings, and the German pilot acknowledged with admiration and a courteous bow the superiority of his captor's skill. The tank encased the crew and lumbered clumsily into battle. The plane, on the other hand, is represented as a tool for expressing the will of the warrior, an extension of his mind, eye, and spirit.

First Battle of the Somme and Bloody April

It is worthwhile noticing from what conditions Northcliffe and Hewlett each were diverting attention. Northcliffe has been rightly condemned for the smokescreen he laid over the catastrophe of the First Battle of the Somme. Hewlett cast a smokescreen over the worst catastrophe of the air war experienced by British flyers to that point. And while the failure of the British to provide an accounting for the high casualty rates of British pilots was criticized at the time and in postwar histories, the idealization of the combat pilot as essentially legendary in stature has remained central to the imagination of the first air war, while the "pluckiness" of the Kiplingesque Tommy has given way to the night-marish images provided by the literary accounts of life in trenches.

To grasp the implications of this difference, it is necessary to have in mind some sense of the military realities behind Northcliffe and Hewlett's accounts. In both instances, the impact of what they were doing comes from a realization not only of what they were failing to mention, but of how they avoided it. This is made clearer by the singu-lar example in Northcliffe of men under fire used to illustrate the easy, nonauthoritarian relationship between officer and enlisted—as opposed to the cruelty of the German officers against their men—and the non-chalance of the soldier when faced with danger, always ready with a quip to ease the tension of the moment:

> Nothing could have been finer or more spirited than the behaviour of the Canadian troops. Many of them "went over the top" with cigarettes between their lips. . . . [A] captain of my acquaintance found himself next to an Irish Canadian soldier crouching amid a whistling of bullets and burst-ing of shells which for the moment made progress inadvisable. Without raising his head the soldier looked at the officer from under his steel hel-met. "Cap," he said, "there's no doubt about it, this is a dangerous war."[15]

The readers on the homefront would have thought of the typical Tommy when they read the account in Northcliffe's book of the soldier who says to his officer as the bullets whiz by, "Cap, there's no doubt about it, this is a dangerous war." But there is another way to read it, using the style of "Tommy-speak" ironically to give voice to a contempt, which if openly expressed to a priggish officer could result in court-martial. Moreover, the soldier's quip showed a nonchalance toward an officer more characteristic of Canadian troops than British.

What the officers told the men along the line to prepare them for the opening day of the Battle of the Somme betrayed the soldiers' innocence and loyalty, even though the line officers could not have known in advance—or refused to imagine—that they were preparing their men for an unprecedented slaughter. The officers repeatedly told the men what their commanding officers had told them: the heavy artillery bombardment preceding the ground assault would decimate the forces in the opposing trenches to such an extent that the infantry would simply walk slowly toward the German lines and engage in what could perhaps be characterized as a mopping-up operation. The officers were talking to volunteers inexperienced in battle. The impression given was that the operation would be rather like a soccer game—exciting, perhaps some scuffling and some injuries, but the artillery would have done the ugly work of the war.

The result was the single worst day in the history of the British military, with 60,000 casualties, 20,000 dead. The artillery shelling prior to the assault and the barrage failed to provide cover and cut the forward German barbed wire. When the British forces went over the top, they walked into decimating machine-gun and mortar fire. So persuaded were the soldiers when they first went over the top that the attack would be an orderly march to claim the opposing trenches that some of them could not comprehend what was happening when they saw their comrades falling to the right and left of them. Some thought they had failed to hear additional general orders that their fellow soldiers had heard. They could not imagine that rank after rank of men was falling because they were dead or wounded.[16] Those who managed to gain the barbed wire in front of the German lines found that the wirecutters they were carrying were insufficient to cut the heavy German wire.

For a different understanding of the quip made by the Canadian soldier to his officer, the best context is provided by the careless sacrifice of the First Newfoundland Regiment, a thousand volunteers from the underpopulated dominion who were essentially eliminated by the end of the first day of the Battle of the Somme. The battle at Beaumont Hamel began when eight British battalions were ordered out of their trenches, down the slope, and then up the facing hill in the initial attack. None got through to the German wire. The circumstances to say the least would have suggested that the assault was a failure and should be called off; but the higher command was removed from the battle itself—physically, by poor communication, and by a failure of imagination. Unable to believe that the initial assault had failed, to imagine that eight battalions had been decimated, they concluded instead that they simply had not received accurate information. They ordered the Newfoundlanders and the First Essex forward to reinforce the British.

The Newfoundlanders were waiting in one of several reserve trenches running parallel to the frontline trench. Intersecting trenches, called communication trenches, connected the reserve and frontline trenches. Usually, reserve troops would move forward in the communication trenches, assemble at the forward trench, and then go over the top. The communication trenches at Beaumont Hamel were clogged with other units awaiting orders. The first Essex moved forward slowly through these; the Newfoundlanders were ordered to go straight into battle from the reserve trench. They exposed themselves to enemy fire behind their own forward position. They had to get through several lines of British wire, go down the dip, up the hill, cut the German wire, and attempt to take their forward trench. There was no artillery barrage to protect them; it was broad daylight, and they were half a mile away from their objective.

The machine gunners began to kill them when they came out of the reserve trench; they kept killing them as they bunched like herded cattle trying to get through the lanes that had been cut in the British wire; a few made it to no-man's land, where more were killed. Not a single man made it to the German wire. Of the 752 men who climbed out of the reserve trench that morning, all 26 officers were killed; 658 enlisted were dead or wounded. The casualty rate was 91 percent. The slaughter took forty minutes.

At the killing field of Beaumont Hamel there is a monument to the Newfoundlanders, but the memorial in the truest sense is the scarred landscape itself. The reserve trenches, frontline trenches, artillery shell holes, and no-man's land were left as they were when the war ended; they are greened in July by the grass that has grown over them, clipped to reveal the depressions. The forces of nature cannot obliterate the outlines of the battlefield, but it has softened them, like a blanket gently laid over the corpse of a dead child. Beaumont Hamel is an uncanny Arcadia, a sylvan field that silently accuses folly and slaughter on an unprecedented scale.

By nightfall the British had 57,470 casualties. The high command thought the assault had been an overall success with some setbacks. In the weeks that followed, General Haig continued to prosecute the assault despite severe losses, and whatever the explanations subsequently made on his behalf, the reality remains that the casualties from the Battle of the Somme were unconscionable and still impossible for the imagination to compass today.

The Canadian soldier who said to his officer, "Cap, there's no doubt about it, this is a dangerous war," might obviously have been expressing something other than a devil-may-care attitude toward the bullets flying past his head. But in Northcliffe's able hands, the comment becomes not an acidly ironic condemnation by a soldier of his officers, but a sign of the pluck of Tommy Atkins. The official story of the war as offered by Northcliffe might best be summarized as depicting Newbolt Man as the chivalric officer commanding Kipling's plucky Tommy Atkins against the uncivilized barbarian indicted in the Bryce Report.

In 1917 there was as much not to tell the public about the air war as there had been in 1916 about the Battle of the Somme. April 1917 is still known in accounts of the history of the air war as "Bloody April," a time when the British suffered their highest casualty rates of the air war to that point. Although some of the British casualty rates for the period have been introduced earlier, they bear repeating here. During that spring the Germans defeated Allied pilots at a ratio of five to one. By the end of April, the RFC recorded 238 men killed or missing and 105 wounded. The starting strength on April 1 was officially given as 849 pilots available, with 496 actually flying. In one month, the equivalent of 70 percent of the pilots who were flying on April 1 had been killed or wounded, or what amounted to 40 percent of the pilots available (operational or in reserve) at the start of the battle. The average flying hours of pilots dwindled from 295 in August 1916 to 92 in April 1917. By way of contrast, the Germans in the Sixth Army Area at Arras between March 31 and May 3 recorded losses to their own pilots of 21 killed, 15 wounded, and 4 missing against the downing of 176 British planes.[17]

During this time, the Allies actually had significantly more planes than the Germans. The high losses were a result of three factors: the Germans had superior planes and the Allies could not produce counterparts to challenge them at a fast enough rate; British pilots were being sent into combat directly from flight school with insufficient training or flight hours; and the pilots were ordered to fly offensive missions—to fly over the German lines to seek the enemy—putting themselves at greater risk than a defensive posture. This was the strategy ordered by Maj. Gen. Hugh Trenchard, who has not escaped criticism for his tenacity in pursuing the offensive at such high casualty rates.

Trenchard cannot be faulted, however, for having to order his men to fly in inferior planes against Germans at the beginning of the Allied offensive in spring 1917. His belief that the use of an aggressive, offensive approach would bring the superiority of British numbers to bear on a German air force that the Allies outnumbered explains the insistence on offensive patrols. The casualty rates also demonstrated very clearly that superior numbers, coupled with the aggression, courage, and a willingness to engage on the part of the pilots, could not overcome the liabilities of poor training and inferior planes.

The Germans had used the winter months of 1917 to hone the skills of organized squadron fighting, and while they had lost their great ace and air-war tactician Oswald Boelcke, Manfred von Richthofen had been given command of Jasta 11—which would become the highest scoring of all the German squadrons—in January 1917.

The stage was set for "Bloody April." On the French side, it was the time of the Nivelle Offensive, the catastrophe witnessed by Billy Mitchell, and which convinced him that the war could be won from the air, particularly by the use of bombers. The losses in that offensive convinced French soldiers to mutiny and march on Paris. And significantly, April was the month the United States declared war, followed by the French request for an American aerial armada.

Making the Image of War

Hewlett's *Our Flying Men* appeared at a propitious time, given the need not only for fresh recruits from Canada and the United States to replace British pilots, but also to feed the image of a new kind of warfare that allowed the traditional characteristics associated with the idealized war hero to manifest themselves.

It is important to consider not only what those writing for Wellington House failed to disclose, but how they framed what they did describe because it reveals how much effective propaganda depends upon a dynamic and mutual involvement of the propagandist with the receiving public, an engagement that can depend upon what the receiving audience is willfully ignoring or refusing to imagine as much as it does upon actual ignorance.

Northcliffe's *War Book* provides a very helpful illustration of this point, one that illuminates a less obvious similarity to Hewlett's approach. Northcliffe's book first appeared against the advent, by the end of 1916, of dissent against the official story voiced by some well-placed and literate line officers. The most dramatic if ultimately ineffective gesture came from Sassoon, whose earliest protests we have mentioned. After recuperating from trench fever, in early 1917 he returned to the front lines around Arras, where he was wounded in April and sent to England to recover in May. In July, supported by antiwar activists and conscientious objectors, including Phillip and Lady Ottoline Morrell, Bertrand Russell, and J. Middleton Murry, Sassoon made public a statement calling for the end of the war which was published in the major British dailies and entered in the record of the House of Commons on July 30. Sassoon fully expected to be court-martialed; instead, he was sent to Craiglockhart War Hospital near Edinburgh to be treated for shell shock.

In calling for the end of the war, Sassoon made his plea on behalf of the soldiers suffering at the front and to protest the complacent indifference of a public more willing to believe the image of the Tommy than imagine the nature of the war:

> On behalf of those who are suffering now, I make this protest against the deception which is being practised on them. Also I believe that it may help to destroy the callous complacence with which the majority of those at home regard the continuance of agonies which they do not share, and which they have not sufficient imagination to realize.[18]

Others also began to condemn the complacency encouraged by the mask of the Kiplingesque image of the Tommy. Richard Henry Tawney had published *The Agrarian Problem in the Sixteenth Century* in 1912. After the war he became one of England's most important economic historians; among his most influential works was *Religion and the Rise of Capitalism* (1926). Tawney was a socialist committed to minimum-wage laws and increasing opportunities. When war was declared, he volunteered and was commissioned; he was wounded in the Somme in July 1916. While convalescing in England, he wrote "Some Reflections of a Soldier," taking aim particularly at the image of the cheerful Tommy as constructed by propagandists. He indicted the British public for accepting such a "ridiculous and disgusting" cartoon as representative of a soldier in combat:

> I read your papers and listen to your conversation, and I see clearly that you have chosen to make to yourselves an image of war, not as it is, but of a kind which, being picturesque, flatters your appetite for novelty, for excitement, for easy admiration, without troubling you with masterful emotions. You have chosen, I say, to make an image, because you do not like, or cannot bear, the truth; because you are afraid of what may happen to your souls if you expose them to the inconsistencies and contradictions, the doubts and bewilderment, which lie beneath the surface of things.[19]

Both Sassoon and Tawney protested against the constructed image of the soldier, and the complacency it encouraged. Tawney offered a remarkably contemporary definition of "image." The reason propaganda works, he pointedly asserted, is not because the public is ignorant and therefore easily duped; rather, it is because the public chooses not to confront the obvious, wishes to be given permission to ignore the grim face of war, prefers to be entertained by an idealized version of warfare that flatters a sense of national values and by implication the worthiness of the individuals born in such a nation. The indictment Tawney makes is not that politicians and the press are lying to the public—which might have made the public's receptivity forgivable—but that the public is surfeiting itself on the candy cane version of the war, and they ought to know better.

The important thing about this insight into "image" is that the positive effect of an image is not necessarily contingent upon the public being unaware of the "truth"; the power of image-making, for instance with regard to politicians, is not so much the absence of negative information about the politician as it is the awareness—on the part of both the public and the political image-makers—that the public can be induced to accept a more attractive picture of the politician despite the information that calls it into question. Tawney took aim at the public's eagerness to consume messages and images of warfare that were obviously prepared for them, their knowing consumption of lies and misrepresentations, and their active participation in giving them cultural currency.

It is not difficult to imagine Tawney recuperating from his wounds while reading *Lord Northcliffe's War Book*, or other cheerful accounts that made the Battle of the Somme into an exciting hunting party, and being moved to the most profound moral alienation as the gap opened between how the homefront wished to delude itself the war was fought, and the hellish slaughter into which he as an officer had ordered his men.

It would be a mistake to assume that just because Tawney wrote as he did, the entire edifice of the war-as-imagined-adventure collapsed; nor is the point that only Sassoon and Tawney denounced the betrayal of the footsoldier by the delusions propagated on the homefront. They are particularly articulate examples of the emerging alienation of the soldier from the homefront, a constructing of the soldiers as "us" and those at home as "they," which became the dominant myth of the war experience from the soldier's perspective: a particular kind of disillusionment to which the best of the war poets and memoirists gave voice, a vision of a sustaining idealism that motivated the soldier but was trivialized by those at home.[20]

Because of the power of those voices, the brevity of the treatment here may seem to give them short shrift, which is by no means intended to underrate their considerable significance for shaping the moral imagination of the war. The focus in this study is on the emergence of the combat pilot; the dissent voiced by Sassoon, Tawney, and others against the constructed image of the ground soldier provides a context for understanding the romantic frame that was hung onto air combat. From the point of view of those interested in maintaining the public's belief in the war-as-imagined, there was a need for another kind of soldier fighting another kind of war to represent British, Canadian, and American liberalism, individualism, and initiative because these qualities were obviated in the face of the slaughter achieved with mechanized weaponry—the shell, the mortar, and the machine gun.

Northcliffe's book provides an example of the methodology against which Tawney so astutely protested. The problem with mechanized warfare was not only that it obviated the individualism of the soldier, but that by doing so it made it much more difficult to promote the vision of the war as fought in civilized ways for civilized purposes, as extending rather than breaking with military tradition. In addition to his strained reassurance that the tank evolved from traditional military weapons such as the battering ram, Northcliffe took pains to demonstrate that the tank does not cross the boundary of civilized warfare:

> They are a real and justifiable means of waging war: they wage it only against soldiers, not against civilians; and the German soldiers find them

terrible enemies. . . . The British Army is justly proud of the daring and success of those who are engaged in this newest from of crushing Militarism.[21]

That last phrase—the "crushing Militarism"—epitomizes Northcliffe's technique of offering to provide an authentic or realistic account of war while at the last moment granting permission to avert the eye from its grimmer aspects. The use of the abstraction to follow the word "crushing," instead of, for instance, the more precise description of "three or four soldiers manning a machine gun," avoids the necessity of addressing how far the realities of modern ground warfare are from a soccer game. Yet a moment's reflection flashes upon the inner eye the picture of a huge, metal vehicle rolling its tracks slowly over four or five young men.

When Tawney accused those on the homefront not of ignorance, but of willfully accepting a sugar-coated image of the war in order to avoid confronting the appalling truth of it, this must have been the sort of trope he had in mind. The trick of diction, converting the object of a weapon from human flesh and blood to an ideological abstraction, encourages an appreciation of the drama of warfare, of its spectacle, while also both encouraging and condoning a singular failure of the moral imagination when it comes to the fundamental reality of warfare. The acceptance of this vision of war is not dependent upon the reader's ignorance of the facts of warfare; it depends upon the reader's willingness to enter into a particular kind of charade with the propagandist, a voluntary enlistment in the process of creating a mutually agreed-upon meaning that obviously masks a harsh reality.

Hewlett also confronted a public that was aware of the air catastrophe she took pains to avoid discussing. The public was described as "distinctly shocked" by the reported losses of twenty-eight planes for April 6 and 7, 1917—the opening days of Bloody April.[22] She adopted the conventional approach for describing the air war, which was to remove the accounts from any connection to the progress of the war, either in the air or on the ground. She concentrated on individual encounters, and on the enthusiasm for the hunt, another conventional metaphor. This focus on prowess and the desire for recognition, or to raise one's score, was taken as wholly admirable. She informed the reader that in order for a victory to "count," the fallen enemy aircraft had to be witnessed by ground observers on the British side of the line. This meant that British pilots who flew offensively over German territory had to accept that usually their victories would not be counted. She quoted the account of one pilot, "I longed to bring down my quarry inside them [his own lines], as no victories count officially unless the machine falls where results can be verified."

In another account, she told the story of a British two-seater that had fired upon and disabled a German plane. Rather than breaking off the battle or finishing off his opponent, the British pilot wanted to bring the plane down behind his own lines in order to get credit for the victory. In response to his efforts to force the German plane in the desired direction, the German gunner continued to fire and killed the British observer, who sat in front of the pilot. Upon landing, the observer was removed from the plane and pronounced dead by the doctor, who said, "He has died a hero, for his victim fell in our lines just as you landed here."[23]

What could under reasonable standards be construed as an entirely unnecessary loss of life, caused by the desire for personal recognition on the part of the pilot, is here rendered as a touching scene of the fallen hero. In fact, the observer who died had no control over his destiny because it was the pilot who made the decision to continue the engagement. This senseless sacrifice can be easily seen for what it is; but Hewlett, as did Northcliffe, gave her readers permission to shut down their moral imaginations.

The Plane as Steed

The precursor for the airplane was from the beginning conceptualized as the horse, a living creature whose spirit was directed by the man who rode him into battle. What appears to us now as simply a fanciful consequence of describing the pilot as a knight—that is, the comparison of horse to plane—did not begin life as a metaphor. The conception of the airplane as a "steed" came first and was a literal, not a metaphoric, comparison. When it became obvious after the outbreak of World War I that mounted cavalry was essentially obsolete, the responsibility for both forward reconnaissance and the equivalent of the mounted assault against the infantry shifted to the air services.

Writing for the *National Geographic* in 1918, the French captain André de Berreota explained that observation planes "possessed the power of exploring the field of battle far beyond that of the cavalry, for which this delicate and dangerous duty had hitherto been reserved."[24] Other aviation commanders also claimed for their service the preeminent military importance previously held by the cavalry. Maj. Joseph Tulasne, chief of the French aviation mission sent to the United States shortly after Congress declared war, assured his readers that the air war would be the decisive factor in the defeat of Germany—especially after the Americans built the planes and trained the pilots needed to replace the depleted Allied ranks:

> As was the case in the cavalry battles of the First Empire, the supremacy wrested from the enemy in the first encounters [after America enters the air war] will hold for many months, and subsequent small reinforcements ordered into the struggle will not be able to regain that supremacy.[25]

Because the combat mission of the pilot evolved from the cavalry, it was widely assumed that men who knew how to ride horses—and especially those trained as cavalrymen—would make the best pilots. An article titled "Who Make the Best Aviators?" (1918) in the popular American periodical *Current Opinion* reported a British study by Doctor Graeme in which he concluded that men trained to ride horses were likely to make better pilots because of their "finer sense and their truer judgment and 'lighter' hands," and, Graeme noted, the Germans "always selected their aviators from the cavalry until recently." Based on these and similar conclusions, British aviators were encouraged to ride horseback even into the 1930s.[26]

Arthur "Archie" Whitehouse, who flew as an RFC observer in World War I and wrote numerous popular histories of the air war, commented on the influence of these assumptions; "hundreds of ex-cavalrymen [both German and Allied] became aerial aces," although he also noted that it was unclear whether this was because riding actually makes a man a better pilot or that trained cavalrymen could be more easily spared than those in other services to transfer to the air force. The latter seems the more likely case: only a small number of those who received the German Blue Max or who became French aces had transferred from the cavalry.[27]

Enough of the best-known aces were ex-cavalrymen to enforce the popular perception during the war that the legacy of the mounted warrior had passed to the pilot. Both Manfred von Richthofen and his brother Lothar transferred from the cavalry. Of his decision to transfer from the cavalry to the flying services, Manfred wrote in his autobiography, "I imagined that, owing to my training as a cavalryman, I might do well as an observer." Of his role as an observer on the Russian front, he said, "Life in the Flying Corps is very much like life in the Cavalry. Every day, morning and afternoon, I had to fly and to reconnoiter" just as his life in the cavalry "had consisted in reconnoitering." But Manfred did not go down in history because he was a particularly skilled scout. Of his later role as a combat pilot he said, "There is nothing finer for a young cavalry officer than flying off to a hunt."[28]

Hewlett praised the French ace Charles Nungesser, who had entered the service in the Second Hussars, as a "good horseman."[29] The Canadian ace Billy Bishop also began the war in the cavalry. In his autobiography Bishop explained why the plane seemed the only way to fight the war as he had intended to fight it:

It was the mud, I think, that made me take to flying. I had fully expected that going into battle would mean for me the saddle of a galloping charger, instead of the snug little cockpit of a modern aeroplane. The mud, on a certain day in July, 1915, changed my whole career in the war.

As both he and his horse stood knee-deep in mud, drenched by an English drizzle, Bishop looked up to see a single-seater plane flying overhead. He asked for an immediate transfer.[30]

Once it was assumed that the air force would replace the cavalry, and that cavalrymen were best suited to becoming pilots, it was but a short step to conceptualizing the plane as a horse—when planes became mechanically reliable. Prior to the war, military commanders in France had concluded that the air services would remain inferior to the cavalry because the plane was unreliable: "Save in very rare cases, the cavalryman can always count on his horse. But the airman has in his motor an instrument that is still delicate, despite progress made to date; its failings can leave him immobilized at any time."[31] The favorable comparison between the horse and the plane was so common by June 1917 that Brigadier General Squiers, in drumming up enthusiasm for the Military Aviation bill, used it without fearing to appear foolish or hyperbolic when he called for putting "the Yankee punch into the war by building an army of the air, regiments and brigades of winged cavalry on gas-driven flying-horses."[32] Popular accounts of air battles used the same metaphor, as when James Middleton, writing for the popular American magazine *World's Work*, described how Guynemer attacked enemy aircraft from below: "he brings his machine up suddenly like a horse standing on its hind legs, and opens fire."[33] Pilots themselves would occasionally refer to their plane as a horse when writing about their exploits for popular consumption. James Norman Hall in *High Adventure* says of the combat plane:

> It seemed living, intelligent, almost human. I could readily understand how it is that airmen become attached to their machines and speak of their fine points, their little peculiarities of individuality, with a kind of loving interest, as one might speak of a fine-spirited horse.[34]

While the comparison of pilot and plane to rider and horse originated in the military as a practical transfer of function from the cavalry, the image of the "cavalry of the air" took on more meaning than a comparison of the ground scout to the aerial scout; it became a cultural sign connoting a continuity of tradition. Just as the medieval knight had evolved into the cavalry, so had the cavalry metamorphosed into the scout plane and combat pilot; air combat could be understood as the latest manifestation of the mounted warrior whose tactical importance extended back to the Norman conquest. Mounted warriors—first the knight and then the officers of the light cavalry—had traditionally been regarded as the military elite; the chevalier embodied the values of the military aristocracy and was the symbol for the continuity of both a culture and the ruling class that dominated it. The failure on the part of many in the military to realize prior to World War I that the advent of the machine gun meant the end of the cavalry suggests a deeply ingrained conviction that future victory would depend upon the cavalry—upon maneuver, skill, and courage in the charge and encounter.[35] In addition, chivalry and the chevalier had gone hand in glove as a cultural ideal for so long that, as Adams comments, the symbolic significance attached to the cavalryman made it difficult to admit that warfare, as with the larger economic and social order, "had passed into the hands of organization men and scientists."[36]

Investing the combat pilot with the role of cavalryman and the plane with the role of the horse offered at the very least a symbolic reprieve from the usurpation of the will of the elite soldier by the advent of mechanization. The image of the plane as a horse distracted attention from implications of recognizing that in the sky the individual warrior is completely dependent upon the machine.

"Machines to Fit the Men"

The British emphasized the continuities between past and present through the "knight in the air" imagery, retaining the conception of rider and steed, an approach consonant with their posture of defending civilization. For the German representation of air combat, the implication was celebrated that the advent of air-to-air combat signified that man and machine had merged, and that as a result the man had become more machine-like—more efficient, more hardened, and hence more "modern."[37]

The American approach, while it drew upon the implications of both the Allied nostalgic romance for the past and German love affair with modern technology, was, on the other hand, something again different. This, at least, was the case with Bennet A. Molter's *Knights of the Air*. Molter was a lieutenant with the French squadron N102. In 1918 he published his account of training and combat flying in support of the aim of recruiting American college men into the air forces. His book is not a memoir; rather, it provides a description of training school and the maneuvers most useful in combat, along with illustrative anecdotes about the top French aces.

In his explanation of the evolution of the combat plane, Molter acknowledged that early in the war planes were undifferentiated in design, and "so it was necessary *to fit the man to the machine*" (Molter's emphasis). But, as the uses of plane in combat became more specialized, so did the planes themselves, "so that the endeavor at the present time is to build *machines to fit the men* who are trained and ready for service as pilots of the several types" (Molter's emphasis).[38] Of the three specializations—observation, bombing, and combat— combat is the elite corps: "The making of a chasse, or pursuit, pilot depends, mainly upon the man's physical and mental equipment, temperament, and adaptability" (52). A careful selection process thus segregates recruits into the three training classes, with those of the superior qualities assigned to training for combat.

In describing the relationship between man and machine, Molter emphasized that the French training placed top priority upon developing "reflexes," a term novel enough to require definition: "It is a sort of subconscious ability to do the right thing at the right time, surely and instantly. . . . It is an intuitive faculty by which our bodily movements are controlled by instinct" (54). As these reflexes were developed and honed, the

> machine becomes almost a part of the finished pilot: he guides it, dodging, twisting and turning, as a bird flies, without conscious effort, leaving his mind and senses free to grasp and record facts and conditions which

require the use of judgment so that reason may shape his larger course of action and determine his future movements. (55)

This account very closely matches the arguments made on the floor of Congress during debate over the Military Aviation Appropriation Bill about the special intelligence and character required of a combat flyer, a reiteration of the military's position that it was college men who should provide the recruits for this special kind of elite service. The additional element in Molter's account is the relationship between such a man, once trained, and the machine. The pilot does not merge with it entirely, but he does become the animating principle for a machine that allows the man to express his finely honed intuitive powers, freeing his equally adept intelligence and reasoning.

Molter's representation of the relationship between a pilot and his plane resolves the tension between man and machine which the advent of mechanized warfare presented, a tension felt especially in the American imagination because of the potential for mechanized warfare raised by the experience of the Civil War. The appeal is heightened by the connection made between the character of the man who flies alone into combat and the ability of the military to maintain that mesmerizing if ill-understood advantage, air supremacy, by which means the United States was determined to conjure victory.

Molter claimed that at the time of his writing, the "Allied flying men hold the supremacy of the war on the Western front" through "sheer will power. It is the combined power of a thousand individual wills, of their daring, their skill and devotion" (101). While acknowledging that the other branches of the air service had their roles to play, Molter said the combat pilot assured the supremacy of the air, and the key factor to the ascendancy of the Allies would be the character of their pilots: "It is on the chasse escadrilles (hunting squadrons) that the supremacy of the air rests, and with it the security of all this is going on, in and behind the Allied lines" (105). The armaments available to each side in the air were about equal, according to Molter. The Allied flyers would prevail because "the Boche fears us, fears to come over our lines, fears to take . . . risks" (102). This was Molter's characterization of the German strategy of preserving their flyers and planes though defensive tactics rather than the Allies' much more costly offensive approach. Molter acknowledged that the individual German pilots were equal in courage to their opponents and the victory was determined by the individual with the superior flying ability—a contest of wills that the Allies, according to Molter, were consistently winning.

To prevail, the combat pilot had to be "imbued with the highest ideals of duty and self-sacrifice. He must have undaunted courage and perfect confidence; he must be cool under any conditions that may arise" (107). Molter merged the characteristics of the man who operates his machine by reflex with the traditional chivalric virtues: "Roland and Oliver were valiant knights, yet each met his fate on the field of honor. War is war and even the most invaluable must sometimes be sacrificed to the insatiable appetite of the horrible beast." The top flyers were men who were not braggarts, "he isn't that kind of man." As the exemplar of the ace, Molter pointed to Guynemer, who was "the greatest of all Aces, Allied or enemy," and reminded the reader that his name was not only a household word in France but was "known to almost every red-blooded boy in American who loves chivalrous deeds and high adventure" (221).

Where Hewlett maintained that it was the man and not the machine that mattered in the outcome, Molter represented air supremacy as depending upon a machine that matched the abilities of an exceptional man with exceptional training. The result was not a "man of steel," hardened into a machine-like cold efficiency, but a man enabled by the machine to bring his character, intelligence, and instincts to bear, enabled, that is, to manifest the traditional valor and abilities characteristic of the romantic vision of the knight. Without such men, air supremacy could not be maintained; and without air supremacy, the implication is clearly made, the stalemate on the ground could not be broken. Upon the abilities of the pilot and the design of his aircraft the outcome of the war depended.

A preference for air combat over service in the ground war was often remarked upon by Molter's countrymen in the Lafayette Escadrille.

They bore witness to the sense that the air war allowed for the expression of individual character or personality in contrast to the realities of the ground war. Many of the original members of the Lafayette Escadrille had served in the French Foreign Legion prior to volunteering for flight school, and they made a point of mentioning the difference in terms of individualism in their published memoirs and letters. Edmond Genet, whose letters were published in the United States in 1918, wrote to his mother in 1916:

> This is the most dangerous branch of the service, Mother, but it's the best as far as future is concerned and if anything does happen to me you all surely can feel better satisfied with the end than if I was sent to pieces by a shell or put out by a bullet in the infantry where there are 75 out of 100 possibilities of your never hearing of it. The glory is well worth the loss. I'd far rather die as an aviator over the enemy's lines than find a nameless, shallow grave in the infantry, and I'm certain you'd all feel better satisfied too.[39]

The sentiment that if someone is going to die there ought to at least be some glory in it might not prove universally attractive as an inducement to join the air service; but the terms in which Genet couched his reasons for enlisting point toward the general significance attached to fighting in a way other than the anonymity inflicted upon the foot soldier in the trenches.

James McConnell, who was also an early member of the Lafayette Escadrille, commented in *Flying for France* (1916) that for Victor Chapman and Kiffin Rockwell, both of whom had served in the ground war for France, flying promised "the restoration of personality lost during those months in the trenches with the Foreign Legion."[40]

In the accounts by Molter, Genet, and McConnell, a distinctly American representation of air combat begins to emerge. The justification of the war in Great Britain as a defense of civilization, fought in civilized ways, looked back to tradition, but the mechanization of warfare on the ground was at odds with both the romance of warfare and the understanding of warfare as a dramatic presentation of the core values associated with manliness and national pride. The airplane offered the opportunity for a more gratifying representation of the machine first as the servant of the man, and second as more like a living being than a mindless mechanism. Given the Fokker Scourge and Bloody April, there was a practical reason for the official story to emphasize the valor and skill of the pilot, considering the inferiority of the early Allied models of combat planes.

While Hewlett emphasized the individualism and superiority of character of the Allied combat pilot, the chief commander for the air force hoped to prevail through sheer numbers, by throwing wing after wing of young, poorly trained, inexperienced pilots at the Germans in the hopes that in the end the superior British numbers would prevail over the enemy's superior training, tactics, and machines. As for the role of weaponry, the outcome in the sky during Bloody April was as much contingent on the machine gun as the failed offensive at the Somme had been.

As with the official story of the ground war, the war in the air was told in a way that masked both the casualty rates and what led to them. The stakes were certainly very high when it came to what role the United States would play in the war. There was considerable political currency to be gained from offering a convincing vision of warfare, one that satisfied the yearning for how war ought to be fought, and for what it ought to represent, and which offered the hope that it might make it possible to avoid the reality of the ground war. At the same time the British and French were urging the Americans to build an air fleet and were assisting in the efforts to recruit American college men into flight training, the RFC had suffered losses equivalent to one-third of its air force. The British version of the air war was a very deadly persuasion.

Molter's account, published in 1918, makes a much stronger case for the design and capabilities of the airplane than Hewlett did. The anxiety that the advent of the machines of warfare would obviate the character of the man who fought is replaced by a vision of a man of character, intelligence, and training. The pilot thus became in popular accounts the member of an elite class taking his place in an elite corps, one that will determine the outcome of the war through air supremacy. The accounts of the earliest members of the Lafayette Escadrille also emphasized that the true expression of individual ability and courage in the war came from flying a combat plane. And if the accounts of the air war coming to the United States from Great Britain masked much that was deadly about air combat, how much more persuasive must have been the accounts of man as master of the machine coming from the Americans who had volunteered for war in the air, even if their accounts were published posthumously. There was glory in war again.

CHAPTER 8

"The Man Is Alone"

Free Lance and Lone Wolf

In flying, more than in any science of war, the man is alone, and on his skill and nerve depends the result.

—Hilda Beatrice Hewlett, *Our Flying Men*

While the combat pilot was lionized at the expense of the observers and bombers, there was also a hierarchy of attractiveness generated by the publicity about those who flew in single-seaters. There were, of course, the aces, but what was most compelling was the "ace of aces" a "lone wolf" or "free lance"—the British or French ace with a "roving commission" or a *chasse libre* who flew alone into combat on voluntary or self-assigned missions. They were portrayed as members of an exclusive fraternity. Each was dependent entirely upon his own will; they sought danger regularly and accepted uneven combat; the war for them was personal—the enemy knew them either by name or by the distinctive designs or colors painted on their planes.

The heroism of the "lone wolf" or the "free lance" was established in the public's imagination early in World War I. As the war progressed, air combat became increasingly a matter of organized patrols and the singularity of the pilot who flew alone under his own command necessarily gave way. But the earliest image had by that time become essentially an icon. The changing realities of warfare did nothing to diminish the idealized vision that had in fact been rather carefully crafted for public consumption.

The earliest representation of air-to-air combat in single-seater aircraft carried with it the essential element of the pilot's discretion. A man alone in a plane could decide for himself whether or not to engage the enemy. This reality was mentioned specifically in the congressional debate over exempting from conscription men who were to become pilots. A man simply could not be compelled into battle in the air for the simple reason that the terms of engagement were established by the pilot himself. This was one of the factors that made volunteering for the air force attractive, with the additional consideration that, while the pilot earned officer status, he was responsible solely for himself and did not have to contemplate sending men who depended upon him to their deaths.

James Norman Hall examined this factor and its implications for testing the character of the man in his *High Adventure* (1918).[1] The two main characters, Drew and the narrator, have arrived as young Americans at the Lafayette Escadrille. The veterans engage the novices in discussion prior to their first sortie, describing various battles which they have survived. Survival "depends on the man. . . . [Y]ou are absolutely on your own. Your job is to patrol the lines. If a man is built that way, he can loaf on the job. He need never have a fight. . . . Oh, he can find plenty of excuses, and he can get away with them." Another veteran challenges this, mentioning someone named Huston who, the reader is given to understand, perfectly matches this description and who is not "getting away with it" because his comrades in arms are aware of his failings. This leads to an argument between the two veterans:

> "Very likely, Huston can't help it. Anyway, it is a matter of temperament mostly."
>
> "Temperament, hell! There's Van, for example. I happen to know that he has to take himself by his bootlaces every time he crosses into Germany. But he sticks it. He has never played a yellow trick. I hand it to him for pluck above every other man in the squadron."
>
> "What about Talbott and Barry?"
>
> "Lord! They haven't any nerves. It's no job for them to do their work well."

This line of conversation continues, leading the narrator to comment that the "life of a military pilot offers exceptional opportunities for research in the matter of personal bravery," ranging from the person who simply has no fear to the "sense of shame" that motivates others.

It is against this consciousness that a combat pilot could determine whether or not he would engage the enemy that the reputations of the ace of aces should be measured. These were men who not only had downed more enemy aircraft than others even though they could act at their own discretion, they also flew voluntarily alone on additional, self-assigned missions.

Americans learned about these extraordinary French and British flyers from accounts in popular American magazines, such as *Literary Digest* and *Mentor*, from reading the *National Geographic*, and from the biographies and autobiographies published both overseas and in the United States. Later in the war, when American squadrons were flying over the Western Front, the attention to the individual flyer changed, taking on an American quality that combined celebrity with the emphasis on teamwork. To understand that evolution, and to appreciate the appeal of the combat pilot to the American imagination in the period leading up to the American commitment to win the war from the air, requires an understanding of the characteristics of the British and French lone-wolf or free-lance ace of aces.

Georges Guynemer, Albert Ball, and William Bishop serve to illustrate the popular understanding of the type because a great deal was written about them. We have examined already Bordeaux's biography of Guynemer, which was translated and published in the United States. To this will be added a second, briefer biography, written for an American audience at the time of Guynemer's death. Guynemer is worthy of attention in an examination of how the American public understood the role of air combat when America entered the war because, as Molter notices, his was a household name in the United States. Albert Ball was the first British pilot to receive the attention given to the German and French aces, and he was widely celebrated; his biography, consisting of a selection of his letters home along with commentary by the editors, was published after his death and was available to the American audience. Billy Bishop was the top ace-of-aces flying for the British. He was a Canadian who was pulled out of combat and made the center of considerable publicity in both the United States and Canada. He was celebrated in the United States, and his account of his exploits ran in the *Saturday Evening Post* before it was published as a book, which became a national bestseller.

The histories of these men—and other ace of aces—are well known. The point here, however, is to examine the narrative conventions that shaped the understanding of their character. There were two basic conventions. One narrative appropriated the nineteenth-century chivalric nostalgia, portraying an impetuous and courageous youth motivated both by duty to nation and filial piety—the free lance. The biographical accounts of the French ace Georges Guynemer and of the British ace Albert Ball epitomize this narrative framework. The second narrative convention appropriated the values of the self-made man, the entrepreneurial parvenu who, by pursuing his personal ambition in unfettered competition with others, ultimately both received reward or profit and benefited the nation: the lone wolf. The autobiographical account of the Canadian ace Billy Bishop epitomizes this narrative.

These differences reflect in part whether the accounts were biographical or autobiographical, and whether they were written about an airman who still flew or were posthumous tributes. An additional factor was the degree to which the accounts were subject to official control. The official interest in shaping the image of the ace is indicated by the status of those who wrote the forewords to Albert Ball's biography, a compilation of letters and commentary published posthumously. Walter A. Briscoe and H. Russell Stannard's *Captain Ball, V.C.: The Career of Flight Commander Ball, V.C., D.S.O.* (1918) includes homages to Ball by Lloyd George, Douglas Haig, Hugh Trenchard, and Brig. Gen. J. F. A. Higgins. And while Billy Bishop gave his account in his own words, *Winged Warfare* (1918) was nevertheless subject to military censorship and was part of a public relations package used to promote Bishop on a recruitment tour of the United States and Canada.

Whether the accounts are autobiographical or biographical, and regardless of whether they adopt the free-lance or lone-wolf narrative, they bear several characteristics in common. They give only glancing attention to the relationship between the conduct of the air war and support for the ground war, for the obvious reason that the Allies, and especially the British, had little positive news to report about the ground battles men such as Ball and Bishop supported from the air. The news about the air war itself was also unwelcome because of the very high casualties inflicted by the Germans during the Fokker Scourge of early 1916, as well as during the spring of 1917, and the spring and summer of 1918. It was especially desirable to avoid these realities given the need in spring 1917 and early 1918 to recruit replacements from the Commonwealth nations and the United States.

The heroes are essentially loners. Little attention is given to deep friendships and the men with whom they flew receive scant attention. This may well reflect the reality that the life-span of most pilots new to combat was a few weeks, and dwelling too much on that reality would require examination of emotions that would be at odds with the celebration and glamorization of the ace of aces, although the emotional toll is not entirely excluded.

What emerges is a highly unrealistic image of warfare as consisting almost exclusively of individuals deciding when they will fly, men who are concerned solely with their next flight and their next encounter, and who are responsible to no one but themselves. To read of these men is to read essentially about one-man wars.

The Duel in the Sky: "To Decide Which Is the Better Man"

The informing trope of the accounts of both the lone wolf and the free lance is the duel, which epitomized the fascination with the air war conceived as individual encounter. The representational conventions of the duel-in-the-sky warrant attention before we turn to the longer biographical and autobiographical accounts of Guynemer, Ball, and Bishop. The duel offered the most convincing proof that the kind of man mattered more than the type of machine he flew, which may explain the fixation with what is—in terms of the contribution it made to the outcome of the war—a meaningless engagement. Stories of duels also emphasized the air war as highly personal, with men who knew each other by name or reputation pitted one against the other. Such a vision obviously resonated with the nostalgia for the chivalric age. Stories of duels were told and retold; new stories evolved as elements of one duel were woven into the story of another, a process recalling the oral transmission of folktales, to which the stories of challenges and duels bore more than a passing resemblance.

Readers of the November 10, 1917, issue of the *Literary Digest*, for example, learned of the death of Max Immelmann. The report falsely attributed his death to his losing a duel with the British ace Captain Ball. The story begins by establishing the conventional connection with the chivalric age:

> The old days when armies ceased fighting to watch their two champions in single combat have come back again . . . no chance meeting of men determined to slay one another, but a formally arranged encounter, following a regular challenge, and fought by prearrangement and without interference. The battle was witnessed with breathless interest by the men of both armies crouched in the trenches.

The account first appeared in the *New York Tribune*, as reportedly told in a letter written by a Canadian infantry colonel, William Macklin, to a friend in New Jersey.

Ball, upon hearing that Immelmann was assigned to a squadron in Ball's sector, said, as if thinking of the dialogue cards in the silent cowboy movies, "This is the chance I've been waiting for; I'm going to get him." He flew over Immelmann's base and dropped his challenge:

> Captain Immelmann:
> I challenge you to a man-to-man fight, to take place this afternoon at two o'clock. I will meet you over the German lines. Have your anti-aircraft guns withhold their fire while we decide which is the better man. The British guns will be silent.
>> Ball.

Immelmann's reply accepting the challenge was soon dropped from a German plane flying over Ball's base.

The story of the encounter is told as a melodramatic showdown, heightening the tension by first placing the "hero" as the underdog who might well lose the fight:

> He was below Immelmann and was, apparently making no effort to get above him, thus gaining the advantage of position. . . . We saw the German's machine dip over preparatory to starting the nose dive.
>
> "He's gone now," sobbed a young soldier at my [Macklin's] side, for he knew Immelmann's gun would start its raking fire once it was being driven straight down.

But "in the fraction of a second, the tables were turned," as Ball executed a loop that brought him above and behind his adversary (a maneuver named after Immelmann, which the article does not mention). Ball unleashed a "hail of bullets" and "Immelmann's airplane burst into flames and dropped." Ball "raced for home," landed, and quickly took off to fly over the burning wreckage, where he "released a huge wreath of flowers almost directly over the spot where Immelmann's charred body was being lifted from a tangled mass of metal." The article closes by noting: "Four days later, Ball, too was killed."[2]

Immelmann flew over the Western Front from spring 1915 to the spring of 1916. He was one of the first to fly the Eindeckers equipped with Fokker's forward-firing machine gun. He was shot down and killed on June 18, 1916, either because, as the Germans claimed, his plane broke up in the sky when his gun shot a propeller blade away, or, as the British claim, his plane was hit by bullets fired from a British observer plane. In his last battle, he was not engaged in a single-handed combat: several planes, both British and German, were involved.

Albert Ball was apparently not one of the combatants; he was shot down a year (not four days) later, May 1917. It is unlikely that the account in the *Literary Digest* refers to some other "Captain Ball" because of the number of planes credited to him: "Captain Ball . . . has only two notches less on the frame of his fighting machine than had the Falcon [Immelmann], who was credited with fifty-one 'downs.'" Immelmann, who was known as the "Eagle of Lille" (not the "Falcon"), was credited with destroying fifteen planes at his death, Ball with forty-four.[3] There was only one "Captain Ball" with such a high number of victories. The man credited by the British with downing Immelmann was Cpl. J. G. Waller, aerial gunner for Lieutenant McCubbin flying for 25 Squadron.

The account of the Immelmann-Ball duel to the death is pure fiction of an especially invidious kind because it uses actual people as the central characters, blurring the distinction between fantasy and reality, making the fanciful seem authentic. It appears to be based on two different episodes, just as was Hewlett's version of the capture of the Fokker. A. J. Insall, in his *Observer: Memoirs of the R.F.C., 1915–1918*, recounted the intention on the part of 11 Squadron late in 1915 to challenge Max Immelmann to single combat. The note, which was prepared but for some reason never delivered, read:

> A British officer pilot is anxious to meet the redoubtable Captain Immelmann in fair fight. The suggested rendezvous is a point above the first line trenches just east of Hebuterne. The British officer will be there from 10 a.m. to 11 a.m. daily from November 15th until 30th, weather permitting. It is understood that only one aeroplane can be sent to meet this challenge, and that anti-aircraft guns may fire at either combatant.[4]

Billy Bishop published an article entitled "Tales of the British Air Service" in the January 1918 *National Geographic*. A friend of Ball's, Bishop recounted an incident when Ball engaged the enemy, who fled; this "disgusted" Ball. "He . . . seized a piece of paper and a pencil which he had with him and wrote out a challenge for the same two machines to meet him at the same spot the next day." Ball showed up, saw the planes, and engaged them when "three more enemy came down from the sky and attacked him. It was a carefully laid trap and he had fallen into it without even suspecting that there was one."[5]

The account of the battle is similar to the Immelmann-Ball story because in Bishop's version, Ball is also at a disadvantage, the "under-dog" in the dogfight: "Turn and twist as he would, he always found one of the enemy on top of him." The two stories are similar in another way: both tell of Ball flying from the scene, landing, and taking off quickly. In Bishop's account, Ball lands in order to make the Germans believe he has been shot down; they land to confirm their victory. As soon as they do, Ball takes off again and heads for the safety of his own base, leaving the frustrated Germans standing beside their parked planes with the motors off.

It is easy enough to see how even one or two stories about formal challenges could spawn any number of variations, weaving the elements until a wholly satisfying version—such as the Immelmann-Ball duel—is fashioned and develops a life of its own. In the same issue of the *National Geographic*, an article by Laurence La Tourette Driggs repeats the story that Ball had shot down Immelmann. Obviously, it took a while to sort out the story of how Immelmann died.

The Immelmann-Ball legend is a consequence of low journalistic standards for verification, coupled with a high degree of government censorship and control over information, the motive of providing sensationalized accounts of the war for eager readers, and the desire to believe that the air war was about heroes dueling in the sky. It is hard to know where the willingness to be waylaid by a fantasy begins and ends.

The Winged Sword of France

Georges Bordeaux was not the only one to represent Georges Guynemer as the boy-knight who sacrificed himself in defense of family and nation. The *Literary Digest* of October 13, 1917, reprinted "The Winged Sword of France," " which appeared originally in the *London Morning Post* when he was listed as missing but his death not yet confirmed: "He is attached to no particular squadron. Instead, he is free to go of his own sweet will to any part of the front, from the Belgian coast to the Swiss frontier. . . . He travels in his personal automobile with his chef."

Guynemer was in fact attached to the famous French squadron, Les Cigognes (the Storks). In a stalemated war, the imagination evidently leaped at the notion that when Guynemer was given a "roving commission," it meant he could move about as he wished, choosing to assign himself to the most dangerous sectors, where he was needed most; moreover he took his own chef with him, sacrificing none of his material comforts to the demands of Mars, and maintaining the habits and tastes appropriate to his class and background.

The boy-knight was known to others, including the enemy; for him, the war was a personal matter, which is why it was so easy to refer to all engagements—not just those that arose from formal challenges—as "duels":

> One day the champion pilot elected to come where the British were. Within twenty-four hours of his arrival the enemy were on the alert for him. The Germans sent up ten machines to catch him. Single-handed he set out for them, and promptly brought down three.[6]

The "free-lance" hero accepted battle when outnumbered and prevailed because of his skill and audacity: "Guynemer hated the word 'luck,'" intones his biographer in the *Mentor*, "perhaps because he was accused of having so much of it." The *Literary Digest* quotes a Paris correspondent for the *New York Tribune* as saying that military observers credited Guynemer's success to "his aerial acrobatics and his absolute lack of fear."[7]

The hero was supposed to decline battle only if he had his opponent at an unfair advantage. The German ace Ernst Udet told of an eight-minute battle with Guynemer: "I try anything I can, but with lightning speed he anticipates all my moves and reacts at once. Slowly I realize his superiority." The favored explanation for why Udet survived is that Guynemer saw Udet's gun had jammed and gallantly let him escape. The other explanation is that Guynemer ran out of ammunition. Udet himself felt that Guynemer broke off the combat because he saw that Udet could no longer defend himself. The episode so affected Udet that he took himself out of combat for several weeks.[8]

Guynemer was also used to illustrate the ideal that the chivalric temperament, while it respected the ties to family, could not be tied by sentiment to them because the hero owed a higher fealty to the nation. Howard Cook, who wrote the biography for the November 1918 issue of a popular American magazine, told of a time when Guynemer was recuperating from wounds: "His parents begged him to rest, so Guynemer compromised by agreeing to establish himself near his family at Compiegne." He kept his Nieuport in a hanger nearby and had one of his sisters arise each day at dawn to determine if it was "Boche weather" or good enough for flying: "And as soon as it was light enough, slyly, like a boy planning mischief against the orders of his elders, the Second Lieutenant Ace came down from his room and mounted his Nieuport for a prospective fray."[9]

Guynemer, we are told, assumed neither of his parents was aware of his deception: "How little he understood the hearts of a father and mother! Father Guynemer has told of the anxieties, the worries lived through during the convalescence. . . . As for the loving Mother Guynemer, she did not dare show her son that she was undeceived by his stratagems" though she watched him go with "tear-dimmed eyes." The implied moral—that Guynemer would not be deterred by familial ties from risking his life repeatedly—is again illustrated when the reader is told Guynemer constantly reassured his parents that he "avoided all risks" and "insisted on his own prudence," when in fact "[n]o peril had been too great for him. He played with danger and looked for it."[10]

It bears repeating that the preferred meanings of these stories are overly determined by the style of the telling. There is a nightmarish quality to the story of a teenage boy (Guynemer was only nineteen) sneaking out of his parents' house—not to meet a girl or smoke a cigarette with his friends, but to go kill someone (as approved by the state) or be killed. Cook writes it as a "boys-will-be-boys" story tinged with a bittersweet sentimentalism, of parents who must give a headstrong boy leave literally to try his wings. By utilizing such trite conventions, Cook does not demand—and the reader presumably does not feel called upon to give—any consideration to the desperate effort to maintain the facade of familial conventionality while the sole occupation for young men is a morning's worth of battle. The anecdote has no less potential for baffling the moral imagination than does any story of the ground war. But no such sense is conveyed; Guynemer's actions fit the fantasy of a "hero" as the individualist who can slip the familial bonds to risk all in the name of a higher duty while at the same time sustaining the deference and respect a loyal son owes his parents.

The affirmation that the true hero was freed from every bond save the duty to nation was communicated by the information that the aces were usually unaffianced bachelors. Nonetheless, there was every indication that the pilot who became an ace would be idolized by women:

> The affection in which France held Captain Guynemer was shown on the French national holiday, last July 14 [1917], when he marched in the parade in Paris carrying the flag of the aviation group. On that occasion he was greeted with outbursts of greeting by the massed people. Women and children impeded his progress with showers of flowers, and finally a police cordon had to be thrown about him in the parade to ward off the worshiping women who sought to embrace and kiss him.[11]

While the hero of the skies could expect women to throw themselves at his feet, he was expected to act as if he had nothing to live for except the next battle.

Albert Ball, V.C.

Walter Briscoe and Russell Stannard in their biography of Albert Ball echo the journalistic conventions used to portray Guynemer as the boy-knight. Ball, who flew over the Western Front between the summer of 1916 and the spring of 1917, was the son of staunchly middle-class parents—his father had been the mayor of Nottingham—and an indifferent student. He enlisted at the start of the war in 1915, and shortly afterwards applied for and received a commission as a second lieutenant, when he transferred to the Cyclists Corps. He soon became enamored of flying, and during the summer of 1915, he paid for his own flight lessons, rising at 3:00 a.m. to ride on a motorcycle the seventy miles to the flight training ground, returning to his base at 6:00 a.m. In the fall, he was transferred to the RFC and continued training through the winter. He was sent to France to fly observer planes in February 1916, and later that spring he began flying single-seat patrols.

Ball was the first combat pilot to become known to the British public with the celebrity attached to the ace (see Figure 9). The *London Gazette* mentioned that Ball had been awarded the Distinguished Service Order in September 1916 but without recounting the action that merited the award. In October Ball was posted home with thirty-one victories and the Military Cross, but the figure was not made available to the press. The public could learn more about Ball from reading French newspapers, which mentioned his achievements with admiration. Despite the lack of detailed information about him, at the time he was awarded the MC, he was treated as a celebrity and lionized in the press. The British public was certainly aware that he was highly decorated and flew for the RFC. He was made the toast of London and his picture appeared frequently in the papers.[12]

Ball returned to the front in early April 1917, assigned to 56 Squadron, which was established to counter von Richthofen's Flying Circus. He was shot down and killed on May 7, 1917, only twenty years old. Ball was credited with downing forty-four enemy aircraft and had won more honors than any other man his age, having received the Distinguished Service Order three times, the Military Cross, the Russian Order of St. George, and the French Legion of Honor. On June 3, 1917, Ball was granted a posthumous Victoria Cross.

In *Captain Ball, V.C.*, Briscoe and Stannard present Ball as a devoted son and brother, a sensitive young man who devotes his off hours to gardening, a skilled pilot who does not hate the enemy, and who sacrifices his life for God and country. While one or two letters are identified as being sent to his fiancée, we learn nothing of her or of their courtship. As with Cook's portrait of Guynemer, Ball is presented as a son who is concerned not to alarm his parents. He reassures them that he avoids unnecessary risk, while at the same time writing them: "if

Figure 9. Albert Ball was represented as the epitome of the British chivalric ace, the "free lance," the individualist who did not hate his enemy but was motivated by duty and the love of nation, family, and God. He built himself a hut away from the living quarters of the base and tended a small garden. From British Imperial War Museum.

anything did happen, as it quite easily may, I expect you and wish you to take it well, for men tons better than I go in hundreds every day." Briscoe and Stannard emphasize the pathos of Ball's sentiments: "His promise to be careful sounds pathetic now we know what risks he took and with what calm he faced the dangers that crowded about him every hour that he was flying over the enemy lines."[13]

Ball's ambition to exceed Guynemer's scores is mentioned but downplayed. What is emphasized instead is his Christian faith, his filial piety, his chivalric respect for the enemy, and his willingness to sacrifice himself for the good of the nation. His biographers point out especially his frequent references to placing his faith in God and sense of duty. Those who knew him "were impressed by his striking sense of duty to his country. They say that he seemed to be conscious of a special responsibility, of a power to do a great service to his country" (181).

In a letter to his mother dated November 14, 1916, Ball wrote from London, during what was to be his last leave, to explain why he had relinquished a posting as flight instructor stationed in England:

> I have offered to go out again. . . . I don't offer, dear, because I want to go, but because every boy who has loving people and a good home should go out and stand up for it. You think I have done enough, but, oh, no, there is not or at least should not be such a thought in such a war as this. (232)

He was so intent on flying over the lines that he declined advancement in rank to major because it would restrict his ability to fly at his own will; yet he did not hate the enemy: "'I only scrap because it is my duty,' he writes his father, 'but I do not think anything bad about the Hun. He is just a good little chap with very little guts, trying to do his best. Nothing makes me feel more rotten than to see them go down, but you see it is either them or me'" (180, 261).

Ball flew into battle in a two-seater in March, April, and May 1916. During those three months, he developed a reputation as an excellent fighter. But it was when he was at last assigned to single-seat scouts that he came fully into his own as the iconic loner who flies into the sky for God and country. He expressed relief at no longer having the responsibility of flying with an observer and felt "free to put himself against all Hun-comers and he was thirsting for battle!" The point suggested by the account is that Ball was able to fly successfully against the Germans even during the Fokker Scourge, which testifies to his abilities as a prudent yet aggressive flyer, and to the superiority of the man over his machine. Again, it is the single-seater combat plane that allows the fullest expression of his abilities and will.

The account is remarkable in one sense because it allows an image of the strain of combat on the pilot. By June 1916 Ball was writing to his parents to remind them that hundreds die every day and to tell them he has built himself a shack to live in near the aerodrome—away from the billets and three miles away from the mess—and has started a small garden. He did this, he writes, because his work was a "nerve pull." His biographers interpret this for the readers as a sign of excellence of character: "A wonderful memory this is—of a boy one moment happy in a garden of his own making, enthusing over the growth of vegetables. . . . and another moment careering through the air chasing and killing Germans" (165). The passage is reminiscent of how Cook attempted to make it seem conventional that Guynemer, a convalescent nineteen-year-old, would sneak around his parents to fly into battle at dawn. The situation described by Ball's biographers is of another adolescent who, faced with the intense stress of air combat and high casualty rates in his squadron, withdraws into a ramshackle wooden shack he hammers together and commences tending peas, interrupting his solitary labors for the regular patrol to kill or be killed. To term this a "wonderful memory" invites the reader to gloss over the glaring implication of a youngster's desperate attempt at finding solace in solitude and in making things grow—of bringing life into a world of ceaseless death.

By July, his biographers report, Ball "was on the verge of a breakdown" (184). He could not however be spared from the Battle of the Somme, which commenced on July 1, 1916: "Tens of thousands of the best of the manhood of the Empire sprang over the parapets on that day to capture the subterranean fortresses that the Germans thought to be impregnable and to perish in the terrible machine gun fire that had to be encountered." Without commenting on the failure of the Somme offensive, and in fact suggesting that it was a success, Ball's biographers point to the ultimate victory in the sky: "Our losses in the air were also inevitably heavy, but the Huns were well beaten there also and lost more than we did" (174). It was during this period—when his nerves were so shattered that Ball was placed for a time in an observer unit—that he received the Military Cross. There is, in short, considerable tension between the desire to portray Ball as plucky hero and the evident signs of strain on a young man facing the unrelenting demands of air combat during a time of high British casualties.

The attractiveness of the personal duel fought with a chivalric restraint and sense of proportion is captured in Ball's account of a one-on-one encounter with a skilled German pilot:

> We kept on firing until we had used up all our ammunition. There was nothing more to be done after that, so we both burst out laughing. We couldn't help it—it was so ridiculous. We flew side by side laughing at each other for a few seconds, and then we waived adieu to each other and went off. He was a real sport was that Hun. (213)

Ball very much epitomized the duelist in the sky who seeks out his opponent. Every night for a fortnight, Stannard and Briscoe report, Ball flew over Richthofen's aerodrome dropping notes to challenge them to a fight. Ball flew in a plane with a red nose cap, which made him clearly recognizable to the Germans. Ball's biographers regard the Germans as cowardly for their failure to accept single-handed combat, especially since the accounts of Ball's last battle indicate that he was significantly outnumbered.

Ball's characteristics were taken as emblematic of the British character and breeding. In one of the many tributes to him, the *Daily Mail* attributed to Ball the "ancient and inbred qualities of our race." Briscoe and Stannard included a long tribute to Ball by Captain Wood of the

Military Aeronautics Directorate. "No man," wrote Wood, "has ever before faced more dangers in a life's span than this man or boy faced in less than two years in France." What motivated Ball, he continued, "was a Duty, and England never had a son who served her more loyally, more truly, and more bravely." He concluded by comparing Ball to Nelson, Napoleon, Kitchener, and Stonewall Jackson: "his name is not less sacred than theirs. He fought as well; none were more chivalrous than he and none lived more truly and cleanly" (306, 314–16).

Albert Ball was an extraordinary warrior by any account. How he was presented by Briscoe and Stannard underlined the qualities deemed most desirable for the public imagination. His role as a young man in love was downplayed; his boyishness, high spirits, and role as a devoted son were emphasized. Personal rather than wholly patriotic motives were hinted at by his flying with a identifying red nose cap on his plane, his ambition to exceed Guynemer's score, and his efforts to taunt the Red Baron into a personal duel. These suggestions of personal motives were very much downplayed, however, in favor of emphasizing the themes of initiative, skill, and courage matched with faith, duty, and patriotism. The biographers omitted reference to the missions in the winter of 1916, when Ball volunteered to fly intelligence agents into enemy territory and, on one occasion, had to force a reluctant spy from his plane. Nor did they emphasize Ball's role as a designer. While on leave in 1917 he worked with the Austin Company to build a plane of his own design. They also omitted any reference to Ball's role as a flight commander, concentrating on his lone patrols instead. And while they mentioned his gardening, they did not note his affection for fine music, poetry, and playing the violin. Finally, in portraying Ball's last battle as an example of the personal nature of the air war—with Germans ganging up on Ball, whom they sought out because of his reputation—Ball's biographers failed to mention that the spring of 1917 was a period of very high British casualties in the air. What his biographers emphasized was the portrait of a boy of energy, pluck, and humility, a loner who placed his skill in the service of his nation, fought—indeed, invited—a personal war, and made the ultimate sacrifice as a result.[14]

Billy Bishop, *Winged Warfare*

Ball and Guynemer were portrayed as epitomes of the free lance, the man who could assign himself to battle, and who was motivated by the desire to fight in the defense of hearth and homeland. Billy Bishop's *Winged Warfare* is an autobiographical account and signals a rather obvious departure from the framing device of the chivalric code. Bishop epitomized the lone wolf; he is a "self-made man," a loner who is motivated by personal ambition (see Figure 10).

William Avery Bishop was born in 1894 in Owen Sound, Ontario, Canada, to a solid, middle-class professional family. His father, Will Bishop, had established a law practice before accepting a political appointment as county registrar. Will and his wife, Margaret Louise,

Figure 10. Billy Bishop, nicknamed "Lone Hawk," epitomized the "lone wolf" representation of the ace. He represented himself as deriving a keen satisfaction from seeing his enemy go down and as motivated primarily by the ambition for high scores in competition with others, particularly Albert Ball. From National Air and Space Museum, Smithsonian Institution.

had four children, and while they were not wealthy, they enjoyed financial security. When the war came in August 1914, Billy Bishop, who was close to being expelled from the military academy he attended for cheating on his exams, enlisted in the cavalry. In 1915 he sought and obtained transfer to the air service.

In seven months of active duty, Bishop became the top Allied ace with seventy-two victories to his credit. He began his service on the Western Front in mid-April 1917; in August he was summoned to a Royal Investiture. King George awarded him the Distinguished Service Order, the Military Cross, and the Victoria Cross. At a later date the king also awarded Bishop the Distinguished Flying Cross. As a result of receiving the DSO, the MC, and the VC, Bishop was lionized in the press and his name and nickname, the Lone Hawk, became well known in Great Britain, Canada, and the United States. In recognition of his propaganda value, the command pulled Bishop out of action in September 1917 after fifty victories and sent him on a speaking tour across North America with the special aim of encouraging recruitment. At the time he set sail for home, he received news that he had been awarded a second DSO and the French had awarded him a Croix de Guerre with palm and the Legion of Honor, making him the single most decorated soldier in the Allied forces. He was offered a contract for a book about his exploits, which he finished during his leave. *Winged Warfare* became an immediate bestseller in the United States. It was also on this leave that he wrote "Tales of the British Air Service" for the January 1918 *National Geographic*, an issue devoted entirely to articles in praise of pilots in the air services. Bishop was given a hero's welcome in Owen Sound and spoke to large crowds in the United States and Canada until he returned to England in January 1918. In short, while Billy Bishop was Canadian, he was presented to Americans as a living, breathing war hero with whom Americans could readily identify at the time when the United States had committed to a large, aerial armada to win the war.

During this leave Bishop traveled to Washington, D.C., to consult with the government on aircraft production. Returning to Canada, he gave a frank talk to the Canadian Club in Montreal, expressing his doubts that the Americans could deliver on their extravagant promises of massive airplane production. He also reported that the French and British were far behind their production schedules. As a result of this speech, Billy Bishop was placed under arrest by the military police on January 12, after he and his new wife, Margaret, had boarded a ship in Montreal preparing to sail for England, where Bishop had been ordered to form his own fighter squadron. Although he was threatened with a court-martial, this was never really likely given his fame and decorations; however, he was given a stern reprimand not because what he said was false, but because it should not have been said publicly.[15] The incident points up the need to read behind the lines of *Winged Warfare*, to understand that while it was written by an outspoken individual, it was nevertheless also subject to the kinds of controls which were naturally exerted over Bishop as a man in uniform.

When he returned to the front in May 1918 leading 85 Squadron, Bishop's record of fifty victories had been surpassed by Jimmy McCudden, who was credited with fifty-seven. Between mid-May and the end of June Bishop brought his total score to seventy-two, a record described by his biographer as "a frenzied killing spree unmatched in the annals of aerial warfare."[16] He was recalled from the battlefield in June by the Canadian government, ostensibly to help organize a separate air branch, but it was likely as well a way to assure that their hero was not killed. When he flew his last mission over the Western Front, he was only twenty-five years old.

Bishop used no chivalric imagery to describe his motives or his encounters with enemy aircraft, and his work lacks a concern for history, personal relations, or patriotism. Bordeaux emphasized the long reach of the Guynemer familial line back to the days of Charlemagne and encouraged his young male readers to apply Guynemer's virtues to the rebuilding of France after the war; Cook emphasized Guynemer's devotion to his family and his duty to the nation. Briscoe and Stannard included an account of Ball's upbringing and education; because the biography includes Ball's letters home, Ball's ties to parents and siblings were presented as a pervasive influence on him.

Bishop's account, on the other hand, begins with his decision to transfer from the cavalry to the air service and ends on the battlefield. We learn nothing of his childhood, his family, or the fiancée whom he married during the same leave he wrote *Winged Warfare*. There are some very sketchy references to other pilots in his or neighboring squadrons, but they remain essentially faceless. Bishop does not offer even brief platitudes on the subject of patriotic duty.

The war for Bishop is very much an account of the Lone Hawk, with heavy emphasis on personal skill and initiative. The most recurrent motif is the description of taking off for battle, the battle with guns blazing in a blue sky, and the return. While *Winged Warfare* cannot be said to have a plot, the theme that runs throughout is one of personal ambition for victories, expressed in terms of a rivalry with Albert Ball:

> Ambition was born in my breast, and although I still dared not entertain the hope of equaling the record of the renowned Captain Ball, who by this time had shot down thirty-five machines, I did have vague hope of running second to him.[17]

Ball and Bishop met in London in March 1917. Bishop had reported to the War Office to receive new orders, frustrated that he could not obtain a posting as a scout on the Western Front. There he met and fell into conversation with Ball, who was on leave. Ball, who was usually reticent, took a liking to Bishop. Soon after Bishop received orders to join Ball's previous squadron, 60, at Filescamp Farm near Izel le Hameau, suggesting that Ball had perhaps used his influence on Bishop's behalf. Ball was assigned to 56 Squadron, which meant he could fly over to visit Bishop, which he did from time to time.

For Bishop, then, Ball was both a friend and a rival. But in *Winged Warfare* Bishop did not mention that he knew Ball as a friend, emphasizing instead only his desire to be at least second best in scores:

> I began to feel that my list of victims was not climbing as steadily as I would have liked. Captain Ball was back from a winter rest in England

and was adding constantly to his already big score. I felt I had to keep going if I was going to be second to him. So I was over the enemy lines from six to seven hours every day, praying for some easy victims to appear. I had had some pretty hard fighting. Now I wanted to shoot a "rabbit" or two.[18]

Bishop's accounts include accepting uneven battle and the occasional personal duel when he knew his opponent. The opportunities for such personal engagements were heightened in the spring of 1917 when Baron von Richthofen's Flying Circus appeared in brightly decorated planes, including the Baron's own famous red Albatros. The British command discouraged such displays, but permitted a few of their top flyers, such as Ball, to paint their planes in distinctive colors. Billy Bishop was also given permission and flew a Nieuport with the front cowling painted blue. Although he was probably unaware of it, Bishop had become a personal target of Baron von Richthofen, and Bishop for his part was eager for an engagement as well.[19]

They met on April 30, 1917, over Drocourt. Bishop was on an afternoon patrol with his commanding officer, Maj. Jack Scott. Flying behind the lines into enemy territory, they came upon a flight of four red Albatrosses. Bishop rightly concluded it was made up of Baron von Richthofen and three of his best flyers. Bishop's bravura is evident in his reason for accepting the uneven engagement: "[A]lthough we knew who they were, we had been searching for a fight, and were feeling rather bored with doing nothing, so after the four we went."

Bishop gives a vivid rendering of the battle:

I opened fire on the Baron, and in another half-moment found myself in the midst of what seemed to be a stampede of bloodthirsty animals. Everywhere I turned smoking bullets were jumping at me, and although I got in two or three good bursts at the Baron's "red devil," I was rather bewildered for two or three minutes, as I could not see what was happening to the Major and was not at all certain as to what was going to happen to me.[20]

The six planes flew "in cyclonic circles for several minutes, here a flash of the Hun machines, then a flash of silver as my squadron commander would whizz by. . . . It was a lightning fight, and I have never been in anything just like it. Firing one moment, you would have to concentrate all your mind and muscle the next in doing a quick turn to avoid a collision." At one point, Bishop got off a clear shot when "von Richthofen flashed by," but at the same time, he saw four more machines descending to the fight, and, not knowing whether they were friend or foe, he "zoomed" up and out of the fray. The four proved to be from the British navy, and they scattered the German squadron. Bishop at first could not find Major Scott and assumed he had been shot down, but Scott rejoined Bishop for the flight home. When Bishop landed, he saw that his machine was very badly shot up, including seven bullet holes that had passed within about an inch of him. "It had been a close shave," Bishop comments, "but a wonderful, soul-stirring fight" (124–25).

The hallmarks of Bishop's style as a warrior are ambition for personal glory, a thirst for the encounter, and the exhilaration of battle, with survival or victory resting on carefully honed skills, innate instinct, quick reflexes, and luck. In May 1917 Bishop returned to England on leave, where he learned he had been granted the DSO. He also learned that Albert Ball had been killed in battle. Bishop returned to the front with his appetite whetted to obtain even greater recognition before his next scheduled leave in July: "By this time I had become very ambitious, and was hoping to get a large number of machines officially credited to me before I left France. With this object in view, I planned many little expeditions of my own" (149–50).

Certainly the most ambitious and controversial of these "little expeditions" came on June 2 when Bishop took off before dawn to attack single-handedly a German aerodrome. According to Bishop's biographer, Ball had been the first to propose such a scheme. He had flown over to Filescamp Farm on May 6, 1917, with a plan for the two of them to take on Richthofen's Circus. Such an attack had never been tried, but Ball felt the element of surprise would assure them success. Bishop agreed to join Ball after his leave, toward the end of May. Ball was killed the day after his visit with Bishop, and Bishop evidently decided to take on the challenge alone. He appears very candid about his reasons: "My record of machines brought down was now in the vicinity of twenty, and I saw I had a rare chance of really getting a lot before going on my next leave— at the end of my second three months at the front." But in a letter to his fiancée, which is not included in *Winged Warfare*, he wrote of his profound grief over the loss of Ball: "They have killed my dear friend, Richthofen and his scarlet gangsters. They are going to pay for this, Margaret!"[21]

According to his account, Bishop flew in the predawn darkness to an unnamed aerodrome he planned to attack—presumably, the last known site of the Flying Circus, which was so called because it could quickly decamp and reappear at another place along the front. Bishop was disappointed when he arrived to find no planes on the ground, either because the aerodrome had been deserted or because everyone was still asleep. Finding himself "in a bad temper" at the misfiring of his plans, Bishop flew along close to the ground in the hopes of coming upon troops and strafing them: "nothing would have pleased me better than to have run across a group of fat Huns drilling in a field, or something of that sort." While he was scouting around, he came upon another aerodrome. At first, he hesitated to attack because he was uncertain of his location and worried about finding his way back to his own lines if he were attacked. He could see seven enemy aircraft on the ground, some of them warming their engines for takeoff. Six of the planes were single-seaters.

Bishop dove from 300 feet and made his strafing attack at 50 feet. There is no hint of either chivalric detachment or deference for the enemy; rather, Bishop was elated at the damage he caused:

one man, at least, fell, and several others ran to pick him up. Then, clearing off to one side, I watched the fun. I had forgotten by this time that they would, of course, have machine guns on the aerodrome, and as I was laughing to myself, as they tore around in every direction on the ground, like people going mad or rabbits scurrying about, I heard the old familiar rattle of the quick-firers on me.

But Bishop could not withdraw because his aim was to lure the scouts into the air. He maneuvered to avoid the machine-gun fire until a plane began to taxi down the runway; just as it left the ground, Bishop opened from behind it at close range:

> There was no chance of missing, and I was as cool as could be. Just fifteen rounds, and it side-slipped to one side, then crashed on the aerodrome underneath. I was now keyed up to the fight, and turning quickly, saw another machine just off the ground. Taking careful aim at it, I fired from longer range than before, as I did not want to waste the time of going up close. For one awful moment I saw my bullets missing, and aimed still more carefully, all the time striving to get nearer. The Hun saw I was catching him up, and pushed his nose down; then, gazing over his shoulder at the moment I was firing at him, he crashed into some trees near the aerodrome. I think I hit him just before he came to the trees, as my tracers were then going in an accurate line.

Two additional fighters took off and threatened Bishop from different directions. Bishop had planned for this eventuality when he noted that there was no wind, which meant that planes would be able to take off in more than one direction. Following his plan, he sought higher altitude but was caught at 1,000 feet; he turned and fired on his pursuer, who crashed to the ground. The other plane now came upon him. Bishop was by now eager to break off battle because he was low on ammunition and he knew the men below would be telephoning other bases for assistance: "But there was no chance of running from this man—he had me cold—so I turned at him savagely, and, in the course of a short fight, emptied the whole of my last drum at him." His opponent broke off the fight, and Bishop headed for home, evading enemy patrols, until he arrived at his own base.

Bishop referred to this episode as a "stunt" rather than a mission. It certainly gained him the recognition he sought:

> Within three or four hours I had received many congratulations upon this stunt, and what I had planned as merely a way of shooting down some

more of the Huns I found the authorities considered a very successful expedition. It pleased me very much—and of course, I have always kept the telegrams of congratulations which I received that day.[22]

Bishop did not mention that this mission earned him the Victoria Cross, nor did he fill in the blanks about how the news of his exploit became known, but that explanation provides significant insight into how fighter pilots were promoted as heroes by June 1917.

Bishop could not have flown the mission without the permission of his commander, Maj. Jack Scott, who by some accounts was very eager to gain recognition for 60 Squadron and recorded victories reported by pilots even when there was no available confirmation. Scott had already recommended Bishop for the Victoria Cross and been turned down. When Bishop landed and filed his report, Scott ordered him into his dress uniform and drove him to meet General Allenby at 3rd Army Advance Headquarters. Scott intended to recommend Bishop for the Victoria Cross again and he wanted Allenby to meet Bishop, and also seems to have been willing to use his connections with friendly members of the peerage in England.[23]

There were those in 60 Squadron who doubted Bishop's veracity. In June 1977 the British Royal Air Force Museum issued a commemorative stamp and envelope to mark the sixtieth anniversary of Bishop's attack on the aerodrome. The museum contacted four of the surviving members of 60 Squadron—Bishop was by that time deceased—to autograph the cover. All but one flatly refused. One of them explained that he doubted the authenticity of Bishop's story and knew other men in the squadron did as well. In 1984, when the doubts about Bishop's account became public, some information was published that seemed to confirm Bishop had attacked the aerodrome. In addition, Whitehouse in his *Decisive Air Battles of the First World War* (1963) offered confirming German evidence that Bishop had strafed an aerodrome, but that he had not downed any planes and had instead retreated.[24] Moreover, German archives do not mention fatal casualties among German airmen along the Western Front for that day.

Against this evidence are the frequent reports that the Germans did not keep especially accurate records and the possibility that while Bishop may have shot down several planes, their pilots were not mortally wounded. In addition, Phil B. Townsend, a pilot with 12 Squadron, reported that in 1918 his squadron occupied the former German airbase at Estourmel. French civilians told him that one morning in 1917 they had seen a British plane attack the aerodrome and shoot down three German planes. There was other evidence from contemporary witnesses that the raid had downed three planes and that two of the pilots were badly shaken up. Bishop's biographer, James McCaffrey, regards this evidence as decisive in resolving any doubts that Bishop flew the mission as he reported it.[25]

The point of revisiting the accounts of Bishop's attack on the German aerodrome is not to revive the controversy over whether Bishop was telling the truth; rather, it is to consider how the ambition for celebrity worked against normal military objectives. Pitting men on the same side, and indeed, in the same squadron, against each other in competition for individual scores could undermine the objective of building esprit de corps and of focusing attention on the enemy. Certainly, there were men in Bishop's unit who mistrusted his reports not only of the attack on the aerodrome but of many of his victories as well. The resentment was deep enough to be long-lived, nursed by some members of 60 Squadron for at least fifty years after the morning Bishop took off alone.

In addition, the ambition for recognition or celebrity led to actions that had little or nothing to do with the war effort itself. Bishop's attack on the aerodrome may have had some effect on morale among German combat pilots, but it had no tactical significance. He correctly referred to it as a "stunt," and one he says he undertook solely to boost his score relative to other British pilots, although the motive of revenge for Ball cannot be ruled out. In general, single pilots seeking combat, and especially uneven combat, solely out of a desire to raise their public profile or out of motives of personal revenge had little to do with the tactics needed to win the war and placed men and their planes at unnecessary risk.

Finally, it is important to notice that the motives of personal ambition and desire for fame and recognition were approved and encouraged by those in command, in this case, Major Scott. This raises the question of why commanding officers thought it worthwhile to promote practices in combat pilots which served no useful military purpose, undermined morale, and created resentment among those who had to rely upon each other in battle.

One clue is provided by the alacrity with which the command pulled Bishop out of harm's way and sent him on a speaking tour. Beyond his general usefulness building morale and confidence on the home-front, Bishop could aid the specific need for recruitment. The need was particularly urgent, and the reason offers one explanation for certain stylistic qualities of *Winged Warfare*. Bishop began his flying career in single-seaters on the Western Front during the Allied offensive, the Battle of Arras, which lasted from April 9 to May 17, during Bloody April.

The casualty rates of Bloody April have been offered earlier. The clue to Bishop's failure to mention any personal relationships with his squadron mates is provided by imagining how Bishop experienced those losses. Bishop's 60 Squadron, along with the neighboring 29, were stationed at Izel le Hameu opposite von Richthofen's Jasta 11 at Douai. The two British squadrons lost more than 100 percent of their flying strength in April with a total of twenty-seven men killed, missing, or taken prisoner, and four wounded or injured in crashes.[26] To have dwelt on who his comrades were would have required Bishop to say how many of them died and how quickly—including his friend Albert Ball. To mention his personal relationship with Ball—as opposed to his references to his rivalry with him—or to dwell on personal descriptions of those in his squadron who were killed would have called upon Bishop to explore emotions that overmastered him—as his letter to his fiancée about Ball's death suggest they did—and which certainly would have detracted from the aim of glamorizing the air war.

When reference to the high casualty rates cannot be avoided, Bishop glossed over the problem, making it appear that the British actually gained the upper hand:

April 6th and 7th were memorable days in the Flying Corps. The public, knowing nothing of the approaching attack which was to go down in history as the Battle of Arras, was distinctly shocked when the British communiqués for these two days frankly admitted the loss of twenty-eight of our machines. We considered this a small price to pay for the amount of work accomplished and the number of machines engaged, coupled with the fact that all our work was done within the German lines. In the two days that we lost twenty-eight machines, we had accounted for fifteen Germans, who were actually seen to crash, and thirty-one driven down damaged, many of which must have met a similar fate.

Bishop explained that it was difficult to gain accurate figures on losses because the British did not record any enemy aircraft as destroyed without "strict verification," a claim certainly not sustained by the account of the raid on the German aerodrome that gained Bishop the Victoria Cross.

Bishop concluded his observation with the comment, intended to reassure the reader: "The Royal Air Force is absolutely unperturbed when its losses on any one day exceed those of the enemy, for we philosophically regard this as the penalty necessarily entailed by our acting always on the offensive in the air."[27] Bishop was offering the official justification, but it should not in all fairness be regarded as mere propaganda. The British evidently fought on sustained by the erroneous belief that the German losses exceeded their own.[28]

Having granted that while the RAF indeed had two bad days, but the Germans had it worse, Bishop returned to accounts of his personal war. One additional aim might be said to be served by this approach. Squadrons 11 and 60 flew Nieuports, which were inferior to the models flown by the Germans, and even to the newer Spads flown by the French or the Sopwith planes that were appearing in naval air units. The accounts of Bishop's skirmishes with and victories over German planes reiterated the message used to respond to criticism of the casualty rates during the Fokker Scourge of the previous year: it was not the machine that mattered so much as the man who flew it, which also distracted attention from the possibility that the strategy employed by the high command wasted human life unnecessarily at a very high rate.

Nor could much more attention have fruitfully been paid to the relationship between the air war and the ground war, given the general aim of painting a positive picture of the war. The Arras offensive was no more successful at breaking the stalemate than the earlier allied offensives had been. The opening offensive against Vimy Ridge had been successfully achieved by Canadian units, an accomplishment so significant that historian James Stokesbury concludes, "It is not too imaginative to say that Canada became a nation on the slopes of Vimy Ridge." But the Arras offensive was the first move in the Second Battle of the Aisne, which opened on April 16, 1917, led by the French general Nivelle. It was this offensive, which cost Nivelle 120,000 men—or a tenth of the French attacking forces—that led to the revolt of the *poilus* and to Petain replacing Nivelle.[29] It was the carnage of the last gasp of this offensive—when the French took the crest of the Chemin des Dames Ridge—that led Billy Mitchell to reach the conclusion that the war could not be won on the ground and had to be won from the air.

While it may have reinforced Canadian national pride to have Billy Bishop emerge as a hero of the same overall offensive that included the taking of Vimy Ridge, it would have not have been worthwhile to dwell on the details of the ground offensive of spring 1917. The Battle of Vimy Ridge was its only successful aspect, and while it was a moment of glory for the Canadians, in general the Canadians serving along the Western Front suffered very high casualties. Of the 600,000 Canadian troops who served in the war, two-thirds became casualties, and one in ten of them died in the war.[30]

The readers of *Winged Warfare*, and especially the young men in Canada and the United States so urgently needed to replace the high casualties in the Allied air services, could not know how much the exaggerated picture of the lone warrior owed to the desirability of avoiding the realities of both the air and ground wars. How much more gratifying is the tale of the hero who flies at his own will, free from the constraints of orders or the need to support the ground war, who fights his own war, seeking the enemy on his own terms, and especially searching for and engaging the archrival, the Red Baron. This conception of warfare not only distracts attention from the progress of the war, it also resonates with cultural preconceptions about how wars ought to be fought and therefore with idealized assumptions about masculinity and society.

The image of the warrior that emerges in *Winged Warfare* bears significant resemblance to the attributes of the individual as *homo economicus*, who without reference to social relations seeks always to maximize pleasure and minimize pain, constrained solely by the limitations of the available resources. As he portrayed himself, Billy Bishop relished battle. Killing the enemy did not bring him remorse, and from time to time he described the pleasure he took in watching the fruits of his own destruction, as planes went down in flames or men on the ground fell under his spray of bullets. Bishop presented himself as a self-made man and a self-sufficient individual, dependent upon neither friends, family, or loved ones, nor upon the sustaining fellowship and teamwork of his squadron mates. He was motivated primarily by personal ambition. Duty was not central to his motives; rather, it was the goad of competition and the desire for reward that made him useful to his nation and its cause. He sought to maximize his pleasure through a reliance solely upon the resources of his own skill, desire, and the technology of the plane and machine gun. For him, pleasure meant combat, victories, and rewards. Ironically, the pain he sought to avoid is not the jeopardy of battle, but being withdrawn from the front. The news that he was being recalled sent him into a frenzy of lone patrols and encounters with the enemy. His is a self-representation that hints at the deeper cultural reservoir of Social Darwinism, which glorified the predatory instinct and competition as the essence of manliness, making the survival of the fittest not simply a neutral fact of nature, but the positive force for social progress.

The "Lone Wolf": Romancing Warfare and Elite Masculinity

The connection between class origins of combat pilots and the kind of war they fought was acknowledged by a French flyer, Jean Beraud Villars, who under the name Lieutenant Marc published *Notes d'un pilote disparu* (1918). The aviators who flew the pursuit planes were essentially privileged because they flew in an elite corps, were spared any kind of hard physical labor with their hands, and engaged in a kind of combat that was highly individualized where valor was still the decisive factor.[31] Although there was an inherent contradiction in the portrayals of the boy-knights (who were depicted as motivated primarily by duty to nation) and the competitive individualists (who were motivated by a desire for personal recognition), these tensions are not acknowledged.

To an extent, however, it would be a mistake not to notice how the narrative frameworks used to describe the pilots with roving commissions allude to the precursor tensions affecting the professional middle class, the parvenu wealthy created by the industrial revolution, and the traditional aristocratic classes whose wealth was based in the ownership of property. The concern that the values of the latter might well be overwhelmed by allowing into the ranks of the gentleman and the officer the sons of the professional middle classes or the wealthy who lacked breeding was expressed in Newbolt's appeal to both types of young boys to prepare themselves as officers. He was well aware that the war had essentially eliminated the aristocratic scions who traditionally formed the officer classes and was quite anxious to assure that admitting the newcomers will be accomplished by socializing them to the traditional values of those who have gone before.

As for these same tensions in the American vein, one has only to think of the novels of Edith Wharton, particularly *House of Mirth*, and the first novel she wrote after World War I—*Age of Innocence*—to be reminded that the encroachments of new money into Old New York created considerable social strain and upheaval. The resistance of the traditional Old New York to the rise of the industrialist and financier who are trying to "break into society" is the essential underlying strain in both works.[32]

A complete social history of the period is beyond the scope of this work; however, both the narrative constructions and the attention paid to class and background in the accounts of the pilots who flew for France and Great Britain—and in the emphasis on the class of those who flew for the Lafayette Escadrille—points toward larger frictions and rifts straining the values of industrialized society. There was a struggle between the traditional and essentially aristocratic values on the one hand and the emerging values of the newer economy. Examples of this tension were prevalent on both sides of the Atlantic. The resistance of the traditional sources of wealth to the encroachments of the parvenu was a not-inconsiderable struggle among the monied classes. The distinct narrative frameworks, which pit the traditional aristocratic chevalier against the "self-made" man, represent this struggle. That they are presented without calling attention to the contradiction is hardly surprising given that the accounts are utilized for propaganda purposes, but it would be a mistake not to notice that the contradictions exist and to consider what larger cultural shifts they signify.

What was important was the portrayal of the combat pilot as an individual in the extreme. Aerial combat demonstrated mastery over the machine rather than making a man either an unskilled operator or a helpless victim of mechanized warfare. Success depended upon the application of both will and intelligence, on making one's own luck.

In some cases, the ace became more valuable as an image than as a warrior. There was an effort to remove Ball from battle and make him an instructor, but he insisted upon returning. The British were more successful at recalling Bishop from battle. None of these inherent tensions and contradictions—between the actual warrior and his value as an image—provoked skepticism or mistrust of the portrait of the lone hero. The accounts in the pilots' own words lent credibility to the earlier accounts promulgated about them, while the control over information assured that contrary accounts would not reach the public.

The emphasis on the combat pilot as a lone warrior made it easier not to mention the grim realities of air combat. Ball's biographers struggle to paste the mask of cheerful boyishness over the signs of the toll taken on him by the stress of air combat and the loss of friends. Guynemer's biographer attempts to paste the mask of adolescent mischief over the chilling account of the recuperating Guynemer obsessed with battle, and his reckless indifference, evidenced by his seeking combat on very uneven terms, is praised as a sign of his indomitable will. In the case of Bishop, the grinning smile of the youthful warrior becomes a grim joyfulness at killing, and it is his only joy, as he suppresses his friendship with Ball and his love for his fiancée. In each case, the emphasis on the warrior's singularity—the chivalric knight, the "lone hawk,"—masks the reality of very young men who, as warriors, are isolated from others and dissociated from themselves.

CHAPTER 9

The Sporting Life

The idealized image of a man who mastered the weapon of warfare, who demonstrated his character and resolve by voluntarily flying into singled-handed combat, appealed to the conventions of an imagined warfare, particularly as it ought to be fought by gentlemen, by those whose breeding, education, and background singularly qualified them to be cool-headed under battle, to sacrifice themselves on behalf of others, and to be officers. This vision was enforced not only in terms of the style of combat but also in the representation of the life the combat pilot led. The conventional picture of a combat pilot on the front was not simply one of comparative ease and comfort compared to the tribulations of the trenches; it was an entirely different form of living altogether, one that coalesced under the imagery of life at a hunting lodge, where guests dined well on linen tablecloths, entertained themselves in the out of doors at various games, and hunted. The corollary between the life of the combat pilot and the leisure activities of the landed classes—horseback riding, tennis, yachting, and hunting—was not simply placed before the public as a metaphor. The skills that derived from these pursuits were seen to suit a man for the role of combat pilot better than any others. The representation of the combat pilot in terms of the underlying conventions of class, background, and a set of competencies made him naturally suited to the individualistic, specialized, and heroic calling of a combat pilot.

As with other aspects of the representation of the combat pilot, the conventions associated with the combat pilot's daily routine at the front gained their potency in no small degree from sharp contrast with the ground soldier. At the time the United States entered the war, much of the effort to compare air combat to sports came from official British or French sources. These writers often struggled to accommodate European sports metaphors to the American idiom, sometimes falling rather wide of the mark. An American who had been among the first to fly with the Lafayette Escadrille, and whose vision of warfare drew heavily on the sports metaphor, was the singular exception. He also broke every convention associated with the gentleman and officer. Bert Hall published his *En l'Air* in 1918 and traveled both the lecture circuit and vaudeville, thrilling and amusing audiences with his account of himself. His image is at the furthest extreme from the image of the boy-knight represented by Ball or Guynemer. He spoke in an entirely American colloquial idiom. His comrades-in-arms would later declare publicly that they regarded him a liar and a bounder, but at the time he was making a name for himself he was known as a decorated war hero who had been among the first to fly with an all American squadron into battle over the western front. His exceptionalism makes him interesting for studying how Americans formed their understanding of the "sporting life" of the combat pilot.

Play Up and Play the Game: War as Soccer

The insistent campaign to convince both the soldier and the public to conceptualize the war as a soccer game, is commemorated today in the uncanny exhibit in the Musée des abris, an underground museum in Albert, France. The visitor walks from the sunlight downstairs into dimly lit converted catacombs. Along the passages and under low arches, exhibits commemorate the troglodyte world of the soldiers who fought the First Battle of the Somme. Mannequins dressed in British uniforms make tea over a small flame, write letters, look through observation tubes, and tend the wounded. One mannequin—a British officer with a soccer ball beside him—represents more poignantly than any other the cruel distance between the war-as-imagined and the war-as-experienced because the men who went over the top on the opening day were very much encouraged to imagine the coming battle as a soccer game.

The seemingly out-of-place exhibit of an officer and a soccer ball commemorates Capt. W. P. Nevill, the company commander of the 8th East Surreys at the First Battle of the Somme. He gave one soccer ball to each of the four platoons under his command, offering a prize to the unit that first kicked its soccer ball to the German lines. As Paul Fussell remarks, Nevill "may have been shrewder than he looked; his little sporting contest did have the effect of persuading his men that the attack was going to be, as the staff had been insisting, a walkover." Accounts of the battle include reports of a soccer ball being kicked—probably by Nevill—toward the German lines when the signal was given to advance. Nevill was killed instantly. Despite this unfortunate example, soccer balls were subsequently kicked from time to time toward enemy lines to demonstrate the sportsmanlike bravado of the Tommies.[1]

The episode was immortalized in verse:

> Where blood is poured like water,
> They drive the trickling ball
> The fear of death before them
> Is but an empty name.
> True to the land that bore them—
> The SURREYS play the game.[2]

Fussell identifies this as an obvious imitation of perhaps the most frequently cited illustration of the persistent comparison of the war with sports: Henry Newbolt's "Play Up and Play the Game." Published in 1898, the poem tells the story of a public schoolboy who learns endurance and competition from playing team sports and then draws upon those lessons when, years later, he is an officer exhorting a badly battered regiment on colonial duty:

> The Gatling's jammed and the Colonel's dead,
> And the regiment blind with dust and smoke;

The river of death has brimmed his banks,
And England's far, and Honour a name;
But the voice of a schoolboy rallies the ranks:
"Play up! play up! and play the game!"

The poem enjoyed enormous popularity. It was frequently included in funeral services for fallen soldiers during World War I, and Newbolt said that it was the one work he was most often asked to recite when he gave public talks.

Newbolt's poem echoes the sentiments of Sir William Fraser commemorating Wellington's victory over Napoleon, "The battle of Waterloo was won on the playing fields of Eton." The emphasis on sports, coupled with an anti-intellectualism, typified not only the British public schools but also American private preparatory schools and colleges catering to the elite classes.

In his study of the relationship between the elite schooling in both England and America and the enthusiasm with which the sons of the ruling classes rushed off to war, historian Michael C. Adams notes especially the connection in America between sports and warfare. Raymond F. Getell, president of Amherst, praised football because it satisfied the "primitive lust for battle" while reinforcing the importance of "organization, cooperation, and the skilled interrelation of individual effort directed to a common purpose." The zealous promotion of school sports led Herbert Branston Gary, an educational critic of the period, to conclude the schools turned out "a useless drone trained only to wield a willow or kick a bladder," which Adams remarked was "a harsh charge but one with foundation" and he argued further that the "sporting ethic was part of an anti-intellectual milieu in which World War One was possible because the formula did not provide any vehicle for questioning the validity of the game."[3]

There is a point to be made here about the role of propaganda in appropriating precursor values in the service of inducing young men to enlist. British (and, for that matter, American) adolescents did not rush off to war because they had played field sports and therefore spontaneously understood the war as an exciting away game, any more than they would inevitably have imagined the war as a crusade simply because they had been assigned *Ivanhoe*. Propaganda campaigns made overt efforts to assert as literally true the fantasy—promulgated in boys' adventure literature by Newbolt, among others—that the battlefield was simply another kind of playing field. For example, a British poster depicted soldiers in the far distance shooting at the enemy and bearing the motto: "Play the greater game and join the Football [soccer] battalion." That the comparison was intended as literal is further illustrated in the analysis of the differences between British and German soldiers offered in *Lord Northcliffe's War Book*. The reason, Northcliffe said, that the German soldier showed no initiative and could only obey in massed numbers is that German boys were not taught to play "individual games" such as football, "which develops individuality." While German soldiers were brave, their bravery differed from (and suffered by comparison with) the "British spirit," which the Germans considered "frivolous and too much akin to sport." The Tommy's lighthearted approach to war as a game was again praised when Northcliffe admired the crew that gave him a ride in their tank. They were "young daredevils" who "enter upon their task in a sporting spirit with the same cheery enthusiasm as they would show for football."[4]

War and American College Football

When the United States entered the war, football rather than soccer was used as the metaphor for warfare, but to a different end. While Northcliffe characterized English football (soccer) as a sport that developed "individuality," the American version, as applied to the ground war, used football to illustrate the need for teamwork in battle. An article in the August 1918 issue of the American popular magazine *Current Opinion* titled "The Advantages of Fear in Battle" asserted the disadvantages of individual heroics in the trenches, emphasizing instead the twin values of fear and anger to both the athlete and the soldier in creating a purposeful solidarity. The reporter reminded his young readers of the exhortations of the coach at halftime in the locker room: "he upbraids the team, pictures the disastrous consequences of defeat and by every means arouses fear and anger, with the result that the men become capable of almost superhuman feats of exertion and endurance."[5] The point made is that the fear and anger felt by the individual soldier on the ground were productively directed toward teamwork, not individuality: "concerted action," not "heroics," is essential to both victory and survival.

Used in this way, the metaphor of football emphasizes qualities at the opposite extreme from those in the combat pilot. Relying upon fear or anger was contrary to accepted military wisdom that the pilot needed a calculating temperament, while the emphasis on being a team player ran counter to the by-then popular conception of the combat pilot as a "lone wolf," although it represented the emerging belief among commanders that victory in the skies depended upon coordinated squadron flying.

The effort to graft the concept of "teamwork" onto the tropes of either the lone wolf or free lance created some confusion in conveying what qualities ought to be singled out as essential to the flight school candidate. Major Tulasne, chief of the French aviation mission to America in 1918, invoked the football metaphor, but without mentioning "teamwork," as part of his effort to recruit American men into the Air Service: "Hundreds of pilots, full of dash, are being trained, and they are going about their work with the same zeal which they formerly displayed on the football field at college."[6] Tulasne reinforced the American recruitment of college football players for the air services but did not draw a connection between how one plays that game and how one fights in the air.

Edward Lyell Fox's article, "U.S. Leads in Air War," in the July 1917 issue of the American popular periodical *Illustrated World* offers a hyperbolic account of the role of the Lafayette Escadrille at the Battle of Verdun the year before and mixes together a variety of sports, some team and some individual. Fox explained the success of the squadron as due to its being composed of

daredevil Americans. You know the type. You have seen them often—making headlong tackles on the football field, diving feet first, spikes flashing, in a wild slide for third base, galloping madly across a polo field, diving from a platform higher than someone else has dared—they are the youth of American and their number is legion.[7]

The appeal to young men of a certain class is suggested by the picture accompanying the article: an unnamed, stern-looking man with dark eyebrows and a moustache, his head encased in a close-fitting dark leather helmet, bearing the caption: "Wasn't He the Greatest End Harvard Ever Had, or the Man who Broke the Record in the 440, or—Well, Never Mind! He has Found a Sterner and More Glorious Sport."

The appeal to male college athletes reflects the serious thinking among military medical advisors about the attributes necessary to the successful pilot. Dr. Norman S. Gilchrist, a captain in the Royal Army Medical Corps attached to the Royal Air Force, studied 100 cases of flyers who suffered nervous breakdown. Dr. Gilchrist's suggested criteria for determining which "high-strung" individuals should be accepted as candidates for flight school clearly reflect assumptions related to class and breeding. Dr. Gilchrist would reject the "nervous, pale faced, introspective, East End clerk, with little or no experience of outdoor exercise and sport, whose habit of life almost compels him to think far too much of himself." The "equally nervous" university athlete, on the other hand, who has been "trained to ignore himself and to control his feelings, trained to act and think of and for others" and is "of good physique and broad in mental outlook" would, however, be acceptable.[8]

British qualifications for a good pilot referred most often to the sports of the elite classes (riding and yachting), but especially to the hunt, and it was generally recognized that a weak physique was not a handicap given the other necessary attributes of quickness, grace under pressure, and intelligent reactions to danger. An article entitled "Who Makes the Best Aviators" in the August 1918 issue of the American popular magazine *Current Opinion* reports that in a study of successful pilots, Dr. Graeme concluded that "previous training in sports is a matter of consequence." The reference is not to football but to "the yachtsmen and the horsemen" because of the "finer sense," "truer judgment," and skills these pursuits develop. Exerting control over one's means of conveyance and utilizing one's intelligence and self-discipline are far more prized than playing on a team, obedience, or a reliance on emotional arousal. The conclusion implicit in Dr. Graeme's study is that the idle pursuits of the privileged class both encourage skills and help develop a temperament uniquely necessary to air combat. The report also remarks upon the man "with splendid physique and apparently unshakable courage" who nonetheless cannot learn to fly well or in some cases at all, while a "'weedy' pale type" may learn to fly quickly and turn out to be a "first-rate pilot."[9] This observation was by 1918 axiomatic. Guynemer's legendary status derived in no small part from the often-repeated account of his frail frame and condition, reportedly caused by his childhood battle with tuberculosis. He had been denied admission to the Ecole Polytechnique because of his poor health and had initially been turned down for military service. Nor was he the sole example. The RAF ace "Mick" Mannock was blind in one eye. Alan John Lance "Jack" Scott, who commanded the famous British 60 Squadron during Billy Bishop's tenure, required two canes to walk because of crippling wounds. He often disobeyed the orders grounding him; the ground crew would lift him into his plane in order to fly missions with the men he commanded. Most notably, none of the veteran American pilots who comprised the Lafayette Escadrille, including the ace of aces Raoul Lufbery, passed the physical for entrance into the newly formed American squadrons once the United States entered the war; for obvious reasons, arrangements were made to set the results aside.

Despite these realities, the targeting of American college football players for recruitment led to some rather odd appeals to team sports as the suitable analogy for air combat. RAF Capt. George F. Campbell's *Soldier of the Sky*, published in the United States in 1918, was aimed specifically at inspiring young men to enlist in the air service. The introductory material explains that Captain Campbell was wounded as an officer in the ground war and rendered unfit for service; upon hearing this disappointing news, he volunteered for air combat. Despite the reality of his infirmity, which posed no limitation to his own flying career, Campbell's account suggested that athletic ability was an essential qualification. Commenting on the role of the scout planes in escorting bomber flights, Campbell said: "You see the same kind of thing in football, where the man with the ball, running down the field, is protected from opponents by the interference of his teammates," a reference that applied equally well to both soccer and American football. He used a less familiar example when he compared the war to cricket:

> All these boys were made of the right stuff, and treated the war as a big game of cricket: all willing to take a chance, and nine times out of ten to give one . . . the chance of a man's life, or "the sporting chance." . . . all the boys being sportsmen at heart. . . . Do you wonder that the Flying Corps is called the "corps elite"?[10]

Campbell's choice of cricket as a metaphor is not well suited for an American audience, but the point about an elite corps made up of members of the social elite is made nevertheless. His reference to the kind of teamwork needed in football is a different kind of emphasis than Fox's undifferentiated enthusiasm for any kind of "daredevil" in sports. Despite the obvious contradictions between Campbell's own history as a flyer and his message about the physical qualifications needed to fly, his focus on teamwork and organized flying rather than the "daredevil" individual is the sign of the shift in emphasis which would characterize flying in the later period of the war.

Air Combat, Big-game Hunting, and the Ace System

The metaphor of blood sports—hunting—rather than team sports was the image most often invoked to describe air to air combat. Hilda Beatrice Hewlett, in her relentlessly cheerful account of the RFC activities on the western front, quoted with obvious relish a gunner in an observation plane who in telling how he shot down an enemy aircraft recalled that he "was spoiling for a fight, for I had bagged nothing lately," and therefore "longed to bring down my quarry."[11] The image was sometimes invoked for the infantry soldier, as when the editor of *The Great*

Advance, a pamphlet published in Great Britain, introduced the interviews with wounded soldiers returning from the Somme by calling them "high-spirited sportsmen" who "tell their battles over in the spirit of a man recounting a fast run with the hounds or a good day's work after big game."

Nonetheless, the comparison seems to appear far more frequently with reference to air combat, most obviously because the style of fighting more readily suggested the hunt. But there was another reason as well: the pilot, unlike his counterpart manning a machine gun or hefting a rifle in the trenches, kept a running tally or score of how many enemies he had killed, wounded, or forced out of battle. The result was to combine the elements of big-game hunting with playing a spectator sport.

The closest sporting analogy to this was the scoring system developed by the Boone and Crockett Club—founded by, among others, Theodore Roosevelt—for comparing the big game killed by the international hunting set. The system, which is still used today, ranks or scores hunters' trophies; for example, the "Lord Rundlesham bison," hanging in the Buffalo Bill Museum in Cody, Wyoming, is ranked twenty-fifth in the world for bison trophies.[12]

The sport of the "Great White Hunter" bears significant resemblance to the system used to publicize the aces. Both ritualized killing, making it a competition among a male elite, who gained public recognition or celebrity because of their trophies. And both depended upon an elaborate system for determining whether a man had a legitimate claim to fame.

As noted earlier, the British never formally adopted the ace system used by the French, Germans, and Americans, which automatically granted special recognition to any pilot who had downed a certain number of planes. But in practice, the refusal to endorse the ace system per se constituted a distinction without much difference, because pilots of the British air service—such as Billy Bishop, Mick Mannock, James McCudden, and Albert Ball—were among the greatest public heroes of the war. The British unofficially considered ten victories as the minimum for ace status rather than the five accepted by the other Allies.[13] All participants had systems for counting coup and recognizing the pilots who distinguished themselves by the number of enemy aircraft they had downed.

The RFC, for example, had four categories used to report "victories," or that a British plane had prevailed over the enemy: Forced to Land (FTL), Driven Down (DD), Driven Down—Out of Control (DDOC), and Destroyed (D). The latter was reported if an enemy aircraft had been seen to crash, disintegrate in the air, or burst into flames in the air. Such distinctions had a legitimate military purpose, but as translated by the press, the word "victory" came to be associated only with the last category, so the public was led to believe that every successful encounter resulted inevitably in death and destruction.[14] The achievements of the pilots mattered for reasons other than the purely military; the military and the press publicized their exploits in a manner reminiscent of the glamour attached to a sport in which one hunter was competitively pitted against another, and their relative scores carefully reported and analyzed.

In addition to determining the category of engagement, two further requirements remained: verification and the determination of which pilot to credit. The various Allied forces had different ways of distributing credit. The British granted partial credit (quarter- or half-points) to all those who assisted in a given victory—a system that encouraged the lone wolf seeking high scores. The American forces, on the other hand, gave full credit for a victory to all those who assisted—which meant, in effect, Americans could gain ace status by cooperating with other pilots.

The competition among pilots for victories and recognition was commonly acknowledged by the end of the war. James T. B. McCudden's posthumous account of his years as a combat pilot, *Flying Fury: Five Years in the Royal Flying Corps*, appeared in the fall of 1918. McCudden ranks fourth among pilots who flew for Great Britain, with fifty-seven victories. Recounting a meeting with Albert Ball while they were both in London on leave in February or March 1917, McCudden said:

Ball seemed rather amused that I wore three ribbons as he did. He said that he thought he would like a French one too, referring to my Croix de Guerre. "By Jove!" I thought, "that man is wonderful." . . . I knew very well that when he went back to France no man was more likely to win a Victoria Cross.[15]

While such avowed glory-seeking today seems to jar with the romantic image of the aces, it did not at the time. Billy Bishop had no compunctions against revealing similar motives to the homefront public in his autobiography. The information that pilots competed against each other for medals and recognition seemed entirely congruent with imagining the air war as both a "hunt" and a game. The scoring system had an immediate analogy in big-game hunting, and, given the celebrity of the aces, war was not simply *like* playing a spectator sport; it *was* one.

The Airbase as Hunting Lodge: The Lafayette Escadrille

What Americans read about life at an air base suggested an elite, private hunting lodge. Early accounts of the Lafayette Escadrille volunteers had a lasting effect on the collective memory of how well the World War I pilots were billeted. In 1917 John Jay Chapman published posthumously the letters written by his son Victor, one of the original Americans to fly with the Lafayette Escadrille. Chapman was born in New York and graduated from Harvard in 1913. The following year found him in Paris where he studied architecture for one year in preparation for admission to the Beaux Arts. In 1914 Chapman volunteered with the French Foreign Legion and served in the trenches along the western front before being transferred to the air service and joining the new American squadron commanded by Major Thenault. He was twenty-seven years old when he died. His father published his letters, along with his own memoir of his son and a number of tributes written by friends.

In a letter dated April 20, 1916, to his stepmother's brother, William Astor Chanler, Chapman described the quarters at their first posting, the former royal spa at Luxeuil Les Bains:

We are finely situated in the ville-d'eaux—eat at the best hotel in town with our officers, live in a "villa" on the hill with an ordnance to clean up, and bathe and drink hot waters. . . . I would you were here to enjoy the countryside, the blossoming fruit trees, and the distant snow-capped hills. The town is old and picturesque. . . . And this morning I saw a stork circling round and round. . . . [James] McConnell says he finds the war quite a fashionable pastime. He winters at Pau [the training field for French aviators], stops off a week or two at Paris, and now, just as the season begins, goes to the summer resort.[16]

Ten days later Chapman wrote to his father of a visit to a nearby squadron to attend the funeral of a pilot. Far from somber, Chapman's letter takes delight in the day's outing: "We lunched . . . with the officers there, and scrumptious food we had, the proprietor of one of the best known restaurants at Geneva being the cook, we were told. Cigarettes, liqueurs, a view of the champs—very small—and the latest model Farman, which had fresh bullet holes from the morning's encounter."[17] While he might have spared his father the mention of the Farman, Chapman, with his artist's eye, is far more eager to comment on the architecture of the surrounding towns and the "little yellow jonquils" that dot the grassy slopes.

The friend Chapman mentions, James McConnell, along with Kiffin Rockwell formed a threesome sent to Luxeuil in April 1916. All three were killed within the year: Chapman was shot down June 23, 1916, Rockwell on September 23, 1916, and McConnell on St. Patrick's Day, 1917.

McConnell was born in Chicago and attended Haverford School in Pennsylvania before graduating from the University of Virginia. He was the land and industrial agent of a small railway in North Carolina until January 1915, when he volunteered for the American Ambulance Service in France. He publicized the work of the Ambulance Service by publishing a number of his letters in *Outlook*, which were introduced by Theodore Roosevelt. Tiring of the role of a mere spectator, McConnell enlisted in the French aviation service.

James R. McConnell's *Flying for France with the American Escadrille at Verdun* was published in the United States in 1917, and in two articles written for *World's Work* that appeared at the same time. His accounts of the squadron's first quarters must have been impressive to readers following the descriptions of the soldier's life on the front:

> Rooms were assigned to us in a villa adjoining the famous hot baths of Luxeuil, where Caesar's cohorts were wont to besport themselves. We messed [ate] with our officers, Captain Thenault and Lieutenant de Laage de Mieux, at the best hotel in town. An automobile was always on hand to carry us to the field. I began to wonder whether I was a summer resorter instead of a soldier.[18]

The image of dashing pilots who fight by day and dine on the finest cuisine and wine by night was widely publicized. Both Chapman and McConnell gave accounts of the French army "moving-picture outfit" that came to film the squadron in flight and in portrait shots for showing in the United States. Popular magazines included pictures of the original volunteers, often with articles written by the American pilots.

Even when the accommodations were less luxurious, the living arrangements of the Lafayette Escadrille seemed more like a lodge or camp than a barracks. When posted to the Somme, McConnell and his mates were appalled by the poor quarters and the mud, but they quickly dispatched two to Paris with a truck, and they returned with cooking utensils, a stove, and other equipment, and "as a result, life was made bearable."

The sense that even under somewhat trying conditions, the combat flyers made their quarters into comfortable if rustic camps was conveyed by others who flew with McConnell. In May 1918 *Scribner's Magazine* published the "War Letters of Edmond Genet: The First American Aviator Killed Flying Officially the Stars and Stripes." A book version, also published by Scribner's, appeared at the same time. Describing the squadron living quarters in the Somme in a letter written February 13, 1917, Genet complained slightly of the cold in the sleeping quarters, but described the common living area as "a mighty attractive little den." He wrote his mother he had "drawn and painted vivid scenes of aerial combats . . . and here and there I've made other pencil drawings of girls." He describes the doors draped with blue-and-brown curtains, white curtains on the windows, and a painting of an Indian head, the emblem of the Lafayette Escadrille. The room included a piano, which four or five of the squadron members could play, and a victrola that played both French and American records. He assured his mother, "We eat splendidly all the time," and that the easy social relations between commissioned and noncommissioned flyers was "sociable and jolly."[19]

Tally, Ho! Accounts of the Dawn Patrol

The best way to convey the picture of squadron life is to draw together the accounts from various sources to construct a typical day in the life of a combat pilot as it was represented to the public at home. In what follows, such a day is traced from the dawn patrol through to the end of the day, drawing upon a number of accounts in publications readily available to the American public. What is striking from reading these accounts is how similar they are in so many respects. They coalesce into a generalized picture of a comfortable, ordered, sociable, and civilized life punctuated by the call to the hunt. The way of life was the "sporting life," a way of fighting war entirely congruent with how a gentleman and an officer ought to combine his leisure time with the call to duty.

American readers learned about the rituals and thrills of the dawn patrol from books and articles written by those who flew into combat for the Lafayette Escadrille or the RAF. "Awakening" the dawn patrol was done by a servant: in Campbell's *Soldier of the Sky*, there is a polite knock on the door, and a "Four-thirty, sir"; in McConnell's account of the Lafayette Escadrille, it is "C'est l'heure, Monsieur." James Norman Hall's hero in his fictionalized autobiography *High Adventure* recalls that on the day of his first sortie, "Tiffin, the messroom steward, was standing by my cot with a lighted candle in his hand. The furrows in his kindly old face were outlined in shadow. His bald head gleamed like the bottom of a yellow bowl. He said, 'Beautemps, monsieur,' put the candle on my table, and went out, closing the door softly."

Descriptions of dressing include the accompaniment of music suitably reflecting that the Americans were flying for the French. McConnell dresses to the warbling of a pilot in the next room singing, "When That Midnight Choo-Choo Leaves for Alabam'." The music on the phonograph as Hall prepares for his first flight is "Chanson sans Parole," followed by "O' movin' man, don't take ma baby grand!"—a combination that gives Hall a "mixed up feeling" that he finds "impossible to analyze." Obviously, the mood is not one of hurry, crisis, or alarm, and every provision has been made to accommodate the tastes of the young Americans. On a chilly morning elsewhere along the front, Campbell does not recount listening to music upon arising. Instead, he shouts, "Orderly, bring me some breakfast!" while he washes up. Again, the picture is of a man of privilege being catered to.

In these accounts the next scene is typically at breakfast. Joining his mates in some quiet talk about the morning's orders, Campbell tucks into a breakfast of eggs and fried toast. Despite the tension and excitement felt by the flyers, one among them, Lewis, is late. He comes rushing in, half dressed, grabs a mouthful of food, and hurries after his mates.

In McConnell's account of the American squadron, there is a bit of joking about losses at the poker table the night before, and a pilot is teased who shows up wearing wooden shoes and pajama pants. "Don't you know an aviator's supposed to be chic?" Hall describes the yawning nonchalance and mild complaining about the early hour among the pilots, who down hot chocolate before heading into the darkness. The pilots flying with Hall don a variety of headgear, which helps relieve the tension: "The sudden transformation of a group of typical-looking Americans into monsters and devotional old ladies, gave a moment of diversion."

After being awakened, being catered to, listening to some music while dressing, a bit of joking, and a studied disregard for military discipline when it comes to wearing a uniform, the men take off into the sky.

Typically, there is at most a very slight reference to the men receiving any orders. The emphasis is on a studied nonchalance before the flight, and when the men are in the air, the focus is on the zest and thrill of the hunt, or upon portraying very serious errors as the subject of humor. In his account of the dawn patrol, Campbell writes that his flight encounters antiaircraft fire going over the line. His group engages two enemy aircraft. He puts his "nose down suddenly, and thus getting up an enormous speed, I 'zoomed' up straight at him. This threw him off a bit, I think, for he turned and putting his nose down, started going like blazes from me." Below him, he sees another enemy aircraft driven down in a spin, until it crashes and bursts into flames. The patrol returns through antiaircraft fire—"Gad, but it was hot! One shell burst right under my left wing, rocked the plane, and sent my heart up into my mouth." The thrill of the hunt over, the men indulge in the simple joy of flying and showing off their skills. Once back on their own side of the lines, they practice stunt flying, "a series of antics and evolutions that delight the boys in the trenches and behind the lines below." The squadron arrives back at the base in time for lunch, and a second patrol at 2:30, with a return in time for a leisurely dinner to discuss the day's events.

On his first dawn patrol, Hall encounters antiaircraft shelling, becomes disoriented, mistakenly heads toward Germany for a time, and is finally rescued by another pilot in another Spad who guides him back to base. When they land this savior chides him: "If I had been a Hun! O man! you were fruit salad! fruit salad, I tell you! I could have speared you with my eyes shut." Back at the base, J.B., the other novice, is so nervous he attempts to light the cork end of his cigarette and recounts an ordeal similar to Hall's. Over lunch, the two come in for considerable ribbing.

On his patrol McConnell watches as Raoul Lufbery downs an enemy aircraft with a direct hit: "As it turned over, it showed its white belly for an instant, then seemed to straighten out, and planed downward in big zigzags. . . . I watched it burn a moment or two." He is relieved to return to base, lands in time for lunch and a nap or a game of cards. Around one o'clock, there is a second sortie, which returns in two or three hours. The more energetic pilots may assign themselves a third patrol, while the others remain behind against the possibility of a phone call ordering them into the sky to intercept intruders. Otherwise, the men are free until dinner.

The similarity of the accounts leaves the impression of thrills, adventures, and narrow escapes that intrude twice a day into an otherwise comfortable life. There are more thrills for those who want them, and the impression is therefore given that to a great extent, a man's fate is in his own hands. At any rate, the question of one's fate is in these accounts apparently at issue for only four to six hours out of a day, and one has something to say about the outcome—a stark contrast to being on the receiving end of an artillery barrage, a gas attack, or machine-gun fire.

The similarity of the accounts, the conventions associated with squadron life, the impression one gains from reading numerous sources published at about the same time, cannot but have made an impression on those reading on the homefront. The implications of this consistency can be grasped perhaps most quickly by anyone familiar with the postwar film *Dawn Patrol*, first filmed by Howard Hawks in 1930, and remade in 1938 with Basil Rathbone, David Niven, and Errol Flynn, where the devil-may-care approach to war in the air as a blood sport gives way to nervous breakdown, grief, and mourning as more and more untrained pilots are sent off on dawn patrols never to return. Even without the potency of that film, the casualty rates alone for both the Lafayette Escadrille and the RFC would suggest that much was hidden behind the conventional depictions of young men who enjoy the thrill of the hunt, who build a sense of camaraderie out of their narrow escapes and the joking they take about it, and who live a life of leisure in between the thrill of the chase.

Leisure Time and Status Signifiers: Tennis, Anyone?

Accounts of life at the base reinforce the elite status of the combat pilots, particularly emphasizing their role as representatives of the leisure class who have volunteered themselves to the nation or an ideal. Mascots are often mentioned—usually dogs, but from time to time the choice was more exotic. The most famous mascots were the two lions named Whiskey and Soda, raised from cubs and kept by the Lafayette Escadrille. They were often photographed and written about and became a hallmark for the squadron; for example, they are mentioned in letters of Stuart Walcott published in the *National Geographic* issue of January 1918, which was devoted to information about the air war. Walcott was a senior at Princeton when he volunteered for the French Flying Corps in January 1917 and was posted temporarily with the Lafayette Escadrille. The month before he was shot down and killed, and in a letter dated November 1, 1917, he wrote his father that one of the squadron mates brought Whiskey in "to wake me up, and my eyes no sooner opened than my head was buried under the covers. Whiskey is a pet—a very large lion cub—which has unfortunately outgrown its utility as a pet and was sent yesterday, with its running mate, Soda, to the zoo, at Paris, to be a regular lion."[20]

Billy Bishop's description also mentions animals, but as one might expect from his temperament, they are targets of a general aggressive rowdiness. Bishop offers numerous accounts of dinners with invited squadrons which end in drunken rough-and-tumble fights, or in his accounts of practical jokes played against one or another of his squadron mates, some of them potentially dangerous. This coarser mentality is also revealed in the significant amount of time Bishop and his squadron mates spent harassing the animals on the farm next to their camp, painting pigs or geese various colors, or trying to get them to do tricks, or giving ducks alcohol and watching their antics, until the death of a drake brought an end to it. They were able to engage in this pointless amusement because they could pay the farmer when the animals became overstressed or died.

Keeping animals as pets or mascots signified a status enviable to the average ground soldier. Looking after an animal is a time-consuming activity with little utility apart from the personal satisfaction gained from it, which was undoubtedly considerable for men under such stress. Providing food and care for an animal—particularly two lions—suggests surpluses of food, shelter, time, money, servants, skill, personal freedom, and the energy needed to learn about the mastery and care of such rare animals.

Other pursuits also reflected the tastes of the leisure class, generally those requiring considerable time and effort to master, comprised of special and complicated rules, or requiring a certain kind of dress and decorum to practice. Billy Bishop mentions horseback riding and regular tennis games at the base in the afternoon; in one instance, the match was interrupted when six machines were ordered to fly, and the men took off in their white flannels. McCudden describes his pleasure in a game called "Bumple-puppy" played with tennis rackets and a ball tied to the top of a pole—rather like tether ball. On their days off, the men Bishop flew with would either sleep all day, roam about the orchard in silk pajamas, visit friends stationed nearby, or drive into the nearest town for lunch at a café and shopping. Accounts by Bishop and others refer to favorite bathing spots in nearby streams, or describe the men digging canvas-lined trenches that were filled with water to form individual bathing spots. Time was also spent hunting, usually birds, but some accounts mention hunting rabbits, or wild boar. Bishop describes shooting pigeons, for which they made a reimbursement payment, a practice that was "much encouraged, as it was the best practice in the world for the eye of a man whose business it is to fight mechanical birds in the air."[21]

Considerable care seems to have been taken at least by some commanders to assure the men were well entertained. McCudden includes an account of an invitation to dine with 56 Squadron in June 1917. Cocktails were served at 8:00, followed by dinner, and the music of a fifteen-piece orchestra. When Major Blomfield formed the squadron in the winter of 1917, he had gone to the principal London orchestras to ask if any of their musicians were being called up. In this way, he acquired excellent musicians, among them the first violinist for the Palace Theatre. Major Blomfield also made a habit of trading skilled men who were not musicians for musicians in other units—as, for example, a nonmusical coppersmith for a musician coppersmith. "Such is the spirit that will finally win the war, though to those who don't know the British Army, it might sound frivolous." The visit convinced McCudden that he should join the 56th, and Major Blomfield agreed to apply for him.[22]

In the evening, McConnell's squadron preferred intelligent conversation, cards or chess, and an early retirement: "After dark, we go down to the villa for dinner. Usually we have two or three French officers dining with us besides our own captain and lieutenant, and so the table talk is a mixture of French and English." In addition to discussing aviation, and learning which pilots have been killed or captured, the conversation turned to broader subjects:

> with our cosmopolitan crowd, one can readily imagine the scope of the conversation. A Burton Holmes lecture is weak and watery alongside of the travel stories we listen to. Were O. Henry alive, he could find material for a hundred new yarns, and William James numerous pointers for another work on psychology. . . . In France there's a saying that to be an aviator one must be a bit "off."[23]

After dinner, the party retires to the "next room," where some men play poker or chess, others play the piano or American ragtime on the phonograph, still another may play with the squadron dog. By nine o'clock most of the men have turned in.

Servants and batmen, renowned European chefs, mascots, orchestras, formal dinners, stimulating conversation, tennis, shooting game, horseback riding, strolls through orchards in silk pajamas, swimming, or bathing—all were signifiers of the elite status of flyers.

There were other less appealing signs of consciousness of caste and class, particularly race prejudice, which the flyers shared with their society in general, but which cannot be overlooked because of its relationship to the construction of the idealized flyer as a member of the elite, as male, and as white. Billy Bishop calls his black dog "Nigger." The position assigned to novice flyers—the highest altitude, away from the fray, to be on watch against reinforcements—is called by McConnell "nigger heaven." The phrase to "sweat like a nigger" was evidently used to mean "engage in hard manual labor." In a similar vein, McCudden is upset to find Portuguese soldiers in his squadron's favorite swimming hole: "needless to say, the water in that place never recovered its pristine clearness, nor odour."[24] Examples of this sort of prejudice are not common in these accounts, but when they occur the demeaning references are employed with the full confidence that the reader will not be disaffected by them, a sign not so much of the caste consciousness of the flyers in particular as of their era, which makes it no more palatable in retrospect.

Trophies

The image of the "hunt" would seem to make trophies a logical part of the representation of squadron life, but in the accounts written during the war either by members of the Lafayette Escadrille, or by those who flew for the RAF and published in the United States, one finds no mention of the memorials and trophies that seem to have been a regular feature of squadron living space, at least according to accounts of the RAF. The common room typically had souvenirs taken from planes shot down over Allied territory. Duncan Grinell-Milne, who gave an account of his own life in the RAF in *Wind in the Wires*, wrote the introduction to the 1968 edition of McCudden's *Flying Fury*. He provides a nostalgic description of the common area for 56 Squadron. It was a rectangular green-painted hut with an officers' mess and an anteroom furnished with "a couple of well-worn settees and some easy chairs crowding about a half-size billiard-table, an upright piano in the corner where the Squadron orchestra gathered on guest nights; at the far end the cast-iron stove that roared red-hot on wintry days." On one wall was a framed plywood board. "Above it was fixed the wooden propeller from a captured aircraft; black canvas crosses cut from other vanquished enemies drooped to either side; and upon the board itself were inscribed the score or so names of those who had won distinctions since the Squadron's first forming. Ball's name headed the list; McCudden's stood out just below. Each was followed by the initial letters of decorations awarded."[25]

The desire to have a souvenir taken from a downed plane may

account for the extra risks pilots sometimes took to force enemy aircraft into Allied territory. Kiffin Rockwell, one of the original members of the Lafayette Escadrille and the pilot credited with downing the squadron's first enemy aircraft, is thought to have been killed because he became reckless when he saw a German two-seater flying over Allied lines. In his account of Rockwell's last fight, McConnell speculated: "I can imagine the satisfaction he felt in at last catching an enemy 'plane in our lines. Rockwell had fought more combats than the rest of us put together, and had shot down many German machines that had fallen in their lines, but this was the first time he had had an opportunity of bringing down a Boche in our territory." In his excitement Rockwell presumably dove too close to the enemy aircraft, apparently nearly colliding with it, and was killed by an incendiary bullet. McCudden recorded his disappointment in a similar situation attacking a German two-seater over Allied lines. He brought it down, but over German lines: "I was rather disappointed with the fellow, because I thought I had him in our lines, and of course it is the ambition of every youthful pilot to down a Hun in our lines—and then land a crash alongside, as most people usually do, much to the evident amusement of the Huns, if they are alive."[26]

The squadron walls of 56 were bedecked with the crosses taken from enemy aircraft, as undoubtedly were those of other squadrons, a way of demonstrating the relative prowess of both individual members and the squadron as a whole. As with any trophy, but particularly trophies from the hunt, the dark German crosses and the propeller signified extraordinary skill, daring, the pleasure of fulfilling a difficult goal and thereby gaining special recognition. The black crosses on the wall might well have carried the stigma of ignoble booty-taking; they were coded instead to signify the courage and even recklessness that set one flyer apart from another, making him an elite among the elite. Nevertheless, the difficulty posed by the practice in terms of public relations is perhaps indicated by the silence about this subject in the accounts written during the war. While mention may be made of a pilot's desire to bring a plane down in Allied territory, references to the taking of souvenirs to display in the squadron "trophy room" are rare.

Another kind of "trophy" mentioned in postwar accounts but not during the war was the display of various women's lingerie hung as "trophies," as was described at Billy Bishop's squadron. The suggested equation of male heterosexuality with conquest and aggression, and the categorizing of it as a sign of competitive superiority similar to having a higher "score" than others in terms of having shot down more planes, is very much contrary to the image of civilized sexual restraint offered in Newbolt's image of the Happy Warrior, but does reflect assumptions about male promiscuous sexuality that seem common enough in contemporary terms. It is worth pausing to consider that combat flyers were discouraged from committed involvement with a woman back home— engagements or marriage—on the grounds that too great a concern for returning to her would undermine his willingness to take extraordinary risks. The legacy of this assumption lingers, for example, in the popular film *Top Gun*, where the first pilot to "wash out" is one with pictures of his wife and kids in the cockpit. A culture that teaches young men that not only their manliness but their very ability to survive in combat depends upon not cultivating deep and lasting heterosexual relations (and never mentions the even deeper taboo against homosexuality), and which credits the strength of the nation to its having won two major world wars, will inevitably influence young men to construct their sexuality around indifference and aggression.

An additional feature of the "trophies" was that they became luck tokens; for example, the American ace Elliot White Springs, whose *War Birds* will be examined at greater length in a subsequent chapter, has his central character include an entry in his diary about the best luck token, which is a nylon stocking taken from a virgin by the light of the full moon. The "magic" is primitive and imitative: having stolen a girl's virginity, one has the necessary potency and shrewdness to anticipate and conquer one's male opponent.

The relationship between combat pilots and women was simply not mentioned in the accounts of them written during the war, although it was generally understood that wearing a pilot's uniform made one particularly attractive to women. Nevertheless, some pilots gave the advice in published accounts that it was best to avoid both strong drink and women if one wished to survive because of the need for a clear head when in combat. Postwar representations introduced the theme that attachment to a woman was a destructive distraction, or that meaningless sexual conquest was a sign of particular potency; for example, the silent film *Wings* makes the love of a woman the root cause for the deadly enmity that grows between two close friends who fly in the same squadron; the 1938 version of *Dawn Patrol* celebrates the drunken sexual adventures of the two lead characters.

Elite Warfare as Blood Sport

In the United States, the potency of the characteristics of the combat pilot as elite hunter came from the sharp contrast between the desired or idealized attributes of the pilot imagined as a gentleman hunter and the foot soldier imagined as the player on a team. For the combat pilot, the preference was for specialized skills over brute strength; intelligent calculation in the face of danger over a mere emotional responsiveness; and personal initiative over conformity. What is at issue is not merely *difference*, but the implied *superiority* of the pilot when compared with the infantry soldier. The man capable of fighting in the air was deemed to be necessarily a breed apart, and therefore it was assumed that the elite class would most likely produce him.

Hunting obviously differs from other sports because its purpose is killing. Used as an analogy to warfare, blood sports have at least the virtue of pointing the imagination in the general direction of the most essential aspect of warfare, while the comparisons with soccer or American football rather obviously intend the opposite effect. But having said that much in favor of the comparison, it is just as necessary to notice that unlike hunting war intends to kill human beings. The analogy with blood sports invites the imagination to ignore this, to render the enemy not simply faceless, but inhuman—a "rabbit" or "quarry" to be bagged.

The linking of war and team sports differs in another way from the connections with blood sports, particularly with regard to the object of the game and, by analogy, of war. What makes a game such as soccer or football worth playing is the notion of a worthy opponent or of equally matched teams. Something is taken away from the pleasure of victory if the score is overly lopsided. Comparing a war to a team sport therefore makes it harder for the public to hold in mind the reality that any decent political or military leadership will seek by whatever means to avoid engaging a worthy opponent. It is an understatement to notice that World War I was a miscalculation of grotesque proportions because essentially equally matched, industrialized nations engaged one another. Military tradition may grant enormous respect to overmatched opponents—such as the Zulus of Africa or the Plains Indians of America—who managed to fight extremely well and to win certain engagements; but ultimately, the day was won because one side had the Gatling gun or an unlimited supply of rifles and the other side did not. The heavy emphasis on comparing ground combat with a particular team sport—English soccer and American football—not only served to fire the imagination of schoolboys with no knowledge of the realities of warfare but much experience with the pleasures of chasing each other and a ball around a muddy field; it also served, because of the implication that "teams" ought to be equally matched, to distract public attention from the most obvious question raised by the conduct of the war, which was the competence of both the politicians who had led the nation into such a war in the first place and of the military command that seemed incapable of responding to the resultant morass.

In big-game hunting, the notion of being equally matched has little or nothing to do with whether or not the competition is worthwhile or interesting. The notion of an equal match is absurd on one count because only the hunter wishes to engage in the sport; the aim of the hunted is to avoid the encounter. This presumed difference of motive lends intrigue to hunting for wild game, because it requires tracking an elusive animal who is presumably interested in flight rather than fight. The hunter's skill is demonstrated by the ability to track an animal in its own environment and to get close enough to bring it into range of a gun. That condition being met, one would have to be more than a little obtuse to suppose that the bison, elk, or mountain goat had even odds against the skilled hunter; the same principle also applies to the hunt for dangerous game. The point is that in all cases the presumption has to be that the hunter with a loaded gun who finds his prey will lose out only if he is unlucky, makes a mistake or miscalculation, or lacks sufficient skill; with predators at the top of the food chain (such as the lion) or a temperamental browser that is larger than the hunter (such as the male elephant), the consequences of the miscalculation are simply greater than with other game.

Team sports and the hunt for trophy animals establish different criteria for testing manhood. In the former, character is demonstrated by playing fair, cooperating with the team, causing injury only by accident, and acknowledging the equality that exists among competitors— the handshake at the end of the game. The character of the trophy hunter is demonstrated by the skill in tracking unsuspecting prey, killing selected targets in a calculated and skilled manner, enforcing the perception of the human superiority over all other forms of life, both those that are harmless and those quite dangerous when aroused, and demonstrating that one's trophy is superior to the animals killed by one's rivals. In team sports, a person participates in order to share victory with the team; big-game hunters are in it for themselves, to gain recognition for their prowess when pitted against a wild animal in its own element.

In one respect, the comparison of the war with big-game hunting shares a similarity with the team-sports analogy because it, too, distracts attention from the role of politicians and military commanders. But that end is reached by a different route. To conceive of ground soldiers as playing soccer or football encourages civilians to think of themselves as cheering on the home team; it reminds everyone that the whole point is that one's side prevail. But to conceive of combat pilots as big-game hunters means the warrior fights for his own sake, and far less clearly as the member of a national "team." Imagining combat pilots as Great White Hunters competing with each other for trophies obscures the recognition that young men are placed in harm's way because of political decisions that led the nation into the war, and that they fly into combat because they are ordered into the sky to achieve military objectives.

On the contrary, the implication seems to be that the nation has provided men with an enviable opportunity to join an elite class by proving themselves exceptional to transfixed onlookers.

As heroes, the combat pilots garnered much deserved admiration, but it should not be overlooked how much of the praise afforded them reproduced precursor social beliefs about breeding and position. The achievement of the combat pilots were contextualized along class lines, reinforcing a system of social relations that elevated to the top of the hierarchy those whose predatory instincts were refined by the cultivation skills and taste, even in the midst of war. Volunteering to fly into combat in the killing fields of the sky for both personal recognition and as a service to the nation, and returning to a game of tennis after a lunch prepared by the squadron chef, epitomized how a gentleman ought to go to war.

Ultimately, the representation of the combat pilot as essentially an individual who fought the war on his own terms with little or no attention to military organization, so obviously cultivated early in the war for consumption on the homefront, proved difficult to dislodge from the public's imagination because it had been so often reiterated. The references to the desirability of college men who played football was an early omen of this change, but the new emphasis that resulted from fusing the earlier image with that of a team player did not emerge until the end of the war as an American hybrid, a subject taken up in a later chapter.

War as Sport in the American Idiom

The American who during World War I most promoted among American audiences the image of air combat as a game, as an entirely enjoyable sport, was Weston Birch "Bert" Hall, one of the original members of the Lafayette Escadrille, joining it in April 1916. In popular histories, he has come down to us as a liar and a self-promoter, a reprobate who was asked to leave the Escadrille because he cheated at cards and failed to pay his debts. He is characterized as a rogue, a soldier of fortune, and a celebrity hound; in short, a warrior at the furthest extreme—

in terms of the values assigned to the warrior—from the chivalric knight or the gentleman hunter.

These negative opinions of him were not generally known when he published the first of two books about his experiences: *En l'Air! Three Years on and above Three Fronts* (1918). What was known was that he was an original member of the Lafayette Escadrille and a decorated airman. During the time he was with the Lafayette Escadrille (which was at that time called the Escadrille Americaine), between April 1916 and November 1916, he was credited with downing three enemy aircraft and was awarded the Medaille Militaire and the Croix de Guerre with three palms. Between November and December 1916, when he was assigned to the French E103, he was credited with his fourth confirmed victory, and was awarded another Palm to his Croix de Guerre. The citation described him as a "clever, energetic, and courageous pilot, full of spirit."[27]

When Hall returned to the United States sometime in the fall of 1917—either having been separated from the French Air Service or, as many claim, having deserted—he was a decorated war hero. His memoir is an interesting account because of all those published at the time, it cannot be said to have been written for any other motive than the interests (profit) of the author. In other words, Hall was not using it to promote a recruitment tour on behalf of Britain or France, nor was it an "official history," subjected to the controls of his commanders. He was promoting himself as a celebrity.

Given the often bitter criticism of Hall, particularly for his tendency to fabricate accounts of himself, *En l'Air!* seems remarkably constrained, even if it is obvious that he glosses the truth about his relations with his comrades-in-arms. His style is totally lacking in the refined and romantic touches brought to bear by other chroniclers of the Lafayette Escadrille. This reflects his difference in background from Chapman, Hall, and McConnell. He was the son of a cavalry man who had served in both the Civil War and with the Mexican army. Hall, who admired his father because of his military career, worked as a farmhand, lacked formal education, and left home to seek his fortune while still a teenager.

He worked as a chauffeur and as a "human cannonball" for a circus before signing on as a merchant seaman prior to World War I. The outbreak of the war found him as a taxi driver in Paris; he was one of the first Americans to enlist in the French Foreign Legion.

His memoir is straightforward and unsentimental, while sparing the reader most of the gory details of combat. He takes the stance of a male adventurer who both sees the humor of war and who takes on its grimmer aspects with determination. While he presents accounts in which he is the central player, he is less inclined to gloat or express glee at the destruction he causes than is Billy Bishop in his account.

Of the dangers of flight school Hall says dismissively, "Many amusing incidents happened to us here; but very few were fatal." What he does not mention is that he lied that he was an experienced flyer in order to get into the flight school, and when given a plane to fly he cracked it up because of his total ignorance. He also gives amusing accounts of life at the front, telling of one occasion when a German officer who landed at the base tried to brazen it out by asking in perfect French if he could borrow some petrol. He recounts a time when a fur glove fell from the sky. A few days later, a German plane flew over and another glove dropped, with the note saying that the "finder might as well have the pair."[28]

Hall writes in colloquial American English, which stands in sharp contrast to the elevated diction of the biographers of Ball and Guynemer, or the polished English of Chapman, McConnell, James Norman Hall, and Genet. His account of a narrow escape concludes, "I arrived O.K. after one of the closest shaves I ever had." He claims that he "encountered Captain Boelke daily" and had the good sense to "keep out of his range." About this prudence, he observes philosophically, if not drolly, "A good pilot can always defend himself in a single combat affair" (69).

There is little commentary on those with whom he flew and even less self-reflection. He gives a very clear indication, however, of the strain on those who flew for the Lafayette Escadrille when he says of their having been assigned to the Somme: "By this time the Lafayette

Escadrille was getting pretty well shot to pieces. The fierce flying and fighting in the Vosges district had now cost us, among many, two of our best, for Kiffin Rockwell and Norman Prince were both killed inside of a month of each other" (90). When they arrived at the Somme, Hall met his former commanding officer, Captain Harcourt, who was in charge of Escadrille 103, "and so it came about that I was able to join him, which pleased me very much." This is all that Hall has to say on the subject of his leaving—or being asked to leave—the Lafayette Escadrille in November 1916.

Hall is, however, more direct than many other accounts in reporting both the strain of battle and the mortality rates:

> A great many men have nervous breakdown or heart troubles and are sent to a separate hospital where they are treated by specialists and well rested before they are sent back. The life of an aviator at the front is very short. No one knows the exact figures, but I have heard it put at about seventeen hours of actual flying. (94)

Perhaps this description explains why Hall was with the 103 for only a month. He had put in a request to accompany the French aviation mission to Romania. He arrived in Paris to receive his new orders on December 16, 1917.

Hall is typically blunt in debunking the notion that air-to-air combat is a chivalric duel: "At the beginning [of the war] there was some chivalry among them [the Germans] but not anymore." And he takes the point even further in what for him counts as introspection into the question of killing another human being:

> Some people have asked me about this business of killing the other fellow. I can't speak for other aviators, but I never really wanted to kill another man—if he was a man. But you cannot call the German a man; he is only a savage. It is simply a case of getting him before he gets you. . . . As I have said, there was at first quite a bit of chivalry in the aviation but that has ceased. (105)

What makes the German less than a man is that he does not fight "at equal odds." The tactic of fighting as a group means that they "cannot be classed as fighters man to man. They fight only in organizations. They are made to fight by discipline and not by overflowing courage. . . . Their machines are good but the men are deficient" (102).

Unromantic as Hall's version is, he nonetheless shares with both the "lone wolf" and the "free lance" the commonly held belief that the expression of virility was manifested in the single encounter, man to man. Cooperation, teamwork, fighting as an "organization"—these are understood not as a more efficient way to fight an air war, but as a sign of the typical stereotype of the German soldier, someone bred to obedience, who fights because of his disciplined role within the group rather than out of personal courage.

After he left the 103, it is difficult to know what exactly Bert Hall did. He seems to have gone with the French aviation mission to Romania in January 1917 and to have returned to the United States, with the stated intention of joining the American Air Service, sometime before September 1917. He reportedly went instead on the lecture and vaudeville circuit to tell about his exploits, wearing the medals he had won and one or two he had not. Apparently he did not remain in the United States. On April 12, 1918, he married an entertainer, Della Byers, in Paris and evidently remained there until the Armistice, a fact that seems odd if he were in fact listed as a deserter from the French aviation service, as some accounts assert.[29]

Hall's willingness to separate himself from the war is also at odds with his devil-may-care regret that the war must some day end, along with his brazen hope that his exploits might earn him the reward of some unnamed benefactor who will save him from ever having to work again:

> It's a fact that flying was so fascinating and so agreeable that we couldn't stay away from it long. I got homesick every time I had leave and I wanted to get back to my pals and the excitement. There is a fascination about it that ruins a man for anything else. I know that I will never be much good at work again.

Before I finally left for America I had, all told, three years of genuine sport. I don't know how much longer the war will last and my only idea is that I will have to go to work when it is over. I hate to think of it. Perhaps some kind philanthropist will put us on a pension. I hope so, as work would be an awful shock after so much pleasure and so many good times. (96–97)

Hall gives a much earthier account of squadron life than his better-heeled counterparts. Describing their billets on the Somme, he gives far less attention than any of the others who described their lives there to the actual accommodations and far more to the bar and gambling: "We had a shower, bath, electric lights, plenty of wood for heat, and a bar. The benefits of the bar went to buy reading matter, and there was also a sort of casino where we played poker, bridge, and a few good old 'prayer meetings' as the dice games were called." Where other accounts maintain a discreet silence, he is unblushingly direct in pointing out that the flyers "have the pick of the fair sex. Our marraines, or godmothers, sent us lots of nice things which were duly appreciated." Without a break in the text, he described other appreciated entertainment: "We had moving-pictures once a week in the hangars, all the latest films." Of the frequent leaves to Paris he says, "It sure was one continuous party from the day we arrived . . . until the last minute of the third day. It made flying seem like loafing. 'Let's go back to the front and get some rest,' we would say as we left Paris" (95–96).

Hard drinking, hard gambling, and promiscuity were not the attributes of the gentleman flyer included in the other accounts of the Lafayette Escadrille. Hall's description of squadron life is closer to the grain found in Billy Bishop's account, but Bishop never crosses the line from describing rowdy hijinks within the squadron to portraying gambling or skirt chasing.

It is not difficult to imagine why the older Hall would rub many of the young Americans in the Lafayette Escadrille the wrong way. He was cut from coarser cloth and became known early on as a person who fabricated accounts of himself. But an additional factor besides his character should not be overlooked. The Lafayette Escadrille was privately funded. As Hall points out, he along with the other officers bought their own food and were expected to be self-supporting. Hall, who lacked the financial resources of his richer colleagues, was a shrewd card player, and he may have relied upon this skill and other forms of gambling to make up for the deficiency. The criticism of him from other members of the squadron included writing bad checks and failing to pay off his debts—essentially unthinkable to any gentleman. In their callow insensitivity, the men of inherited wealth in the squadron may not have recognized that Hall simply lacked the financial wherewithal to be a privately funded volunteer, and he may have been rather desperately trying to cover that lack. He himself offered the seemingly cavalier observations, "Money was the least of our troubles, as one did not expect to live long enough—so why worry about finance" (95).

Hall has come down through the histories of the Lafayette Escadrille as the black sheep of the squadron. His second account of himself in the war, *One Man's War*, published in 1929, has been generally derided for its discrepancies with *En l'Air* as Hall's effort to "prove how one man can be in two places at the same time." He is cast not as a "lone wolf"—he never became an ace—but as a soldier-of-fortune, a man whose motives were wholly at odds with the ennobling and idealized motivations of the other original members of the Lafayette Escadrille. That is as it may be. But he shared with them the realization that the Lafayette Escadrille was an example of the elements of celebrity and publicity as essential components in the emergence of air combat as an admired even enviable form of warfare.

Hall is worthy of attention in that particular cultural aspect of the history of air combat for three reasons. First, he was a living embodiment of the vision of air combat as a game, a kind of sport, a combination of thrills and humor. Second, he legitimized a particular kind of masculinity—hard drinking, hard gambling, womanizing, and scrapping for a fight—which was a counterbalance to the refined image of the gentleman warrior typical of the accounts that bore the stamp of caste and breeding, and a vision of the combat pilot that bears an uncomfortable resemblance to the mentality that led to the Tailhook scandal. Third, he was so clearly a self-promoter. He invented himself for public consumption and in the vernacular, and not only in print or on the lecture circuit. Immediately following the war, he produced and starred in a Hollywood film *A Romance in the Air*, and in 1920 he made another film, *Border Patrol*. He traveled the road to promote these films, lecturing to the audience before each screening. He seized upon the celebrity of the combat pilot—the product of recruitment and publicity campaigns—for his own profit and benefit. He thus represents at the far extreme what was to emerge as characteristic of combat pilots—their celebrity, or their value as an image.

PART III
DEATH AND TRANSFIGURATION

I know that I shall meet my fate
Somewhere among the clouds above;
Those that I fight I do not hate,
Those that I guard I do not love;
My country is Kiltartan Cross,
My countrymen Kiltartan's poor;
No likely end could bring them loss
Or leave them happier than before.
Nor law, nor duty bade me fight,
Nor public men, nor cheering crowds,
A lonely impulse of delight
Drove to this tumult in the clouds;
I balanced all, brought all to mind,
The years to come seemed waste of breath,
A waste of breath the years behind,
In balance with this life, this death.
    —W. B. Yeats, "An Irishman Foresees His Death"

CHAPTER 10

"As Swimmers into Cleanness Leaping"

Primitive Instinct, Civilized Character, and the Hero's Fate

The emergence of a conception of social evolution—of progress based upon rationality, morality, and technology—appropriated biological theorizing to social vision, a vision that divided history, the peoples of the world, and individuals themselves along the poles of "primitive" and "civilized," as driven by natural impulse or as shaped by the constraints of reason. This way of mapping history and geography placed civilization squarely in European control, a flattering vision that was, according to most social historians, dashed by the reality of the Great War. The larger point is that the construction of the war as a crusade made Great Britain, France, and ultimately the United States defenders against a threat to civilization itself.

The Great War presented a challenge to the optimism that Europe had cornered the market on "civilization." Germany, which had seemed to epitomize intellectual and artistic cultivation, now seemed entirely barbaric. The advent of the war itself made it seem that thinking about "civilization" had been wrong or at least taken a wrong turn. And the reality of trench warfare certainly undercut any precursor ideas about how wars would be conducted along lines reflective of civilized constraint and obviated the notion that the soldier's character determined his destiny.

Given the polarity of "civilization" and "primitive," there was a marked tendency toward deciding that "civilization" was the problem and "primitive instinct" was the solution, or more precisely, the necessary purgative—perhaps the greatest example imaginable of making the worst seem the better cause.

It is this tendency with regard to legitimizing the ground war—of making a place for it in the imagination—which makes the advent of the aces gain particular significance. Because they, uniquely among the representations of the warrior, were insistently represented as being in charge of their own destinies, as choosing combat, and as prevailing through strength of character and skill. Their death was neither accidental nor the result of simply waiting like trembling sheep for the axe to fall. While the realities of the trenches required a reinvigoration of the ideal of the "primitive" as necessary to survival, the combat ace epitomized the vision of the true hero, one who bore about him all the virtues of civilization and who was therefore its most obvious defender.

The best illustration of the need to represent combat pilots in this way is the British treatment of the death of the German ace of aces, Baron von Richthofen. In the intense effort to assure that the official story of his death was that he was shot down by another pilot—rather than by ground fire—can be traced the significance attached to the vision of pilots as masters of their fates.

But before that particular episode can be fully illuminated, the larger context that gave it meaning must necessarily be established. We begin for that reason with a consideration of how the values of the "primitive" were pitted against the weakening values of "the civilized" by cultural commentators, the medical profession, and the emerging science of psychology. As our interest is primarily in how the general public or the popular imagination received these ideas, the focus will be on how these ideas were sifted and shaped for a popular audience. Along the way, we will compare briefly how the ground soldier was represented in Great Britain, the United States, and Germany in terms of his reliance on primitive instincts in order to reflect upon how cultural values shape the understanding of masculinity.

"Civilization" Is the Enemy, War the Necessary Purgative

While the general aim of British domestic propaganda was to justify Britain's aims in the war as a defense of civilization, there was another, somewhat contradictory justification offered by the intelligentsia, one that welcomed the war as purging society of the weakening effects of the surfeits of civilization. In his cultural history of Great Britain during World War I, Samuel Hynes finds that within the literary and intellectual elites, there were those who framed the coming of war as the solution to the threat to traditional English life perceived by the major Victorian social critics—Carlyle, Disraeli, Arnold, and Ruskin—and which Carlyle had named "The Condition of England." It was Edmund Gosse who, according to Hynes, in the fall of 1914 first voiced the sentiment that the Condition of England was a social disease for which the war was the cure. As the preeminent man of letters of the Edwardian literary establishment, Gosse's welcoming of the war as the antidote for the excesses and decadence of the era helped frame the thinking of other intellectuals in England. War would force men from the lap of luxury into physical deprivation and the spiritually improving conditions of self-sacrifice and dedication.[1]

Gosse voiced this vision in his essay, "War and Literature," which appeared in the *Edinburgh Review* in October 1914. It begins by declaring the purgative value of war:

> War . . . is the sovereign disinfectant, and its red stream of blood is the Condy's Fluid that cleans out the stagnant pools and clotted channels of the intellect. I suppose that hardly any Englishman who is capable of a renovation of the mind has failed to feel during the last few weeks a certain solemn refreshment of the spirit, a humble and mournful consciousness that his ideals, his aims, his hopes during our late past years of luxury and peace have been founded on a misconception of our aims as a nation. . . . We have awakened from an opium-dream of comfort, of ease, of that miserable poltroonery of "the sheltered life." Our wish for indulgence of every sort, our laxity of manners, our wretched sensitiveness to

personal inconvenience, these are suddenly lifted before us in their true guise as the spectres of national decay; and we have risen from the lethargy of our dilettantism to lay them, before it is too late, by the flashing of the unsheathed sword.[2]

There were others who in various ways lent their voices to this astonishing and disturbing view, what amounted to a mood of cultural decadence used to express the hope that the war would purge the culture of "decadence," coded to mean effeminacy in men, a summing up of the reactionary responses that condensed around the public scandals and various litigations involving Oscar Wilde.[3]

Rupert Brooke's "Peace" certainly reflected much of this response to war as an opportunity to cleanse both the spirit and the body, a chance to reclaim manhood put to the service of honor, an especially clear message conveyed in the first octave of his most famous poem:

> Now, God be thanked Who has matched us with His hour,
> And caught our youth, and wakened us from sleeping,
> With hand made sure, clear eye, and sharpened power,
> To turn, as swimmers into cleanness leaping,
> Glad from a world grown old and cold and weary,
> Leave the sick hearts that honour could not move,
> And half-men, and their dirty songs and dreary,
> And all the little emptiness of love![4]

Brooke saw action only briefly at the start of the war and died of a non-combat-related infection aboard a French hospital ship off the coast of Lemnos. He had been on his way to the Dardanelles. His collection *1914 and Other Poems* was published in 1915 and by 1920 had been reprinted twenty-eight times. His *Collected Poems*, published in 1918, went through sixteen impressions in the following ten years. He was certainly one of the most admired poets to write of the war, not only among the public, but among British soldiers as well.[5]

What might be called the "Purgative School" represented the war as an opportunity for true manhood to reassert itself, a chance to cast off luxury, social indifference, and sexual effeminacy, the unhealthy byproducts of Edwardian civilization. While Germany may have been the "enemy without" who gave occasion for the testing through fire, the "enemy within" was the more significant canker in the rose, the more important disease to be blasted away.

The Enemy Is Civilization:
"Reverting to the Primitive" in America

The fascination with purgatives and unsheathed swords might be taken as revelatory of little more than the overwrought imaginings of a repressed and ingrown Edwardian intelligentsia, a set of exclusively Albion concerns; however, when the United States entered the war, a comparable theme was sounded, but one that reflected clearly that Gosse and Brooke were writing at the beginning of the war and largely about how they imagined the war would be conducted. By the time the United States entered the war, almost three years later, romanticized notions of warfare as a test of manhood were completely dispelled.

In order to gain some sense of how this idea was presented to the American public, the inquiry into the American version of warfare and the primitive instincts will focus on the August 1918 issue of *Current Opinion*, a popular American periodical. It offered three articles about the character of men needed to fight the war. Two took up the theme of war as hygienic, serving as both a purgative and a restorative for men who had been rendered retiring or effeminate by the demands of civilized life. This view was presented to the American public as the considered belief not of literary critics, but of Sigmund Freud and of noted medical doctors. These articles apply essentially to the vision of the ground war and the experience of those who fought it.

A third article in the same issue discussed medical findings about the temperament required to be a successful combat pilot. One need only read the three articles to grasp why in the popular imagination the combat pilot became such a source of psychological relief and positive identification.

The article, "Reversion to Primitive Emotions as a Result of the War," endeavors to present a synopsis of two essays written by Sigmund Freud in the spring of 1915, six months after the outbreak of war: "The Disillusionment of the War" and "Our Attitudes Toward Death."[6] Before we consider how the editor presented the ideas of Freud to the American readership of *Current Opinion*, a few words ought to be said about the essays themselves and what motivated Freud to write them.

According to his biographer Ernst Jones, Freud had initially been captivated by the general war fervor. Freud had said that "for the first time in thirty years, he felt himself an Austrian," a reference, among other things, to his sense that the participation of Austrian Jews in the war—including his two sons—would have an integrative function for Jews in general, improving their acceptability. In the opening weeks of the war, Freud found himself quite swept away, declaring, "All my libido is given to Austro-Hungary." His early enthusiasm waned with Austrian losses, and his hope turned to Germany.[7]

Freud summed up his understanding of what the war represented in a letter written at the end of 1914 to Dr. Frederik van Eeden, a Dutch psychopathologist and man of letters who disagreed with Freud's theories but who maintained a long-standing acquaintance with him. The letter was published in German by van Eeden in a weekly periodical, *De Amsterdammner*, on January 17, 1917. In it Freud argued that the "cruelties and injustices for which the most civilized nations are responsible" in the war, as well as the "different way in which they judge their own lies and wrong-doings and those of their enemies," and the "general lack of insight" demonstrate the validity of the central thesis of psychoanalysis: the "primitive, savage and evil impulses of mankind have not vanished in any of its individual members, but persist, although in a repressed state, in the unconscious . . . and lie in wait for opportunities of becoming active once more." Moreover, the intellect or reason is feeble, "a plaything and tool of our instincts and affects."[8]

Freud's "The Disillusionment of the War" reflects upon the prewar belief in progress. "Progress" was conceived as demonstrating an evolutionary process represented by three general stages: the primitive, the barbaric, and the civilized, with the civilized defined as both the most advanced state and one epitomized by the white, European races. While offering a critique of this optimism as itself illusory, Freud also reproduced its underlying assumptions. He associated the "primitive" with the instinctual. The "instincts" are universal in all men, they represent "primal needs," and while these cover a range of human impulses, two of them include selfishness and cruelty, which civilized social organization converts through cultural influences to altruistic behaviors. Freud here reproduced the discourse that legitimated pitting the "civilized" nations of Europe against the "primitive" peoples suited for colonization. The construction of the world as divided between the "primitive" and the "civilized" became an explanatory model useful for representing history as uniform, evolutionary with a purpose, and favoring Europe; it was also a kind of a "map" of the world, a configuration that determined who stood "outside" history in a natural or primitive state and who were the makers of history, with the former becoming part of "history" once they could be made the beneficiaries of more advanced societies. The discourse of the "primitive" and the "civilized" also served as a guide to the human psyche, which contains this history as a synchronous internal history and map: the forces of "civilization" curb and control the "primitive" instincts. The "problem" the war posed to the social consciousness of Europe, the disillusioning factor, as Freud saw it, was quite literally that it was occurring among civilized nations, instead of being directed, as Europeans had led themselves to believe war should and would be, toward civilizing and pacifying primitive peoples or barbaric nations.[9]

An additional source of the disillusionment was the conduct of the war itself, because, Freud argued, it violated civilized expectations— a general belief in restraint that pictured war, if it did come,

> as a chivalrous passage of arms, which would limit itself to establishing the superiority of one side in the struggle, while as far as possible avoiding acute suffering that could contribute nothing to the decision and

granting complete immunity for the wounded who had to withdraw from the contest, as well as for the doctors and nurses who devoted themselves to their recovery. There would, of course, be the utmost consideration for the non-combatant classes of the population—for women who take no part in war-work, and for the children who, when they are grown up, should become on both sides one another's friends and helpers.[10]

Freud's understanding of the effect of the war on social consciousness draws a line between the "primitive" and the "civilized." He joined those who saw in the war a stripping away of the veneer of civilization to reveal the underlying primitive impulses that have been masked by the repressive forces of culture.

With this brief introduction, we turn to how the *Current Opinion* article represented Freud's ideas to the general readership. "Reversion to Primitive Emotions as a Result of the War," as its title signals, focuses popular understanding on this aspect of Freud's analysis, appropriating it to the purpose of inspiring men to see the war as a positive opportunity to cast aside the repressive and emasculating restraints of "civilization."

The article focuses particular attention on the Freudian dichotomy distinguishing "primitive man" from "civilization," with civilization functioning to suppress the primitive qualities of masculine nature, particularly as they relate to aggression and sexuality. "War," the article summarizes, "strips off the . . . deposits of civilization and makes the primitive man in us reappear." This sounds as if it might lay the foundation for a thorough indictment of warfare, but instead the accusations are laid at the feet of civilization, which because it requires men to suppress their primitive instincts makes them—and here the article quotes Freud—"live above their means" and become "civilized hypocrites."

The attendant "distorted [masculine] characters" result from "inhibited impulses" which seek opportunities to express themselves. These aggressive impulses are not suppressed in the primitive man, who demonstrates a straightforward willingness always to "kill a stranger" and who denies the possibility of his own death. These impulses have simply been "covered by a thin veneer of 'civilization'; all are ready to break out, with pristine vigor, if afforded opportunity." Realizing this, Freud asks (rhetorically), "Shall we not turn around and admit the truth?"—which is that "civilization" has masked or repressed these primitive impulses. Here the article quotes Freud at length:

> War . . . forces us again to be heroes who cannot believe in their own death; it stamps all strangers as enemies whose death we ought to cause or wish. . . . Shall we not admit that in our civilized attitude towards death we have again lived psychologically beyond our means? . . . Were it not better to give death the place to which it is entitled both in reality and in our thoughts and to reveal a little more of our unconscious attitude towards death which up to now we have so carefully suppressed?

Freud is quoted to enforce the disparaging conclusion that civilization softens the spirit:

> We do not dare to contemplate a number of undertakings that are dangerous but really indispensable, such as aeroplane flights, expeditions to distant countries and experiments with explosive substances.

Men do not "dare" these things because they feel tied to the apron-strings of mothers and wives, and the corollary obligations to one's children:

> We are paralyzed by the thought of who is to replace the son to his mother, the husband to his wife, or the father to his children, should an accident occur.

"Civilization"—understood here as essentially the result of there being women and children in the world—thus makes a man insipid because he fears to risk his own death. What seems implicitly condemned is the man who seeks secure (and hence dull and routinized) employment to assure that he can provide for the bourgeois family, who conforms to social convention and seeks safety in numbers. War strips away the "veneer" of the professional middle class: a man can only become fully a man again when called to the dangers of the battlefield.

What is taken as the most important aspect of Freud's analysis is the dichotomy that pits the "primitive," the instinctive, the willingness to kill another, the belief in one's immortality, and the positive values of risk, progress, and "truth" against "civilization," "hypocrisy," fear of one's own death, familial love and attachment, and "inhibitions" about killing others or risking one's own life.[11]

The role of "civilization" in suppressing the natural or primitive masculine nature is reiterated in the second article in the same issue of *Current Opinion:* "The Advantages of Fear in Battle: Courage of the Soldier Not So Important as Heroic Souls Think," a report on a study by Dr. George T. W. Patrick on the role of fear in battle.[12] Patrick framed the issue as did Freud, arguing that modern society suppresses the primal masculine instincts:

> Fear and courage are deep-seated elemental emotions and there has been very little change in respect to them in historic times. Modern invention and modern science have made a new world for us. They have changed our manner of living, they have changed our environment. . . . They have surrounded us with comforts and conveniences and luxuries. They have improved beyond belief our food, our clothes and our homes; but both the human body and the human mind are about the same as they were thousands of years ago.

This analysis reiterates the belief—or fear—that the blessings of civilization are emasculating, but Patrick is closer to Gosse than to Freud in assigning the cause to the comforts made possible by science and technology rather than to mothers, wives, and children.

Dr. Patrick is quoted as reassuring on the point that the essential masculine instincts remain and are permitted to flourish once a man goes off to war:

Writers on the war tell us that when the blacksmith, the farmer, the teacher, the salesman, meet at the training-camp, put on their suits of khaki, get into the swing of military life . . . [they] become new men, strange to their friends and to themselves. But this is not quite accurate. They become not new men, but old men, racially old, old fighters. . . . Pugnacity and ferocity in the life of the civilian may never be exhibited, but they are there as slumbering instincts. Let the occasion arise, let the environment be favorable, and these old passions will blaze into life again.

Dr. Patrick seems to approve of war because it permits "old passions" to blaze. The point singled out for emphasis has to do with the role of fear in warfare:

One of the delusions on the subject of battle, encouraged by a defective psychology, relates to heroes. An army of heroic souls would be undisciplined, liable to defeat and certainly incapable of mass-action in the technical sense. The fact is that fear in the soldier is of advantage because it stimulates concerted action, the tendency to cling to the regimental or company formation, to obey the word of command. One must be an extreme individualist to act heroically, which means stepping out of the crowd, doing the exceptional. Team-work is the tendency of the timid. Let no soldier, therefore . . . have any fear of fear. Fear is good for him.

The observation indicates that by August 1918 the conditions of trench warfare were sufficiently known to prevent Northcliffe's version from being taken as entirely credible or desirable. Northcliffe pitted the initiative, inventiveness, and zest for war exhibited by the British, Canadian, and American soldiers against the unimaginative, obedient character of the German soldiers, who could only act en masse. But the latter qualities are seen as essential to fighting in the trenches, while the individualistic qualities praised by Northcliffe are seen as a liability.

If the attributes that are taken as least desirable in the ground soldier are reversed, they provide a profile of the attributes assigned to the combat pilots: the "hero" is the "extreme individualist" who "steps from the crowd"; one who is interested neither in "team-work" nor constrained by the bonds of obedience to strict military discipline; one who can exhibit "pugnacity and ferocity," and who relies upon his own initiative rather than upon orders; one who survives not because he uses fear to seek safety in numbers but because he casts fear aside to confront the enemy alone. In other words, the essential attributes assigned particularly to those combat pilots who obtained "roving commissions" seeking the enemy on their own initiative.

That the appeal of the ace resided in the stark contrast between his role and that of the infantryman is reinforced by the third article in the August 1918 *Current Opinion*, "Who Makes the Best Aviators?" It asserts at the outset that the determining factor in air combat is the individual rather than the machine: "much of the trouble ascribed to machines and motors is due to individuals." Claiming that there is a distinct "flying temperament," the article summarizes the findings of Dr. H. Graeme Anderson of the British air service:

> The ideal aviator must have good judgment, he must be courageous, and not upset by fear, even if conscious of the perils of his lot. He must be cool in emergencies, able to take quick and careful decisions and to act accordingly. His reaction times must never be delayed—he must be ever alert, as mental sluggishness in flying spells disaster.

It is difficult to imagine how any man between eighteen and thirty—which, the article states, is the ideal range of ages for becoming a pilot—who read the three articles could possibly want to be anything other than a combat pilot, or how any reader who remained behind on the homefront could feel anything except the strongest positive identification with pilots' heroic attributes. Taken together, the articles suggest that the man who avoids war is to be pitied only slightly more than the man who goes but winds up in the infantry; the man to be envied and admired is the one who can qualify to be a pilot. The full realization of masculine virtues—the risk and initiative of the hero who is in command of his own fate—is reserved for him.

The advent of the ace salvaged the warrior from the image of a man who had to rely on fear and unthinking conformity to survive in a modern, mechanized war. In addition the ace obviated the choice Patrick and Gosse both argued had to be made between "civilization" (meaning material progress and its comforts) or "war," which permits a man to be a man because the decadent and emasculating corruptions of "civilized" living are purged. The fruits of science and technology—in the form of the plane mounted with a machine gun—served to enhance rather than supersede the expression of civilized violence; technology, in other words, made it possible to be an admirable fighting man.

The *Current Opinion* articles also illuminate why cloaking combat pilots in the mantle of the chivalric knight proved such a popular reassurance. Freud, Patrick, and Gosse all seemed to agree that the cost of civilization was too high; it required a man to "live beyond his means" in the sense that he could not be fully realized as a man unless the "veneer" of civilization was relinquished. But Freud's definition of "civilization"—or the rot within it—differed from both Patrick and Gosse. What is wrong with the Freudian Civilization is not that it has too many material comforts; rather, it is a repressive social order that requires a man either revert to the primitive—abandoning the "civilized" life—or become a "distorted personality."

This is not much of a choice. Newbolt Man promised altogether the more attractive option with the image of the Happy Warrior. The image of "primitive man" or of the Freudian hero is of someone motivated by the desire to kill repeatedly or habitually—a sensibility that Freud quite rightly noted is not generally admired in civilized society. On the other hand, the chivalric virtues were made by Newbolt and others into both the source and the epitome of civilized behavior. Far from being a sign of emasculation or inhibition, civilized conduct originated with the knight and continued always to be practiced by the elite class. The warrior, or more precisely, the officers, represented the influence of the ruling class and therefore possessed those refined sensibilities that tempered violent aggression through a code of honor calling for fair play and Christian restraint. Conceiving the pilot as a knight-errant therefore obviated the need to choose between a primitive manhood and the Freudian repressive "civilization." Because Newbolt Man was a warrior, he was also the progenitor and guardian of all civilized values, and responsible for passing the guerdon to his son. In the Happy Warrior, aggression, violence, civilization, procreation, and the family exist in a necessary harmony.

Victims and Warriors:
Cultural Constructions of Masculinity

The infantry soldier, immobile and pinned down with his comrades in a trench while being bombarded, was so common an image on both sides of the Western Front that it is possible to ignore the differences in the accounts and particularly what they reveal about cultural definitions of masculinity; but these finer distinctions warrant attention because they bring into even sharper focus the appeal of the combat aces to the imagination in terms of an idealized mastery of one's destiny as opposed to a primitive reactivity.

The most significant factor is the comparative importance of "chance" in the odds of survival for the ground soldier and the pilot. The perception that the ground soldier was a mere victim of impersonal weapons meant that chance, rather than the test of courage, was the decisive factor. In this equation, who one was had little or nothing to do with how one met one's fate. The implication that came with associating the ground warrior with the "primitive" was ultimately that the ground soldier in a highly mechanized war was not a heroic agent of his own history and the destiny of civilization, but was instead caught up in what amounted literally to the machinations of history.

How the experience of the ground soldier was understood—and is understood—reflects considerable cultural differences in how masculinity was idealized. British pilot Cecil Lewis, whose postwar account of his experiences as a British pilot in *Sagittarius Rising* (1936) is one of the very few pilot's memoirs which is also memorable literature, emphasized the distinction between the infantry who endured assaults and the pilot who sought battle, but he interpreted both as forms of courage:

> Courage takes various forms. With us it lay more in audacity than in tenacity. We admire in others the qualities lacking in ourselves, so the Infantry admired our nerve while we admired their phlegm. Speaking personally, I think I should have gone out of my mind under a heavy trench bombardment. My instinct in an emergency has always been to do something—attack or run away. To sit and wait to be blown to pieces requires characteristics I have not got, so I can never honour enough the plodding men who bore the burden of the war, who gave us victory (for what it proved to be worth) because they stuck it.[13]

Lewis identified what the infantry endured as a sign of character, as requiring an act of courage, but it was a courage that placed one's fate well beyond one's control: "to sit and wait to be blown to pieces."

Recent American representations, by way of contrast, emphasize the soldier as passive recipient, prevented by the nature of mechanized warfare from functioning as a soldier in any traditional sense.[14] The experience of the ground soldier under artillery barrage is held up as a singular example of victimization and helplessness rather than as exemplary of a courage of endurance. Ronald Shaffer, in his *America in the Great War,* concluded his account of how soldiers reacted under artillery bombardment with the observation: "under bombing and artillery attack, troops felt utterly helpless, incapable of responding to what was being done to them, uncertain, paralyzed." Similarly, David M. Kennedy in his *Over Here: The First World War and American Society* commented that "many men wrote of their sense of outraged helplessness while being shelled" and pointed to the "feeling of impotence" as the singular characteristic of the men who fought on the ground.[15]

The conclusions of social historians reflect how the American soldiers described their senses of themselves in battle. Shaffer based his conclusions on published nonfiction accounts, including letters and diaries. He quoted as typical a letter by Lt. Hervey Allen, who wrote: "To be shelled is the worst thing in the world. It is impossible to adequately imagine it. In absolute darkness we simply lay and trembled from sheer nerve tension." And a similar account by Corporal Pierce: "I am soon a nervous wreck. I lose control as the bombardment wears on into hours. . . . I want to scream and run and throw myself. . . . When I hear the whistle of an approaching shell, I dig my toes into the ground and push on the walls of the dugout."[16]

What is suggested in the equation between artillery bombardments and paralyzed helplessness is not so much an indictment of war itself as of how it was conducted; that the artillery barrage and aerial bombardment against troops in fixed positions meant that the soldier could not act as a soldier. William L. Langer commented, "shellfire has always seemed a bit unfair to me. Somehow it makes one feel so helpless, there is no chance of reprisal for the individual man. The advantage is all with the shell and you have no comeback."[17] Similarly, Alan Seeger, whose very popular collection of poems celebrating the experience of war earned him the title in some quarters of "the American Rupert Brooke," wrote to his father that he disliked the experience of artillery bombardment because he objected to "being harried like this by an invisible enemy and standing up against all the dangers of battle without any of its exhilaration or enthusiasm."[18]

These accounts imply a conception of what warfare is supposed to be and, therefore, how a soldier ought to behave. He should be able to see his opponent, not be assaulted by an "invisible enemy," and he should be able to react to his opponent, to "fight back." In the absence of those opportunities, the soldier appears to cease to be a soldier, ceases even to have the qualities of courage and tenacity that Lewis ascribed to him; instead, the characterization is one of a helpless victim, trapped, with no choices to make.

This characterization differs markedly as well from that offered in the best-known account of trench warfare, Erich Maria Remarque's *All Quiet on the Western Front*, where a particular kind of agency is gained from the stripping away of the trappings of civilization. In one scene, the small band of men at the center of the narrative come under heavy bombardment:

> Beside us lies a fair-headed recruit in utter terror. He has buried his face in his hands, his helmet has fallen off. I fish hold of it and try to push it

back on his head. He looks up, pushes the helmet off and like a child creeps under my arm, his head close to my breast. The little shoulders heave. . . . I let him be.

The scene reintroduces a recurrent theme in the novel, which is that the war brings forward in the men capacities for nurturing their comrades, seen here specifically as if the experienced soldier is a parent tenderly comforting a frightened child.

As the barrage subsides the narrator rouses the recruit from his terror, reassuring him, "You'll get used to it soon."

Gradually he comes to. Then suddenly he turns fiery red and looks confused. Cautiously he reaches his hand to his behind and looks at me dismally.

I understand at once: Gun-shy. . . . "That's no disgrace," I reassure him: "Many's the man before you has had his pants full after the first bombardment."

The indictment handed down in *All Quiet on the Western Front* is not that the war rendered the men who fought it passive or deprived men of their masculinity, making them impotent victims. The arc of a man's experience in the war is a reversion to babyhood and dependency as the necessary precursor to being reborn into a male society governed by primal instinct. The war, says the narrator, "has transformed us into unthinking animals in order to give us the weapon of instinct." The animal here identified is one who survives in a pack, in company with others, not the lone hunter: "It [the war] has awakened in us the sense of comradeship, so that we escape the abyss of solitude."[19] If there is any positive value identified by the narrator as arising from the experience of war, it is the collective experience of being forced to endure by instinct for survival:

Distinctions, breeding, education are changed, are almost blotted out and hardly recognizable any longer. . . . It is as though formerly we were coins of different provinces; and now we are melted down, and all bear the same stamp. . . . First we are soldiers and afterwards, in a strange and shamefaced fashion, individual men as well. It is a great brotherhood, which adds something of the good-feeling of the folk-song, of the feeling of solidarity of convicts, and of the desperate loyalty to one another of men condemned to death, to a condition of life arising out of the midst of death. . . . If one wants to appraise it, it is at once heroic and banal—but who wants to do that?[20]

The sense that "first, we are soldiers" is heroic because it is achieved under such singular circumstances and banal because of its commonness. The chief foe of humanity is not identified as how the war was fought—the impersonality of the artillery barrage. The enemy in *All Quiet on the Western Front* is the war itself and the callous indifference of the older generation who encouraged their sons to enter the maw of death.

The differences in how the ground soldier of the Western Front has been understood reveal both prewar expectations about how a war ought to be fought and the changed conception of the significance of warfare and the warrior formed since World War I. Lewis in his postwar account honored the courage of the soldiers' tenacity with the bitter awareness of the futility of the war itself, as World War II loomed on the horizon. Recent American historians, attentive to the traditional American polarities of "individualism" and "dependence," or of "the self-made man" and "victimization," notice the representation of the soldier as "victim" and "helpless." Remarque finds dignity in the soldiers' capacities to respond to each other in caring, even motherly ways, and in the survival value of reverting to the instinctual behavior of the hunting pack.

The differences in the representations undermine easy equations between a natural masculine instinct for violent aggression and the inevitability of warfare because they rather clearly indicate that how masculinity is understood is a product of cultural understandings, beliefs, and imaginings. More specifically for our purposes, the differences in how the ground soldier was represented are indices in both the United States and Great Britain of how far short the experience of the trenches fell from the idealized conception of the hero who carried the weight of civilization on his shoulders.

The Combat Pilot as Master of His Fate

It is in contrast with the ground soldier, then, that the combat pilot gains cultural potency as an image. The combat pilot was a warrior who could see his enemy and fight back. Central to the appeal of this image was the belief that when war is conducted in this way, the warrior held his fate in his own hands because it was his native abilities and character—not impersonal and implacable force—that determined the outcome of the encounter.

This way of understanding the combat pilot was conventional, often repeated, and held as an article of faith by many of the pilots as what distinguished them from their hapless countrymen trapped in the trenches. Sholto Douglas was a British combat pilot in World War I, served as an air marshall for the RFC during World War II, and subsequently became head of British Airlines. In 1963 he published what he intended would be the first volume in his autobiography. *Years of Combat* is an account of his childhood and especially of his service in World War I. Reflecting upon his thoughts as an experienced pilot in March 1918 Douglas comments:

> success . . . depended, far more than in any other forms of fighting, on individual skill, nerve and courage. In fighting on the land or at sea it was largely a fluke, dictated by pure chance, whether one came through with a whole skin or fell by the wayside. One sat in a hole in the ground on land, or behind a sheet of armour plating at sea, and it was purely a matter of chance whether a bullet or a shell hit you or the man standing next to you. But that was far from being the case in fighting in the air. If you were alert and watchful and able to think a split second faster than the man against whom you were fighting, and if you could shoot a shade straighter and with an ounce or two more nerve, then ninety-nine times out of a hundred you were able to beat your opponent. But it was up to the individual to do that, and chance played only a comparatively small part in the encounter. . . . I felt that if I were killed in the air it would be very largely because of my own stupidity or lack of skill.[21]

Similarly, Sir Walter Raleigh, who wrote the official British history of the air war, said:

> Those who were privileged to watch the performance of our flying men in the war know that there is developed in them a temper not less remarkable and not less worthy of cultivation—the temper of the air. War in the air demands a quickness of thought and nerve greater than is exacted by any other kind of war. It is a deadly and gallant tournament.[22]

While these observations were written after the war, they reflect the popular understanding of the combat pilot that emerged during the war. The qualities the British felt distinguished the combat pilot from ground soldiers were echoed by the Americans. In one of his letters Victor Chapman wrote, "this flying is much too romantic to be real modern war with all its horrors. There is something so unreal and fairlylike about it, which ought to be told and described by Poets, as Jason's Voyage was."[23]

Conveying the positive image of the pilot as in command of his own destiny was not, however, left to arbitrary or haphazard means. In May 1917 Lord Northcliffe agreed to be assigned to the British war mission to the United States. Some indication of the British influence on the American representation of the combat pilot is perhaps gained from reading James Middleton's article, "Manhunters of the Air." Middleton reports the episode that earned the RFC pilot Colonel Rees the Victoria Cross and concludes with the remark, "Colonel Rees is now in this country, cooperating with our Government in the development of our air fleet."[24]

Middleton's representation of the air war reproduces Northcliffe's version of the ground war. National character is symbolized by how individuals fight: The French and British pilots, as well as the Americans who fly with the Lafayette Escadrille, possess superior virtues and abilities that cannot be fostered in a military autocracy; they are qualities nurtured only in nations that emphasize personal initiative and other liberal values. The resort to the morally inferior tactics of cheating, ambush, ganging up, and running from a fair fight simply reveal the

German pilots as the uninspired, machine-like bullies and cowards inevitably developed by a Prussian culture. Unquestionably, the altogether better qualified and morally superior Allies will prevail.

Middleton advises his readers: "The airplane . . . presents new problems of morale which the German military philosophy has not prepared for." He repeats the oft-stated belief that the German military trains its infantry "as more or less inarticulate units in a huge machine. Initiative is notoriously not the prime quality of the German soldier. He fights as a mass, shoulder to shoulder, under the constant supervision of his officer." It is this "native lack of German initiative" which "explains the fact that practically all the fighting takes place over the German lines." Middleton agrees that there are distinct advantages to this strategy—that their planes do not fall into enemy hands and their wounded pilots land in their own territory. But Middleton obtusely brushes these aside as mere excuses for a general lack of the needed virtues:

> This all seems sound logic but, as is usual in all German tactics, it ignores the moral and spiritual side. A policy of waiting to be attacked hardly serves to develop that dash and spirit and eagerness for adventure which, above all, comprise the efficient airmen.

Naturally, these virtues reside with the Allies because aerial combat "is emphatically individual; the aviator must do his own thinking, meet sudden situations with instantaneous decisions of his own." That British and French pilots "penetrate" fifteen or twenty miles into German territory accounts for their "superior prowess" because it has made them "far more skillful and intrepid than the Germans."

No reader could tell from these conclusions that a mere four months earlier the outnumbered German air forces, relying on a defensive strategy and formation flying, had decimated the British RFC, which followed an offensive strategy. The resort to disciplined tactics and formation flying simply confirmed for Middleton the mental conformity and unwillingness to fight on equal terms characteristic of the German fighter: "the German aviator, though he is commonly less resourceful and skillful than the French, is not lacking in courage. But he still prefers, even in the air, something akin to that close formation to which he is accustomed on land. This is the reason that he usually flies in squadrons." The unwillingness to fight on equal terms is also indicated by the resort to ambush and deception.

Middleton reiterates the point at the end of the article, when he reports the encounter that earned Rees the Victoria Cross. Rees managed to fight his way clear of ten German planes by bringing down three and putting the remaining seven to flight. Middleton has no trouble explaining why the Germans were in a group of ten: "The Germans much prefer to fly in squadrons, and take particular joy in overwhelming an enemy by sheer force of numbers. It is the old German land tactic once more applied to the air."

By war's end, the desire to believe that in the air war the warrior's character determines his fate had taken a firm hold over the popular imagination in the United States. The belief led, as one might reasonably expect, to some rather strained locutions, none more so than that offered by Laurence La Tourette Driggs in his introduction to Eddie Rickenbacker's autobiography, which Driggs ghostwrote. Readers were introduced to *Fighting the Flying Circus* with this hyperbole:

> Never once in all his fighting career did Captain Rickenbacker permit an enemy pilot to injure him!
>
> This remarkable fact at once forces the conclusion that our American Ace of Aces was not only superior to the enemy airmen he vanquished, but by saving himself for the continued service of his country he was superior to all those rival expert duelists who, despite their extraordinary ability as pilots and sharpshooters, yet unfortunately lacked that necessary judgment to preserve from wounds their valuable persons for further encounters with the enemy.[25]

Driggs insists by inference that skilled pilots who are severely wounded or killed in combat have themselves to blame, and he goes even further in suggesting that it amounts to something like disloyalty to the nation—

a putting oneself first rather than submitting one's temper to prudent restraints in order to serve the nation as a warrior without getting killed. This absurdity reflects in part that Driggs is juggling two contending factors. One is the celebrity associated with America's ace of aces, the other is the military's judgment that the glamorizing of the daredevil flying of the "lone wolves" worked against military aims, particularly as disciplined tactics dependent upon formation flying took hold. Strained though Driggs's tone of pietistic judgment may seem, his effort to celebrate Rickenbacker as both an individualist and an exemplar of military self-discipline takes to an extreme logical conclusion the reasoning used to elevate the role of the pursuit pilot to an exceptional form of combat. Most notably, Driggs reinforces a fantasy—already well developed by the end of the war—of a hypermasculine prowess that made the combat pilot a man who held his fate in his own hands.

A Hero's Death: Baron von Richthofen

A significant number of the top aces who flew over the Western Front were killed in combat, and given the symbolism attached to the character of the combat pilot, it is not surprising that considerable attention has been paid to discovering or to speculating upon how the aces met their fates. Particularly significant are those instances when a famous pilot may have been downed by ground fire rather than having lost a duel in the sky.

The most impressive example is the controversy over the death of Germany's most famous ace, Manfred von Richthofen. Known as the Red Baron, the Ringmaster of the Flying Circus, he flew his last flight on April 21, 1918 (see Figure 11). He was downed while flying in low pursuit of a British plane over Australian lines near Vaux, in the region of the Somme. A dispute soon arose over whether his death could rightfully be claimed by Capt. Roy Brown, flying with the 209 Squadron, or by gunners with the 53rd Australian Field Artillery. The conflicting claims quickly became controversial and remain so to this day among those who maintain an intense interest in the history of the war in the air over the Western Front, and in von Richthofen's career in particular.

Figure 11. A stern Manfred von Richthofen was represented as the epitome of German "efficiency." He continued the development of German air combat, which relied on organized and disciplined defensive tactics. From Military History Institute.

The point of reviewing the conflicting claims over von Richthofen's death is not to establish which service ought to receive the credit; rather, it is to notice that there was such an intense controversy and one that continued well after the war had ended. It mattered little to Richthofen himself whether he was killed by a bullet from the air or from the ground; nor can one identify what strictly material military aim might have been served by assigning credit either way. This is especially borne in on the imagination of anyone who visits the site near Vaux where Richthofen crashed. It lies east of Amien in the rural region along the valley of the Somme River. The chimney of an abandoned brick kiln is the only landmark in a landscape that in the summer offers the eye rolling fields of golden ripening grain. Richthofen's plane crashed near the kiln. There is nothing in view to indicate that this sector had any particular military value, nor does the landscape offer any obvious evidence that a long and bloody trench war was fought here. His death did not change the course of a battle or turn the tide of a war.

Considering the number of men who died in this sector, and how many remains of the dead have inevitably been incorporated into this gentle earth, the quarreling over how one individual lost his life seems grotesque and absurd. The death of Richthofen, for instance, might have been represented as a sign of how effectively the air service and the ground artillery coordinated their efforts, giving credit to the pilots for luring Richthofen close to the ground, or driving him down, possibly wounded, into the range of the waiting Lewis guns. There is an uncanny oddness about both the persistence with which each service tried to gain credit, and the insistence upon not only claiming it for the air service, but upon making sure that Richthofen received a hero's funeral. To appreciate that oddness, and how much it ultimately reveals about the need to assure that the combat pilot was understood as the master of his fate and not at the mercy of chance, requires a review of the circumstances of von Richthofen's demise.

Because he carried identification in his wallet, Richthofen was immediately identified by the Australian and New Zealand soldiers who gathered around the plane, which fell on the Allied side. As Richthofen's body bled from multiple wounds, souvenir hunters began stripping the plane of its identifying marks, its cowling, brass clock, petrol tank, the instruments, the red fabric covering the plane, guns, and propeller—the latter of which was made into a number of paperweights—as well as Richthofen's boots, gloves, and identification disk.

As a sign of how important the dispute was over how he had been downed, Gen. H. S. Rawlinson, commander of the British Fourth Army, ordered two separate postmortem examinations. The first of these, conducted on the night of April 21 by a two medical officers from the RAF, concluded death had been caused by a bullet that had passed from the right side and exited half an inch below the left nipple, that the bullet could not have hit the spine, and that the wound could not have been caused by ground fire. On the morning of April 22, four medical officers, representing the Australian Army and Air Force Medical Services and the British Fourth Army, conducted the second postmortem, which contradicted the first. They concluded that the fatal bullet had come from the right and slightly in front of Richthofen, glanced off his spine, and exited on the left side of his chest. Those who examined the body during the second postmortem disagreed with the RAF officers that the fatal bullet could not have come from the ground.

An obvious further indication of the significance attached to this interservice rivalry was given five days later, when despite the conflicting medical reports, a dispatch from Gen. John Salmond at RAF headquarters gave credit for downing Richthofen to Capt. Roy Brown and a recommendation of a bar to add to his Distinguished Service Cross. One month later, however, General Rawlinson sent through Maj. Gen. John T. Hobbs his personal thanks to Gunner Robert Buie of the 53rd Australian Artillery for having downed Richthofen.[26]

The gruesome rivalry for credit and the relentless souvenir hunting—which continued even as Richthofen's body was prepared for burial—gives some indication of the celebrity attached to the Red Baron. At twenty-five Richthofen was an international hero, credited with eighty victories, his exploits featured in newsreels as well as magazines and news articles on both sides of the Atlantic. The German command, concerned that their top ace would be killed, had suggested that he accept a ground position, such as an inspector, but he had refused. The Allies were just as aware of how significant his death would be. It would provide a boost to the harried British flyers and demoralize their German counterparts. To make sure of the latter, a photograph was taken of Richthofen's body with the intention of dropping prints over German airbases as evidence of his death.[27]

The day following his death, Richthofen was buried with full military honors in the local cemetery of the village of Bretangle, with full press coverage. The funeral was notably an RAF affair. The procession from 3 Squadron was led by an honor guard of twelve soldiers, followed by official mourners, an infantry platoon, other soldiers, and townspeople. The coffin was borne by six RAF officers. As his coffin was lowered into the grave just outside the village, a thirty-six-volley salute was fired by the honor guard, while a line of officers filed past to pay their last tribute and to lay flowered wreaths on the grave, pictures of which were dropped from RFC planes onto German airbases (see Figure 12).

The cross placed at the head of the grave was fashioned from a four-blade propeller.[28] That night, French villagers, angry that a German had been buried in their cemetery, desecrated the grave and took the propeller that had been used as a cross. Another was soon provided by General Sir John Monash, who warned the mayor of Bretangle that further interference with the gravesite would lead him to remove his headquarters from the vicinity. There were no further incidents.[29] The evening of the funeral, an RAF pilot flew over von Richthofen's base to drop a photograph of the grave and a note to say that their commander had been shot down the day before and had been "buried with full military honours."[30]

Reports of Richthofen's death, along with pictures of the funeral, were disseminated widely in Europe and in the United States. The publicity provoked the German press to what could only be understood as a narrow-minded and ungenerous outburst against the funereal honors granted to their fallen hero. The *Deutsche Tagezeitung* offered this commentary by Count Reventlow:

These honors are nothing but the manifestation of British self-advertisement of their "chivalry" [or sportsmanlike knightliness]. . . . For our part we cannot consider the honors given to the remains of von Richthofen as sincere. The English press is full of them, and with characteristic blatancy blares about British magnanimity. But they say nothing about the huge prizes of money that were offered to the pilot who could kill Richthofen. In fact, these must have amounted to an enormous sum. And this explains the bitter and "noble" controversy [over whether RAF Captain Roy Brown or an Australian artillery unit should get credit for the victory] which raged around the corpse of the fallen pilot, for there was cash waiting for the one who inflicted the fatal wound and brought the German machine to earth.[31]

Figure 12. Photograph of Manfred von Richthofen's grave at Bretangle. The British had a propaganda field day with the death and funeral of Baron von Richthofen; pictures of his grave with a note explaining that he had been buried with military honors were dropped over German bases. From British Imperial War Museum.

Such hamfisted propaganda reveals an unwillingness or inability to recognize that messages aimed at the home audience could be quoted verbatim by Germany's enemies—as these comments were in the United States—and used as evidence of the Germans' lack of civilized refinement.

The Germans were upset that their hero had been buried by the British on French soil rather than sent home—where they would have given him an even more heroic burial. In 1925 this demand was met. At the request of Richthofen's mother, his remains were brought to Germany. Large crowds gathered at the train stations in Germany to see the train bearing his coffin, and the body entered Berlin with considerable ceremony. The procession through the Berlin Gate to the final resting place in the Invaliden Cemetery was the "most widely attended service in the history of the German capital."[32]

The reaction of the Germans to the British ceremony and honors reflects the understanding on both sides that the Red Baron had tremendous iconic value. His death and the honors accorded him gave the British an opportunity to demonstrate precisely the chivalric values that Reventlow identifies as scarcely veiled gloating. In his account of the funeral written for *National Geographic*, L. L. Driggs concluded by quoting from the comments of C. G. Grey—who wrote the foreword to von Richthofen's diary when it was published in English.

> There is not one in the corps who would not gladly have killed him [von Richthofen]. But there is not one who would not equally gladly have shaken hands with him had he been brought down without being killed or who would not so have shaken hands if brought down by him. . . . He was a brave man and a clean fighter. May he rest in peace.

"Who can now say," asks Driggs to draw the obvious point, "the day of chivalry is passed?"

Assigning the cause of death to an RAF pilot obviously made it possible to draw upon the already familiar chivalry of the knights of the air and reinforce its significance for the public at home and the watching world. The British were keenly aware that the exact way that

Richthofen met his end mattered a great deal in terms of the significance assigned to it. Testimony is given to this awareness by Robert Buie, the gunner credited by General Rawlinson with downing von Richthofen. Writing in 1961 at the age of sixty-eight, Buie, who felt there was never any doubt that ground fire had brought down von Richthofen, recalled the visit he received on May 9, 1918, by General Sir William Birdwood. "He shook hands vigorously with me and remarked that it would have been more fitting had Richthofen been brought down in the air engagement and a great pity also, that he wasn't just wounded and taken prisoner," and then he called Richthofen "a very gallant man" who was nonetheless "better out of the way" because of how successful he had been at downing British planes.[33]

General Birdwood's speculation about the various desirable ways that von Richthofen might have been brought down reflects the interest in the propaganda value of the outcome. The propaganda value of his having been shot down by an RAF pilot was articulated at the time in an issue of the British periodical *Aeroplane:*

> His death is bound to have a gravely depressing effect on the German Flying Service for obviously the younger and less brave will argue that if a von Richthofen cannot survive their chances must be small. Equally his death is an encouragement to every young French and British pilot who can no longer imagine that every skillful German pilot that attacks them is von Richthofen himself.[34]

The morale factor was certainly highly significant as a factor in the RAF's insistence that they claim credit for downing von Richthofen. Two aspects were relevant to morale. The first, which is less immediately obvious than the second, had to do with the desire on the part of the commanders to emphasize squadron discipline over the glamorized vision of individual heroics. Capt. Roy Brown, a Canadian, was in command of the patrols that day and it was he who was credited with downing von Richthofen. He was protecting the newest pilot in his flight, and a friend, 2d Lt. Wilfred R. May. As an irony of history, Manfred von Richthofen's cousin Wolfram had just been assigned to his command. Both commanders had ordered their respective fledglings to stay high above the fray, observing the battle. May, who had been flying above the circling Wolfram, could not resist the easy target, dove on him firing and missed. The two novices wound up in the middle of the fight they had both been observing. Wolfram, whose plane was damaged, made a hasty retreat, leaving May exposed to the Fokkers that quickly surrounded him.

The insistence by the RAF on awarding Brown the exclusive credit for downing Richthofen reinforced the growing importance assigned to group discipline and teamwork. Brown's role in seeking to save the least experienced pilot in the flight, and the lesson of what happens to inexperienced pilots who take lightly the advice of their commanders, were probably not lost on any of the pilots in the sector.

The additional and more obvious morale factor is revealed by May's comment that as terrified as he was to find himself being pursued, "Had I known it was Richthofen, I should probably have passed out on the spot."[35] The remark indicates how potent Richthofen was not simply as an efficient commander and combatant, but as the symbol of an overwhelming skill. The value to morale cannot be underestimated of demonstrating that even the most deadly of the German aces could be brought down by another pilot acting to protect a squadron mate.

The dispute over which service should get credit, the scavenging of souvenirs from both the plane and Richthofen's body, the contradictory autopsy reports, the RAF funeral with full military honors, the insistence that the gravesite be preserved over the objections of the local townspeople elevated the significance of Richthofen's death, assuring him legendary status not only for Germans, but for those from the British and Commonwealth nations, and Americans as well. It might seem odd to make such a hero out of one's opponent. Certainly, had his demise been deemed the result at the time of a hail of machine-gun and rifle fire from ground troops, his death would have provided a far less potent message, making Richthofen the victim of something like blind fate, or of the same implacable and anonymous forces as the ground soldier.

On the other hand, for a pilot of his standing to have been brought down by another pilot because of a failure in judgment, or a mistake in tactics, brought home a better lesson for RAF pilots. The lesson needed to fit the prior symbolic constructions attached to the World War I aces, which ran against portraying them as fighting in conjunction with ground forces or as relying upon the ground forces at all. In context, it would have been extremely difficult for the RAF to share the credit with the ground forces, and because of that resistance, the attributes of the aces were reinforced. In the RAF representation of the matter, Richthofen's death demonstrated that in the air war the outcome depended upon the individual's skill and judgment—with the added monition that it depended upon military discipline as well.

The intensity of the dispute over the manner of Richthofen's death illustrates the depth of feeling associated with the distinction between the ground soldier and the pilot, the importance assigned to the ability to separate the kind of war experienced on the ground from the "temperament of the air." The dispute carried within it the contested cultural territory over the values and mores of the industrialized age and, as a corollary, the contested definitions of masculinity.

The most significant aspect of the accounts of von Richthofen's last day, apart from the continuing argument over how he died, is that what happened is obscured by the fog of war; yet, there is a keen unwillingness to acknowledge that as the ultimate reality. The need to know why such a skilled pilot as the Red Baron would allow himself to be exposed to ground fire at such close range remains. Was he still alive when the gunners opened fire on him? Or was he already dead, or nearly so? Was his judgment clouded by anger because he was unable to finish off quickly an obviously inexperienced pilot?[36] That need is the most obvious indication of how important the idea was that the aces were in command of their own destinies, that upon their will and judgment the outcome was determined. If the understanding of the ground soldier as one who was stripped clean of civilized repressions gave support to the emerging modernist critique of civilization, the aces gave proof for a countervailing cultural conservatism that saw the warrior as one epitomizing the highest expression of masculine nature tempered by reason and restraint, a man whose character determined his fate.

CHAPTER 11

American Pilots as Symbols
of American Democracy

Until the United States entered the war, Americans who flew into battle did so as members of either the French or British armed forces. Once war was declared, the Lafayette Escadrille was absorbed into the American forces, and new American pilots flew for the United States, either in American squadrons or attached to British squadrons. The advent of the war created the opportunity to transform American pilots into heroes in a national and democratic idiom, to make them living symbols of American democracy.

The new pilots arriving on the Western Front in the last year of the war encountered a reality very different from the air war as advertised. The illusion that a combat pilot held his fate in his own hands confronted the harsh reality that in the fall of 1918 the Allies suffered their greatest losses of the air war. The continuing appeal of the image on the homefront owed much to the technology of communications, and to a reiterated representation, a consistent way of telling the story, which became commonplace and conventional by the end of the war. An additional element lent the image particular authenticity: by the end of the war, pilots were regularly engaged in creating a projected image of themselves as individualistic heroes, reproducing the stereotypes they had internalized for the benefit of the camera, in press interviews, or their autobiographies.

The published accounts of two American pilots illustrate the change from the earlier British reticence about involving pilots in creating their own celebrity, a change the British had also undergone in promoting Billy Bishop's autobiography. The participation of America's ace of aces, Eddie Rickenbacker, in making a faked film documentary about air combat illustrates how the lines between reality and fantasy were blurred by the participation of the pilots themselves in overt propaganda, while the publicity surrounding the death of Quentin Roosevelt illustrates how the idealized image of the boy-knight was appropriated to make meaningful the death of a young American flyer and score a propaganda coup over the Germans. Together they provide an insight into how, after the United States entered the war, pilots were converted into symbols of American democracy.

Black September 1918

The impression Americans on the homefront formed of the air war in 1918 was free of accurate information about the heavy Allied air force losses during what came to be known as Black September 1918, when the combined German air and naval air forces along the Western Front and over the North Sea accounted for the largest losses in a single month among the Allied air forces, exceeding by a considerable factor the casualty figures of April 1917. From January 1918 to the Armistice in November, the RAF had 3,700 combat casualties over the Western Front; in September alone, there were estimated British combat casualties of 588, with 316 killed or missing. Some sense of the increased casualty rates is gained from comparing them with the losses between July 1 (opening of Battle of the Somme) and November 1916, which came to 499 pilots and observers. Some estimates indicate that the average pilot life in France during 1918 was less than six weeks, and that 64 percent of pilots on active duty were killed, wounded, or missing before the end of their first eight-month tour of duty.[1]

The problems of 1918 for the Allied air forces along the Western Front were similar to those of 1917. Inexperienced British pilots continued to fly offensive patrols; they faced a German air force that had increased the number and quality of planes in response to the U.S. entry into the war, and employed tactics that relied on effective discipline and training. British pilots who had sufficient training, in the words of chroniclers of Black September, just to "fly his aircraft straight and level" faced experienced opposite numbers: "To be thrust into the maelstrom of a whirling air-battle was often something which the embryo scouting pilot did not survive." Nor did the British have a model of fighter equal to the capability of the German counterparts.[2]

The Pilot Appropriated: Published Accounts

Against these realities ought to be measured the participation of pilots in reproducing the stereotypes of air battle for the popular imagination. Early on, the accounts of duels in the sky reflected the imaginative renderings of intelligence officers writing publicity for the press in ways which to the pilots' eyes significantly misrepresented their experiences. Sholto Douglas's recollection of how he managed to elude the formidable duo Oswald Boelcke and Max Immelmann on December 29, 1915, offers an excellent example because it differs markedly from accounts of it published during the war. It also provides an unusual example of how a pilot responded to reading two different accounts of a remarkable encounter, one published in the British press and one written by his opponent.

On that day, Douglas was the pilot, flying reconnaissance with Lieutenant Child, while David Glen was flying escort, when they were attacked by six Germans. Glen was shot down, leaving Douglas and Child alone to fend off their six pursuers. Child shot down three. They were harried, outnumbered, running low on fuel, and their engine had been hit. Douglas headed for Allied lines, putting the plane into a spiral dive and flying just above trees, still pursued by enemy aircraft. Childs strafed Germans soldiers, presumably to fend off ground fire. Miraculously, the trailing Fokker abandoned the chase about a mile from the Allied lines.

A report of this encounter was carried in the *Times* of London a week later, January 6, 1916, under the heading: "A Risky Air Dive. British Pilot's Fine Exploit. Six Machines to Two." Commenting on it,

Douglas says: "Some of the fanciful phrasing in this official account, which was obviously written by an Army Intelligence Officer who was not very familiar with the Flying Corps, reads in a somewhat quaint fashion, and parts of it have twists of humour that must surely have been quite unintentional." The report of the fight explained that "its pilot [Douglas] decided that escape could only be sought by a very risky dive to within 20 ft. of the ground—risky in that it necessitated a descent by very steep spirals at a speed of quite 100 miles an hour, with little room to recover. Only very delicate and confident handling could ensure the success of this manoeuvre, which only the absence of other means of escape could justify." Douglas comments: "There was no delicacy about what I did with the B.C.2c on that particular occasion: I was tearing around for all I was worth, intent only on getting away from those Fokkers, and I was much too scared ever to be aware of the confidence with which I was so pleasantly credited" (120). The official accounts faithfully reproduced the British official response to the Fokker Scourge, which was to claim that the outcome of the duel in the air was determined by the quality of the flyer rather than the technology of the plane.

Douglas later learned that two of the Fokker pilots were Oswald Boelcke and Max Immelmann. About a year after this encounter, Boelcke's diary was published in Germany. Douglas's friend Wilfrid Freeman had the account of the encounter with Douglas translated and sent it to him. Douglas included Boelcke's account in his autobiography; this is how Boelcke described the encounter:

That was a fine fight. I had to deal with a tough fellow, who defended himself stoutly. But I forced him on to the defensive at once. Then he tried to escape me by turns, etc., and made an effort to get at me on my weak side. He did not succeed, but the only success I scored was forcing his machine even further down. . . . Finally he could defend himself no longer, because I had mortally wounded his observer. It was now a comparatively easy job to shoot the fellow down, but when we got to eight hundred metres I ran out of ammunition because I had previously used some of it on two others. That was his salvation. We now circled around each other, but neither could do the other any harm. Finally Immelmann came to my aid, and the fight began all over again. I kept on attacking merrily, so as to confuse the Englishman. We managed to force him down to one hundred metres and waited for him to land, but he went on flying about like a madman all over the place, with the pair of us behind him. I tried to cut off his further progress by flying at him, etc.; then my engine gave out, and I had to land. I could just see my opponent disappearing behind the next row of trees and thought he would land there; I was very delighted and, arming myself with a Verey pistol [for firing flares]—I had no other weapon at hand—I rode across on horseback to take the fellow prisoner. But he had flown on. . . . Then in the evening there came a report that the Englishman actually flew over the trenches at a height of one hundred metres and got home. Smart of the fellow; he won't have many imitators! Immelmann could not go on shooting at him because his gun jammed. That was no victory, but a joyous scrap. (121–22)

Douglas was amused by the difference between the report of this "joyous scrap" and what actually occurred. Boelcke believed he had killed the gunner because Child "was facing backwards and firing over my head" and he "became so physically sick through the violence of the way in which I was having to toss our aircraft about that he finally fell over and threw up all over me. This made things more than a little awkward because his vomit came all over my helmet and goggles, temporarily blinding me. I had to fly the rest of the way back without goggles." Some of the flyers in Douglas's squadron told him that he had been recommended for the Victoria Cross. He did not disagree when the Wing Commander denied the recommendation on the grounds that the VC was supposed to be rewarded for unselfish bravery, and Douglas was just saving his own skin. "That, I consider, is a fair enough comment on the whole affair."

Douglas's account is compelling as he tells it, but the factors most significant for him—terror, the revolt of the body at the stress of the battle, being temporarily blinded by vomit, and sheer luck—would not fit well with the image of air combat both the British and the Germans sought to convey to the homefront.

The Uses of Film

A significant technological factor in the involvement of the pilots themselves in producing publicity about air combat was the emergence of cinema photography as a tool for documenting the battlefield. The demand for moving images—"moving" both in the sense of motion and emotion—and the impossibility of filming under battle conditions ultimately involved pilots in staging stunts and battles.

Victor Chapman, in a letter dated May 14, 1916, described the visit to Luxeuil of a press reporter and a cinema photographer. Chapman and the other pilots staged a bombardment mission, with the planes flown by the Lafayette Escadrille demonstrating how they protected French bombers—which were also filmed—with each scout plane diving just in front of the cameraman, who remained on the ground. Chapman commented that the film would be shown in the United States later in the summer. He concluded, "Kiffin and Berty Hall were much peeved to think that some _____ person was going to make heaps of money out of it and we'd risked our necks for nothing. (None of us like to manoeuvre so close together . . .). 'Think of the honor,' said I. 'Oh no, give me the cash and keep it,' said Bert." The publicity shots and filming were followed by an "eight or ten course" lunch with some very good wine. As for the reporter, "I know he'll write up a most enraptured account of us."

A month later, Chapman had reason to regret the playful enthusiasm with which he had initially greeted the publicity. The airfield and the nearby town of Bar-le-Duc were bombed, with forty civilians killed, ten of them children. "Yes, this is what comes of getting notoriety," he wrote. "There were disgusting notices about us in the papers two days ago,—even yesterday. I am ashamed to be seen in town today if our presence here has again caused death and destruction to innocent people [a reference to earlier bombing at Luxeuil]. It would seem so." In a letter written the following day, Chapman seemed to have eased his conscience, noting that Petain's General Staff had just moved to the area, and that would account for the targeting.[3]

Nevertheless, assigning such high visibility to the Lafayette Escadrille invited special attention from the Germans, just as the celebrity attached to Manfred von Richthofen and the Flying Circus made him a special target. It was believed that publicizing both squadrons and individual pilots carried a benefit that outweighed the usual military value attached to maintaining secrecy about the squadrons or the anonymity of the pilots.

The demand of the newsreel camera for exciting footage made it very easy to cross the line from demonstrating the kinds of maneuvers planes engaged in when on a mission to staging a battle in the sky. The opportunity presented itself a month before the Armistice when the "Hat-in-the-Ring" squadron, the most famous and successful of the American squadrons, managed to capture a German Hanover. Eddie Rickenbacker in his *Fighting the Flying Circus* reported that Capt. Merian C. Cooper, an official cinema photographer, asked to film a staged battle between the squadron pilots and the Hanover, and arrangements were made for him to be flown in a Liberty plane with his camera strapped in. Reed Chambers was assigned the role of the German pilot, while Thorn Taylor played the gunner, "dressed in villainous-looking garments." Eddie Rickenbacker was the American pilot who engaged and shot down the Hanover (see Figure 13).[4]

The script called for the German observer to commit suicide; Taylor was to throw a dummy out of the plane while he ducked out of sight: "This would portray the very acme of despair of the Boche aviators, who, it would be seen, preferred to hurl themselves out to certain death rather than longer face the furious assaults of the dashing young American air fighters." It would also gloss over the reality that German flyers by this time were equipped with parachutes while Allied and American pilots were not.

As for the American role in the film:

In my old Spad No. 1, with the Hat-in-the-Ring insignia plainly inscribed on the side of the fuselage and the red, white, and blue markings along wings and tail sufficiently glaring to prove to the most skeptical movie fan that this was indeed a genuine United States airplane—I was to be Jack the Giant Killer.

Using earlier footage of an "enemy" squadron flying by in the far distance, the impression intended was that Rickenbacker encountered an entire squadron and finished them off single-handedly, after a furious battle involving tracer and flaming bullets, which would be picked up by the camera even in daylight. When Rickenbacker delivered the staged *coup de grace*, Taylor released lampblack from the Hanover, intended to convince "even the dullest intellect" that the plane was about to burst into flames; then, flares positioned under the wings were ignited to simulate fire. Thorn tossed the dummy overboard and ducked down, while Chambers released more lampblack and took the plane into a slow, spiraling fall to the earth.

29656

Figure 13. Lt. Eddie Rickenbacker in the cockpit of a Spad. 94th aero squadron, Rembercout, October 18, 1918. America's top ace is shown here in a publicity still taken at the time of the filming of his fake battle with a captured Hanover. From Still Picture Branch, National Archives, 111-SC-29656.

The filming was not without its dangers. It was canceled the first day because the Liberty bearing camera and photographer crashed on takeoff. On the second day, during the filming, the pilots had to be careful to avoid the bullets coming from the stunting planes and be sure of their own aim, be aware of their maneuvering, and yet manage to stay within the eye of the camera. The greatest danger, however, came from the use of a real German plane. When the group drifted over a French airfield, French artillery commenced firing at the Hanover and a number of fighters took off to assist Rickenbacker's Spad. Chambers put the plane into a dive, heading for a landing at the French aerodrome, while Rickenbacker flew close by, signaling to the French planes that he was bringing in a surrendered plane. After landing, Rickenbacker explained the situation, and everyone had a good laugh, except for Chambers and Taylor, who looked rather the worse for wear. The film made that day was, according to Rickenbacker, later shown in the United States.

The film was made in late October 1918. By this time it was taken for granted that American combat pilots would and indeed ought to participate in publicity about themselves and that there were no significant issues involved in making wholly contrived propaganda. The men who flew had a very clear sense of how the public back home—even the "dullest intellect"—imagined the war, and what fantasies about the air war it would be easiest, not to mention most desirable, to feed. It was very rare to have a captured aircraft, and it was valuable for military reasons because the pilots could practice engaging it, gaining an understanding of its capabilities and weaknesses. Yet the interest in staging a battle to encourage the public's taste for melodrama outweighed the risks to such a valuable prize of war.

The Valuable Element: A Plot

The impact of the visual image of air combat came not simply from the authenticity of the moving image, but from the application of a conventional plot to the encounter of enemies, a rationalization that proved impossible with documentary footage of the ground war. The most memorable scene in the first feature-length documentary not only of the

Western Front but of warfare was staged. *The Battle of the Somme* was released in London on August 21, 1916. The film signaled a shift in official thinking, which initially saw photographers and the cinema camera as a threat to military security. Documentary footage of the battlefield was instead understood as a way to engage the public's support for the war by giving them a realistic picture of the level of sacrifice endured by the men along the front. While some public figures, particularly those in the clergy, felt that such direct encounters with the images of war from the safety of a cinema house would degrade the public's sensibilities, there was a general feeling among the average citizen and the governing elites that the documentary served the useful purpose of helping people—especially women with sons, brothers, and husbands at the front—understand the war and gain some sense of release from wondering how loved ones had died.[5] The documentary also aimed at inspiring a zeal for the war or arousing the complacent to a better sense of commitment.

The technical limitations of the camera determined how the "reality" of the front was represented. The footage was taken by two cameras fixed on tripods. They could take pictures only of what moved past the camera's eye and could not capture actual battle. Of the impression made by the film, Samuel Hynes observes:

> The reality . . . is expressed in the very structure of the film. . . . It is, for
> example, a film without a narrative line, made up of disconnected vignettes,
> in which guns fire, men march, other men wait, wounds are treated, an
> English soldier offers a cigarette to a German prisoner. There are no con-
> tinuing characters, and no defined individuals; all faces are the same face,
> dirt-smeared under a tin hat, taut with anxiety or nervously grinning.
> (122–24)

There is also a lack of visual continuity, with guns firing in various directions at an unseen enemy out of the frame, so that it is difficult to grasp where the "enemy" is supposed to be.

The sole exception in the documentary to this disconnected fragmentation is, Hynes notes, the one depiction of death in battle. The camera is positioned behind an earthen parapet, taking pictures from behind of a few soldiers going "over the top." One man falls at the top and slides back down the sloping earth, another falls on the left, and two more farther away. This is the scene from the film most frequently mentioned by critics and it stands out vividly in the minds of those who can recall seeing it as a child. The stills from this sequence are used often to illustrate the real Battle of the Somme in history books or in newspaper and magazine articles commemorating the battle. It is, however, the one scene that was staged, memorable because it is also the one scene that has a comprehensible structure, one that "seems to enact the idea of battle and sacrifices," which makes it naturally appealing to historians or journalists looking for an icon of battle. It breaks from the dominant image of the war, which was "not a matter of individual voluntary acts, but of masses of men and materials moving randomly through a dead, ruined world towards no identifiable objective; it is aimless violence and passive suffering, without either a beginning or an end—not a crusade but a terrible destiny" (125).

The concocted air battle between Rickenbacker and the Hanover gained meaning for the viewing public because it had a plot where the hero triumphed over evil, the demoralized "evil" German gunner who for the filming wore a predictably black flight suit and helmet with fiendish-looking goggles. The American is clearly the captain of his fate; the German, though a formidable enemy, lacks the essential moral fiber to prevail.

While Rickenbacker's account makes the filming into a rather amusing "lark," it was a lark with the serious purpose of representing the air war favorably to American audiences. The filming of a staged air battle in October 1918 marks the beginning of both a technological capability and a way of representing the air war on film that ultimately conditioned the public's taste not simply for the images of air wars as they are fought, but for those images packaged in a way that reproduced Americans' most significant and positive fantasies—that Americans were the rescuing heroes who encountered dangerous but morally unworthy opponents, and that victory came because of superior character, skill, and moral restraint.

Without that narrative frame to lend meaning to the images, watching the latter-day manifestations of air war would lack the thrill and gratification many Americans associate with not only a film such as *Top Gun*, but with the pictures of American planes flying off to bomb Baghdad, the battlefields of Kuwait, Belgrade, and the surreal landscape of Afghanistan. The receptivity to the images derives from the long association of air combat with a particular narrative, and with the equally long tradition of blurring the distinction between fantasy and reality in representing air wars.[6]

The American Boy-Knight: Quentin Roosevelt

Quentin Roosevelt did not actively participate in reproducing the conventional image of air combat, starring himself as a hero, as did Eddie Rickenbacker. But as the youngest son of Theodore Roosevelt, who had been in the public eye since he was a child, it was inevitable that his death as an aviator in battle would be used to make him into a symbol of national aspirations. He was represented as the epitome of the "boy-knight," but one with a particularly American and democratic accent. And he was transfigured in death into not only a national symbol, but a weapon to be used in the propaganda war against the Germans.

Quentin was exposed to a double pressure: one coming from the attention the press gave to him as the son of Theodore Roosevelt, and the other and more personal, from his family's—and especially his father's—expectations of him. These were particularly onerous expectations to place upon a young man who left college when the war broke out in his sophomore year, a young man of great charm with poor eyesight and, by all accounts, a not very skilled pilot.

Given who their father was, there was little doubt that the four Roosevelt sons would serve in the war. Theodore Roosevelt began angling for his son's commissions at the same time he sought one for himself. He saw to it his son Kermit enlisted in the British Army, where he served in Mesopotamia until he transferred into the U.S. forces in France. Both Theodore Jr. and Archibald received early commissions through preferential treatment by Pershing. Quentin also intended to seek a commission, but his poor eyesight disqualified him. On April 16, 1917—in the midst of the controversy over his request for a division—Roosevelt wrote to Newton Baker asking him to assure Quentin a position in the air services of the U.S. Signal Corps.[7] Baker replied, assuring Roosevelt he would act on his behalf, saying, "it would give me pleasure to think that your boy is there and a part of our establishment." On April 22 he wrote to tell Roosevelt that Quentin had been accepted to flight school. Quentin had memorized the eye chart in order to pass the medical exam.[8]

Quentin arrived on August 14, 1917, at the American flying school at Issoudun and was assigned the duty of supply officer, and later as the commander for the mechanics. The tent-city, which became a morass in the fall and winter, was home to Quentin and a number of his friends from Groton. He shared rooms in the home of Roosevelt family friends with one of them, Hamilton Coolidge, when he was unable to get away on leave to Paris, where his sister Eleanor maintained an apartment while working with the YMCA. He was popular with the mechanics, and occasionally led them on nighttime "requisitioning" raids to neighboring bases. He was spoken of universally as cheerful, gay, and popular, and as a good administrator if an indifferent flyer.[9]

By Christmas, Quentin was diagnosed with pneumonia, contracted in the deplorable conditions of the base. He spent about three week recuperating with Eleanor and completed his recovery while gambling in the south of France (171). While he was in Paris, two of his brothers, Archibald and Theodore, wrote to tell him they thought he was a "slacker" because of the four brothers, he had yet to see battle, a communication that caused considerable consternation in the Roosevelt family, particularly when Theodore Sr. learned of it. He cabled Quentin, "We are exceedingly proud of you," but the insecure Quentin was nevertheless affected by the accusations, even though they were unfair. Despite his efforts to get a frontline assignment, the USAS continued to suffer from a shortage of planes (186–88).

Quentin finally received orders to the front in mid-June, and had his first encounter with the enemy on July 6 while flying escort for an observer. He downed his first plane and escaped from two others. The account of his victory was carried in the press dispatches, which gave his father no end of delight. "The last of the lion's brood has been blooded!" he wrote to his son Ted. While the press accounts made it seem as if Quentin had fulfilled the role of a chivalric hero who engages the enemy against uneven odds, the facts were that Quentin had been blown into the clouds by a wayward gust, and when he re-emerged, he sought to rejoin his formation. As he approached it from behind, he belatedly realized it was a group of German planes. "I was scared perfectly green," he wrote to his fiancée, Flora. He decided to seize the opportunity to fire upon them and with luck managed to get one before the others turned on him (191–92). His good fortune, coupled with his enthusiastic nature, made him overconfident. Eight days later, Quentin was dead. He had been flying in the rear of his formation when he broke away and rose alone to meet a group of German planes. He was killed by two machine-gun bullets to the back of his head.

The Germans seized upon the propaganda opportunity afforded by the death of so prominent a pilot. They buried Quentin with full military honors, marking his grave with his propeller for a cross, inscribed with "Roosevelt," and they printed in major German newspapers a fully detailed account of his last battle, reports that were translated into English and widely published in the United States.

In the United States, Quentin was memorialized as a sweet-natured, intelligent child given to "boyish pranks" and a love of the outdoors who had willingly given his life for his nation. A loving reminiscence, written by Rev. Ambler M. Blackford, was published in the *Outlook*. Blackford had been Quentin's teacher and mentor at the Episcopal High School in Alexandria, Virginia, a boarding school Quentin attended when he was eleven. He wrote, "never have I met another like Quentin—certainly not at that age." He spoke admiringly of Quentin's love of reading and power of concentration, a boy who loved to ride horseback and to take long walks, a boy who "seemed to learn as much from nature as he did from his books." He was also given to a number of pranks related to animals. He shunned publicity even though he was often in the public eye. Blackford quoted from a number of letters Quentin sent him while he was in Europe in 1909. Quentin described the Velázquez "Infanta Marguerita" at the Louvre as "the cunningest thing I ever saw," was moved by the stained-glass windows in the Gothic cathedrals, and enjoyed his Latin lessons with "an old Corsican monk." He also wrote to his schoolmaster of his excitement at attending a airplane show: "you don't know how pretty it was to see all the aeroplanes sailing at a time. . . . It was the prettiest thing I ever saw." Blackford reminds the reader of the irony that Quentin's plane crashed to earth about twenty miles away from the place where nine years earlier he had been thrilled by the aeroplanes at Rheims.[10]

The lingering over the details of Quentin's boyhood—his intelligence, his little pranks, his love of the outdoors, his cultivation—echoes the sentiment attached to earlier boy-knights: Albert Ball, Victor Chapman, and Georges Guynemer. But Quentin, unlike his predecessors, gained his status because of who his father was and not because of his own achievements. He was on the front too short a time and died having downed one enemy aircraft; he fell short of the criteria established for elevating flyers to public celebrity as "aces," or even as men of exceptional capability. It was as the son of Theodore Roosevelt that Quentin was made a symbol of the American spirit, an individual of an elite background who nevertheless epitomized the essential values and strengths of democracy. In the service of transforming Quentin into a national symbol, his grieving father played his part.

A month after Quentin's death, one of his classmates from Groton, Bill Preston, brought a cross he had made to the site, accompanied by Colonel McCoy, a friend and former aide to Theodore Sr., and Father Duffy. They found Quentin's downed plane near his grave, parts of it stripped by German and American soldiers looking for souvenirs. Visits to his grave by advancing American troops became too frequent and dangerous—the area was exposed to German artillery—and it was declared off-limits.[11]

The attention paid to Quentin Roosevelt's grave reflected the profound loss his death represented to his immediate family and friends; but beyond that, people in Europe and the United States were acutely aware of this death. Of the more than two thousand letters of condolence sent to Sagamore Hill following the news of Quentin's death, many were from heads of state, but many more were from ordinary individuals, and some were from the men who had served under him. There was great personal identification with the youngest of the Roosevelt boys and with how he had died, in no small part because the nation had watched Quentin grow from the "White House baby" into a young flyer.

His identification as the son of Theodore Roosevelt was very much part of the memorial tributes. President Crawford of Allegheny College, who visited Quentin at his camp in France, reported Quentin's reply to Crawford's observation, "Lieutenant, there are large numbers of Americans who are very proud of the way the four sons of Theodore Roosevelt are acquitting themselves in this war." "I shall never forget," Crawford said, "how his face lighted up as he made reply, 'Well, you know it's rather up to us to practice what father preaches.'" Crawford reinforced the reference to Quentin's parents: "Colonel and Mrs. Roosevelt have certainly made a great sacrifice in giving such a son to the cause of human freedom. Their sacrifice and sublime fortitude ought to be an example to many."[12]

Quentin's death was used to symbolize the difference between the democratic United States and the autocratic Germany. The U.S. press hammered away at the point that while the six sons of Wilhelm II were shielded from the war and given safe command assignments, the four sons of Theodore Roosevelt, former president of the United States, were in the fighting, and one of them had been killed in combat (see Figure 14). The article "Transfigured Youth" gave to Quentin the encomium: "In his sacrifice his fellow-countrymen have beheld the symbol of America's young manhood offered to the cause of liberty." That Quentin died "fighting against odds" is also "a type and symbol of American manhood." Quentin's qualities—a willingness to sacrifice his life, the courage to fight even when outnumbered—are starkly contrasted with the protection enjoyed by the sons of the German royal family: "No family in Germany has been safer so far in this war than the Hohenzollerns."

ROTOGRAVURE SECTION

Chicago Sunday Tribune.

THE WORLD'S GREATEST NEWSPAPER

AUGUST 4, 1918

ROTOGRAVURE SECTION

Col. Theodore Roosevelt

Capt. Kermit Roosevelt

Maj. Theodore Roosevelt Jr.

Quentin Roosevelt.

Capt. Archibald Roosevelt

THE DIFFERENCE BETWEEN DEMOCRACY AND AUTOCRACY—In the frieze above are the kaiser and his six sons, all of them members of the military caste which sends other men to death in battle but which keeps at a safe distance from the front itself. All of the kaiser's sons have high military commands in theory, but none of them is ever close enough to the front to be in actual danger. The crown prince, a notoriously erratic and irresponsible military officer, is given credit for generalship which is actually the work of other commanders. Col. Theodore Roosevelt's sons, who fight for principle and not for love of conquest, are, on the other hand, in the very thick of fighting. Quentin, pictured here, was killed in an aeroplane duel on July 14. Capt. Archibald is in a hospital in France with a broken and paralyzed arm and with a leg badly wounded by shrapnel. Maj. Theodore Jr. was recently reported wounded, and Kermit, who has been serving with the British forces in Mesopotamia and has been decorated for gallantry in action, recently left the British forces to become an officer in the American artillery in France.

Figure 14. "The Difference between Democracy and Autocracy," published in the *Chicago Herald Tribune* on August 4, 1918, contrasts Theodore Roosevelt and his four sons (including the dead Quentin) with the sons of the Kaiser. On his last flight, Quentin Roosevelt left his "tail" position in formation to fly alone against pursuing enemy aircraft. His death was used to celebrate "democracy," in which the sons of the elites participate in war, over the German "autocracy," which protected the sons of the Kaiser. From Theodore Roosevelt Collection, Harvard College Library.

Noting that Quentin was joined by his three brothers and an uncle in volunteering for the war, the article declares their service as epitomizing an American brand of royalty: "All the sons of a sovereign people are princes of the royal household, and they have proved in this war that there is no royalty equal to the royalty of the common people."[13]

The use of Quentin's death to heap approbation of the royal family for sending men to a war they would not fight themselves was published not only in the United States but in Germany. Theodore Sr. had the satisfaction of learning that the pointed comparison had caused dissension in the German ranks. Wilhelm II abdicated on November 9. At the same time there was a Republican sweep of the U.S. Senate, fueled by the demand for unconditional surrender from Germany, a campaign in which Theodore Roosevelt had played an important role. He could comfort himself with the belief that the death of Quentin—or more specifically, what it was constructed to mean—had influenced the outcome of the war.[14]

A Father's War

Theodore Roosevelt's conception of the Great War was as much shaped by the war-as-imagined as were those of his English counterpart, Henry Newbolt, both of whom lived the war vicariously through their sons, and both of whom found their image of war shattered by the reality of it. Where Newbolt sought for his son and son-in-law the life of the knight going off to war, Roosevelt sought for his sons what he had sought in his own life—a time when it could be lived as a "crowded hour." This was one of Roosevelt's favorite phrases and was selected by his daughter, Alice, for the title of her autobiography. The original source is *Verses Written During the [Seven Year's] War [1756–1763]* by the British poet Thomas Mordaunt: "One crowded hour of glorious life / Is worth an age without a name." It was quoted (and thereby popularized) by Sir Walter Scott in *Old Mortality* (1816). Roosevelt wrote his eldest son and namesake in France, "You are having your crowded hours of glorious life." When he received news that Quentin had downed a German plane, he wrote to his daughter Ethel, "Whatever now befalls

Quentin he has now had his crowded hour, and his day of honor and triumph."[15]

All of his sons had their "crowded hour": Archibald was wounded and decorated; Roosevelt wrote to him to convey his sense of pride, "Well, now we know what it feels like to have a hero in the family." Ted was gassed and took a bullet in his legs and was also decorated; Kermit was awarded the Military Cross before he transferred to the United States Army. They all returned, except Quentin.

On July 17, 1917—just a little over a year after Quentin left— Roosevelt received word that his plane had been shot down behind German lines. He nevertheless insisted upon giving a scheduled keynote address to the New York state Republican convention. On July 22 he received word by telegram from President Wilson that Quentin had been killed. He was twenty-one years old when he died.

Roosevelt felt deeply the loss of Quentin and his grief lends poignancy to his otherwise mawkish public rhetoric. Roosevelt transfigured Quentin into the symbol of national pride and character, the embodiment of the Fallen Warrior.[16] In 1918 he dedicated his book *The Great Adventure* to "All who in this war have paid with their bodies for their souls' desire."[17] It was another of his favorite phrases. In his letter to Senator Chamberlain of April 12, he made his case for his leading a volunteer division with the words: "Let us pay with our bodies for our souls' desire."[18] He could not have known it would be not his epitaph, but the one he implicitly offered to his son.

In his book Roosevelt begins by calling life and death parts of the same Great Adventure—a term often used to recruit men for the war, and which carried the implication that it was better to die young living a life of adventure than to linger into an uneventful old age. He tells of a letter written by the wife of a soldier at the front to a mother whose son "had fought in the high air like an eagle, and like an eagle, fighting had died." The letter said, "I hope my two sons will live as worthily and die as greatly as yours." Roosevelt approves the sentiment: "There spoke one dauntless soul to another! America is safe while her daughters are of this kind."[19]

The second chapter, "The Men Who Pay with Their Bodies for Their Souls' Desire," starts with, "In a great war for the right, the one great debt owed by the nation is that to the men who go to the front and pay with their bodies for the faith that is in them" (268). He praises the "young Galahads" who "when they have found the grail have too often filled it with their own hearts' blood." And then he gives a more overt tribute to his son without naming him:

> Some have been driven by a sense of duty to do the best there was in them in a task for which they have no natural desire. Others eagerly welcome the chance to sweep straight as a falcon at the quarry which may be death; and these may come back with broken wings; or they may never come back, and word may be brought to the women who weep that they must walk henceforth in the shadow. (271)

Roosevelt uses the phrase "men who pay with their bodies for their heart's desire" both to dedicate the book and to title the chapter that includes this eulogy to his son. The significance of the phrase for him is suggested by a letter he wrote his son Theodore on May 30, 1917: "I do not sympathize with the proverb:—'God keep you from the werewolf and from your heart's desire.' It is best to satisfy the heart's desire; and then abide the fall of the dice of destiny." It is clear from the context that Roosevelt meant this for himself—as he did when he used the phrase "heart's desire" in his letter to Senator Chamberlain. The letter is in response to a letter his son had sent portraying the family as bears. Commenting on his efforts to get his remaining sons (Kermit and Quentin) their commissions, Roosevelt says, "The big bear was not, down at the bottom of his heart, any too happy at striving to get the two little bears where the danger is; elderly bears whose teeth and claws are blunted by age can far better be spared."[20]

Roosevelt was willing to risk the "werewolf" and seek his heart's desire; and he wished the same upon his sons. Even Alice Roosevelt Longworth felt the tension in her father's love for his sons while at the same time arranging for them to go to war. Describing him in June

1917—when all his sons shipped out—she says: "He talked . . . about the four boys with a grim elation at the thought that they would soon all be in the war. He said how certain it was that several, perhaps all, would be wounded, perhaps killed."[21]

But Roosevelt was not an essentially callous man. He grieved for his son and survived him by only five months. How much of his death was attributable to his grief can be inferred from his letters and the memoirs of those close to him. The toll is clear.

What distinguishes Roosevelt is not that he had sent his sons to war and had by his own beliefs and actions made it unthinkable for them not to go to war. Nor is it that as a consequence three of his sons were wounded and one was killed. What he did as a father is what the nation did then and has done since. What distinguishes him is that he was fully conscious of the role he had played in convincing his sons to go to war, in inspiring in them a "soul's desire" for which they paid with their bodies. This is revealed most clearly in a letter he wrote in response to a friend of Quentin's, Mary L. Brown, who had written to express her condolences:

> you told us something about our son Quentin that we would never other-
> wise have known. I need not say to you that it is a very sad kind of joy that
> your letter gave me. To feel that one has inspired a boy to conduct that
> has resulted in his death, has a pretty serious side for a father—and at the
> same time I would not have cared for my boys and they would not have
> cared for me if our relations had not been just along that line.[22]

It is tempting to view Roosevelt as a freak of nature, a man who was so extraordinarily obsessed by militarism and imperial ambition that Chronos-like, he devoured his own children feeding the maw of war. Certainly that is Frederick Palmer's ultimate judgment. He comments on the help Baker gave "in keeping with the father's and the son's wishes, to have Quentin hastened to France, where this youngest cub was to have the soldier's death which the old lion had craved." Palmer draws this grim portrait of Roosevelt at the same time he praises the work of

Baker for his successful efforts to convince and frighten American males between the ages of twenty-one and thirty to register for the draft; and the efforts of the War Department, Chiefs of Staff, and college presidents to convince young men of Quentin's age to volunteer for officer's training. It is easier to see Roosevelt as a monster of nature who visits upon his son the death in battle he himself had sought rather than as merely the reflection of his era in the mirror.

In the final analysis, neither a president nor a congress sends the young to war, nor do their mothers and fathers; the nation does, either by the general clamor for war or the inarticulateness of those who know better when the drums of war begin to beat. Whenever young men and women go into combat, it is because we have sent them. We depend upon their willingness to pay for their soul's desire with their bodies. The question is whether or not it is possible to become conscious of the cultural influences, values, and memory that arouses that desire, that make the war-as-imagined seductive to both parents and their children. And to wonder, if we find Roosevelt too harsh a portrait of ourselves to contemplate, what in the long run either the legacy of war or the indifference to it might make of us.

CHAPTER 12

Death Wears a Romantic Mask

The Allies were more and more interested in adopting the tactics of the German air force and putting them to use in offensive battle—the very tactics that had led commentators to label the Germans "cowards." The change in battle tactics required a change in how the war was explained to those on the homefront, and from this effort emerged a distinctive American idealization of the combat pilot—an "ace" who was at once a celebrity, a leader, and a team player.

The changes in how the American flyer was represented are best approached through three different examples. First, how the public was prepared for a change in understanding how the war in the air was fought, and for giving positive credit to the Germans; second, how war hero Eddie Rickenbacker was transformed into an exemplary model of the national hero, the American version of the ace, while at the same time another decorated flyer, the highly individualistic Frank Luke, was essentially held up as exemplary of how *not* to go about fighting in the air. Third, the reasons why an American pilot, Elliot White Springs, was disillusioned by his experience in the war, and especially with the idealized vision of the "lone wolf."

While the way combat pilots were depicted changed, what did not change was a romanticism that elevated the symptoms of stress to examples of a hypermasculinity, a devil-may-care freedom in approaching the invitation to death. This vision as a consequence elevated as wholly exemplary of masculinity what in another context would have been defined as the consequences of despair, stress, guilt, and fear. It is the romance of the single encounter, the duel, which has endured, rather than an awareness of the high cost of the air war on the individuals who fought it.

The American Approach to War in the Air

September 1918 was a turning point for the use of air power in combat. In August 1918 Col. William "Billy" Mitchell was placed in command of the U.S. First Army Air Service (USAS). He was planning the largest combined air assault in history along the Chateau-Thierry sector and gained French support for it. Under his command were combined forces equaling approximately 700 fighters, 400 observation planes, and 400 bombers, which were to support 500,000 Allied ground troops in attacking the German salient at Saint-Mihiel. They confronted a German force of 213 German aircraft: 72 fighters, 24 bombers, 105 reconnaissance, and 12 photographing planes.

Although they reinforced these numbers after the assault began, the Germans remained significantly at the disadvantage in terms of numbers. Nevertheless, they inflicted significant losses. As already noted, September 1918 was the worst month for Allied air casualties in the entire war—and just six weeks before the Armistice. In the final analysis it was the sheer number of Allied planes, coupled with the inability of the Germans to replace their lost pilots quickly and their lack of fuel, which made it impossible for the Germans to sustain their superiority. The British replaced their losses with new men recruited from the Commonwealth nations, and the infusion of the American forces also added to the numbers which could be thrown against the Germans.[1] The analysis of the final months of the air war makes it obvious that it, like the ground war, had become a war of attrition rather than one that depended upon the skilled encounter in single-handed duels. Moreover, Mitchell's coordinated assault required formation flying for specific objectives related to ground support, a military purpose at the opposite extreme from the lone wolf on a roving commission.

Deadly Expectations

The men who flew later in the war bore witness to the influence of the publicity and celebrity of the earlier aces. In *Decisive Air Battles of the First World War*, Archibald Whitehouse said that in 1918, "hundreds of young, inexperienced but high-spirited youths" entered the Allied air services "hoping to emulate Albert Ball, Guynemer, McCudden, Nungesser, or Billy Bishop." Using impassioned terms understandable in a veteran who flew over the Western Front, Whitehouse emphasized the high cost when the imagined nature of air combat met the reality:

> The result was what might have been expected. The experienced performers fattened their scores against the newcomers, or their improved mounts outperformed the equipment flown by the other side. It was in the summer and autumn months of 1918 that dozens of inspired young men either went down in flaming cockpits or fought their way to glory in the "ace" column. It was unclassified murder, a period in which military aviation was criminally employed, when so many fine men were sacrificed needlessly to furnish "victory" headlines.[2]

Accusations that high casualty rates in the air services amounted to murder had been voiced early in the war. In March 1916, Noel Pemberton-Billing, a former Royal Navy pilot, was elected to Parliament, where he charged that pilots were being murdered because of poor organization and inefficiency, allegations that led to official judicial inquiries into the administration and command of the RFC. But Whitehouse was referring to September 1918.[3]

The shift in emphasis away from the lone wolf in the representation of the air war to the homefront must necessarily be measured against the grim toll that the air war was taking on Allied pilots, and the raised expectations of the novice pilots themselves, whose imaginations had been fed on the stories by earlier combat pilots.

In terms of the American public's understanding of the air war, Laurence La Tourette Driggs was one of the more influential popularizers of the air war-as-imagined. Born in 1876 into a family that traced its paternal lineage to the Dutch settlers, educated at the University of Michigan and the New York University law school, Driggs was a trial attorney and a New York state assistant attorney prior to the war. After an unsuccessful bid for a New York Republican congressional seat, he purchased a cattle ranch in Texas. The outbreak of the war in Europe found him in Germany, where he volunteered his services to the U.S. consulates in Munich and Bavaria, and ultimately in Switzerland.

Driggs had a keen interest in aviation before the war, and by 1914 he had collected what was reportedly one of the largest aviation libraries in the world. In 1916 he visited all of the aircraft factories and flying schools in England, and in 1918 he visited every British flying squadron on the Western Front. At the same time, he organized the American Flying Club for pilots who had flown over enemy territory, and he visited American squadrons and came to know many of their pilots. During the war Driggs wrote numerous articles about air combat for both American and European magazines, two nonfiction books on aviation, and one adolescent fictional adventure, *Arnold Adair: American Ace* (1916). After the war, Driggs formed three regional airlines that became the parent companies for American Airlines. Driggs was very involved in promoting public interest in the potential for both the military and commercial usefulness of aircraft. He organized the first airplane races in the United States, including the first transcontinental air race from New York to San Francisco in 1919. He also organized and was given the commission to command the first National Guard air squadron.[4]

Driggs's background, knowledge, and interests made him a reliable and useful conduit to the public for official information, ideas, and publicity, and it is in the service of those interests that his writing about the American air force is best understood, not the least example of which is Eddie Rickenbacker's *Fighting the Flying Circus* (1919), for which Driggs was the ghostwriter.

Driggs's access to official sources of information makes the change in how he characterized the air war for American audiences particularly significant. In his articles for popular American magazines written during the war, Driggs joined other correspondents in describing the combat pilots as men whose combats in the sky rival "in romance the exploits of the knights of King Arthur,"[5] but he used the chivalric imagery infrequently and then only as a rhetorical ornament; it was not his essential framework for shaping his narrative.

Not long after the appearance of American squadrons in Europe, U.S. readers discovered in the pages of popular magazines a changed assessment of both the appropriate conduct of the air war and the quality of German air combat strategy. Driggs offers this instruction in two articles published in the winter of 1918: "Aces of Aviation," which appeared in the January 30, 1918, issue of *Outlook*, and "How Battles Are Fought in the Air" published a month later in *Harper's Magazine*.

Driggs offered a confused account, wishing on the one hand to reiterate the conventional emphasis on individual temperament and judgment. On the other hand, he had to acknowledge the importance of German disciplined flying. In the *Outlook* article Driggs published "for the first time in America" a complete list of the "aces" (those who had brought down five or more planes) and their victories through December 1, 1917. He noted the German total (1,093) was well in excess of the French (567). Driggs was troubled by the realization that the figures he obtained (from, he tells the reader, published sources on the Continent) fail to support the impression given in newspaper accounts in the United States of Allied air superiority:

> Confronted now with this official score after three years of war, we not only realize the mistake we have made in blandly accepting newspaper reports announcing our supremacy in the air, but we begin to estimate with due caution the size of the task that is before us.

The figures demonstrated that the Germans had been able to defeat as many planes as the Allies with half the number of pilots. Driggs concluded that German air tactics, and particularly squadron flying, were primarily responsible for this. He correctly identified the flight tactics developed by Boelcke and improved by Richthofen: the members of a squad harry the enemy aircraft until the squadron leader sees an opening and attacks. Although Driggs does not mention it, this strategy protected or shielded the inexperienced pilots. Driggs interpreted the strategy as providing the flight leader a cheap form of glory because the "credit" for victories went to him. In asserting that this tactic provided the leader a victory "without risk or danger to himself," Driggs overlooked the statistics he had just presented—which indicated that a very high proportion of Germany's most able pilots were dead.

But while he used the rhetoric conventionally employed to denigrate the moral fiber of the Germans and elevate the initiative and dash of the Allies, he was compelled to conclude the organized tactics of the Germans were superior to the individualism of the Allied flyers:

> With the Allied airmen this successful system is imitated only so far as the enemy's tactics compel them to follow it. Every man is for himself among the Allied air fighters, and overwhelming odds are recklessly disregarded to a most melancholy degree, as is evidenced by the heavy and growing losses among the French and British flyers.

For Driggs, assumptions about the Germans notwithstanding, the lesson was quite clear. One was implied: that the Air Service ought to become a separate branch of the military command. The other he made explicit:

> It is the opinion of Anglo-Saxons that German temperament and characteristics do not lend themselves so nicely as do ours to the science of aviation. Yet, despite this racial handicap, their airmen hold their own against overwhelming numerical odds. Verily, an ounce of brain is worth a pound of brawn.
>
> German tactics are permeated with that detestable word "efficiency." . . . Team work, formation fighting, shameless avoidance of an equal contest, venturing over enemy lines only with strong support, permit the few thus banded together to hold their own against the preponderating but scattered free lances of the Allies. . . . The sooner this unpalatable but relentless truth is realized, the sooner will we adopt methods to cope with these of Germany and then the sooner will our peace with honor come.

One can almost hear Driggs gritting his teeth as he acknowledged that the racially inferior, autocratic, and machine-like Germans were actually superior in the way they prosecuted the war to the altogether more attractive Allies—with their individualism, chivalric regard, and sportsmanlike fairness.[6]

Driggs was implicitly suggesting an American approach to the war, one that does not allow itself to follow the "chivalric" mentality into making combat pilots little more than "free lances," but that combines an equal regard for individualism with a pragmatic imitation of German organization, strategy, and tactics.

In the *Harper's Magazine* article, Driggs urged his readers to take the blinders off and recognize the intelligence that informed the German tactics. "We are hasty," he wrote, "if we assume . . . cowardice, or even weakness, in the German Air Service." He acknowledged Boelcke's role in designing the German tactics, and to indicate the sound thinking behind them, he quoted from a letter sent by Boelcke to his mother (and first published in Germany):

> It has been said that German airmen never fly over hostile lines. As regards chasing-machines [fighter planes], that is true; but it should be remembered, first, that our new Fokkers have some features which we ought to keep to ourselves; and, second, that our object is only to prevent hostile aeroplanes from carrying out their observations. It is for these reasons that we prefer to wait for them where we expect to meet them.

Driggs endorsed the German reasoning and elaborated each of Boelcke's points. Protecting both the plane and the pilot made eminent sense, so "the apparent cowardice of the German pilots may, after all, be better military strategy than our own 'free lance' style of adventurous combat." Driggs also defended the Germans against the charge that their pilots were "unsportsmanlike" because they refused "to accept combat on equal terms." Driggs as much as said that this attitude is more rational than the hot-headed willingness to accept battle when the odds are against victory and saner than stimulating the public imagination to the expectation that pilots will seek their death that way:

> So many instances of this are seen that our pilots are inflamed to an impulsive contempt of their adversaries and recklessly dive upon overwhelming odds. If successful, this bravery is hailed with satisfaction by press and people. If the "overwhelming odds" naturally overwhelm, melancholy reference to one more missing aviator is recorded in our official reports.

In drawing the logical conclusion, Driggs dropped entirely any concession to a presumed distaste for adopting the methods of the Germans; he told the reader to stop staring at the shadows in the cave, be pragmatic, and accept the realities of air combat:

> Contemptuously ignoring German methods has been a costly blunder of our allies. Rather to the opposite extreme should we go, imitating shamelessly every point of value possessed by the enemy, whether in machine construction or in air tactics. We can begin where they have arrived. At an equality there, any improvements we add will advance us so much toward superiority.[7]

Driggs's accounting of German superiority reflects the impact on air combat of Oswald Boelcke's tactics and training program at the time that Germany regained air superiority in 1916. In *Knight of Germany*, he stressed teamwork, and described how much difficulty he had convincing the young pilots in his command that individual scores were not important; what was important was that the squadron won the credit. Boelcke was exasperated by the resistance of younger pilots, who were seeking their own medals, victories, and celebrity, to the concept of organized fighting.[8]

Eddie Rickenbacker: America's Ace of Aces

Driggs's most important work in terms of his lasting influence was ghostwriting Eddie Rickenbacker's memoir. Despite Rickenbacker's claim in his later autobiography, *Rickenbacker: His Own Story* (1967), that *Fighting the Flying Circus* was not ghosted, the evidence is that he approached Driggs, who agreed to ghostwrite it from Rickenbacker's notes and a diary he kept during the war.[9] Driggs's remarkable observation in the preface bears repeating because it is consonant with the articles he wrote during the war and gains emphasis from comparison with them: "Never once in all his fighting career did Captain Rickenbacker permit an enemy pilot to injure him!" He offers the appraisal of Rickenbacker as one cool-headed enough to grasp the value of "saving himself for the continued service of his country," which made him superior to his opponents who "lacked that necessary judgment to preserve from wounds their valuable persons for further encounters with the enemy."[10]

The 94th "Hat-in-the-Ring" Squadron ended the war with sixty-nine victories, more than any other American squadron. It was the first American unit to send planes over enemy lines and the first to produce an American ace, Douglas Campbell. The squadron logged more hours over enemy lines than any other American squadron and brought down the last German plane to fall to American fire in the war.

Rickenbacker was assigned to a combat squadron for seven months and was hospitalized for two of them following surgery on his ear. During the five months he flew in combat, he was credited with twenty-six confirmed victories, a record unequaled in both world wars for the number of victories in such a limited time. He was awarded the Distinguished Service Cross with nine Oak Leaves, the French Legion of Honor, and the Croix de Guerre with four palms, and in 1930 the Congressional Medal of Honor for action in September 1918. After the war he helped found Eastern Airlines, and during World War II he served as a valued and respected advisor to the U.S. Army Air Forces.

Rickenbacker came from poor origins and was not a "college man." He had been a famous race-car driver before the war and volunteered for the Air Service, but was felt to be unsuitable because he was older than most volunteers and because his knowledge of machines would, in the minds of those most closely associated with training pilots, make him fearful to fly once he understood how the airplane worked. Certainly his lack of education and background were disqualifying factors given the class prejudices of the time. He was initially made a mechanic and chauffeur for General Pershing, until he was picked out by Billy Mitchell to help form the first American squadron to fly over the front.

By the end of the war Rickenbacker had come to embody American liberal pragmatism, the ideal of the self-made man, of democratic teamwork, and of public celebrity as the just reward for personal achievement. He received numerous offers to capitalize on his fame, including movie contracts, which he turned down because he refused to "degrade both my stature and the uniform." He was, by the end of the war, that thoroughly contemporary American product, a celebrity: both a man and an image of one.

Fighting the Flying Circus represents Rickenbacker in a manner reflective of Driggs's concern for finding a way to combine the symbolism of individualism, initiative, and skill with the requirements for a more efficient approach to air combat dependent upon discipline and organization. Rickenbacker arrived at the 94th Squadron and met heroes of the Lafayette Escadrille whom he had read about: Raoul Lufbery, at the time America's top ace, and James Norman Hall, who had by that time published his account of flying with the Lafayette Escadrille in *High Adventure*. Rickenbacker was awed upon meeting these heroes in the flesh: "We had all heard of these boys and idolized them before we had seen them. I cannot adequately describe the inspiration we all received."[11]

Hall had written eloquently of the new spirit being formed among airmen, a combination of idealism and a zest for the adventure of life:

> There was not a man there who was not ready and willing to give his life, if necessary, for the Allied cause, because he believed in it; but the admission could hardly have been dragged from him by wild horses.
>
> But the adventure of the life, the peculiar fascination of it—that was a thing which might be discussed without reserve, and the men [of the Lafayette Escadrille] talked of it with a willingness which was most gratifying. . . . They talked a new language and were developing a new cast of mind. . . . I thought of the time which must come soon, when the air,

as the sea, will be filled with stately ships, and how the airservice will develop its own peculiar type of men, and build up about them its own laws and its own traditions.[12]

This individualistic vision of a new type of man who is tested in a new way seemed uppermost in Rickenbacker's account of his first flight over enemy lines:

A feeling of elation possessed me as I realized that my long dreamed and long dreaded novitiate was over. At last I knew clear down deep in my own heart that I was all right. I could fly! I could go over enemy lines like the other boys who had seemed so wonderful to me! I forgot entirely my recent fear and terror. Only a deep feeling of satisfaction and gratitude remained that warmed me and delighted me, for not until that moment had I dared to hope that I possessed all the requisite characteristics for a successful war pilot. Though I had feared no enemy, yet I had feared that I myself might be lacking.[13]

Anyone flying into battle for the first time would have cause to be afraid. The point is how Rickenbacker interpreted the fear to himself; that is, Rickenbacker's sense of elation was directly related to meeting the test of manhood shaped by reading accounts of lone-wolf pilots.

Rickenbacker wanted to become America's top ace, and he provides considerable insight into how focused the American squadrons were on the scores of individual pilots. In his account of September 15, Rickenbacker encountered five German planes and shot one down in flames. Immediately upon landing, he drove to the balloon section to get confirmation of his victory for both that day and the day before. He was eager to learn if he had become the top ace. He gave a careful accounting of the scores to that point: When Raoul Lufbery had been shot down and killed with eighteen victories, Paul Baer, who had flown with the French and had nine victories, was called in by his commanding officer, William Thaw, who now commanded an American group. Thaw talked to him about the "opportunity before him as America's leading Ace [flying with an American squadron]. He advised Baer to be cautious and he would go far." Baer was shot down and slightly wounded behind enemy lines two days later. Frank Baylies, flying with the French Cigognes, held the title with thirteen until he was shot down in June 1918; he was followed by David Putnum with twelve victories, who was shot down in September. While Rickenbacker was not indifferent to the deaths of these men, his interest was also keenly in scores and who held ace status. His most immediate competition who was still alive and flying had six official victories, but with the two that Rickenbacker had shot down, he would now lead the list. Still, he had a superstitious fear of achieving the title because all the previous titleholders were dead or captured: "I wanted it and yet I feared to learn that it was mine."[14]

Despite this conventional emphasis, Rickenbacker is represented as developing a primary concern for the overall performance of the squadron. His motives are juxtaposed with the career of Frank Luke, a member of 27 Squadron, who epitomizes the reckless, daring, high-strung individualist. Luke had gone down in aviation history as a "balloon buster" (see Figure 15). He downed fifteen observation balloons—which were particularly difficult targets to hit and survive the attack because they were heavily protected—as well as four German airplanes before he was killed in action. In his last combat mission, he was flying against orders and facing both a recommendation for the Distinguished Service Cross and a court-martial when he finished. He was the first American flyer to win the Congressional Medal of Honor and the Distinguished Service Cross.

Luke's combat missions lasted only nine days, during which time he logged thirty hours of flight time and became America's top ace. Luke characteristically peeled off from squadron formation to fly on his own; he was on a self-assigned patrol when he brought down his first balloon, which meant he was given that kind of mission as a specialty. On his last flight, he was flying on his own after having been grounded for insolence to a superior officer. He attacked a number of German balloons and came under attack. He crashed in a German-occupied village, where he was quickly buried.[15]

Rickenbacker was given command of the 94th Squadron at the same time that Luke was given an honorary dinner for his achievements. When Rickenbacker learned that Luke's record meant that the 27th Squadron led the 94th by six victories, he hurriedly assembled his pilots and together they resolved, "No other American squadron at the front would ever again be permitted to approach our margin of supremacy." Every pilot felt that the "honor of his squadron was at stake." Rickenbacker then called a meeting with the mechanics, informed them of the pilots' resolve, and told them it would be only by their "wholesouled help" that the squadron could succeed. Rickenbacker also consulted himself on the kind of leader he wanted to be: "I should never ask any pilot under me to go on a mission I myself would not undertake. . . .

Figure 15. Frank Luke gained his reputation as a reckless and courageous pilot in the "lone wolf" tradition during his very short career. From Still Picture Branch, National Archives, 111-SC-23127.

I would accompany the new pilots and watch their errors and help them to feel more confidence by sharing their dangers." The next morning, as a test of his new mentality and resolve, Rickenbacker went on a lone patrol and returned an hour and a half later with two more victories to his credit. Within a week the 97th had once again become the top-scoring American squadron, and Frank Luke was dead.[16]

Rickenbacker described Luke as an "excitable, high-strung boy," whose "impetuous courage was always getting him into trouble. He was extremely daring and perfectly blind and indifferent to the enormous risks he ran." The point could not be more clearly made that hot-headed, impetuous free-lance flying brought death to the self-centered and reckless individual, while thoughtful foresight, leadership, and resolve brought success to both the individual and the unit.

Essentially, the focus on the individual in competition with other individuals is transferred to unit pride, a desire for the squadron to outdo other squadrons. In the account of Rickenbacker's leadership goals, there is the same indifference to the larger aims of the war which characterized the accounts of earlier aces, and the same celebration of the competitive ambition aimed at others fighting on the same side. This competitive spirit is altered to include attention to teamwork and mutual resolve within the squadron. As with football, the team gets credit for winning, and the team cannot win unless everyone contributes, but the greatest celebrity goes to the quarterback who both leads and inspires the team.

Rickenbacker's approach linked the aims of the squadron or the character of the pilot with cultural traditions, as did both the British and French accounts of their top aces. But the reference point is not history, chivalry, the aristocracy, or the code of the gentleman. Rickenbacker is represented as having invented a new kind of air combat based implicitly upon the American desire to be number one through competition and teamwork, and to gain personal celebrity and recognition by demonstrating superior skill or ability within the constraints established by the corporate entity, whether conceived as a "team" or a squadron. The larger goal of victory is achieved not through self-sacrifice for the greater good—which is the chivalric model—but by inspiring unit pride and striving for greater levels of personal achievement.

The vision of air combat offered in *Fighting the Flying Circus* combined the Allied and especially British love of the individualist and the sportsman with the German attention to unit cohesion and discipline. Where the Germans were represented as succeeding because they were by nature given to following orders, the American model is shown to succeed because the leader sought for and obtained mutual assent to a specific goal intended to increase the participants' sense of pride and to gratify their ambition. Success comes from adhering to the economic metaphor Driggs used as axiomatic for the Germans: "The maximum of success with the minimum of risk." It was a principle equated earlier in the war with the deplorable German "efficiency," an approach to combat that was taken to reflect a moral flaw in the German character made all the more obvious by the gentlemanly "chivalry" and willingness to engage shown by the Allied pilots. The Americans were seen as "fighting" the German Flying Circus in a new way, by adapting the German methods to the democratic and more aggressive Yankee spirit.

"Super-Airmen," a Breed Apart

Neither the physical nor psychological tolls of battle were made a significant part of the popular understanding of air combat to anywhere near the extent that "battle fatigue" became understood as a condition of the ground soldier. The absence of attention to the psychological toll of air combat made it difficult—if not impossible—for readers to interpret the accounts of exploits in the air as symptoms of combat stress or despair; this, in turn, had consequences for interpreting the taking of extraordinary risks as a sign of hypermasculinity, as defining the men who flew into battle as "a breed apart," or as possessed of a special "temperament of the air."

In Great Britain during the war, military medical opinion was divided over the effects of battle on pilots. As was the case with "shell shock" or "neurasthenia" in the ground forces, not every doctor agreed that there were legitimate, debilitating psychological as well as physical factors affecting the ability of combat pilots to continue to fly. While accurate statistics are not available on the number of airmen who were affected by the equivalent of neurasthenia or battle fatigue, reasonable inferences can be drawn that the effects were considerable, certainly from the photographs of the careworn faces of aces such as Charles Guynemer and Oswald Boelcke.

The official British history of the air war gives statistics for 1916 showing that the "effective service" for combat pilots was "no longer than two and half months," compared with four months for flyers in observation units, and three and a half months for a day-bombing pilot. This did not mean that the life expectancy of a combat pilot was less than three months; the figures represent all the reasons why a pilot would be unable to fly, including (in addition to mortality) wounds, illness, and emotional or psychological problems.[17] In October and November 1918 medical journals in Great Britain and the United States published the conclusions about combat stress in pilots of Capt. Norman S. Gilchrist, M.D., from examining one hundred cases that had come under review by the Royal Air Force Special Medical Board.[18] Gilchrist used "break-down" to describe those men who were found to be "permanently unfit," which meant for some unfit to fly for at least six months; for most, it meant for years. The men examined included both those who were in training as pilots (63) and those who had combat experience as combat pilots (33), observers (3), and balloon officers (1). Since Gilchrist did not make distinctions in assigning the symptoms, it is difficult to know the extent to which he was reporting the effects of battle as compared to the effects of training. Moreover, he was interested primarily in developing a way to identify men who were poor candidates for flight school; hence, his study is of limited value in providing a fully developed perspective on the effects of combat stress on pilots.

Nevertheless, his figures are suggestive. Of the thirty-three quali-fied pilots he examined, twenty were found to have psychological break-down, identified as "nerves," loss of confidence, or a general nervous breakdown. The same findings were reported for two of the three quali-fied observers and of the one balloon officer. Of the twenty qualified pilots, ten were found to have "lost their nerve" after crashing (one crash was ascribed to the effects of alcohol); two after the experience of flight; six as the "stress of service"; and two as the result of "stress of service" in a malarial country (German East Africa).

The chief reasons pilots were found unfit for duty were psychological, including nervousness and loss of confidence, as well as symptoms of air sickness: faintness and nausea. For combat pilots, the symptoms in some cases were related to head injuries sustained during battle. Gilchrist found that in over 52 percent of those examined (both trainees and experienced pilots) the higher cerebral functions were affected, with symptoms including loss of memory, concentration, judgment, temper, affections, and reaction time; and there was a high incidence of dreams, nightmare, obsessions, and hallucinations. Gilchrist acknowledged that sometimes these symptoms were the concomitant of concussion, but whether the causes were physical or psychological, he recommended that the experienced flying officer with these symptoms be given two or three months rest and, with the absence of symptoms, returned to light duty.[19]

Temporarily going into a kind of waking trance during a combat flight must surely have been one of the more terrifying symptoms. It was not recognized until after the war as combat fatigue. During the war, the cause was sometimes assigned to oxygen deprivation. There are reports by observers of pilots who, unaware of what they were doing, took the plane straight into an enemy formation. These and other symptoms—including trembling hands, insomnia, and nightmares—reflected the extraordinary stresses of prolonged combat, not the least of which was being pulled from the relative ease of life on the base into brief but very intense encounters in combat. Flying for two or three hours was itself a test of strength and endurance. The planes were difficult to manage. The air in an open, unheated cockpit could be frigid at upper altitudes and, depending on the model of plane, laced with a sickening smell of castor oil. The engines had an intense and deafening drone.[20]

Coupled with the physical fatigue from flying were the debilitating effects of combat and the demoralizing effects from the loss of friends. Men assembling for lunch after a morning's combat were confronted

with the newly empty chairs of those with whom they had shared breakfast earlier in the day. Sometimes a man given up for dead would suddenly reappear several days later, seemingly no worse for wear. The
uncertainty over whether one ought to mourn or continue to hope must
have added considerably to the psychological effects of the high mortality rates in flying squadrons.

The toll on flyers is seen in photographs of the French ace Georges
Guynemer and the German ace Oswald Boelcke, whose physical appear-
ances epitomized how the diarist in Elliot White Springs's *War Birds:
Diary of an Unknown Aviator* described himself in one of his final entries
before he was killed: "Here I am, twenty-four years old, I look forty
and I feel ninety. I've lost all interest in life beyond the next patrol. . . .
I haven't a chance, I know, and it's this eternal waiting around that's
killing me" (see Figures 16 and 17).[21]

Elliot White Springs's final entries for his fictional pilot offer the
best description of the mental breakdown of pilots exposed to frequent
combat missions and the loss of friends in action. Springs influenced
popular cultural conceptions of the air war of World War I in the work
he published after the war. "For years," commented Whitehouse, a long-
time friend of Springs, "Springs' version of front-line flying was the basic
idea of Hollywood epics" and "[p]ulp writers lifted his plots, characters,
and hilarious situations."[22]

Springs's most important work, *War Birds*, was published in 1926.
His is a caustic, illuminating account of how young men volunteered for
war with visions of their individual heroics in meeting the competitive
test of manhood (see Figure 18). Springs and two other Americans,
Lawrence Calahan and John Grider, were assigned for training with the
RAF in England when they were selected by Billy Bishop to join the
squadron he was forming. On May 22, 1918, 85 Squadron flew to France
and settled at a base near Dunkirk. Springs was credited with three victories before he was shot down on June 27. After he recuperated from
his injuries, he was assigned to the American 148 Squadron, promoted
to captain, and made a flight commander. At the end of the war, his
squadron ranked second only to Rickenbacker's 94th "Hat-in-the-Ring"

Figure 16. Georges Guynemer shortly before his death in September 1917, hollow-eyed and wan from the stress of battle. From British Imperial War Museum.

Figure 17. Oswald Boelcke: the stress of battle is evident in the deep lines in his face and his hollow expression. From British Imperial War Museum.

in the number of victories scored by an American squadron. Springs was credited with eleven victories and ended the war as America's fifth-ranking ace. He received the Distinguished Service Cross (United States), the Distinguished Flying Cross (Great Britain), and Medal of Honor (Aero Club, United States).

Springs epitomized the recruit from an elite background thought most desirable by the Air Service. He traced his paternal ancestry to John Springs, a Dutch settler in New York in 1652. His father, Leroy, was a highly successful merchant, manufacturer, and banker. Elliot attended the Franklin Academy, the Asheville School, Culver Military Academy, and Princeton University, where he received his B.A. in 1917. When he returned from the war, he flew as a test pilot for a private company

Figure 18. Lt. Elliot White Springs, 184th Aero Squadron, standing in front of his plane after crash-landing. German enemy aircraft had shot off one wheel and damaged the propeller. From Still Picture Branch, National Archives, 111-SC-24276.

in 1919, then joined the family business in 1920, which was the most prominent textile-manufacturing organization in the South.

Springs's *War Birds* is an example of the literature of disillusionment. While part of this is expressed as a disillusionment with war itself, the other more particular variety is with the "lone wolf" tactics of Springs's mentor, Billy Bishop, who is seen as essentially lacking leadership ability. The book draws upon early entries from Grider's diary, which Springs received after Grider was shot down and killed; the majority of the work is a thinly disguised autobiographical account. For convenience, the central character, who is never named, should be designated as "Grider," because the narrator often refers to Springs as a character in the narrative.

Grider's last entries detail the descent into mental breakdown. Grider essentially considers himself already dead and clings only to the slim hope that he will die with some dignity. He describes his anxiety and fears as he receives his orders at night and cannot sleep. Waiting for the afternoon patrol makes him think he is "going crazy. I keep watching the clock and figuring how long I have to live." He is oppressed by the news of others who have died:

> It gives me a dizzy feeling every time I hear of the men that are gone. . . .
> [W]hen you have lunch with a man, talk to him, see him go out and get
> in his plane in the prime of his youth and the next day someone tells you
> that he is dead—it just doesn't sink in and you can't believe it. . . . I've lost
> over a hundred friends, so they tell me. . . . I'm still expecting to run into
> them anytime.

His fallen friends haunt his dreams when he does manage to sleep.

Grider is kept going only because he thinks cowardice or dishonor are worse than death:

> I only hope I can stick it out and not turn yellow. I've heard of men land-
> ing in Germany when they didn't have to. They'd be better off dead because
> they've got to live with themselves the rest of their lives. I wouldn't mind

being shot down; I've got no taste for glory and I'm no more good, but I've got to keep on until I can quit honorably. All I'm fighting for now is my own self-respect.

Remarkably, Grider then records in his diary the victories tallied by his remaining friends and himself and offers his critique of the various systems for counting coup:

> Clay, Springs, and Vaughn are all piling up big scores. But their scores won't be anything to those piled up on the American and French fronts. Down there if six of them jump on one Hun and get him, all six of them get credit for one Hun apiece. On the British front each one of them would get credit of one sixth of a hun. . . . Cal has five or six now and I've got four to my credit. . . . Springs and Clay have been decorated by the King with the D.F.C. Hamilton and Campbell got it posthumously and Kindley and Vaughn have been put up for it. Cal is going to get it too.[23]

Disillusioned by and about war, overwhelmed by grief over the loss of his friends, and certain that his cracked nerves will be the cause of his own death, Grider nevertheless remains obsessed by the system used to accumulate personal glory, rather like a miser counting his coins in the hottest circle of a Dantesque Hell.

In the fictionalized account *12 O'Clock High* by Beirne Lay Jr. and Sy Bartlett (1948), which was made into a popular film starring Gary Cooper, a World War II bomber pilot's assumption that he was already dead was represented as the necessary mentality.[24] British veteran pilots of World War I also said that their most important asset was a lack of imagination, a concentration on living only for the moment or the day, without looking ahead to what life would be like after the war.[25]

Chief among the imagined horrors was the image of dying in a burning plane. The romantic lore associated with jousts in the air included the sense that the aim was simply to knock a plane out of combat, which seems to have been the case in the earlier stages of air combat. Certainly, from the German perspective, driving a French or British pilot down was as good as killing the pilot or burning the plane because the Allied offensive strategy meant the pilot would most certainly be captured; however, German training especially under Boelcke and Richthofen stressed destroying both the opponent and his plane, with the preferred method being to close on the opposing plane and aim for the pilot or for the fuel tank. Richthofen was especially insistent on trying to send opponents down in flames and chastised those in his command who reported driving down planes without assuring they were on fire.[26] The recollection of shooting down other pilots in flames and the fear of being shot down in flames plagued many pilots, and some of the best-known aces flew with a small side arm intending to shoot themselves if they found themselves doomed in a burning plane.

The realities of air combat make it difficult not to speculate on the extent to which despair motivated other pilots like Springs's hero, Grider. Edwards Park, who flew combat planes in World War II, describes with admiration the achievements of the World War I aces in his *Fighters: The World's Great Aces and Their Planes* (1990); yet he also raises the question of what motivated them. Noting that Charles Guynemer was wounded eight times, crash-landed seven times, and refused the request of his commanders to take a rest, Park asks: "Death wish? Guynemer as much as admitted it. 'What new decoration can you possibly be looking for?' asked an adoring woman when he was in Paris conferring with the Spad people. 'The wooden cross,' he answered."[27] Lee Kennett, in his history *The First Air War, 1914–1918* (1991), links the high casualty rates among combat pilots to a "self-destructive tendency among the great aces of World War I," noting that those "who were the very best at aerial combat had the poorest survival rates."[28] Other aces who did not survive the war also refused opportunities for transfer, rest, or leave—including Albert Ball and Manfred von Richthofen—preferring to push themselves beyond reasonable limits. The foolhardiness of Frank Luke, his evident insistence upon placing himself repeatedly in profound jeopardy, raises the similar question of whether he was motivated by despair and by his grief over the loss of his flying mate in a balloon attack.

Attention to the motives of the World War I combat pilots tends to pathologize the pilots. Park speculates that Guynemer had a "death wish," and Lee ascribes self-destructive tendencies to the pilots. Gilchrist demonstrated a similar tendency in seeking causes for the breakdown of pilots in some set of personal or individual weaknesses, traceable to childhood, rather than in the effects of combat. In reporting the case histories of the men found unfit for service, he reported that 27 percent came from families with what he terms hereditary "unstable nervous temperament"; 40 percent were nervous as children (biting their finger-nails) and avoided the usual "rough and tumble" sports; and 30 percent had a previous history of mental depression, insomnia, and loss of concentration. It is noteworthy that Gilchrist concluded it is irrelevant whether or not these symptoms were the result of "a bomb in battle" or "worry at the office," and failed to clarify how many of the men he examined had these symptoms as a result of either cause. The bias in his reasoning was evident when he noted that some combat pilots who were fit for service had some of these symptoms in their case history, so that the correlations cannot be taken as causal; yet he concluded that the presence of such symptoms and others—such as nightmares as a child—should argue against accepting a candidate for flight school.

Gilchrist mixed together symptoms that may have been the direct result of combat stress with symptoms that may or may not have any relevance to determining whether or not a combat pilot would remain fit for service—such as childhood sleep-walking. This was consonant with the emerging wisdom on the condition generally known as "shell shock" in the ground forces; a tendency, that is, to seek some weakness, either hereditary or in upbringing, that would account for an individual soldier's inability to continue to perform his duties. The tendency to pathologize the symptoms without reference to the effects of the war itself was not entirely uniform; however, there was considerable interest in identifying the root causes for shell shock not simply in the extra-ordinary psychological trap faced by a man raised to obey orders who encounters the horrors of cowering in a trench or being buried by shell fire, but in other psychological factors as well, such as too much cod-dling by the mother during childhood.[29]

While combat stress for the ground soldier was linked with a soldier's inability to fight and was connected with a defect of will through the prewar association of hysteria exclusively with women,[30] combat stress for the pilots became part of the representation of him as a man of indomitable will, even if it was often directed in foolhardy or self-destructive ways. Guynemer was seen as a man of unstoppable will whose infinite drive for aggression was tragically trapped in a mortal body, as a fellow officer said in his tribute to him: "Guynemer was only a powerful idea in a very frail body, and I lived near him with the secret sorrow of knowing that some day the idea would slay its container."[31] His death is therefore a tragic consequence of his character, and a matter of choice, not the result of a despair born of a loss of hope.

Neither the symptoms of combat stress in pilots nor the explanations for them were generally known to the public; instead, those psychological adaptations to the inevitability of death became part of the attributes of the aces that made them a new breed of elite warriors. Moreover, the tendency to seek to account for the effects of stress on pilots by identifying some fatal weakness in the individual reinforced in its own way the popular conception that what accounted for the success of the aces was that they were fully in command of their destiny by reason of their extraordinary personal attributes.

The same month that Gilchrist published his conclusions in medical journals read by only a few experts, W. P. Crozier published "The Super-Airman" in the respected American journal of opinion, the *New Republic.* Crozier offers to answer the question, "By what strange physical and mental power does he overtop the general mass . . . winning his fifty or seventy victories?" Drawing upon the published accounts of the most successful aces of Germany, France, and Great Britain, Crozier attributes the "genius of the air" to keen vision, accuracy of aim, and skill in maneuvering. What sets the ace apart from others who possess these same abilities is that he is "absolute master of his machine" and is "exhilarated by danger and mischance because of his firm conviction that he is and will be the master of every difficulty that can arise." He is confident that his plane "under all circumstances . . . can be made obedient to his will." In addition, he is a highly motivated fighter, one who "has an incomparable will to battle and to victory." In other men, their "passion for battle" and their "supreme confidence" would be "sheer foolhardiness." He observed that Ball "seemed almost to court collisions," while Guynemer "carried boldness far into the realm of rashness." Richthofen, on the other hand, differed in temperament: "masterful, audacious, dominating, but rather colder and more calculating." But all the aces shared "a dominating personality, a will that harnesses all these qualities together in a fierce conviction that he is better than the other man and can destroy him." Crozier speaks with unqualified admiration of the masculine qualities that accounted for the aces: "fierce vitality," "passion and aggressive will," coupled with "cool judgment and a keen eye." He does not dwell on the other similarity linking the men he describes, which is that all except one—Charles Nungesser—were killed in action.[32]

The hypermasculinity assigned to the pilots makes a manly virtue out of what may have been life-jeopardizing decisions that were the product of physical stress, sleep deprivation, loss of memory and concentration, grief, and absolute despair. Other factors related to combat stress have been transformed into emblems of airmen as "a breed apart." The reputation of airmen as carefree drinkers is reinforced by accounts of how often they consumed eggnog before a flight or took it with them. But the combination of eggs and milk was used to ward off nausea caused by the smell of fuel and castor oil, or the pain of ulcers developed as a result of combat, while the rum or brandy served a fortifying function perhaps related to finding courage, but certainly related to the cold experienced while flying in an open cockpit. Some pilots also reported being able to sleep only after narcotizing themselves with alcohol. The stereotype of the airman as holding on to special lucky talismans—a teddy bear, a woman's nylon stocking, or the like—and of his superstitions—especially not having one's picture taken in one's airplane—are also part of the lore associated with the aces. They are symptomatic of a recognition that their fates are not in their own hands.

For many of the aces, the end of the war brought with it a disappointment felt as a restlessness, an inability to settle into an organized way of life. Conditioned by war to think of themselves as having no life beyond the next sortie, and coming back to a world vastly changed by the war, pilots often found reintegration into civilian life difficult. Sholto Douglas looked back as an old man upon his emotional state after the end of the war, when he was a highly decorated combat pilot who had been in command of a squadron: "Life now seemed to be so dull and uninspiring, and I was restless and did not seem to be able to bring my thought to settle constructively." Cecil Lewis identified his rootlessness after the war as an extension of the way he had adapted to the demands of war in the sky:

> The mentality of the postwar years was no different from that of the war itself—an obsession to take the next objective, whether you wanted it or not, whether you were any better off when you got it or not, whether you had any idea of where to go next or not. It gave men the illusion they were getting somewhere, doing something, when, in reality, they were floundering deeper and deeper into chaos. (94)

Without question, the aces of World War I were men of extraordinary achievement in combat, but the terms used to glamorize the aces distracted attention from the stresses of combat, the deficiencies in training and tactics, the limitations of planes, and the reality that the mortality rates were unacceptably high for too many squadrons during too many periods of the war for reasons unrelated to whether or not the pilots who lost their lives or their nerve had bitten their nails as children. Moreover, the stereotype of the aces as admirable "supermen" because they were foolhardy, temperamental, careless of life, ambitious for glory, lived only for the moment, and were obsessed with battle not only upholds a highly limited vision of masculinity, it also obscures the extent to which the characteristics of the aces were signs of extreme stress and a descent into chaos, rather than extraordinary self-control.

Aces as National Emblems

The particular qualities associated with the World War I aces bore the stamp of their respective nations, a representation that carried weight after the war ended and that variously influenced the qualities associated with the American ace, who bore traces of elements associated with the British, French, and Germans. The particular qualities of the American ace come into highest relief when placed in the context of how the other nationalities understood the role of the combat pilot.

An important contribution to sustaining the chivalric-gentleman legacy in Great Britain in the postwar period is Alan John Lance Scott's autobiographical account, published in 1920, of the squadron he commanded, *Sixty Squadron R.A.F.: 1916–1919*. At various periods during the war, 60 Squadron included several of the most outstanding of the British aces such as Albert Ball, Billy Bishop, J. B. McCudden, and W. E. Molesworth. By the end of the war, pilots who flew with 60 Squadron had been awarded one Victoria Cross, five Distinguished Service Orders, thirty-seven Military Crosses, and five Distinguished Flying Crosses. In short, 60 Squadron is deservedly one of the legendary squadrons of World War I, even granting that Scott was actively engaged in gaining publicity and recognition for its pilots throughout the time of his command.

Scott was a determined individual as well as a respected commander. He led 60 Squadron from March through November 1917, with interruptions to recover from wounds suffered in combat or to assume a wing command. Born in 1883, he was educated at Merton College, Oxford, and then entered the law. Shortly after the war broke out, he entered the Royal Flying Corps. In 1915 he broke both legs in a training crash, and from that point on he needed two canes to manage to walk. Although he was initially refused orders to enter combat, he nevertheless managed to join 43 Squadron as a captain, where he needed help to enter and exit the cockpit, but proved himself in combat. When he was posted to 60 Squadron, he went against general orders that confined commanders to noncombat flying and, along with Billy Bishop, engaged nineteen enemy aircraft in one mission. He was wounded but recovered. In November 1917, following his recovery from a second set of wounds resulting from crashing, he was posted to Britain to command the School of Aerial Navigation and Bomb Dropping at Andover. He was decorated during the war, and after the war he became air secretary to Winston Churchill when he was secretary of state for the War Office and the Air Force, and to Churchill's successor. He gave both of them flying lessons. In 1920 Colonel Scott was made a group captain in the RAF and was generally considered to be on his way to becoming a future Chief of Air Staff. His career was cut short when he died in 1922 as the result of a double pneumonia which developed after a skiing holiday at St. Moritz.

Scott started writing the war history of 60 Squadron in 1920, at the time he assumed command of an RAF group and when his star was definitely rising. This was not his first venture into publicizing the achievements of the pilots who flew for 60 Squadron. He is generally acknowledged to have been responsible for assuring Billy Bishop received the VC for his controversial single-handed and unconfirmed attack on a German airbase. New Zealand airman Maj. Keith "Grid" Caldwell, who was both a decorated ace credited with twenty-five victories and the commander of the celebrated 74 Squadron, described Scott as a "splendid choice" to command 60 Squadron because of his excellent leadership administering the unit, maintaining morale, and in combat; however, "his one fault was that being such a gentlemanly sort of chap, he thought the best of everybody and may have been a little tolerant in accepting combat claims from almost everyone when perhaps there was some doubt."[33]

The preface to Scott's history was written by Lord Hugh Cecil, who as a member of Parliament was involved among other matters in preparing a report on the future education of RAF pilots. In his preface, Cecil reinforces the legendary status of the combat pilots, pointing out the "poignant contrast" provided by the comfortable living conditions the pilots enjoyed, the good food and drink, "all the fun and merriment" natural to young men, and the picturesque French countryside: "Yet from this abode of youth and ease and joy the dwellers went forth into the abyss of the air, to face danger at which imagination quails." Cecil praises Scott's history for offering "jewelled memories" of those who fought and died during the war, as the memory of the war begins to fade.[34]

In his account of the air battle during the Battle of Passchendale, Scott inserts a portion of Cecil's report on the future training of RAF officers. The subject is a gentleman's character, and in his discussion of it, Cecil had quoted extensively from Edmund Burke, *Reflections on the Revolution in France* (1790), Cardinal John Newman, *The Idea of a University* (1873), and Lord John Cavendish, "Speech Proposing Mr. Thomas Tounshend for Speaker" (1770).

Scott includes these passages as a tribute to those who died while fighting for 60 Squadron because they "attained very nearly" that ideal. Scott means by that a reference to class, but the source and particular value of the gentleman's virtues are articulated in the passage from Burke's *Reflections on the Revolution in France*, which pits the aristocratic tradition, and conservative "chivalric" values against those of utilitarianism and commercial interests:

> But the age of chivalry is gone. That of sophisters, economists, and calculators has succeeded; and the glory of Europe is extinguished for ever. . . . The unbought grace of life, the cheap defense of nations, the nurse of manly sentiment and heroic enterprise is gone! It is gone, that sensibility of principle, that chastity of honour, which felt a stain like a wound, which inspired courage whilst it mitigated ferocity.
>
> This mixed system of opinion and sentiment had its origin in the ancient chivalry; and the principle, though varied in its appearance by the varying state of human affairs, subsisted and influenced through a long succession of generations, even to the time we live in. If it should ever be totally extinguished, the loss, I fear will be great. It is this which has given its character to modern Europe.[35]

The Passchendale campaign was during Bloody April, 1917. The reader of Scott's account is offered merely a glimpse at the disaster of spring

1917—a long paragraph that deals with the casualties in 60 Squadron, but does not place them in the context of the overall losses to the RFC. Reading between the lines, one can sense the effects of losing "almost twice the strength of the squadron" in two months—or thirty-five officers (a squadron consisted of eighteen pilots and the commander); or of losing ten out of eighteen pilots in three days. Scott also offers· what on the surface appears to be only understated observations—given in a few sentences—of poorly trained pilots and badly constructed planes that broke up in flight. In offering his account of Passchendale, Scott observes the decorum of a gentleman; in the words of Newman, he "carefully avoids whatever may cause a jar or a jolt—all clashing of opinion or collision of feeling."[36]

As a consequence of the disaster of spring 1917, the strategy for aerial combat shifted toward far more highly organized forms of aerial combat, although more characteristically in the German, French, and American forces. Scott seems to point to this change in emphasis when, from all those whom he could have named in particular, he chooses to eulogize by name Capt. F. H. B. Selous, M.C., who died in January 1918:

> As good a flight commander as ever we had, he was a very great loss to the squadron. Without, perhaps, the brilliance of Ball or Bishop he, like Caldwell, Summers, Armstrong, Hammersley, Chidlaw-Roberts, Belgrave, and Scholte, to name a few only of the best, played always for the squadron, and not for his own hand. He took endless pains to enter young pilots to the game, watching them on their first patrols as a good and patient huntsman watches his young hounds.
>
> The character of Selous, like those whom I have mentioned, not to speak of many others whom their comrades will remember, attained very nearly to the ideal of a gentleman's character as described by Burke, Newman, and Cavendish.[37]

Scott draws a distinction between the aces who hunt alone—Ball and Bishop—and the commander who is able to master the leadership needed for a very different kind of combat.

This seems an odd distinction for Scott to make, given his considerable role in promoting Billy Bishop to international prominence as the "Lone Hawk" after his solo raid on a German airfield. The quotations on the "Character of a Gentleman," with their emphasis on deference, fealty, and honor, gain their most pointed meaning for the future training of pilots and their commanders from the implicit contrast between he who fights alone and thereby gains recognition and celebrity and he who fights for the squadron and to protect its members, even if he therefore gains neither recognition nor celebrity.

Scott's *Sixty Squadron* clearly aims to define the combat pilot of World War I and of the future as the embodiment of the Happy Warrior. Scott manages to assure the legacy of combat pilot as gentleman-knight, but also intends to reshape the ideal to one who subordinated himself not only in the sense of swearing fealty to the nation and its cause, but also by foregoing ambitions of individual heroics in favor of effectively leading the flight.

The American forces tended to emphasize "teamwork" rather than "fealty," and were on the whole more drawn to the aggressive or offensive use of air power than the French, but more conservatively than the approach favored by the British. The USAS in 1918 benefited from the French attention to organization, an influence that came not only from their direct advice, but from the experience provided by the men who had flown with the Lafayette Escadrille when they transferred. The American approach was an amalgamation of the British offensive strategy and the French emphasis on organization and planning. And all of them—British, French, and American—had to take note of the considerable advantage demonstrated by the outnumbered Germans.[38]

While the emphasis on squadron discipline in both Great Britain and the United States was learned from the example of the Germans, this emphasis was ultimately assigned different national significance in Germany. While Great Britain legitimized its participation in the war as defending advanced civilization against barbarism, Germany claimed that the conservatism of Britain and France lay like a heavy, repressive hand against the modern energy and spirit of the newer and more vital

Germany.[39] The German aces seemed to embody this spirit. Immelmann, Boelcke, and Richthofen represented a new breed of men who merged with the machine, men of steel both in the sense of what they endured physically but also in the sense of being devoid of emotional remorse, of a strong-willed and highly skilled ruthlessness. This modernist merging of man and machine, in the words of historian Peter Fritzsche, "not only reconciled Nietzsche with industry but made Nietzschean virtue dependent on the mobilization of the industrial arsenal."[40] The image of the aces in the postwar era was appropriated to political purpose, serving to symbolize the resurgent ambition of Germany. Particularly for the Nazis, the aces represented technological mastery coupled with self-reliance and willfulness: "It was a recognizable, derivative version of this patriotic, strong-armed, air-age Germany that went to war in 1939."[41] Thus, while the British continued to represent combat pilots in the chivalric, conservative framework after the war, the Germans extended and deepened the regard for pilots as epitomizing the "modern" spirit of a new German destiny. Neither approach entirely suited the American idiom.

Aces in the American Voice

In the United States immediately after the war, the official concern was with tempering the tendency to associate the individualism of American pilots with a lack of military discipline both in the air and on the ground. The mentality was epitomized in both Billy Bishop's accounts of the rowdiness of the squadron mess and in Springs's account in *War Birds* of the Americans who were seconded to the British air service and picked by Bishop to serve in the squadron he was forming. The heady attention from the hero of the air war certainly compounded the sense of privileged license that characterized the Three American Musketeers, as Springs, Callahan, and Grider regarded themselves. They were wealthy, self-indulgent, and, for the most part, unsupervised. The account of their training period, especially after they were tapped by Bishop, reads like the annals of an unending American fraternity party. Springs paid the rent for a manse in Berkeley Square and for a butler and a cook. The three Americans became the hosts for bouts of heavy drinking, loud parties, an alarming destruction of property, and womanizing. Bishop accepted this behavior indulgently and participated in some of it himself, including the occasional bar fight and stunt flying that terrorized the local civilians.

The official history of the U.S. Air Service refers directly to the attitude of combat pilots as a problem in its final report on the conduct of the war. The war demonstrated that the role of the observer and the observation pilot was "the most important and far-reaching," but recruiting pilots into this branch was made difficult by the popular representation of the "spectacular elements of aerial combat," the celebrity, "and the color of romance" attached to the pursuit pilots. The popular belief that the combat pilots did the most important work of the war "has from the beginning proved a serious handicap to the development of other branches of the Air Service." Pilots assigned to bomber or observation duty tended to "resent" the assignment and felt themselves in a lower caste compared to the pursuit pilots, taking it as a sign of their own inferior ability.[42]

The official history of the air war clearly reflects the desire to counteract the popular conceptions of combat pilots as a breed apart: "The truth is that the flyer is no more temperamental than any other healthy young man and is equally anxious to live up to the best traditions of the profession of arms." The "more conspicuous" insignia and uniforms of the air services explain why they were more often singled out for "breaches of discipline." Accusations that American combat pilots engaged more often in breaches of military discipline than other officers were found to be unsupportable.

At the same time, the report recognizes that esprit de corps is the most important element of success in air combat, and maintaining it requires special leadership. The pilots are volunteers and will use their knowledge only if willing to; they cannot be compelled to fight well. Moreover, the inspirational support provided the ground soldier by being in constant company with his comrades in arms is denied the pilot, who is "alone in the air and is often the final judge of his own conduct under fire." For these reasons, the role of the officers is to serve as "guardians and advisers" to those who are in their command.[43]

The concern in this section of the official history is clearly to counteract the extreme behavior described and endorsed by the popular accounts of the combat aces while at the same time acknowledging that the combat pilot is a member of an elite corps and subject to different treatment and discipline than other servicemen. The report does not so much disavow the image of the pilot as operating outside of normal limits and constraints as seek to channel the energy productively.

Although *War Birds* differs markedly from *Fighting the Flying Circus* in tone and in its final judgment of the war, the two share a common vision of the influence of the ace system on the psychological realities of men who entered the air war expecting it to be about individual competition and celebrity. As with Billy Bishop's autobiography, both Rickenbacker and Springs do not provide an account of the air war that reflects upon its contribution to the ground war; and none of the three uses the narrative frame of chivalry or the Happy Warrior. Instead, the focus is on the entrepreneurial model, the image of the self-made man who proves himself and reaps personal rewards through competitive if deadly sport.

Both the fictional Grider and Rickenbacker come to the realization that squadron discipline is more important and less dangerous to one's fellow pilots than the lone-wolf approach made famous by Billy Bishop. Yet both Grider and Rickenbacker are also preoccupied with the question of scores and tallies; how Springs presents Grider's fixation on scores makes him seem insane, while Rickenbacker portrays himself as taking a healthy interest in living up to the highest expectations for a pilot, only slightly tainted by a superstition that becoming the top ace might be a fatal jinx.

Both integrate the idealized accounts of the aces with their individual personality and background; both try to adapt themselves as warriors to the images of the combat pilot as hero. While Springs's quest is to gain the approval of, and if possible replace, the father figure in the form of the flesh-and-blood hero Billy Bishop, Rickenbacker's need is to live up to the image of the new type of man represented in countless accounts of flyers, and particularly those who flew with the Lafayette Escadrille. Springs finds the war yet another example of the destructive effects of the older generation on the younger—a projection in this instance of his long-standing conflict with father; Rickenbacker, who worked in a bottle factory as a boy to support his widowed mother, is gratified that the war dissolved class barriers and allowed him to participate in a Great Adventure as a part of a democratic fellowship.

The understanding of the pilot gained from these accounts is of a man who succeeds if he is competitive, individualistic, and motivated by ambition and the desire for personal recognition and glory, but who also recognizes the need for integration into a squadron. At his best, he is one who determines his own fate through skill and determination, and through submitting his ambition to military discipline. At worst, he succumbs to the pressure of war and imagines himself as fated to die and determines to make his death an honorable one.

Of the two, Rickenbacker gained the greater popular attention as America's ace of aces. The alternate and weaker strain that made the ace representative of the age of chivalry and hence of a cultural conservatism tied to British origins did not, however, fade entirely from view amid the hoopla. When Rickenbacker returned a hero, a banquet was given in his honor by a group of automobile associations at the Waldorf-Astoria in New York. Among the dignitaries was one of the early advocates of air power as an alternative to the ground war, Secretary of War Newton D. Baker. He offered Rickenbacker this accolade:

> Captain Rickenbacker is one of the real crusaders of America—one of the truest knights our country has ever known. He will find his greatest delight, when the evening of his life comes, in looking back on his experiences. He will never forget the thrill of combat in the clouds where it was his life or his adversary's. . . . [H]is life will always be gladdened as he looks about him and sees men and women and children walking about free and unafraid and when he thinks he has given his best and ventured his own life to bring this about.[44]

The trope "knights of the air" was secured for history, although its resonances were far deeper in British culture than in the United States.

The Romance of the Aces

In the final analysis, the enduring appeal of the ace is epitomized in the duel, the image frozen in time of two men in two planes circling each other, each seeking the advantage, but bound together by an inexpressible intimacy. At the core of the deadly encounter, there was a sympathy, a mutual attraction, which accounts for the continuing power of the aces as symbols for a particular kind of character and courage. Beyond the political or ideological uses to which the images of the aces have been put, beyond the efforts to glamorize the experience of their war for films or pulp fiction, there remains the reality of this empathy at the center of violence and destruction.

The uniquely international brotherhood of the World War I aces resides in this intimate connection. Pilots on both sides give similar accounts of such encounters. The German ace Ernst Udet described meeting with a Spad toward the end of the war:

> After we flew around and about each other nine or ten times, unable to get each other in our sights, I saw my opponent more closely. He wore a scarf flying in the wind and black headcovering and . . . he was clean-shaven. He looked at me for a long time, then raised his right hand and began to wave. I don't know why, but all at once I felt very sympathetic to the man in the Spad. Without a thought, I waved back. This went on for five or six curves. Suddenly I had the strange feeling that I wasn't confronting an opponent but practicing turns with a comrade.

This momentary fraternity ended when a squadron of German planes comes to Udet's aid, and the Spad was chased away.[45]

Cecil Lewis offers one of the rare passages in which pilots reveal they have internalized the image of themselves as the Happy Warrior, have embraced the knight, understood it not as a metaphor, but as their core identity. He provides the self-revelation in his autobiography, published two years before Britain was once again at war with Germany:

> As long as man has limbs and passions he will fight. Sport, after all, is only sublimated fighting, and in such fighting, if you don't "love" your enemy in the conventional sense of the term, you honour and respect him. Besides, there is, as everybody who has fought knows, a strong magnetic attraction between two men who are matched against one another. I have felt this magnetism, engaging an enemy scout three miles above the earth. I have wheeled and circled, watching how he flew, taking in the power and speed of his machine, seen him, fifty yards away, eyeing me, calculating, watching for an opening, each of us wary, keyed up to the last pitch of skill and endeavour. And if at last he went down, a falling rocket of smoke and flame, what a glorious and heroic death. What a brave man! It might just as well have been me. For what have I been spared? to die, diseased, in a bed! Sometimes it seems a pity.
>
> So if the world must fight to settle its differences, back to Hector and Achilles! Back to the lists! Let the enemy match a squadron of fighters against ours. And let the world look on! It is not as fanciful as you suppose. We may yet live to see it over London.[46]

Cecil Lewis, the Happy Warrior, handed off to the next generation the image of the warrior engaged in unending warfare, transcending the limitations of life by embracing death found in the face of a man who looks much like oneself, bound to him by the intimacy of death understood as a kind of love; a clean, unbroken invitation to glory and proof of manhood passed from Achilles, to Roland, to the aces of World War I, to the flyers who would soon after Lewis wrote, fly in the Battle of Britain.

In both popular accounts and as the subjects of serious military analysis, the aces seemed to fall into two general types: those who were rash, impetuous, and reckless—Albert Ball, Georges Guynemer, Frank Luke—and those who were careful, calculating, and concerned with tactics—Oswald Boelcke, Manfred von Richthofen, Mick Mannock, and Rene Fonck.[47] The dashing, devil-may-care, reckless image of the aces was the most resilient in the popular imagination, along with that of a man in charge of his own destiny, testing his individual virtues against those of his opponent. The aces were represented as actively seeking to engage and reengage in this Dance of Death, as men who did not fear death, and, implicitly, as men who sought it. Their romantic power over the imagination came from the sense of them as men who chose to die as heroes, found an elation in battle, and lived only for the moment. Because most of the famous aces died in the war, they were literally immortalized as warriors; they never grew old, never revealed the flaws and frailties that emerge from living in ordinary times, and, with few exceptions, left behind neither widows nor progeny. They seemed to be serious versions of Peter Pan, who never grew up and always sought the Great Adventure, sweeping from the sky upon his archenemy. They seemed to embody the fantasy of men who had escaped the paltry limitations of middle-class civilization, unfettered by the claims of hearth and home, of getting and spending, who therefore daily acted upon the masculine drive to place their lives at risk.

The emphasis on duels in the sky masked the nature of air combat: the high mortality rates, and the high rates of psychological breakdown. Aviation historian Mike Spick credits the promotion of the chivalric imagery in autobiographical accounts to the guilt aces felt about achieving their high-scores through the "method of the assassin"—sneaking up on a plane unawares—or the revulsion they felt when they remembered the sight of an opponent falling from the sky in flames. The need for a "mental self-protection" helps to account for the romanticized versions of air combat; in addition, accounts of skillful maneuver in one-on-one bouts in the sky make for more exciting reading than descriptions of pouncing on some unsuspecting plane flown by an inexperienced pilot with a life expectancy measured in days, not weeks or months.[48]

Democratizing War

> The clock in Bush's study struck seven, and within minutes all of
> the television networks were reporting anti-aircraft fire and falling
> bombs over the capital of Iraq. "This is just the way it was scheduled,"
> Bush said calmly.
>
> —U.S. News and World Report Staff, *Triumph without Victory* (1992)

While exploits of the aces restored the glory to war in the popular imagination, the lessons learned from World War I struck serious military thinkers as suggesting that future wars would be conducted from the air, but that they would rely increasingly on strategic bombing, at the opposite extreme from romantic medieval jousting lists. The high costs of the Great War along with the technological advances in airplanes and bombs suggested that future wars should not be determined solely or even primarily by the flower of the nation's male youth, but carried to the homefront in long-range bombers. While in the popular imagination the concept of violence tempered by civilized constraints was embodied in the vision of the youthful encounter in the sky, those in charge of imagining future wars transferred the concept of how to fight a war in defense of civilization to theories that idealized the deterrent threat of bombing cities as epitomizing the civilizing effects of warfare.

In the postwar era, theorists and popularizers on both sides of the Atlantic argued that future wars would be determined by the bombing of cities. While such visions were presented as prophecies of the inevitable, there was a thinly disguised underlying implication of desirability, that waging war against civilian populations was how war not only would be but ought to be fought in the future. The unmitigated slaughter of the nation's male youth would be avoided by terrorizing the opposing civilian population into demanding surrender from their leaders, or it would defeat the enemy by disrupting the industrial capacity to wage war. The threatened aerial bombardment of cities would serve a civilizing function as a deterrent for future wars, while strategic bombing in the event of war would also civilize the violence of modern warfare by assuring that wars were short and decisive.[1]

The moral and imaginative leap is significant in shifting the appropriate means for defending civilization from the civilized violence of air-to-air duels to the strategic and terror bombing of cities. When warfare became uncongenial to providing evidence for the inevitability of caste, breeding, and skill as signs of the natural leader, and when the odds of surviving became next to nil, the battlefield lost its appeal. The idea of strategic bombing was legitimated among military analysts because the civilian population was assigned the key responsibility for starting and ending wars—what Billy Mitchell referred to as "democratizing" warfare.[2]

Forebodings: Henley-Page Bombers, or How a Gentleman Fights an Air War

Unique testimony to the transformation of the idealism of the warrior from the combat pilot to the bombing crew is found in a manuscript housed in the British Imperial War Museum, the wartime diary of Maj. William Ronald Read, MC, DFC, and AFC. Willie Read was born in 1885, the eldest son of a wealthy Hampstead family. Both of his parents died when he was twelve, and he was raised by guardians, along with six siblings, in considerable affluence. Having attended Jesus College, Cambridge, he was commissioned into the King's Dragoon Guards in 1908. In 1913 he was sent to the Royal Flying Corps, and in August 1914 he was with the first British squadron sent to the Western Front. He survived the war and lived the life of a bachelor Edwardian amateur adventurer and traveler, dying in 1972. His account of his role in the first air war is noteworthy; he was assigned to plan what would have been the first air attack on Berlin and was quite disappointed when the war ended too soon for him to execute the order.

Read's diaries provide a fascinating insight into the evolving nature of aerial warfare and the reactions of a thoroughly British gentleman and individualist to the emerging nature of air combat. In December 1915 he was sent from his squadron on the front to Britain to organize his own squadron. He felt "very sad about going home" because he had "such a ripping five months in the squadron." In April 1916 he returned to the front in command of 45 Squadron. But by October 26 his enthusiasm for air combat had waned and he thought of applying to return to his old regiment. The immediate cause seems to have been the toll on the men in his command, including ten men missing, killed, or otherwise out of action between October 22 and October 26. The planes were unreliable, the billeting for the men was poor, and while moving to new quarters in December, the trucks carrying their equipment were either hit by a train or drove into a ditch. High winds carried off some of their canvas hangars or tore others to pieces. For this delay he received considerable criticism from his superiors for his inefficiency. By December Read's entries include complaints about the "awful dud lot of pilots from England," some of whom are "Not fit to wear the pilot's badge" and who do not know how to fly. His entry for December 7, 1916, reflects upon how he was perceived by his commanding officers: "Trenchard has suggested . . . that I am not a success out here and that I'm rattled over my losses in the squadron." Read permitted himself a rare moment of demoralization, complaining: "Everyday I am straffed by Wing and Brigade for this and that, in fact whatever I do is wrong." Responding to the rumor that he will be sent home, Read wrote of his commanding officers, "They are a lot of overfed pampered pets who sit on their bo-hinds and fling out horrid abuse at any hard working devil trying to do his bit." In April he put in for and was granted transfer to the Dragoons, which he did not much enjoy. In September he was transferred again to begin training with a RNAS Hanley-Page bombing squadron.

Once he settled into commanding a Hanley-Page squadron in August 1918, Read became the kind of officer he had ideally sought to be. He wanted to "promote a proper adventurous and more daring spirit" among his men and therefore requested permission to assign himself missions—an unusual request because squadron leaders were not supposed to fly any combat missions. He received permission to fly one mission per week, which brought upon him the criticism of other squadron leaders who perceived him as simply bucking for a D.F.C. He was undaunted by the criticism, saying, "I love this flying [on a raid to Metz]. . . . [T]here is a feeling of incompleteness if I do not fly at all."

Read settled into an entirely enjoyable life near Roville, hunting quail, hares, and the occasional boar at a nearby French estate; touring the countryside by car at night with the way lit by Very lights; playing soccer; ordering concerts and theatricals for the squadron; inviting other wing commanders for dinner with songs and drunken revelry; going to the private cinema at 100 Squadron—in general, living what came to be regarded as the prototypical life of a pilot in a flying squadron. What made his ease of mind possible, in addition to the considerable opportunities for leisure pursuits, was the low casualty rates for the night-bombing missions. He was responsible for the well being of the men in his command, not for their deaths.

In April 1918 Read mentioned discussions of plans to bomb Berlin, which at first seemed logistically impossible. In May he offered if all else failed to volunteer for a solo bombing flight to Berlin. In November he was ordered to take six Hanley-Page bombers to Bohemia and find a landing place north of Prague to establish a staging field for bombing Berlin. Read noted that he could not predict how the Czechs would react, given there is a state of "general revolution," but he looked upon the mission as "a grand adventure and if successful will beat anything the air force has done in the war." On November 8 Read was preparing to fly ahead of the other planes alone to locate a suitable landing place and then arrange for support supplies to be sent by rail from Trieste. He was keenly interested to learn on November 9 that an ultimatum for surrender had been issued because if the Kaiser refused, everyone would have been hotly in favor of bombing Berlin; but if he accepted, obviously, Read would miss his grand adventure. The plans to bomb Berlin continued to be discussed even after the general revelry broke out following the announcement of the Armistice, but Read was ultimately deprived of his opportunity.

Commanding a Hanley-Page night-flying squadron appealed to

Read because it so closely matched the ideal vision of an Edwardian gentleman-officer at war. The lifestyle was essentially that of a country gentleman, there was a sense of personal contribution to the war effort, scope for individual demonstrations of courage, opportunities for promotion, and, above all, his leadership did not include sending untrained men on dawn patrols in inferior airplanes to their inevitable deaths. There is no lack of personal courage in Read, and there was a zest for combat in the early days of the war, when the Lewis machine gun became part of his plane. But the casualties then were low and came more from crash landing or other mistakes than from air-to-air combat. Deaths were sufficiently rare that pilots on either side were careful to inform each other by dropped messages of the fates met by enemy pilots.

When he returned to the front with his own squadron, Read encountered much altered conditions. Night-bombing accommodated far better his sense of how a war ought to be fought. While he felt pangs of conscience over the possibility that his bombs would kill innocent civilians, he rationalized it as an inevitable aspect of war. His entry after a bombing mission into Ghent reads: "Know the probabilities are that it fell on quarters inhabited by Belgians and it seems to me that it is a merciful dispensation of Providence that my conscience does not accuse me of being a murderer. Thank goodness one's conscience is forgiven these things in wartime." By the end of the war, his fondest ambition was to fly solo to Berlin and bomb it—a gesture more symbolic than meaningful, yet tellingly directed toward civilians rather than combatants.

The Idea of Strategic Bombing

The development of a strategic bombing capability as the way to resolve the stalemate along the Western Front had been part of the American agenda in seeking to build the largest aerial armada in the world when the United States entered the war. The request included in the Ribot cable was intended to provide for the deployment of bombers, and Billy Mitchell's encounter with Hugh Trenchard persuaded him, as it did some members of the Bolling Commission, that strategic bombing was the key to ending the war. Indeed, Trenchard was mobilizing commanders, including Major Read, to plan the bombing of Berlin.

But the American imagination was not prepared to accept the idea of terror or morale bombing—that is, bombing directed toward the enemy's civilian population. For one thing, the propaganda campaign leveled against German barbarism pointed not only toward the atrocities against civilians in Belgium and other occupied territories, but to the Zeppelin raids on the cities of Great Britain. The evidence that the Prussian mentality was essentially barbaric was based precisely on the point that they intentionally waged war against unarmed civilians, including women and children. Newton Baker was appalled at the idea of bombing cities and made it clear that his vision of a vast aerial armada winning the war did not include it.

As the United States entered World War I—and hence, began the venture that would lead it to emerge as the world's dominant military power by the end of the century—the idea took root in the public's imagination that America's military dominance could be achieved through the reliance on air power, which would both represent the essential American spirit and obviate what a democracy cannot ultimately sustain for long—high losses on the ground. It is also clear that key military planners, including the very influential Billy Mitchell, foresaw that this vision would eventuate not from duels in the sky between evenly matched combatants, but from carrying the war over the lines of battle and directly to the enemy's population.

The Military Aviation Appropriation Bill included funding for bombers, but it was passed quickly and with little debate. The descriptions of the kind of air force the United States would build was both glittering and vague, reinforcing in the public's imagination the one kind of air combat that had been glamorized in the press, in books, and on the screen: air-to-air combat. This form of warfare resolved post–Civil War anxieties that mechanized weaponry would subsume the individual, making him little more than an extension of the machine. It restored to combat traditional visions of war as a test of manhood, and, as Americans were lionized for their roles in both the Lafayette Escadrille and the American squadrons flying over the front, American combat flyers were made the embodiments of American national pride and aspirations, demonstrable proof of the superiority of American democracy.

The attractiveness of strategic bombing, while it might initially seem to be at the opposite end of a spectrum of warfare conducted along the lines romanticized in the duels in the sky, derived much of its potency from the promise that it, too, would embody many of the same values. The arguments in favor of strategic bombing echoed those earlier utilitarians who favored mechanized weaponry, that is, the argument that the threat of mechanized warfare would be so onerous that it would prove to be a deterrent, and when deterrence failed, mechanized warfare would both lower the number of casualties, and have such tremendous destructive power that the enemy would soon capitulate, thereby shortening the length of a war.

This line of reasoning was obviously rather severely challenged by the first venture into mechanized warfare on the scale fought in Europe between 1914 and 1918. It must have appeared to many military analysts a simple exercise in logic to conclude that, with the advent of improved technologies for building airplanes, the same principles could be applied to strategic bombing, and that where the thinking had failed rather demonstrably when it came to an even encounter on the ground, it would succeed if the war was carried to the civilians in cities.

There was, of course, the problem of the public's reservations about conducting war directly against civilians. It jarred against the vision of the United States as riding to the rescue, saving civilization from itself, while demonstrating the moral superiority of the American character.

How that public morality was changed to accept the strategic bombing of cities as worthy of American military power is beyond the scope of this study, except to offer a few observations relating to the origins of America's dream of becoming a dominant power through reliance on air power.

The strategic bombing of European cities in World War II by the U.S. forces was made morally palatable within the context of total warfare by the assurances offered to the American public that the bombing was aimed at military targets only. American technology was held up as so advanced as to permit specific targeting using the Norden bomsight. There is a scene, for instance, in the Hollywood movie remake of the World War II documentary *Memphis Belle* which is not in the original documentary. In the Hollywood film, the navigator siting a target in Germany tells the captain that the military target is close to a school, and that to be certain they do not hit the school, the plane will have to make another pass—a highly dangerous maneuver because it requires flying back into the oncoming planes also targeting the same site, while under fire from German attack planes and from artillery on the ground. The captain agrees, the plane circles to make another pass, and the navigator, using the Norden bombsight, drops the load. This may seem to be an effort to gild the lily and make the bombing of German cities more acceptable to audiences watching the remake long after the event; however, the captain of the *Memphis Belle*, who was an advisor to the Hollywood version, says the incident did in fact occur.

Convincing the public that American planes only sought out military targets and relied on precision bombing reflects the continuing influence of a public morality that assumes warfare will be conducted with civilized constraint. This confidence depended upon the ability to suppress information to the contrary during the war, but it is also the case that the United States was keenly interested in avoiding the targeting of civilians. The Allies decided to attack Dresden toward the end of the war, a city with no significant value. The 790 British Lancasters that bombed the city on the night of February 12 created a firestorm that swept away all in its path, engulfing eight square miles. They were followed in the daylight of February 13 by 450 American B-17s, who were supposed to bomb the railyards, but dropped their bombs on the city instead because the smoke obscured their target. It took them eleven minutes to drop enough bombs to destroy another eight hundred acres, inflicting on the population what one historian has termed "a havoc that no other city had ever endured as the result of one raid."[3]

The news of the results, and the international outcry against the firebombing of Dresden, were distressing to USAAF Chief of Staff Gen. "Hap" Arnold, who had been present at the creation of the dream of American air power. At the time the United States entered World War II in 1941, he advocated sending bombers immediately to Europe to bomb the German homeland, reflecting the military planning in the years since 1918. When he learned of Dresden and a following raid on Chemnitz, he contacted Maj. Gen. Carl Spaatz, who headed the Eighth Air Force, demanding to know, "Does this represent a change from American policy of bombing selected industrial structures to one of bombing cities?" Spaatz replied that it definitely did not.[4]

The strategic bombing of cities obviously stretched to the limit the belief that the use of air power to determine the outcome of a war could be reconciled with earlier conceptions of warfare as defending civilization through civilized constraint, or as a proof of manhood and national character through the encounter of equally skilled warriors. The rationale was stretched even further in the bombing of Japan. Upon hearing that the incendiary bombing of Tokyo had inflicted the greatest damage of any attack in military history, General Arnold congratulated Gen. Curtis E. LeMay who had ordered the attack, an evident departure from Arnold's earlier qualms. But for LeMay, the bombing of Japanese cities simply extended the idea that strategic bombing should undermine the industrial capability of the enemy:

> We were going after military targets. No point in slaughtering civilians for the mere sake of slaughter. Of course, there is a pretty thin veneer in Japan, but the veneer was there. It was their system of dispersal of industry. All you had to do was visit one of those targets after we'd roasted it, and see the ruins of a multitude of tiny houses, with a drill press sticking up through the wreckage of every house.[5]

While one's gorge rises at the general's use of the word "roasted," it is his unflinching description of precisely what incendiary bombing, and nuclear bombing, do. LeMay is clearly a utilitarian, a pragmatist: "The whole purpose of strategic warfare is to destroy the enemy's potential to wage war," and there is "nothing new about this massacre of civilian populations." It was common practice in the barbarian era.

Distasteful though it may be to recognize, LeMay is voicing the lesson learned from World War I. Throughout his account, LeMay is plagued by the thought that mothers of the men he sent into battle will write to him to accuse him of killing their sons. Saving his nation from domination by another and saving the lives of his men requires carrying the war directly to the enemy's civilian population. It was LeMay who ordered the planes into the sky which dropped the atomic bombs on Hiroshima and Nagasaki, and his utilitarianism extended to the use of nuclear weapons: "to worry about the morality of what we were doing— Nuts. A soldier has to fight. We fought. If we accomplished the job in any given battle without exterminating too many of our own folks, we considered that we'd had a pretty good day" (383).

The important consideration to bring to LeMay's crude defense of the use of nuclear weapons is that it was not universally accepted as a justification for dropping the atomic bomb at the time he published his memoirs in 1965, and LeMay knew it. He inveighs against those "young kids who don't know any better," who "demonstrate against the military," and "a lot of old fools who ought to know better. They are worried to death about our dropping nuclear weapons." But, he snorts, "In SAC [Strategic Air Command] our bombardiers aren't worried about it" (382).

LeMay's utilitarianism, his bluntness, was anticipated in the dark parody of the frothing Gen. "Buck" Turgidson, played by George C. Scott in Stanley Kubrick's *Dr. Strangelove* (1964). It was a period when the reliance on nuclear deterrence was increasingly questioned, and the use of indiscriminate bombing in North Vietnam, and the dropping of bombs using napalm and agent orange on civilian populations aroused public consternation in the United States and abroad. The bloom was off the rose in terms of the American public's love affair with the use of air power.

Persian Gulf War

Yet on January 16, 1991, the American public, which polls had shown were generally opposed to a shooting war against Iraq, reacted with what was widely reported as "euphoria" to television pictures of the first prime-time war, which showed Iraqi artillery fired into the night sky, defending against an air attack by the U.S. Air Force. For day after day, beginning with twenty-four-hour coverage on the major networks, Americans were shown pictures of young pilots climbing into beautifully designed planes, especially the futuristic F-117 Stealth bombers, and videotape footage of precision bombs falling precisely on their targets.

The images of the war were masterfully controlled by the USAF in ways that suppressed the less desirable images of air warfare and foregrounded those that resonated with the romance of the first air war. Although they were in the first bombing mission to Baghdad and dropped the lion's share of nonprecision bombs on the battlefield, there were no pictures of the B-52 bombers, nor were reporters allowed to interview their crews or given access to their bases. The B-52s are associated with America's nuclear capability, and the news that they would refuel in India set off public demonstrations there. The Saudis indicated they would not allow B-52s to take off from their airports. The symbolic potency of the B-52s in the region was too potentially negative to allow for any publicity surrounding them. The American public had to content itself with seeing schematic blueprints, line drawings, or file film. There were no pictures of the B-52s operating in the theater of war, although the soul-searing effect of the tons of bombs dropped from them onto Iraqi soldiers trapped in bunkers is widely credited with their surrender in large numbers.

Americans saw plenty of pictures of precision weapons heading right for their targets, even though they accounted for only about 12 percent of the tonnage dropped, and the total tonnage exceeded all that dropped by the Allies in World War II. They were sheltered from images of precision weapons that missed their targets, and because great care was so obviously exercised to assure that only military targets were hit, the public was assured that the deaths of civilians were lamentable but morally excusable as "collateral damage"—the equivalent of Major Read's temporizing to soothe his conscience at the knowledge his bombs had killed innocent civilians: "thank goodness one's conscience is forgiven these things in wartime."

With the images of B-52s suppressed, attention focused almost exclusively on the glamour of American planes taking off and landing. Particularly compelling were those of the Stealth bombers taking off into either the setting or the rising sun (who could tell?), with the pilot giving a thumbs-up just before he roared into the sky. It was a reprise of the image of aces as told originally during World War I, and as retold many times; it was *Dawn Patrol* come true, only this time without all the deaths of young pilots.

The public was not made aware that the modern air force flies as a literal armada, sometimes stretching seventy miles across the sky, with different highly specialized aircraft assigned specific missions necessary to the success of the mission, a highly coordinated form of attack. What they saw were individual pilots flying into battle; rarely was even a small formation shown. And while most advanced planes require both a pilot and a weapons' operator, the impression most often given was of a single individual climbing into his plane, the most advanced technology in the world, to do combat with Saddam Hussein. It was made all the better, of course, by the reality that the Iraqi air force ceased to be a threat within a few hours of the opening of the war. It was an air war in which very few pilots were killed in the air.

Still, the pilots were called fighter pilots and the planes used impressed the eye as fighter planes—that is, planes that engaged in air-to-air combat. The most familiar to the American public was the F-14 Tomcat, featured in *Top Gun* (1986), starring Tom Cruise. The film celebrated the revival of air-to-air combat training in 1969 at the Navy Fighter Weapons School, training that had been dropped because advanced weaponry seemed to obviate its necessity, until the assumption was proven incorrect in the skies over Vietnam. The Navy rented F-14s to Paramount Studios, and one F-14 fighter pilot, Art Scholl, was killed in the making of the film.

The film revived the excitement of air-to-air combat and the attractiveness of combat pilots, and identified the F-14 with high-tech duels in the sky. Notably, it emphasized the need of a talented but head-strong individual to submit to squadron solidarity. Equally notable for the continuity with the original stereotypes of the aces was the connection between masculine aggression in the skies and sexual attractiveness. No larger ethos of the warrior was presented.

The glamour associated with *Top Gun* was attached to an airplane used for bombing missions in the Persian Gulf War. All of the planes that roared off the runways or carrier decks were used for bombing; the Stealth bomber, the most glamorous of them all, was just that: a bomber designed to evade radar in order to bomb cities.

The advantages of the visual impression to controlling the public's reaction to the war cannot be overestimated. Gone from view were the offensive, large, negatively identified B-52s; present to the eye were fighter planes with young pilots, thumbs up, taxiing down the runway at dawn, and upon their safe return climbing from their planes, helmets in hand, looking both fashionable in their flying gear and very, very cool.

Moreover, they were fighting against an archenemy in defense of civilization. Pres. George Bush initially defended military action against Saddam Hussein on very practical grounds: control over oil fields upon which the United States depended. But this was met with the outcry "No Blood for Oil." Meeting with Margaret Thatcher, Bush was introduced to the long-in-the-tooth messages used by Great Britain: military action in the Persian Gulf was a defense of civilization against a new Hitler, who practiced barbaric atrocities against both minorities within his own borders and innocent civilians in Kuwait. Appeasement was unthinkable. It was not long before the press picked up the general outlines, and Saddam Hussein was transformed into Hitler, his invasion of Kuwait into a threat of the direst portends to civilization, and the actions of the United States and its Allies into the creation of a New World Order based upon civilized values.

This justification, along with the reality that the television cameras could take pictures around the clock and transmit them all over the world, required that the images of the war—which the military controlled—represent it as conducted along civilized lines, governed by civilized constraints. American know-how in high technology aircraft coupled with clean-cut American men who knew how to fly them would bring order once again. While the technology for reporting the war had changed, the messages they conveyed—and the images they were allowed to convey—were a reprise of the justifications for war and for establishing the acceptable way of fighting them which had initiated America's entry into the arena as a world power.

The specter of a protracted ground war waged against a formidable enemy in a difficult terrain was raised consistently during the military buildup that preceded the air campaign, a reprise that echoed most immediately with Vietnam, but which ultimately resonated with the received images of the Great War, whose carnage and stalemate had made the option of conducting war from the air seem an ideal alternative to Americans and created the conditions for imagining America as the world's major air power.

The air force has had a long history of managing the images of air campaigns because the promotion of the original image of the ace dueling in the sky was itself borne of a publicity campaign, a form of warfare that from the beginning has had a powerful utility as a propaganda device. The traditions associated with that legacy place constraints on the uses of air power which are directly related to both the projection of force as a civilized violence and the representation of the pilot as the embodiment of national character and aspirations.

This aspect of the legacy of the first air war also presented itself in the Persian Gulf War. On February 25 airplanes attacked Iraqi soldiers fleeing Kuwait City in anything they could manage to commandeer. The result was a three-mile-long stretch of what would come to be known as the Highway of Death along the Mutla Ridge. The planes attacked the front and rear of the column, and the next day television cameras filmed images of burned-out and abandoned cars, trucks, jeeps, and buses, some of them loaded with the spoils of war—furniture, television sets, clothing, perfume, and cigarettes. While most of those in the column apparently abandoned their vehicles and escaped, the televised images of burned-out vehicles, some containing charred bodies, were transmitted to a watching world.

There was an intense outcry in the United States in response to the appalling images because as one history, published shortly after the war ended, put it, "Americans do not engage in 'turkey shoots.'" Gen. Norman Schwartzkopf was furious at the suggestion that Americans engaged in wanton destruction of unarmed and fleeing soldiers who were not in military vehicles. The public reaction to the pictures of Mutla Ridge are thought by a number of analysts to have played an important role in the decision to end the war without pursuing the Iraqi ground forces to annihilation, a decision that was also made in response to pressures from Saudi Arabia and Egypt to call an end to the war once the Iraqis had fled Kuwait.[6]

The idea that "Americans do not engage in 'turkey shoots'" was a reference primarily to the concept of the use of air power. Without dwelling on the use of B-52s to pulverize Iraqi soldiers sweating it out in their bunkers as an example of an uneven use of power equivalent to a "turkey shoot," the point to be made is that combat planes represent a particular set of contraints in warfare, an important factor in the condemnation of the attack along the Highway of Death.

This set of constraints played an important role in another way, one that while it was widely reported in the British papers was not in the United States. The pilots themselves in both the British and American forces indicated to their superiors that they did not wish to receive further orders to engage in a similar attack. Pilots, of course, face the same military charges for refusing direct orders as does any other soldier; however, combat pilots from the beginning have been regarded as both officers and the members of an elite corps. They are highly trained, and their effectiveness in the airplane depends very much on will and initiative even if they are also extensions of a highly technical and computerized weapon of war. To indicate that they did not wish to receive further orders for a certain kind of combat carried weight. While both General Schwartzkopf and President Bush rejected the criticism of the attack as an example of "wanton destruction," the pilots themselves felt that what they had been asked to do was outside the constraints on the use of punishing force from the sky.

Their reluctance to engage in such conduct was widely reported in the British press and used as a reason why the war was not further prosecuted than it was. This brought a public outcry against the government for attempting to use men in uniform as the excuse for what was a political decision. In the United States, no such attention was drawn to the unwillingness of American pilots to engage in annihilation attacks; the criticism from some quarters for ending the war earlier than a decisive victory has been blamed on the sensitivity President Bush felt toward the public criticism of the conduct of the war in response to the pictures of the carnage at Mutla Ridge.

The success in the Persian Gulf was widely represented as having "laid to rest the ghost of Vietnam," a phrase suggestive of many possibilities, but in the context of how success was achieved in the Persian Gulf the lesson seemed to be that the American public's reluctance to engage in war could be overcome if the campaign was conducted in the name of "civilization," relied upon air power rather than ground soldiers—and there were few, if any, casualties on the ground once those forces were deployed—and the air campaign was conducted along lines that allowed for a moral idealism about air wars to prevail. It was permissible to bomb cities so long as the images shown to the public made it obvious that precision bombing was used, the precision was "pinpoint," the only civilian casualties were incurred by accident, big bombers were out of sight, the airplanes used looked like combat fighters, and the individual who emerged from the cockpit was a handsome, clean-cut young man wearing an outfit that bespoke his virility and competence operating a highly technical machine.

NATO Forces Bomb Serbia

The Persian Gulf War realized the fantasy of air power as imagined at the time the United States faced with considerable dread the prospect of sending a million conscripts to fight in a stalemated foreign war. The positive images of an air campaign associated with the Persian Gulf War laid the groundwork for the bombing of targets inside Serbia, particularly the sustained attacks on Belgrade, in the spring of 1999. Again, the *casus belli* used to legitimate the first-ever use of NATO forces in combat was that Slobodan Milosevic was a second Hitler engaged in atrocities equal in intent if not dimension to the Holocaust. The compelling images of peasants forced from their homes and onto rural paths, fleeing with their meager belongings piled onto tractors—and looking as if they had been living in a time warp since 1914—and the resonance of the Balkans with the history of World War I, connected the action of Milosevic with both wars. The essential requirements for the conduct of the war were, first, not to involve the United States and other NATO forces in a ground war in Kosovo; second, to use air power to force Milosevic to capitulate; third, to have no American casualties during the air campaign; and fourth, to adhere to the morality of a civilized restraint in the use of violent force.

The problem that presented itself was that Milosevic neglected to capitulate within the expected several days. What this meant for NATO was that it had run out of legitimate military targets by about the fourth day of the campaign. Gen. Wesley K. Clark, NATO's supreme commander, demanded 2,000 targets in order to obviate the need for a ground war while sustaining pressure on Milosevic. NATO turned to bombing tobacco factories, hotels with gambling casinos and other interests owned by friends of Milosevic, as well as electric grids and bridges.[7] In short, NATO crossed the Rubicon that had marked the boundary of acceptable targets for precision bombing. This seems to have been a return in a scarcely veiled way to one of the original aims of strategic bombing during World War I and developed since, which is to so demoralize the populace that they overthrow the enemy's leadership. Winston Churchill's delicate way of phrasing it to his bomber commanders in World War II was "bombing German cities, simply for the sake of increasing the terror, though under other pretexts." Churchill was recommending a review of the policy following the public outcry after the night bombing of Dresden.[8]

With the bombing of Belgrade, the solution to the repugnance felt immediately following World War I at the loss of so many soldiers—which began in the Balkans—was realized; the war was carried directly to the civilian population in the hopes that the enemy's government would collapse while sparing the lives of any NATO soldiers or flyers. It was an ideal war from the military's point of view, allowing for the conduct of the war to seem to match the justness of the cause. The idea that some precision weapons aimed at military targets went astray and fell on the homes of citizens or on their cars was legitimated as accidental, and therefore as not crossing the boundaries of just conduct. In this regard, the ability to claim that the bombing of the Chinese embassy was just a stupid mistake caused by incompetence enhanced rather than detracted from the justification of the continuing bombing of Belgrade because it reinforced the idea that any civilian casualties were simply a regrettable cost.

The air campaign against Belgrade demonstrated the military's capacity to represent in a positive light to the American public the bombing of nonmilitary targets in a city for a protracted period of time against an enemy nation that poses no direct military threat to the United States, nor holds any resources significant for the national defense, nor occupies a highly strategic position. Regardless of how one might feel about the legitimacy of the cause behind the NATO campaign, the implications for the conduct of future wars should not escape attention.

9/11/01 and After:
Defense of Civilization and War from the Air

The September 11, 2001, attack on the World Trade Center and Pentagon was an event of such portent that the full consequences and significance of both the attack itself and the response can scarcely be calculated. Yet the perspective provided by history and, in this particular instance, how America understood its first step into the world as a dominating air power, can help gauge the implications of how the United States responded.

When terrorists who were widely assumed to be acting as part of the Al-Qaeda network attacked two American embassies in Africa in 1998, the audacity and damage were shocking, and directed no less against both American symbols and citizens than the attack on the World Trade Center on September 11, 2001. After the embassy attacks in 1998 President Bill Clinton called upon Americans to prepare for a long and sustained campaign against terrorists; he ordered missile attacks against a factory in Sudan supposedly used to produce chemical weapons for Al-Qaeda and against Al-Qaeda training camps in Afghanistan. These attacks seemed misguided, lacking in utility, and, to many, merely an effort to distract attention from the Monica Lewinsky scandal. While Osama bin Laden and his cohorts had declared war upon the United States, the United States could scarcely tear itself away from the fascinating questions about cigars and how history could have been changed by a decent dry cleaner long enough to notice the attack and counterattack.

The 1998 attack provides a useful point of comparison to the reactions to the attack of September 11. President Clinton did not, in response to the bombing of American embassies, declare that civilization itself required defense. Nor was the defense of civilization invoked after the first bombing attack on the World Trade Center in 1993. That was followed by a search for the culprits, a trial, and sentencing. In other words, it was understood as a violation of domestic law, and not as an act of war.

In September 2001 Pres. George W. Bush, echoing his father's justifications for the Persian Gulf War, declared that civilization itself was at risk after the attack of September 11. It was a tried and true metaphor, one that had been invoked during both world wars to justify the Allied cause. It must have seemed only natural to President Bush, reeling from the devastating and unprecedented attack, to extend the metaphor and declare that the United States was now engaged in a crusade.

The immediate outcry from the Muslim world which greeted his use of both "civilization" and "crusade" must have shocked White House advisors into recognizing the difference between a metaphor and its source in history. In a sense, the invocation of warfare to defend civilization from the "east" had come full circle. The imagery owed its origins to the legitimizing discourses of imperialism; it was appropriated as a *casus belli* by the Allied powers, and particularly Great Britain, to paint Germany as neither civilized nor "western," as sharing more with the barbarian and Muslim "East" than with Europe. The romanticism of the Victorian era, which revived the imagery of the knight-errant as the epitome of Victorian masculinity, provided the cultural context for applying the image of the mailed and mounted warrior to World War I—at least initially, until the realities of trench warfare rendered the image ridiculous except for the "knights of the air."

At the beginning of the twenty-first century, both President Bush and his foe, Osama bin Laden, reinvoked the image of crusade not as an abstracted and decontextualized metaphor, but as a reprise of the historical realities of 1000 A.D. In an odd and uncanny way, both leaders mirrored the other in their justifications. The embarrassing consequences for President Bush were almost instantly recognized. The word "crusade" dropped from his arsenal of images, while "defense of civilization" morphed into "defense of civilized values," which, the president acknowledged, are subscribed to by Christians, Muslims, and Jews alike. The insistence upon naming the world's three major religions, of course, validated the divisions of the world imposed by Osama bin Laden himself (who called for a new crusade against Jews and the West), while having the effect of excluding all other major belief systems, and all those who adhere to civilized values without also adhering to any major religion.

Underlying the president's initial impulse to frame the threat as one against "civilization" and its corollary, the Judeo-Christian tradition, was a political foundation no less significant than the relationship between the Victorian chivalric revival and the defense of aristocratic values against the encroachments of the parvenu class. The alarm that western values (as embodied in western civilization) are besieged and in need of defense had been sounded by conservative voices in America prior to the attack on September 11, ranging from the political theorist Samuel Huntington to the cultural conservatives Lynne Cheney and

William Bennett. In the case of the cultural conservatives, the attack prompted them to extraordinary levels of stridency in condemnation of both "multiculturalism" and of colleges and universities that sponsored teach-ins where criticism of the United States was voiced. The implied proposition that western civilization is superior to the Muslim, especially in the Levantine, was sounded soon after September 11 by Bernard Lewis in *What Went Wrong: Western Impact and Middle Eastern Response* (December 2001), and explicitly by conservative Italian Prime Minister Berlusconi in a major speech (September 2001).[9]

Defining the attack on the United States as an attack on civilization itself made the defense of civilization—or its later iteration, civilized values—the *casus belli* for both America's armed response and for calling upon NATO signatories to support the United States in its war effort. The sign that the attack represented an attack on civilization was that it had been aimed primarily at civilians (the World Trade Center and not the Pentagon became the visual symbol of the attack) with a wanton disregard for the value of human life, both in the hijacking of the planes with the intent of killing the crew and passengers, and by targeting the World Trade Center. Subsequently, the Taliban's disregard for human rights, particularly of women and girls, was added as a sign of their barbarism. This provided an additional justification, beyond the protection they afforded to Osama bin Laden and the Al-Qaeda network, for unseating their regime.

The attack on the United States, the radical extremism of the Taliban, and the demonstrable lethality of the Al-Qaeda network are undeniably violations of both human rights and the accepted international justifications for the uses of force. What is at issue here is not to deny those realities nor to dissect the history of the involvement of the United States in creating the conditions on the ground in Afghanistan which proved so fertile a nest for vipers.[10] Rather, the point is to trace the "defense of civilization" as a *casus belli*—how the justification resonates with the history of the United States and how it relates to the conduct of the war against Afghanistan, a war conducted primarily from the air.

A defense of civilization as a justification for war implicitly entails the combatants who invoke it in a civilized approach to the violence of warfare, especially with regard to the proportionality of the response and the protection of civilians. This level of constraint has, since the Persian Gulf War, been built into the American image of how war is waged from the air. The capacity both to show constraint with "pinpoint targeting" and to save the lives of American ground troops is an apparently happy marriage of the honorable code of engagement, epitomized in Melville's Englishman of the Old Order lamenting the loss of the *Temeraire*, with the pragmatic praise of technology expressed by his Utilitarian.

The optimism that air power enables the United States to wage war with civilized constraint was frequently presented to the American public not as a hoped-for ideal, but as an obvious fact. Articles appeared from October through December 2001 in American political commentary magazines and in major newspapers with the reassuring titles or headlines, "Humanity of the Air War: Look How Far We Have Come," "New Warfare: High-Tech US Arsenal Proves Its Worth," "Bull's-Eye War: Pinpoint Bombing Shifts Role of GI Joe," "Use of Pinpoint Air Power Comes of Age in New War," and "US Is Prevailing with Its Most Finely Tuned War."[11]

In stark contrast to these reassurances are the facts: the United States introduced both the largest conventional dumb bomb in the world into the theater of war (the "daisy cutter") and used fuel-air explosives, which have a far greater destructive capacity than conventional bombs. In addition, the civilian death rates in Afghanistan, using reliable nonmilitary sources, were evidently significantly higher in proportion to the munitions used than those in the American-led NATO attack on Belgrade and its environs.

In the 1999 campaign to defend Kosovo, far more sorties were flown with far fewer civilian casualties. It is estimated that in the 1999 campaign to defend Kosovo, 500 civilians were killed. The estimates by nonmilitary sources for the deaths in Afghanistan through January 1 range from a conservative 1,000 to 1,300, to 4,000.[12]

The factors that account for this difference make it difficult to sustain the romantic vision of a "high-tech" war that protects civilians by "pinpoint" or "bull's eye" weapons:

First, the United States relied far more heavily on bombers in the campaign against Afghanistan than in the 1999 campaign, when the more glamorous Navy fighter-bombers flew the most sorties. In other words, there were fewer sorties but very heavy munitions delivery in the Afghanistan war. In the opening week, bombers (B1s, B52s) dropped over 80 percent of all munitions: 500 Global Positioning System–guided and laser-guided bombs, 1,000 Mk-82 "dumb bombs," or unguided bombs, and 50 cluster bombs. Navy fighter bombers made up the rest of the munitions dropped, totaling 2,000 bombs, during the first week. The proportions during the first week are estimated at 55 percent unguided, 45 percent guided. Carpet bombing did not begin until late October and is not included in these figures.[13]

Second, in the attack on Afghanistan, the United States relied far more heavily on Global Positioning System (GPS) guidance than was the case in the Kosovo campaign, which relied on the more accurate laser-guidance for "smart bombs." This was more significant than it might have otherwise been because the military targets were in the middle of built-up urban areas, a strategy adopted by the Russians, who sought to protect what were then their bases during their failed invasion of Afghanistan. These bases had since been occupied by the Taliban. About 50 percent of GPS-guided munitions fall outside of the desired imaginary circle around the target, a matter of 32 to 42 feet. This means that 50 percent fall beyond a 2,100-square-foot area. Even those that fall with the acceptable radius wreak considerable damage on nontargeted sites.[14]

Third, the United States deployed a higher percentage of cluster bombs in the Afghanistan war. A "cluster bomb" is a Combined Effects Munitions (CEM) because it can be used against both human beings and armored vehicles, and it can be used to start fires as well. A CBU-87 weighs 1,000 pounds and contains 202 "bomblets," called BLU-97/B, which are dispersed over an area of 100 by 50 meters. About 7 percent of the "bomblets" fail to explode on contact. They become unexploded ordnance, or the equivalent of landmines, particularly lethal to small children attracted by their bright yellow casings. They are additionally attractive because they resemble in size and color the food rations that were dropped over Afghanistan at the same time that cluster bombs were deployed.[15]

Fourth, some bombing targets were in residential areas in cities of greatest population density. While one-third of Afghanistan is unpopulated, and as of 1999 Afghanistan had only one-third the population of Yugoslavia, the bombing was targeted at the major population centers of the few major cities, some of which have population densities greater than Belgrade. The targets themselves contributed to the greater likelihood of civilian casualties. While the aim in the bombing of Belgrade was to use force to achieve a resolution of the conflict over Kosovo, the aim in Afghanistan was to remove the Taliban regime and to kill members of the Al-Qaeda; hence, the targeting included sites in residential areas with the intent to destroy individuals rather than only destroy the infrastructure (which was bad enough in the case of Belgrade). Assassination from the air seems less likely to destroy targeted individuals than the older system of sending in the Special Forces or the CIA, but it puts American lives at less risk. It obviously required placing civilians in harm's way.[16]

Fifth, pilots were given orders to seek out and destroy "targets of opportunity." To fleeing refugees, it seemed that bombs were falling on anything that moved—trucks, taxis, ambulances. The lower levels of accuracy automatically entailed in siting "targets of opportunity" was compounded by reliance for intelligence on armed Afghans on the ground who sometimes used American air power to settle old scores with rivals, as was evidently the case on at least two occasions.[17]

As for heavy ordnance used in the theater of war, the press sometimes referred to "thermobaric" and "daisy cutter" as if they were the same kind of bombs. They differ in both design and purpose. Four BLU-82 slurry bombs ("daisy cutters") were used in Afghanistan; none were used in the Balkan campaign in 1999. Daisy cutters weigh 15,000 pounds, making them the world's largest conventional bomb. The size of a small car, the bomb is delivered from the back bay of a cargo plane, the MC-130, flying at high altitude. The warhead contains 12,600 pounds of a detergent "slurry" (ammonium nitrate, aluminum powder, and polystyrene). It is detonated just above ground, clearing an area of 300 to 900 feet, producing a flash and sound perceptible at long distances. It produces an overpressure of 1,000 pounds per square inch (psi). Developed originally to clear jungle for helicopter landing pads in Vietnam, they were used in the Persian Gulf War against entrenched troops for both their destructive capacity and for their terrifying psychological effect.[18]

Fuel-Air Explosives (FAEs), or thermobaric bombs, were used in Afghanistan on March 3 in the assault at Gardez against enemy forces entrenched in cave bunkers. FAEs produce an overpressure of 427 pounds psi and a temperature of 2,500 to 3,000 degrees Centigrade. People at ground zero are literally crushed to death, while others caught in the blast wave traveling at 9,800 feet per second are suffocated by the vacuum. Thermobaric bombs were first developed by the United States for use in Vietnam and were used in the Persian Gulf War; the advanced model used in March was barely out of the design stages. Two separate charges are used to detonate the container of volatile gases, liquids, or powdered explosives. The first charge bursts open the container above the ground, scattering the contents as an aerosol cloud. The second detonates the cloud, creating a fireball followed by a massive shockwave.[19]

While the thermobaric bomb is laser-guided, it hardly fits the picture of what Americans usually imagine when the words "pinpoint" or "bull's eye" are used. The thermobaric bomb is compared with disturbing regularity to tactical nuclear weapons. A paper published by the Foreign Military Studies office at Fort Leavenworth, Kansas, concludes: "a fuel-air explosive can have the effect of a tactical nuclear weapon without residual radiation." This echoes the opinion of a military analyst writing for a Russian military magazine: "In its destructive capability, it is comparable to low-yield nuclear weapons."[20]

Arguing in January 2001 that because "FAEs blur the distinction between low yield nuclear weapons and conventional weaponry," the British Campaign for Nuclear Disarmament (CND) called upon the United Kingdom's government to renounce any further development because it would "encourage other nations to breech their own obligations under international law and develop similar Weapons of Mass Destruction," that is, nuclear, biological, and chemical weapons.[21]

The use of thermobaric bombs in Afghanistan, while it was not the first time they had been used, seems somehow to have inched the United States closer to the blurring of boundaries predicted in the CND report. The Pentagon's confidential Nuclear Posture Review, whose contents were leaked in March 2002, included plans to develop what one reporter called "a new generation of smaller, super-hardened nuclear weapons to smash through rock and concrete and attack deep underground bunkers where enemy states could build weapons of mass destruction."[22] Evidently, in defending civilization against the uncivilized, it is permissible to use weapons of mass destruction because obviously anyone building weapons of mass destruction must necessarily be an enemy of civilization. Again, one is confronted with an uncanny mirroring of the very mentality against which civilization is supposedly pitted.

The boundary that is in danger of being crossed is that of proportionality. While the mainstream press on both sides of the Atlantic described the thermobaric and daisy-cutter bombs in awestruck tones, there seemed to be little of the deeper understanding of their use which is required to raise the appropriate questions about levels of response. The benchmark of "nuclear weapons" seems to be the accepted limitation on the legitimacy of munitions dropped from planes on troops. This may explain why the press seized upon the descriptions of thermobaric bombs as essentially like nuclear weapons, but without the radioactive consequences.

The apparent lack of understanding of these weapons, coupled with the lack of any framework capable of raising the issue of proportionality of response, meant that no serious public discussion of their use would arise. It may well be that in the sense that their use shortened the war and spared American lives, the use of daisy cutters and thermobaric bombs did not exceed the limits of proportionate response. The point is that no public discussion of the concept of proportionality was raised; the public was not made conscious of it as an issue requiring responsible judgment. This silence was matched by the effort on the part of the military to control access to the theater of war, and especially to images of the destructive consequences of American air power. In October 2001 the U.S. military purchased the rights to all the satellite war images from the Denver-based Space Imaging, Inc. For similar reasons, American bombs tried to put the Al-Jazeera television studio in Kabul out of business. The major television networks in the United States did not seek to know the civilian casualty counts, and the Pentagon was not interested in offering them. Concerns about civilian casualties were dismissed as the unfortunate cost of war, or as not subject to "independent" confirmation, or caused by the Taliban and not by American bombs. In one notable instance, military press officers simply denied that an entire village had been destroyed by American bombs despite the accounts by its occupants who managed to survive and reporters who saw the bomb damage. As for casualties among enemy soldiers, the military simply denied that they were taking body counts.[23]

During the assault on Afghanistan the military sought to control the images of the destructive power of American bombers and their payloads while the pacesetter press and opinion weeklies reassured the American public that America conducts only "high-tech" air wars, and that "high tech" is synonymous with "pinpoint" or "bull's eye" targeting. Civilian casualties, while lamentable, were dismissed as both inevitable and accidental. No constraints, short of using "weapons of mass destruction" (at least for the time being) were regarded as worthy of discussion when it came to the theater of war. Meanwhile, in Europe and elsewhere, there were graphic press accounts of children dismembered by bombs in front of their parents' eyes, extended families of thirty or forty wiped out in one night's bombing, and wounded civilians in ambulances bombed on the way to the hospital.

Americans are being asked to accept that America engages in what James Der Derian calls "virtuous war," represented by the reliance on technology to refine and control the use of violence.[24] The argument can legitimately be made that the failure to raise the appropriate moral questions has a desensitizing effect on the public. The low American casualty rates and the quick resolution of conflict make wars seem easy, and therefore, pave the way for more wars. Certainly, this seems to be the hopeful conclusion drawn by President Bush and his advisors.

The failure of the mainstream press, and especially of the network news, to press the difficult questions constitutes a complicity with power. But the reality is that information about casualties, destructive consequences, weaponry, and strategy are readily available to those who have sufficient initiative to seek it out. Reports in the American pacesetter press and, to a greater extent, in the foreign presses provided a picture for those with sufficient imagination of what the Afghans were enduring; organizations concerned with disarmament, peace, and defense alternatives had a wealth of information available on their websites. What was lacking was a focal point for public analysis of the information, or the public will to seek it actively.

The effort to control information and images illustrates that the military is not convinced that the public is "desensitized" to warfare; on the contrary, the control signifies the fear over the potential waning of support should the public be confronted with the carnage of warfare, coupled with clear reporting and analysis of the meanings of "collateral damage," "GPS guidance," and "high-tech" bombs. Far from having been laid to rest, the "ghost" of Vietnam, from the point of view of the administration and the Pentagon, determines the control over information, as does the memory of the reaction to the images of the Highway of Death along Mutla Ridge.

The war against Iraq began as this study was going to press. A few observations will necessarily have to suffice in lieu of a more extended analysis of how the presentation of this latest air war drew upon the legacy of America's dream of civilized violence.

The Bush administration was unable to make a compelling case that Iraq constituted a sufficient imminent threat to legitimize a preemptive strike. Despite opposition to the war in the streets around the world and in the United States, by America's traditional European allies in the Cold War as well as Russia and China, and in the formal chambers of the UN, the United States and its allies launched a war against Iraq which began on March 19, 2003, and ended with President Bush announcing victory on May 2, 2003.

The decision by the Pentagon to embed reporters meant the public's view of the war was essentially confined to what a small, mobile ground force encountered. Nevertheless, the story of the conquest of Iraq in short order with low coalition casualties depended upon the use of overwhelming power from the skies.

While General Tommy Franks, who headed the U.S. Central Command, initially called for 500,000 troops, civilian policy makers advocated a far smaller force. As one official put it, the ideal was for "less ground-centric and more air-centric" planning. The advocates for prevailing from the air argued prior to the war that the Navy and Air Force would be able to deliver up to 1,000 strike sorties per day, with 90 percent of the ordnance "precision guided."[25]

The decision to rely heavily on air power coupled with covert operations and a smaller ground force resulted in a war in which there were 15,500 strike sorties, or less than half those flown during the Persian Gulf War, with 27,000 bombs dropped—a dramatic difference from the 265,000 dropped in 1991. The difference is accounted for by increased use of smart weapons, amounting to 67 percent compared with the less than 12 percent in 1991, a much smaller Iraqi army, and no Iraqi air cover.

By April 14 more than 300,000 troops were in the region, though not all of them were deployed, including 255,000 from the United States. There were 121 dead among the American soldiers, compared with just over 300 in 1991. Neither the Iraqis nor the coalition forces provided casualty figures for Iraqi combatants.

While the war was a success given its limited aims—to topple the regime of Saddam Hussein with low casualties among the coalition ground forces—the toll in civilian casualties yields a very different picture of what a victory means in modern warfare. The U.S. military will not provide information about the civilian casualties, nor will Congress order it. Yet even the American television audience became aware to some extent of the death and destruction visited upon civilians. Viewers of other news outlets—including the BBC, but especially Middle Eastern satellite news broadcast by Al-Jazeera (Qatar), or from Abu Dhabi (UAE), Amman (Jordan), or Beirut (Lebanon)—saw far more graphic evidence of men, women, and children injured or killed. Iraqi estimates placed the number of civilian dead at 600, and those injured at more than 4,000. Additional casualties, however, mounted from diseases related directly to the effects of the war, death and maiming from the bomblets released by cluster bombs, violence associated with looting, the lack of medical supplies and hospital facilities for those injured in the war, and with conditions not related to the war but equally life-threatening.

The disproportionate ratio of civilian casualties to those of the coalition forces reflects what is now a normal condition of modern warfare. At the same time that President Bush declared victory over Iraq, the Save the Children Foundation issued its annual report on the state of the world's mothers, which focused on protecting women and children in war. The report noted that "close to 90 percent of war casualties now are civilians, the majority of whom are women and children. That compares to 5 percent a century ago."[26]

The report references ongoing strife in Sierra Leone, Burundi, Sri Lanka, and other destabilizing nations. But the reality is that the nation with the most advanced military wages war in a way that yields far higher casualties among civilians than among its own soldiers, and reduces the infrastructure to such an extent that civil order and security, food supplies, water, electricity, hospitals, and medical supplies are denied to civilians. The atrocities in the world's hidden wars are the result of direct and intentional assaults on the civilian population. While the American approach to fighting war involves seeking to avoid directly targeting civilian populations from the air, it does not involve seeking actively either to protect civilians, remove them from the conflict, or provide for security in occupied areas.

The example made to the world of this American mentality with regard to civilian casualties came on Monday, April 7, 2003, when a B-1B bomber dropped four precision bombs on a restaurant in the Monsour district of Baghdad because it was believed that Saddam Hussein and members of his family were meeting in an underground bunker. CNN and other American networks repeatedly showed the crater left by the bomb while speculating on whether or not Saddam Hussein had been killed. In some of the footage, a man was shown falling into the arms of another man and weeping. No explanation was provided even though the footage was played and replayed numerous times.

On Arab satellite networks, the scenes of the crater were explained as a bombing of a neighborhood by American planes. Usually, there was no mention made of the belief that Saddam Hussein was hiding beneath the restaurant. The emphasis was on the damage to the surrounding neighborhood. The explanation of the man collapsing was that he and others had been digging with their hands in the cement rubble because he could hear the voice of his young son Mohammed. The cries stopped, the man shouted, "Mohammed is gone," and fell into the arms of a friend overcome with grief and shock.

Young Mohammed falls into the category of "collateral damage." Presumably, his death was not considered worth reporting in the United States because it was accidental rather than actively intended—as would be, for instance, the kidnapping of a child to serve as a soldier in Uganda. This level of reasoning is a distinction without a difference to the watching eyes of the world.

The American capacity to remain disinterested in "collateral damage" derives ultimately from the same capacity recorded by Major Read when he acknowledged that his bombs must inevitably fall on civilians but that as it was war, his conscience could be free of the self-recrimination that he was a murderer. It is precisely because Mohammed was buried under rubble caused by a precision bomb dropped from the sky—and therefore his death was unintended—that attention in the

United States can be turned away from him and his father and toward the tantalizing question of whether or not Saddam Hussein is dead and if so, whether or not his DNA could be identified.

The legacy of the American use of air power allows for what in this instance should best be described cynically as a pragmatic moral clarity about civilian deaths: Americans are invited to view a grieving father with a clear conscience.

The legacy that makes the combat pilot a symbol of national strength and virility was definitely on President Bush's mind when he ordered a tailor-made flight suit and climbed into the cockpit of a S-3B Viking for a short hop from California to the deck of the carrier USS *Abraham Lincoln* to address the troops returning to their home port. "Yes, I flew it," he beamed to reporters as he emerged from the plane onto the flight deck.

The explanation that he flew in a jet because the *Abraham Lincoln* was out of the range of a helicopter proved bogus, and the American public was given the lame explanation that President Bush just wanted to see the flight deck as landing pilots would. That did not explain, however, why the ship was turned so that the picture would not show the California shoreline and the camera would not have to shoot the picture into the sun.

Nor did it explain why President Bush had not availed himself of the opportunity to land on a flight deck during the war in Vietnam. One week before his graduation from Yale (1968) he had been assigned to the Texas Air National Guard. There was the strong suggestion of wire-pulling to assure the young Bush did not have to serve in Vietnam, along with the criticism that following his initial training as a pilot, he failed to report to duty because he was otherwise occupied working for a political campaign.

Lisa Shiffren, in a *Wall Street Journal* article titled "Hey, Flyboy," reinvoked the nostalgia for the American ace when she gushed that President Bush looked "virile, sexy, and powerful." Senator Robert Byrd (D-W.Va.) took another view in a speech to the Senate titled "Making the Military a Prop in Presidential Politics":

American blood has been shed on foreign soil in defense of the President's
policies. This is not some made-for-TV backdrop for a campaign commercial. This is real life, and real lives have been lost. To me, it is an
affront to the Americans killed or injured in Iraq for the President to
exploit the trappings of war for the momentary spectacle of a speech. . . .
I do question the motives of a deskbound President who assumes the garb
of a warrior for the purposes of a speech. . . .War is not theater, and victory is not a campaign slogan.[27]

The war in Iraq demonstrates the consequences of the dream of civilized violence for the American imagination. It allows on the one hand
a sense of innocence with regard to the destruction wreaked or unleashed by American might. The destruction of the cultural sites of Iraq
by looters while American soldiers stood by was equivalent in potential
symbolic power to the condemnation of the Germans which followed
upon the burning of the library at Louvain or the destruction of cathedrals. But the Bush administration approved of the looting as evidence
that the Iraqis were exercising their "freedom" for the first time in
decades. The reality that war from the air takes a disproportionate
toll on civilians while sparing the lives of ground forces echoes Billy
Mitchell's favorable conclusion that air war would democratize warfare.
But Americans are shielded from the implications of the reality because
the bombs dropped are "precision" bombs and hence a highly civilized
form of violence, a vision promoted by American news media no less
than by the Pentagon.

One legacy of America's first air war is thus the continuing belief
that air war is a purer form of warfare, one that allows America to extend
the benefits of its democracy to the world as if it is defensive of our
own national security while maintaining a sense of innocence or at least
absence of guilt when waging uneven war against enemies vaguely defined as both "evil" and an imminent threat.

A second legacy was literally embodied in President Bush when
he climbed into the cockpit to fly to a carrier to address troops returning from war. President Bush decided that projecting the image of the

combat pilot was more potent than his role as commander-in-chief emerging from a helicopter in a suit and tie.

With that decision, the symbolism of the combat pilot in the American imagination has come full circle, from a dream based upon neither knowledge nor material capability to a surrealism. What began as an image that seemed to be real has become an image essentially divorced from reality, referencing a fantasy of a nation appropriated for political ends.

What is missing from the initial dream of civilized violence is the traditional conception of civilization itself. The basis for the condemnation of the German terror campaign in Belgium was that it constituted war directed against civilians and hence marked the Germans as barbarians, as did their destruction of cultural sites. It was that belief that civilization entailed culture, law, protection of the weak, and fair play which provided the foundation for the lionizing of the aces as latterday knights. Absent that traditional vision, we are left with the image of the combat pilot, emptied of any larger reference except as a symbol of virility and national pride, hijacked for political purpose and used to celebrate a war in which the civilian casualties far outweighed the losses to coalition soldiers and the civil order was reduced to anarchy.

There seems, at the opening of the twenty-first century, to be no public consensus about what ought to constrain the largest air force in the world using conventional weapons, and an air force unlikely to be challenged. The constraint in the past has been the watching eyes of the public, who take the air war as signifying the highest ideals of the American projection of force in order to be a civilizing influence upon the world. The sustaining influence of that image remains a powerful constraint against the arbitrary use of strategic bombing, a constraint that will ultimately be tested by the skilled efforts to construe strategic bombing of nonmilitary targets as meeting the idealized vision of wars fought from the sky within the limits of civilized violence. At present, the very definition of "civilization" has been appropriated by the conservative side of the political spectrum in the United States. A failure to retrieve the concept from so narrow a faction—and the corollary inability to foreground the underlying progressive idealism about the intrinsic value of human life contained in the concept—means simply that the grounds for awakening the public conscience, that powerful influence on those who shape the public imagination of warfare, will be lost.

Notes

Introduction

1. The contribution of the American involvement in the air war of World War I is largely overlooked or given far less attention than other aspects of the war in accounts of the long-lasting effects of that war on America: see, for instance: Harries and Harries, *The Last Days of Innocence*, and Zieger, *America's Great War.*

Michael S. Sherry's *The Rise of American Air Power* gives some attention to World War I, but places primary emphasis on World War II for the origins of American air power. An equally excellent account of the fascination with the airplane in times of peace and war on both sides of the Atlantic is provided by Robert Wohl in *A Passion for Wings*. A valuable contribution to the study of the first air war in the American imagination is found in Dominick A. Pisano et al., *Memory and the Great War in the Air.*

The representation of the American air war has tended to be in the form of biographies of the exploits of various aces, as this study reviews. The larger significance of the dream of achieving American victory through air power, born during World War I, has, however, not been recognized.

1. "We Were Dealing with a Miracle"

1. Arnold, *Global Mission*, 53; see also Glines, *Compact History of the United States Air Force*, 73; Holley, *Ideas and Weapons*, 41.

2. Palmer, *Newton D. Baker*, 1:287; Pershing, *My Experiences in the World War*, 1:28.

3. Palmer, *Newton D. Baker*, 1:288.

4. Quoted in ibid., 1:291.

5. Arnold, *Global Mission*, 53.

6. Ibid., 54; Holley, *Ideas and Weapons*, 45.

7. Holley, *Ideas and Weapons*, 42.

8. Arnold, *Global Mission*, 54; Levine, *Mitchell*, 98.

9. Arnold, *Global Mission*, 49.

10. Levine, *Mitchell*, 91, 96–97; Hurley, *Billy Mitchell*, 25–26.

11. Arnold, *Global Mission*, 49–50.

12. Holley, *Ideas and Weapons*, 46–47; Hurley, *Billy Mitchell*, 27–28.

13. Maj. E. S. Gorrell to Col. R. C. Bolling, Oct. 15, 1917, and Lt. Col. V. E. Clark, memo to Chief Signal Officer, Sept. 12, 1917; both quoted in Holley, *Ideas and Weapons*, 135.

14. Holley, *Ideas and Weapons*, 61.

15. Ibid., 70–73.

16. Vander Meulen, *Politics of Aircraft*, 12, 24. Vander Meulen is far less critical of Coffin than are his numerous detractors.

17. *National Cyclopaedia of American Biography* (J. T White, 1926), 54; Coffin quotation from Biddle, *Barons of the Sky*, 76.

18. Freudenthal, *Aviation Business;* see Hughes Report, Report of Aircraft Inquiry (1918), 29.

19. March, *The Nation at War,* 202–3.

20. Beaver, *Newton D. Baker and the American War Effort*, 58.

21. Holley, *Ideas and Weapons*, 61: "Officials in the United States generally assumed that the report received from the Bolling Commission would unleash the productive capacity of the nation to create aerial flotillas capable of sweeping the Germans from the skies. But during the spring and summer of 1917 the military authorities directed no effort toward establishing an effective organization to continue making the decisions begun by the Bolling Mission. Here is evidence of their failure to appreciate at that time the dynamic nature of aircraft design. Freezing design at one point for any prolonged length of time would result in producing obsolete aircraft, a liability in combat. When the Bolling decisions were made this was not fully understood if, as is doubtful, it was recognized at all. The realities of combat were to drive the point home all too clearly."

Quotation on Air Service policy from Air Service, American Expeditionary Force, memo no. 21, July 15, 1918, quoted in Holley, *Ideas and Weapons*, 122. Also in Toulmin, *Air Service, American Expeditionary Force*, 144.

22. Arnold, *Global Mission*, 62; Glines, *Compact History of the United States Air Force*, 76; Biddle, *Barons of the Sky*, 103–5; Holley, *Ideas and Weapons*, 121, 125.

23. Holley, *Ideas and Weapons*, 119, 121.

24. Ibid., 125; Arnold, *Global Mission*, 67–68.

25. Harries and Harries, *Last Days of Innocence*, 201.

26. Biddle, *Barons of the Sky*, 98–99.

27. Holley, *Ideas and Weapons*, 136, 138.

28. March, *The Nation at War*, 207.

29. Pershing, *My Experiences in the World War*, 1:161; March, *The Nation at War*, 204.

30. Vaughn, *Holding Fast the Inner Lines*, 212–13; Freudenthal, *Aviation Business*, 50; Vander Meulen, *Politics of Aircraft*, 37.

31. Freudenthal, *Aviation Business*, 50–54; Biddle, *Barons of the Sky*, 106.

32. Freudenthal, *Aviation Business*, 61.

33. Vander Meulen, *Politics of Aircraft*, 40.

34. Freudenthal, *Aviation Business*, 58.

35. Palmer, *Newton D. Baker*, 1:290.

36. Ibid., 1:287, 291.

37. March, *The Nation at War*, 21–22.

38. Palmer, *Newton D. Baker*, 1:289, 290.

39. Ibid., 1:290–91. Palmer reports that the military appropriation bill had the support of the General Staff, which is contradicted by both Arnold and Holley.

40. Beaver, *Newton D. Baker and the American War Effort*, 58.

41. Palmer, *Newton D. Baker*, 1:279.

2. "Did You Ever Buy a Pig in a Poke?"

1. Quoted in Palmer, *Newton D. Baker*, 1:289.

2. "Program for Building of Government Aircraft Stated," 16; "U.S. Acquires Aviation Field in France to Train Flyers Graduated in America," "Broad Plans Made to Train Our Airmen," 3; *New York Times*, June 4, 1917.

3. "He Says with Aircraft We Can Win War," sec. 2, p. 4; also "Cheering Crowds Greet Pershing Arriving in Paris," and "German Airmen Kill 97, Hurt 437 in London Raid." The full text of Coffin's statement is printed in the *Official Bulletin*, June 15, 1917, 5.

4. "He Says with Aircraft We Can Win War."

5. "Fliers Can Win War, Senators Are Told," sec. 4, p. 4.

6. Editorial, *New York Globe*, June 15, 1917.

7. "Delays in Getting Both Airplanes and Aviators," sec. 4, p. 4.

8. Biddle, *Barons of the Sky*, 92–93; Freudenthal, *Aviation Business*, 41–42; Vander Meulen, *Politics of Aircraft*, 26–28.

9. "Put the Yankee Punch into the War!," 2; subsequent quotes are from the same source. See also "$600,000,000 Asked for Huge Air Fleet," sec. 10, p. 8.

10. "Great U.S. Air Fleet Urged by Secretary Baker," 2; subsequent quotes are from the same source.

11. "President Ready to Back Up Aircraft Program," 1.

12. "America Pledged to Air Supremacy."

13. "Air Corps of 150,000 Men Needed, Says Howard Coffin," *Official Bulletin* 6.

14. "The Conquering Air Fleet"; *Cong. Rec.*, 65th Cong., 1st sess., July 14, 1917, 5577.

15. Dewey, "Americans Fly in France," 33–34.

16. "Great Fleet of U.S. Airships in 1918 Would Defeat Germany, Declares French Aviator," 10.

17. "A Call for Airplanes."

18. *Cong. Rec.*, 65th Cong., 1st sess., July 14, 1917, 5592.

19. Palmer, *Newton D. Baker*, 1:293.

20. *Cong. Rec.*, 65th Cong., 1st sess., July 14, 1917, 5591.

21. "Aeronautics. Speech of Hon. Murray Hulbert, of New York, In the House of Representatives, Saturday, July 14, 1917," *Cong. Rec.*, 65th Cong., 1st sess., July 20, 1917, 5871–75.

22. *Cong. Rec.*, 65th Cong., 1st sess., July 16, 1917, 5604.

23. Ibid., July 14, 1917, 5611.

24. *Washington Post*, July 16, 1917; reprinted in *Cong. Rec.*, 65th Cong., 1st sess., July 16, 1917, 5625. Ironically, the *Post* suggested information that would be useful to the Germans. In opposing the plan to create a separate air service, the editorial argues that planes are used for tactical purposes to support the army and navy. This could be interpreted as suggesting the plans do not include developing a separate arm devoted to strategic bombing.

25. *Washington Post*, July 18, 1917; reprinted in *Cong. Rec.*, 65th Cong., 1st sess., July 19, 1917, 5788.

26. *Cong. Rec.*, 65th Cong., 1st sess., July 18, 1917, 5728.

27. Ibid., 5730.

28. "Senate Insurgents Block Aviation Bill," *New York Times*, June 19, 1917, sec. 11, p. 1.

29. "Hampering the Government," sec. 8, p. 2.

30. "Senator Owen Replies," sec. 3, p. 4.

31. "At Last the Airplanes," sec. 8, p. 1.

3. A Matter of Class

1. Representative Wood, *Cong. Rec.*, 65th Cong., 1st sess., July 14, 1917, 5603.

2. Representative LaGuardia, ibid., 5604.

3. Representative Kahn and Representative Hulbert, ibid.

4. Representative Gordon, ibid.

5. Representative Lenroot, ibid.

6. Senator Curtis, Senator Chamberlain, and Senator Hardwick, *Cong. Rec.*, 65th Cong., 1st sess., July 18, 1917, 5727.

7. Senator Hardwick, ibid.

8. Senator Reed, ibid., 5732; Senator Vardaman, ibid., 5730.

9. "Hampering the Government," 8:2.

10. *Cong. Rec.*, 65th Cong., 1st sess., July 21, 1917, 5907.

11. Senator LaFollette, ibid., 5907, 5908.

12. Senator Norris, ibid., 5907, 5908.

13. See Kennedy, *Over Here*, 148, 150, 153.

14. Wells, *The War That Will End War*, 29.

15. Quoted in Kennedy, *Over Here*, 18; Mark Sullivan, *Our Times*, 296; *Cong. Rec.*, April 25, 1917.

16. Quoted in Kennedy, *Over Here*, 22.

17. Secretary of War Newton Baker made the distinction between what conscription symbolized in militaristic as opposed to democratic nations: "Militarism is . . . the designation given to a selfish or ambitious political system which uses arms as a means of accomplishing its objects. The mobilization and arming of a democracy in defense of the principles on which it is founded, and in vindication of the common rights of man, is an entirely different thing." Quoted in Sullivan, *Our Times*, 296n.

18. See Dewey, "The Social Possibilities of War," 577; and Kaplan, "Social Engineers as Saviors," 347–69. Cited from Kennedy, *Over Here*, 50.

19. Quoted in Clifford, *Citizen Soldiers*, 33.

20. Quoted in ibid., 66; see *New York Times*, Aug. 12, 1915.

21. Much of this was ideological eyewash, which is not to say that those who promulgated it did not believe it themselves. Nonetheless, the Plattsburg Idea was both elitist and racist. General Wood barred blacks from the Plattsburg training camps because he balked at the idea of military training for men "with whom our descendants cannot intermarry without producing a breed of mongrels; they must at least be white." In addition, those who advocated universal military training felt it would serve to assimilate the "hyphenated Americans"— European immigrants—to the values of the United States (as understood by those who controlled military training). As for the gender issues, it goes without saying that women were regarded as automatically excluded from military training. See Kennedy, *Over Here*, 148–49, 161.

22. Palmer, *Newton D. Baker*, 1:223.

23. Clifford, *Citizen Soldiers*, 235.

24. Ekirch, *The Civilian and the Military*, 169–70, 184.

25. Palmer, *Newton D. Baker*, 1:222.

26. Clifford, *Citizen Soldiers*, 243–44.

27. Harries and Harries, *Last Days of Innocence*, 100.

28. Quoted in Schaffer, *America in the Great War*, 186.

29. Palmer, *Newton D. Baker*, 1:198–99.

30. Quoted in Beaver, *Newton D. Baker and the American War Effort*, 29; Johnson, *Pioneer's Progress*, 253. Cited in Roosevelt, *Letters*, 1184, fn for 6203.

31. W. Wilson to N. D. Baker, March 27, 1917, Baker Papers, cited in Beaver, *Newton D. Baker and the American War Effort*, 29.

32. N. D. Baker to W. Wilson, February 7, 1917, Wilson Papers; J. Parker to N. D. Baker, February 8, 1917, Baker Papers; quoted in Beaver, *Newton D. Baker and the American War Effort*, 27.

33. Beaver, *Newton D. Baker and the American War Effort*, 30, quoting from minutes of the Council of National Defense, March 24, 1917, Daniels Papers; Daniels Diary, March 24, 1917; N. D. Baker to W. Wilson, March 29, 1917, Wilson Papers.

34. Beaver, *Newton D. Baker and the American War Effort*, 30.

35. Woodrow Wilson, "From the Diary of Thomas W. Brahany. Tuesday, April 10, 1917," in Wilson, *The Papers of Woodrow Wilson*, 42:31; Longworth, *Crowded Hours*, 246.

36. Roosevelt to Chamberlain, April 12, 1917, *Letters;* subsequent quotes are from the same source.

37. Baker to Roosevelt, April 13, 1917, in Roosevelt, *Letters*, note to letter 1174.

38. TR to Baker, April 23, 1917, in Roosevelt, *Letters*, letter 6203, 1176–84.

39. "Moral" and "morale" were often spelled the same at this time; in addition, they were sometimes used as synonyms—as seems to be the case with Roosevelt.

40. Baker to Roosevelt, May 5, 1917, in Roosevelt, *Letters*.

41. "Wilson's Proclamation," *New York Times*, May 19, 1917, 1; subsequent quotes are from the same source.

42. "Clemenceau Pleads for Col. Roosevelt," *New York Times*, May 28, 1917.

43. TR to Augustus Peabody Gardner, June 6, 1917, in Roosevelt, *Letters*, 1199.

4. "They Made Grand Copy"

1. Information about the Thiepval Memorial and grounds from Holt and Holt, *Holts' Battlefield Guides*, 19–201; Winter, *Sites of Memory, Sites of Mourning*, 105–7.

2. It is estimated that if the British casualties of that day stood in a line, separated from each other by only an arm's length, the line would stretch for thirty miles. This and other casualty estimates from Holt and Holt, *Holts' Battlefield Guides*, 2–12; other estimates from Stokesbury, *Short History of World War I*, 156.

3. Bowen, *Knights of the Air*, 18; Fussell, *The Great War in Modern Memory*, 37.

4. Bowen, *Knights of the Air*, 36; Fussell, *The Great War in Modern Memory*, 9.

5. Bowen, *Knights of the Air*, 69.

6. Douglas, *Years of Combat*, 153.

7. Ibid., 109.

8. "Statements in Parliament," July 19, 1916, 46; quoted in Kennett, *The First Air War*, 155.

9. Garros is generally credited with the particular development in air combat that led to the emergence of the pursuit pilot in World War I. He is also credited by some as being the reason why the term "ace" entered the American vocabulary to mean a pilot who had shot down five planes. When he had downed five planes, Garros was awarded the Legion of Honor, and French as well as British newspapers referred to him as an "ace," then a popular Parisian term for

anyone of notable athletic prowess. An American journalist in Paris heard the term in connection with Garros, assumed it meant any pilot who had scored five victories, and, according to some historians, it was used by journalists with that meaning from that time forward. Whitehouse, *Decisive Air Battles*, 86.

10. Lippmann, *Public Opinion*, 5–11; subsequent page numbers appear in the text.

11. Kennett, *The First Air War*, 68–69.

12. Ibid., 72.

13. Trenchard, quoted in ibid., 110; Lewis, *Sagittarius Rising*, 47.

14. Kennett, *The First Air War*, 110.

15. Account of Fokker scare in ibid., 110–11.

16. German sign quoted in ibid., 72.

17. McCaffery, *Billy Bishop*, 44, 48–49; Callender and Callender, eds., *War in an Open Cockpit*, 15.

18. Quoted in Whitehouse, *Decisive Air Battles*, 176.

19. McCaffrey, *Billy Bishop*, 117; Callender and Callender, eds., *War in an Open Cockpit*, 15.

20. 172 Americans ultimately served in other French squadrons, and they are known collectively as the Lafayette Flying Corps.

21. Parson, *The Great Adventure*, 13.

22. Ibid., 15.

23. Ibid., 16; Jablonski, *Warriors with Wings*, 39.

24. Jablonski, *Warriors with Wings*, 35, 39.

25. Whitehouse, *Decisive Air Battles*, 213–11; quoted in Bowen, *Knights of the Air*, 100.

26. Whitehouse, *Decisive Air Battles*, 212–13.

27. De Sieyes, "Aces of the Air," 9.

28. Ibid., 5.

29. Rickenbacker, *Fighting the Flying Circus*, 12–13.

30. Nordhoff and Hall, *Falcons of France*, 1.

5. *Casus Belli*

1. Whitehouse, *Legion of the Lafayette*, ix–x.

2. Jablonski, *Warriors with Wings*, 7.

3. Gordon, *Lafayette Escadrille*, 3.

4. See Keegan, *The Second World War*, 10–30.

5. Read, *Atrocity Propaganda, 1914–1919*, 29, 30. Read is quoting from the report of a commission ordered by the German Reichstag in 1924 to investigate violations of international law during World War I. The report, *Volkerrecht im Weltkrieg, II*, was filed in 1927.

6. Sanders and Taylor, *British Propaganda of the First World War*, 142–43.

7. Ibid., 146.

8. Report of the Committee on Alleged German Outrages (London: His Majesty's Stationery Office, 1915), hereafter cited as Bryce Report.

9. Peterson, *Propaganda for War*, 53, 60; Read, *Atrocity Propaganda, 1914–1919*, 30. The account of the burning of the Louvain library is from Col. Frederick Palmer, *With My Own Eyes* (1934), 305, cited in Peterson, *Propaganda for War*, 60.

10. French Ministry of Foreign Affairs, *Germany's Violations of the Laws of War*. The copy in the Cornell University Library is a gift from Sir Gilbert Parker.

11. Marshall, Parker, Thompson, and Gibbs, *Thrilling Stories of the Great War on Land and Sea, in the Air, Under the Water*, 32, 116, 118; subsequent page numbers appear in the text.

12. French Ministry of Foreign Affairs, *Germany's Violations of the Laws of War*, vii–viii.

13. Ibid., xii.

14. Marshall et al., *Thrilling Stories of the Great War on Land and Sea, in the Air, Under the Water*, 32.

15. Ibid., 112.

16. "Remember Belgium: Enlist To-Day" (1915), Imperial War Museum poster 5075, reproduced in Dutton, "Moving Images?," 43–58.

17. "The Scrap of Paper" (1914), Imperial War Museum poster 5083, reproduced in ibid.

18. Posters reproduced in Paret, Lewis, and Paret, *Persuasive Images*: Ellsworth Young, "Remember Belgium" (1918), 21; H. R. Hopps, "Destroy This Mad Brute" (1917), 25; Fred Spear, "Enlist" (1915), 27.

19. Campbell, *Reel America and World War I*, 60.

20. Campbell, *Reel America and World War I*, 98; Ward, *The Motion Picture Goes to War*, 55–56.

21. Campbell, *Reel America and World War I*, 97–98; Ward, *The Motion Picture Goes to War*, 56.

22. Campbell, *Reel America and World War I*, 97.

23. Ibid., 96.

24. Ward, *The Motion Picture Goes to War*, 57.

25. Vaughn, *Holding Fast the Inner Lines*, 210.

26. Campbell, *Reel America and World War I*, 100.

27. Campbell, *Reel America and World War I*, 94.

28. Rockwell, *War Letters of Kiffin Yates Rockwell*, 116.

29. McConnell, *Flying for France with the American Escadrille at Verdun*, 96–97.

30. Rockwell, *War Letters of Kiffin Yates Rockwell*, 163.

31. Ibid., 165–66.

32. Genet, *War Letters of Edmond Genet*, 235–36.

33. MacLeish, *The Price of Honor*, 9.

6. Civilized Warfare and the Gentleman-Knight

1. Newbolt, *Tales of the Great War*, 248–49.

2. Hynes, *A War Imagined*, 27.

3. "Harmsworth, Alfred Charles William, Viscount Northcliffe," in *The Dictionary of National Biography, 1922–1930*, ed. J. R. H. Weaver (London: Oxford University Press, 1937), 401.

4. Jane Anderson, "Looping the Loop over London," in Anderson and Bruce, *Flying, Submarining, and Mine Sweeping*, 2.

5. Sassoon, "The Poet as Hero," 199, quoted in Hynes, *A War Imagined*, 156.

6. Ford, "Arms and the Mind," 78–79. The quotation and context is from Hynes, *A War Imagined*, 105–6.

7. For the impact of the war on the cultural imagination, see Fussell's seminal study, *The Great War in Modern Memory*, and the more recent analysis by Hynes in *A War Imagined*.

8. Fussell, *The Great War in Modern Memory*, 18–24.

9. Hynes, *A War Imagined*, 101, 103, 132.

10. Dutton, "Moving Images?," 43–58.

11. Parliamentary Recruiting Committee, "Britain Needs You at Once" (1915); Parliamentary Recruiting Committee, "Take Up the Sword of Justice: Join Now" (1915). See Dutton, "Moving Images?"

12. Girouard, *Return to Camelot*, 290.

13. Girouard, infra.

14. Adams, *The Great Adventure*, 105.

15. Fussell, *The Great War in Modern Memory*, 26, quoting from Howarth.

16. Newbolt, ed., *The Later Life and Letters of Sir Henry Newbolt*, 314–15, quoted in Hynes, *A War Imagined*, 304.

17. Newbolt, *Book of the Happy Warrior*, vi-vii.

18. Ibid., 278.

19. Adams, *The Great Adventure*, 105.

20. Sir Henry Newbolt, letters, to Alice Hylton, Aug. 12, Aug. 14, and Dec. 25, 1915, to M., March 28, 1918, and to Emma Coltman, March 31, 1918, in *Later Life and Letters of Sir Henry Newbolt*, ed. Newbolt, 213–14, 219, 247–48.

21. Newbolt, letter to Alice Hylton, Oct. 6, 1918, in *Letters*, ed. Newbolt, 255.

22. From an article by historian Carl Russel Fish, writing on behalf of the Creel Committee (NBHS) for *History Teachers Magazine*, quoted in Gruber, *Mars and Minerva*, 133.

23. Vaughn, *Holding Fast the Inner Lines*, 205–6.

24. Raymond Fosdick to family, June 9, 1918, in Fosdick Papers, quoted in Kennedy, *Over Here*, 216.

25. Quoted in Genthe, *American War Narratives*, 97, quoted in Kennedy, *Over Here*, 215.

26. Kennedy, *Over Here*, 212.

27. Driggs, "Plane Tales from the Skies," 849.

28. Richthofen, *The Red Air Fighter*. Citations from Arno Press edition; subsequent page numbers appear in the text.

29. Lieutenant Henri Farre, illustration, "The Forty-Fifth Victory of Guynemer, Knight of the Air," *Ladies Home Journal*, Sept. 1918, 10.

30. Park, *Fighters*, 49–50; Whitehouse, *Heroes of the Sunlit Sky*, 279–82.

31. Bordeaux, *Georges Guynemer*, 11; subsequent page numbers appear in the text.

7. Mechanized Warfare and the Man

1. Hawthorne, "Chiefly about War Matters by a Peaceable Man." All citations from *Nathaniel Hawthorne*, ed. Woodson, Simpson, and Smith; subsequent page numbers appear in the text.

2. Melville, "The *Temeraire*," and "A Utilitarian View of the *Monitor*'s Fight," 37–40.

3. Sherry, *Rise of American Air Power*, 6.

4. Woodrow Wilson, speech at Brooklyn, New York, May 11, 1914, in *Papers of Woodrow Wilson*, 30:15, cited in Cooper, *Warrior and the Priest*, 269.

5. Edward M. House, diary entry, Feb. 12, 1913, in *Papers of Woodrow Wilson*, 27:113, cited in Cooper, *Warrior and the Priest*, 268; Hibben and Herrick quoted in Kennedy, *Over Here*, 179.

6. Cooper, *Warrior and the Priest*, 310; Woodrow Wilson, prolegomenon to peace note, ca. November 1916, *Papers of Woodrow Wilson*, 40:70–71.

7. Leonard, *Above the Battle*, 97–110.

8. Northcliffe, *Lord Northcliffe's War Book*, 86.

9. Ibid., 44.

10. Stokesbury, *Short History of World War I*, 156.

11. Hynes, *A War Imagined*, 50; Younghusband, *A Soldier's Memories in Peace and War*, 187–88.

12. Northcliffe, *The War Book*, 47–48.

13. Hewlett, *Our Flying Men*, 36.

14. Crozier, "The Super-Airman," 279; Whitehouse, 95; Bowen, *Knights of the Air*, 79.

15. Northcliffe, *The War Book*, 64.

16. Account of surviving veteran, Battle of the Somme (film), Historial de le Grand Guerre. Peronne, Picardy.

17. Morrow, *The Great War in the Air*, 234; Franks, Guest, and Bailey, *Bloody April . . . Black September*, 110–11.

18. Sassoon, *Diaries, 1923–25*, 173–74, quoted in Hynes, *A War Imagined*, 175.

19. Tawney, "Some Reflections of a Soldier," 104, quoted in Hynes, *A War Imagined*, 117.

20. Hynes, *A War Imagined*, 119.

21. Northcliffe, *The War Book*, 93–94, 96–97.

22. Bishop, *Winged Warfare*, 71.

23. Hewlett, *Our Flying Men*, 11, 16–17.

24. Berreota, "Flying in France," 13.

25. Tulasne, "America's Part in the Allied Mastery of the Air," 3.

26. "Who Make the Best Aviators?," 197; see also Kennett, *The First Air War*, 116.

27. Whitehouse, *Decisive Air Battles*, 183; Kennett, *The First Air War*, 116–17.

28. Richthofen, *The Red Air Fighter*, 46–47; remark on hunting, quoted in Bowen, *Knights of the Air*, 119.

29. Hewlett, *Our Flying Men*.

30. Bishop, *Winged Warfare*, 21.

31. "L'Aeroplane et la cavalerie-Opinions allemandes," *Revue Generale de l'Aeronautique militaire theorique et pratique* (1911), 179, translated and quoted in Kennett, *The First Air War*, 106.

32. Bowen, *Knights of the Air*, 148.

33. Middleton, "Manhunters of the Air," 521.

34. Hall, *High Adventure*, 43.

35. Sherry, *Rise of American Air Power*, 7.

36. Michael Adams, *Great Adventure*, 69.

37. Fritzsche, *Nation of Fliers*, 59–101.

38. Molter, *Knights of the Air*, 52; subsequent page numbers appear in the text.

39. Genet, *War Letters of Edmond Genet*, 177.

40. McConnell, *Flying for France with the American Escadrille at Verdun*, 21.

8. "The Man Is Alone"

1. Hall, *High Adventure*, 115–16; subsequent quotes are from the same source.

2. "German Falcon Killed in Air Duel," 60–61; subsequent quotes are from the same source.

3. Whitehouse, *Decisive Air Battles*, 97; Bowen, *Knights of the Air*, 88; Park, *Fighters*, 44.

4. Quoted in Kennett, *The First Air War*, 172, from Insall, *Observer*, 75.

5. Bishop, "Tales of the British Air Service," 27, 33.

6. "Guynemer, Ace of the Aces," *Literary Digest* (October 13, 1917): 56.

7. Ibid., 55; Cook, "Georges Guynemer," 6.

8. Park, *Fighters*, 50.

9. Cook, "Georges Guynemer," 4–5.

10. Ibid., 5–6.

11. "Guynemer, Ace of the Aces," 55.

12. Whitehouse, *Heroes of the Sunlit Sky*, 166–68; McCaffery, *Billy Bishop*, 47.

13. Briscoe and Stannard, *Captain Ball, V.C.*, 159–60; subsequent page numbers appear in the text.

14. Whitehouse, *Heroes of the Sunlit Sky*, 165–68.

15. McCaffery, *Billy Bishop*, 164–65.

16. Ibid., introduction, n.p. (second page).

17. Bishop, *Winged Warfare*, 91.

18. Ibid., 114.

19. McCaffrey, *Billy Bishop*, 104.

20. Bishop, *Winged Warfare*, 123; subsequent page numbers appear in the text.

21. McCaffrey, *Billy Bishop*, 110–11, 113; Bishop, *Winged Warfare*, 155.

22. Bishop, *Winged Warfare*, 157–62.

23. McCaffrey, *Billy Bishop*, 130, 133.

24. Whitehouse, *Decisive Air Battles*, 344.

25. McCaffrey, *Billy Bishop*, 204–5.

26. Morrow, *The Great War in the Air*, 234.

27. Bishop, *Winged Warfare*, 69–70.

28. Morrow, *The Great War in the Air*, 234.

29. Stokesbury, *Short History of World War I*, 232, 234–35.

30. Ibid., 231.

31. Cited in Morrow, *The Great War in the Air*, 204; Villars, *Notes d'un pilote disparu—1916–1917*, 211–12.

32. Wharton, *Age of Innocence* and *House of Mirth*.

9. The Sporting Life

1. Fussell, *The Great War in Modern Memory*, 27. He includes an account of a football kicked toward the Turkish guns on the lines near Beersheeba in November 1917.

2. Poem on the margin of an undated field concert program in the Imperial War Museum; quoted in ibid.

3. Adams, *Great Adventure*, 41–42.

4. Northcliffe, *War Book*, 86, 94.

5. "The Advantages of Fear in Battle," 106.

6. Tulasne, "America's Part in the Allies' Mastery of the Air," 1.

7. Fox, "U.S. Leads in Air War," 667.

8. Gilchrist, "An Analysis of Causes of Breakdown in Flying," 401. A report of the same findings was published in the *New York Medical Journal* (Nov. 23, 1918): 906–7.

9. "Who Makes the Best Aviators," 107.

10. Campbell, *Soldier of the Sky*, 119, 47.

11. Hewlett, *Our Flying Men*, 11.

12. Tompkins, *West of Everything*, 186.

13. McCudden, *Flying Fury*, 290.

14. McCaffrey, *Billy Bishop*, 196–97.

15. McCudden, *Flying Fury*, 667.

16. Chapman, *Victor Chapman's Letters from France*, 172.

17. Ibid., 174–75.

18. McConnell, "Flying for France with the American Escadrille at Verdun," 45.

19. "War Letters of Edmond Genet," *Scribner's Magazine* 63 (May 1918): 520.

20. Walcott, "Life Story of an American Airman in France," 86.

21. McCudden, *Flying Fury*, 183, 184; Bishop, *Winged Warfare*, 191, 174.

22. McCudden, *Flying Fury*, 159–60.

23. McConnell, *Flying for France*, 53.

24. McCudden, *Flying Fury*, 183.

25. Duncan Grinell-Milne, foreword to new edition, McCudden, *Flying Fury*, vi.

26. McConnell, "Flying for France: Further Experiences of an Aviator in the American Escadrille in France," 505; McCudden, *Flying Fury*, 135.

27. Gordon, *Lafayette Escadrille*, 75.

28. Hall, *"En l'Air!,"* 44, 59; subsequent page numbers appear in the text.

29. Whitehouse, *Heroes of the Sunlit Sky*, 51; Gordon, *Lafayette Escadrille*, 74.

10. "As Swimmers into Cleanness Leaping"

1. Hynes, *A War Imagined*, 11–12, 16.

2. Quoted in ibid., 12.

3. Ibid., 16.

4. Brooke, *Collected Poems of Rupert Brooke*, 101.

5. Hynes, *A War Imagined*, 300.

6. Freud, *Thoughts for the Times on War and Death* (1915), including "The Disillusionment of the War," "Our Attitudes Toward Death," and "Letter to Dr. Frederick van Geden," in *Reflections on War and Death*, reprinted in *Standard Edition of the Complete Psychological Works of Sigmund Freud*, 14:273–303. Subsequent citations are from the *Standard Edition*.

7. Quotations from Jones, *Life and Work of Sigmund Freud*, 2:172; see also Reif, *Freud*, 311–15.

8. Sigmund Freud, letter to Frederick van Eeden, Vienna, Dec. 28, 1914, in Freud, *Standard Edition of the Complete Psychological Works of Sigmund Freud*, 14:301–2.

9. Freud, "Thoughts on War and Death," in ibid., 276.

10. Ibid., 278.

11. "Reversion to Primitive Emotions as a Result of the War," 109–10. The *Current Opinion* article reveals how Freud was explained to the public and what emphasis was placed on Freud's reflections. This raises the question of why an article about Freud appeared in a popular American periodical. Freud was not a household name at the time. Moreover, as he was Austrian, he was not the most likely source to look to for an analysis of the war which would be looked upon favorably in the United States. The *Current Opinion* article begins with some throat-clearing about this, noting that while there might be some prejudice against printing ideas from the opponent side, the fact was that *Current Opinion* was demonstrating the open-mindedness and liberality of a democratic and enlightened society in doing so. All of this is suggestive of additional research into how the article came to be placed in *Current Opinion*. One reason for raising the question is that Edward Bernays was attached to the CPI. Sigmund Freud was his uncle. Bernays, who was to become the doyen of public relations after the war, both relied upon and was highly instrumental in popularizing the ideas of his uncle. See Tye, *Father of Spin*.

12. "The Advantages of Fear in Battle," 106; subsequent quotes are from the same source.

13. Lewis, *Sagittarius Rising*, 137.

14. See also Mosse, *Fallen Soldiers*.

15. Shaffer, *America in the Great War*, 158; Kennedy, *Over Here*, 211.

16. Ibid., 158–59.

17. Langer, *Gas and Flames in World War I*, 24, quoted in Kennedy, *Over Here*, 211.

18. Alan Seeger to Father, Dec. 11, 1914, in Seeger, *Letters and Diaries of Alan Seeger*, quoted in Kennedy, *Over Here*, 211.

19. Remarque, *All Quiet on the Western Front*, 273–74.

20. Ibid., 271–72.

21. Douglas, *Years of Combat*, 277.

22. Raleigh and Jones, *War in the Air*, quoted in Douglas, *Years of Combat*, 46.

23. Chapman, *Victor Chapman's Letters from France*, 181.

24. Middleton, "Manhunters of the Air," 521; subsequent quotes are from the same source.

25. Rickenbacker, *Fighting the Flying Circus*, vii.

26. Titler, *The Day the Red Baron Died*, 233.

27. Ibid., 100, 198.

28. Burrows, *Richthofen*, 204.

29. Titler, *The Day the Red Baron Died*, 221.

30. Burrows, *Richthofen*, 205.

31. Driggs, "Aces Among Aces," 575; second version/translation in Burrows, *Richthofen*, 205.

32. Titler, *The Day the Red Baron Died*, 275.

33. Ibid., 235.

34. Quoted in ibid., frontispiece.

35. Ibid., 115; Burrows, *Richthofen*, 199.

36. Titler, *The Day the Red Baron Died*, 131.

11. American Pilots as Symbols of American Democracy

1. Morrow, *The Great War in the Air*, 317–18.

2. Franks, Guest, and Bailey, *Bloody April . . . Black September*, 113–14.

3. Chapman, *Victor Chapman's Letters from France*, 178, 183, 184.

4. Rickenbacker, *Fighting the Flying Circus*, 255–60; subsequent quotes are from the same source. The unedited footage is available in the National Archive.

5. Hynes, *A War Imagined*, 124; subsequent page numbers appear in the text.

6. Robertson, "Air Wars," 133–46.

7. Roosevelt had changed his mind about enlisting Quentin in the British air force because it was not clear whether or not this could legally be done unless Quentin renounced his citizenship. See TR to Cecil Spring Rice, April 16, 1917, in Roosevelt, *Letters*, 1174.

8. Palmer, *Newton D. Baker*, 206; Renehan, *The Lion's Pride*, 138.

9. Renehan, *The Lion's Pride*, 155–59; subsequent page numbers appear in the text.

10. Blackford, "Quentin Roosevelt," 211–13.

11. In February 1918 Quentin's mother visited the gravesite. She arranged to have a fountain placed there and ordered a stone marker bearing the phrase from Shelley's *Adonais:* "He has outsoared the shadow of our night." But that was not to be Quentin's final resting place. In July 1943 his older brother, Theodore Jr., died while on duty in France and was buried at Sainte-Laurent-sur-Mer near Normandy. A year later, Quentin was moved from his grave near Chemery to rest beside his brother; his headstone was brought back to the Roosevelt family home at Sagamore Hill. Renehan, *The Lion's Pride*, 206–7.

12. Crawford, "Quentin Roosevelt—An Incident," *The Outlook*, August 28, 1918, 211–13.

13. "Transfigured Youth," 511–12, *The Outlook*, July 31, 1918.

14. Renehan, *The Lion's Pride*, 247.

15. TR to TR Jr., Oct. 20, 1917, and TR to Ethel R. Derby, July 12, 1918, in Roosevelt, *Letters*, 1245.

16. Mosse, *Fallen Soldiers*.

17. *The Great Adventure* first appeared as a series in *Metropolitan Magazine*.

18. TR to Senator Chamberlain, April 12, 1917, in Roosevelt, *Letters*, 1171.

19. Roosevelt, *The Great Adventure*, 263–64; subsequent page numbers appear in the text.

20. TR to TR Jr., in Roosevelt, *Letters*, 1199.

21. Longworth, *Crowded Hours*, 255.

22. TR to Mary L. Brown, July 26, 1918, in Roosevelt, *Letters*, 1355.

12. Death Wears a Romantic Mask

1. Franks, Guest, and Bailey, *Bloody April . . . Black September*, 118.

2. Whitehouse, *Decisive Air Battles*, 205–6.

3. Morrow, *The Great War in the Air*, 177–78; Franks, Guest, and Bailey, *Bloody April . . . Black September*, 111.

4. "Laurence La Tourette Driggs," entry in *The National Cyclopaedia of American Biography* (Ann Arbor, Mich.: University Microfilms, 1967), 216.

5. Driggs, "Plane Tales from the Skies," 849.

6. Driggs, "Aces of Aviation," 184–86.

7. Driggs, "How Battles Are Fought in the Air," 416–22.

8. Spick, *The Ace Factor*, 51.

9. Kelly, note on authorship of *Fighting the Flying Circus*.

10. Rickenbacker, *Fighting the Flying Circus*, vii.

11. Ibid., 13.

12. Hall, *High Adventure*, 19–20.

13. Rickenbacker, *Fighting the Flying Circus*, 6.

14. Ibid., 193–94.

15. Whitehouse, *Heroes of the Sunlit Sky*, 81–89.

16. Rickenbacker, *Fighting the Flying Circus*, 205–6.

17. Kennett, *The First Air War*, 166; cf. Raleigh and Jones, *War in the Air*, 5:425.

18. Gilchrist, "Analysis of Causes of Breakdown in Flying," 401; the same findings were published as Norman S. Gilchrist, "Causes of Breakdown in Flying," *New York Medical Journal* (Nov. 23, 1918): 906–7.

19. Gilchrist, "Analysis of Causes of Breakdown in Flying," 401.

20. Kennett, *The First Air War*, 146.

21. Springs, *War Birds*, 267–68; see also Davis, *War Bird*.

22. Whitehouse, *Heroes of the Sunlit Sky*, 133.

23. Springs, *War Birds*, 274.

24. Lay and Bartlett, *Twelve O'Clock High!*, 95.

25. Kennett, *The First Air War*, 148.

26. Fritzsche, *Nation of Fliers*, 93–94.

27. Park, *Fighters*, 50.

28. Lee Kennett, *The First Air War*, 170.

29. Miller, "The Mother Complex," 115–28.

30. Showalter, *The Female Malady*, 167–94.

31. Kennett, *The First Air War*, 170.

32. Crozier, "The Super-Airman," 278–80.

33. D. W. Warne, introduction to Scott, *Sixty Squadron RAF*, viii.

34. Ibid., xiii–xv.

35. Ibid., 74–75.

36. Scott, quoting Newman, in ibid., 78.

37. Ibid., 73–74.

38. Franks, Guest, and Bailey, *Bloody April . . . Black September*, 244.

39. Ecksteins, *Rites of Spring*, 64–72.

40. Fritzsche, *Nation of Fliers*, 62.

41. Ibid., 217.

42. "Observation Flying and Its Importance," in *United States Air Service in World War I*, ed. Maurer, 1:104–5.

43. "Temperament," in ibid., 1:89–90.

44. Rickenbacker, *Rickenbacker*, 152–53.

45. Fritzsche, *Nation of Fliers*, 88.

46. Lewis, *Sagittarius Rising*, 45–46.

47. Spick, *The Ace Factor*, 61.

48. Ibid., 6.

Epilogue

1. Sherry, *Rise of American Air Power*, 22–46.

2. Ibid., 30.

3. Morrison, *Fortress without a Roof*, 377.

4. Ibid., 378.

5. LeMay and Kantor, *Mission with LeMay*, 384; subsequent page numbers appear in the text.

6. U.S. News and World Report Staff, *Triumph without Victory*, 396.

7. Robertson, "Strange Case of the Missing Chinese Embassy," 194.

8. Morrison, *Fortress without a Roof*, 378.

9. Huntington, *The Clash of Civilizations and the Remaking of World Order*; for Lyn Cheney, see American Council of Trustees and Alumns, http://www.goacta.org; for William Bennett, see American for Victory over Terrorism, http://www.goavot.org; Lewis, *What Went Wrong*; for reports of Berlusconi's speech, see Black, "Scorn Poured on Berlusconi's View as EU Tightens Security Links," and Foot, "An Enemy of Democracy."

10. See Rashid, *Taliban*; Bodansky, *Bin Laden*; and Cooley, *Unholy Wars*.

11. Robbins, "Humanity of the Air War"; Kaplan, "New Warfare," 34; Ricks, "Bulls-Eye War," 1; Schmitt and Dao, "Use of Pinpoint Air Power Comes of Age in New War," 1; and Tyson, "US Is Prevailing with Its Most Finely Tuned War," 1.

12. Conetta, "Operation Enduring Freedom," 1–2; Herold, "A Dossier on Civilian Victims of United States Aerial Bombing of Afghanistan."

13. Conetta, "Operation Enduring Freedom," 1.

14. Ibid., 2.

15. Ibid., 3; "Cluster Bombs in Afghanistan," 1–2.

16. Conetta, "Operation Enduring Freedom," 3.

17. Herold, "Dossier on Civilian Victims," 11; Conetta, "Operation Enduring Freedom," 3.

18. "BLU-82 'Daisy Cutter'"; "BLU-82B"; Conetta, "Operation Enduring Freedom," 2.

19. Chamberlain, "Thermobaric Warfare," 1.

20. Ibid., 1; "Backgrounder on Russian Fuel Air Explosives (Vacuum Bombs)."

21. Chamberlain, "Thermobaric Warfare," 2.

22. Cornwall, "US Begins Work on 'Super-hard Bunker Buster' Nuclear Bombs."

23. Lawrence, "A War Without Witnesses"; Campbell, "U.S. Buys Up All Satellite War Images"; "It Just Did Not Happen"; Parry, "A Village Is Destroyed and America Says It Never Happened."

24. Der Derian, *Virtuous War*.

25. Rowan Scarborough, "Size of Force on Ground Key in Plan for Iraq War," *Washington Times*, April 26, 2002.

26. Save the Children Foundation, *State of the World's Mothers 2003: Protecting Women and Children in War and Conflict* (New York: Save the Children Foundation, May 2003), 9.

27. Robert C. Byrd, "Making the Military a Prop in Presidential Politics," speech on the floor of the U.S. Senate, May 6, 2003, available at http:/www.senate.gov/~byrd_speeches_2003may.

References

Adams, Michael C. C. *The Great Adventure: Male Desire and the Coming of World War I.* Bloomington: Indiana University Press, 1990.

Adams, Paul. "The Story of the Lafayette Escadrille, as told by Sgt. Clyde Balsley." *The Bellman* (July 20, 1918): 68–72.

"The Advantages of Fear in Battle: Courage of the Soldier Not So Important as Heroic Souls Think." *Current Opinion* 65 (Aug. 1918): 106.

"Air Corps of 150,000 Men Needed, Says Howard Coffin." *Official Bulletin*, July 19, 1917, 6.

"America Pledged to Air Supremacy." *New York Times*, July 5, 1917, sec. 4, p. 5.

Anderson, Jane, and Gordon Bruce. *Flying, Submarining, and Mine Sweeping.* London: Sir Joseph Cariston and Sons, 1916.

Arnold, H. H. *Global Mission.* New York: Harper and Brothers, 1949.

"At Last the Airplanes." Editorial, *New York Times*, July 23, 1917, 8:1.

Bacheller, Irving. "The Merry Jest of the Airman." *The Independent* (Jan. 26, 1918): 143, 156.

"Backgrounder on Russian Fuel Air Explosives ('Vacuum Bombs')." *Human Rights Watch*, Feb. 15, 2000. http://www.hrw.org/press/2000/02/chech0215b.htm.

"Battles of Two-Seaters and Single-Seaters in the Sky." *Current Opinion* (Sept. 1918): 174.

Beaver, Daniel R. *Newton D. Baker and the American War Effort, 1917–1919.* Lincoln: University of Nebraska Press, 1966.

Berreota, Captain Andre de. "Flying in France." *National Geographic* 33 (Jan. 1918): 9–26.

Biddle, Wayne. *Barons of the Sky: From Early Flight to Strategic Warfare, The Story of the American Aerospace Industry.* New York: Henry Holt, 1991.

Birley, J. L. "The Principles of Medical Science as Applied to Military Aviation." *The Lancet* (May 29, 1920): 147, 256.

Bishop, Major William A. "Tales of the British Air Service." *National Geographic* 33 (Jan. 1918): 27–37.

———. *Winged Warfare.* Edited by Stanley M. Ulanoff. 1917; Garden City, N.Y.: Doubleday, 1967.

Black, Ian. "Scorn Poured on Berlusconi's View as EU Tightens Security Links." *The Guardian* (Oct. 4, 2001): 4.

Blackford, Ambler M. "Quentin Roosevelt: Some Reminiscences Recorded by One of His Teachers." *The Outlook* (Oct. 9, 1918): 211–13.

"BLU-82 'Daisy Cutter.'" *Guardian Unlimited.* Special Reports. Daisy-Cutter Bombs. 2002. http://www.guardian.co.uk/flash/0586058891600.html.

"BLU-82B." Federation of American Scientists: Military Analysis Network. http://www.fas.org/man/dod-101/dumb/blu-82.htm.

Bodansky, Yossef. *Bin Laden: The Man Who Declared War on America.* New York: Random House, 1999.

Bordeaux, Henry. *Georges Guynemer: Knight of the Air.* Translated by Louise Morgan Sill, with an introduction by Theodore Roosevelt. New Haven: Yale University Press, 1918.

Bowen, Ezra. *Knights of the Air.* Alexandria, Va.: Time-Life Books, 1980.

Briscoe, Walter A., and H. Russell Stannard. *Captain Ball, V.C.: The Career of Flight-Commander Ball, V.C., D.S.O.* London: Herbert Jenkins, 1918.

Brooke, Rupert. *The Collected Poems of Rupert Brooke.* Introduction by George Edward Woodberry. New York: Dodd, Mead, 1959.

Burrows, William E. *Richthofen: A True History of the Red Baron.* New York: Harcourt, Brace and World, 1969.

Byrd, Robert C. "Making the Military a Prop in Presidential Politics." Speech on the floor of the U.S. Senate, May 6, 2003. http://www.senate.gov/~byrd/byrd_speeches_2003may.

"A Call for Airplanes." *New York Times,* July 22, 1917, sec. 1, p. 1.

Callender, Gordon W., Jr., and Gordon W. Callender Sr., eds. *War in an Open Cockpit: The Wartime Letters of Captain Alvin Andrew Callender, RAF.* West Roxbury, Mass.: World War I Aero Publishers, 1978.

Campbell, Captain George Frederic. *A Soldier of the Sky*. Chicago: Davis Printing Works, 1918.

Campbell, Craig W. *Reel America and World War I: A Comprehensive Filmography and History of Motion Pictures, 1914–1920*. Jefferson, N.C.: McFarland and Company, 1985.

Campbell, Duncan. "U.S. Buys Up All Satellite War Images." *The Guardian* (October 17, 2001): 1.

Chamberlain, Nigel. "Thermobaric Warfare." Campaign for Nuclear Disarmament Briefing Paper, Jan. 11, 2001. http://www.cnduk.org/briefing/thermo.htm.

Chapman, John Jay. *Victor Chapman's Letters from France*. New York: Macmillan, 1917.

"Cheering Crowds Greet Pershing Arrival in Paris." *New York Times*, June 14, 1917, 1.

Clifford, John Garry. *The Citizen Soldiers: The Plattsburg Training Camp Movement, 1913–1920*. Lexington: University Press of Kentucky, 1972.

"Cluster Bombs in Afghanistan." *Human Rights Watch Backgrounder*, Oct. 2001. http://www.hrw.org/backgrounder/arms/cluster-bck1031.htm.

Conetta, Carl. "Operation Enduring Freedom: Why a Higher Rate of Civilian Bombing Casualties." Briefing Report #11: Project on Defense Alternatives, Jan. 24, 2002. http://www.comw.org/pda/0201oef.html.

Congressional Record. Washington, D.C., 1917.

"The Conquering Air Fleet." Editorial, *Washington Post*, July 14, 1917.

Cook, Howard W. "Georges Guynemer: The Winged Sword of France." *The Mentor* 6 (Nov. 6, 1918): 1–11.

Cooley, John K. *Unholy Wars: Afghanistan, America, and International Terrorism*. 2d ed. London: Pluto Press, 2000.

Cooper, John Milton, Jr. *The Warrior and the Priest: Woodrow Wilson and Theodore Roosevelt*. Cambridge: Harvard University Press, 1983.

Cornwell, Rupert. "US Begins Work on 'Super-Hard Bunker Buster' Nuclear Bombs," *The Independent* (London): 16.

"A Courteous Ambush in the Air." *Literary Digest* (May 13, 1916): 1382.

Crozier, W. P. "The Super-Airman," *New Republic* (Oct. 5, 1918): 278–80.

Davis, Burke. *War Bird: The Life and Times of Elliott White Springs*. Chapel Hill: University of North Carolina Press, 1987.

"Delays in Getting Both Airplanes and Aviators." *New York Times*, June 17, 1917, sec. 8, p. 4.

Der Derian, James. *Virtuous War: Mapping the Military-Industrial-Media-Entertainment Network*. Boulder, Colo.: Westview Press, 2001.

De Sieyes, Captain Jacques. "Aces of the Air." *National Geographic* 33 (Jan. 1918): 5–9.

Dewey, John. "The Social Possibilities of War." In *Characters and Events: Popular Essays in Social and Political Philosophy by John Dewey*, vol. 2, ed. Joseph Ratner, 551–60. New York: Henry Holt, 1929.

Dewey, Stoddard. "Americans Fly in France." *The Nation* (July 12, 1917): 33–34.

Douglas, Sholto. *Years of Combat*. London: Collins, 1963.

Driggs, Lawrence La Tourette. "Aces Among Aces." *National Geographic* (Jan. 1918): 568–80.

———. "Aces of Aviation." *Outlook* 118 (Jan. 30, 1918): 184–86.

———. "Heroes of Aviation." *Outlook* 118 (Jan. 16, 1918): 94–97.

———. "How Battles Are Fought in the Air." *Harper's Magazine* (Feb. 1918): 416–22.

———. "Plane Tales from the Skies." *Century Magazine* (April 1918): 849–57.

Dutton, Philip. "Moving Images? The Parliamentary Recruiting Committee's Poster Campaign, 1914–1916." *Imperial War Museum Review* 4 (1989): 43–58.

Ecksteins, Modris. *Rites of Spring: The Great War and the Birth of the Modern Age*. Boston: Houghton, Mifflin, 1989.

Ekirch, Arthur Alphonse. *The Civilian and the Military*. New York: Oxford Unversity Press, 1956.

———. *Progressivism in America: A Study of the Era from Theodore Roosevelt to Woodrow Wilson*. New York: New Viewpoints, 1974.

"Fliers Can Win War, Senators Are Told." *New York Times*, June 15, 1917, 4:4.

Foot, Paul. "An Enemy of Democracy." *The Guardian* (Oct. 2, 2001): 18.

Ford, Ford Madox. "Arms and the Mind." *Esquire* 94 (Dec. 1980): 78–79.

"Four Aces and a Joker." *The Independent Harper's Weekly* (Feb. 2, 1918). Unnumbered photo essay between pages 178 and 192.

Fox, Edward Lyell. "U.S. Leads in Air War." *Illustrated World* (July 1917): 667–72.

Franks, Norman L. R., Russell Guest, and Frank W. Bailey. *Bloody April . . . Black September*. London: Grub Street, 1995.

French Ministry of Foreign Affairs. *Germany's Violations of the Laws of War, 1914–1915*. Translated by J. O. P. Bland. New York: Putnam's Sons, 1915.

Freud, Sigmund. *The Standard Edition of the Complete Psychological Works of Sigmund Freud.* Vol. 14. Edited by James Strachey. London: The Hogarth Press and the Institute of Psycho-Analysis, 1957.

Freudenthal, Elspeth E. *The Aviation Business: From Kitty Hawk to Wall Street.* New York: Vanguard Press, 1940.

Fritzsche, Peter. *A Nation of Fliers: German Aviation and the Popular Imagination.* Cambridge: Harvard University Press, 1992.

Fussell, Paul. *The Great War and Modern Memory.* London: Oxford University Press, 1975.

"Gallant Feats in the Blue." *Literary Digest* (Nov. 16, 1918): 58, 62–63.

Genet, Edmond. *War Letters of Edmond Genet: The First American Aviator Killed Flying the Stars and Stripes.* Edited by Grace Ellery Channing. New York: Scribner's Sons, 1918.

Genthe, Charles V. *American War Narratives, 1914–1918: A Study and Bibliography.* New York: David Lewis, 1969.

"German Airmen Kill 97, Hurt 437 in London Raid." *New York Times,* June 14, 1917, sec. 4, p. 4.

"German Falcon Killed in Air Duel." *Literary Digest* (Nov. 10, 1917): 60–61.

Gilchrist, Norman S. "An Analysis of Causes of Breakdown in Flying." *British Medical Journal* (Oct. 12, 1918), 401.

Girouard, Mark. *The Return to Camelot: Chivalry and the English Gentleman.* London: Yale University Press, 1981.

Glines, Lt. Col. Carroll V., Jr. *The Compact History of the United States Air Force.* New York: Hawthorn Books, 1963.

Gordon, Dennis. *Lafayette Escadrille: Pilot Biographies.* Missoula, Mont.: Doughboy Historical Society, 1991.

"Great Fleet of U.S. Airships in 1918 Would Defeat Germany, Declares French Aviator." *Official Bulletin,* July 19, 1917, 10.

"Great U.S. Air Fleet Urged by Secretary Baker; May Turn Tide of War for Her Allies." *Official Bulletin,* June 18, 1917, 2.

Gruber, Carol S. *Mars and Minerva: World War I and the Uses of the Higher Learning in America.* Baton Rouge: Louisiana State University Press, 1975.

"Guynemer, Ace of the Aces." *Literary Digest* (Oct. 13, 1917): 52–57.

Hall, Bert. *"En l'Air!" Three Years on and above Three Fronts.* New York: New Library, 1918.

———. "Fast Fighting and Narrow Escapes in the Air. "*American Magazine* 86 (1918): 43–44, 102.

Hall, James Norman. *High Adventure.* Atlantic Monthly Company, 1917; reprint, New York: Arno Press, 1980.

"Hampering the Government." *New York Times,* July 10, 1917, 8:2.

"Harmsworth, Alfred Charles William, Viscount Northcliffe." *Dictionary of National Biography, 1922–30,* ed. J. R. H. Weaver, 397–403. London: Oxford University Press, 1937.

Harmsworth, Alfred Charles William, Viscount Northcliffe. *Lord Northcliffe's War Book, with Chapters on America at War.* 1916; enlarged ed., New York: George H. Doran, 1917.

Harries, Meirion, and Susie Harries. *The Last Days of Innocence: America at War, 1917–1918.* New York: Vintage Books, 1997.

Hawthorne, Nathaniel. "Chiefly about War Matters by a Peaceable Man." *Atlantic Monthly* (July 1862): 403–42. Reprinted in *Nathaniel Hawthorne: Miscellaneous Prose and Verse,* ed. Thomas Woodson, Claude M. Simpson, and L. Neal Smith. Columbus: Ohio State University Press, 1994.

"He Says with Aircraft We Can Win War." *New York Times,* June 14, 1917, 2:4.

Healy, Patrick, and Glen Johnson. "Opposition Advances Closer to Kandahar." *Boston Globe,* Dec. 2, 2001, A30.

Herold, Marc W. "A Dossier on Civilian Victims of United States' Aerial Bombing of Afghanistan: A Comprehensive Accounting," December 2001. http://www.cursor.org/stories/civilian_deaths.htm.

Hewett, Sgt. "An Aerial Soldier of Fortune: Sergeant Hewitt's Own Story of Life in the Lafayette Escadrille." *Air Travel* (Feb. 1918): 251–55, 286–87.

Hewlett, Beatrice. *Our Flying Men.* London: T. Beaty Hart, n.d.

Holley, I. B., Jr. *Ideas and Weapons.* Washington, D.C.: Office of Air Force History, 1983.

Holt, Tonie, and Valmai Holt. *Holts' Battlefield Guides: The Somme.* London: T. and V. Holt, n.d.

Hughes Report. *Report of Aircraft Inquiry (1918).* Washington, D.C.: U.S. Justice Department, 1918.

Huntington, Samuel P. *The Clash of Civilizations and the Remaking of World Order.* London: Touchstone Books, 1997.

Hurley, Alfred F. *Billy Mitchell: Crusader for Air Power.* 2d ed. Bloomington: Indiana University Press, 1975.

Hynes, Samuel. *A War Imagined: The First World War and English Culture*. New York: Collier Books, 1990.

Insall, A. J. *Observer: Memoirs of the R.F.C., 1915–1918*. London: Kimber, 1970.

Jablonski, Edward. *Warriors with Wings: The Story of the Lafayette Escadrille*. New York: Bobbs-Merrill, 1966.

Johnson, Alvin. *Pioneer's Progress: An Autobiography*. New York: Viking Press, 1952.

Jones, Ernst. *Life and Work of Sigmund Freud*. Vol. 2. New York: Basic Books, 1955.

Kaplan, Fred. "New Warfare: High-Tech US Arsenal Proves Its Worth." *Boston Globe*, Dec. 9, 2001, 34.

Kaplan, Sidney. "Social Engineers as Saviors: Effects of World War I on Some American Liberals." *Journal of the History of Ideas* 17 (1956): 347–69.

Keegan, John. *The Second World War*. New York: Viking Penguin, 1990.

Kelly, David. "Note on authorship of *Fighting the Flying Circus*." *WWI Aero*, no. 160 (May 1998).

Kennedy, David M. *Over Here: The First World War and American Society*. New York: Oxford University Press, 1980.

Kennett, Lee. *The First Air War: 1914–1918*. New York: Free Press, 1981.

Langer, William L. *Gas and Flames in World War I*. New York: Knopf, 1965.

Lawrence, Felicity. "A War Without Witnesses." *The Guardian* (Oct. 11, 2001): 21.

Lay, Bierne, Jr., and Sy Bartlett. *Twelve O'Clock High!* 1948; Reynoldsburg, Ohio: Buckeye Aviation Book Company, 1989.

LeMay, General Curtis, and MacKinlay Kantor. *Mission with LeMay: My Story*. Garden City, N.Y.: Doubleday, 1965.

Leonard, Thomas. *Above the Battle: War-Making in America from Appomattox to Versailles*. New York: Oxford University Press, 1978.

Levine, Isaac Don. *Mitchell: Pioneer of Air Power*. 1943; New York: Duell, Sloan and Pearce, 1958.

Lewis, Bernard. *What Went Wrong: Western Impact and Middle Eastern Response*. New York: Oxford University Press, 2001.

Lewis, Cecil. *Sagittarius Rising*. London: Peter Davies, 1936.

Lippmann, Walter. *Public Opinion*. 1922; New York: Free Press, 1965.

Longworth, Alice Roosevelt. *Crowded Hours*. New York: Scribner's Sons, 1933.

Marc, Lieutenant [Jean Beraud Villars]. *Notes d'un pilote disparu—1916–1917*. Paris: Hachette, 1918. Translated by S. J. Pincetl and Ernest Marchand as *Notes of a Lost Pilot*. Hamden, Conn.: Archon, 1975.

March, General Peyton C. *The Nation at War*. New York: Doubleday, Doran, 1932.

Marshall, Logan, Sir Gilbert Parker, Vance Thompson, and Philip Gibbs. *Thrilling Stories of the Great War on Land and Sea, in the Air, under the Water*. L. T. Myers, 1915.

Maurer, Maurer, ed. *U.S. Air Service in World War I*. Vol. 1. Maxwell Air Force Base, Ala.: Albert F. Simpson Historical Research Center, 1978–79.

McCaffery, Dan. *Billy Bishop: Canadian Hero*. Toronto: James Lorimer and Company, 1988.

McConnell, James M. "Flying for France: Further Experiences of an Aviator in the American Escadrille in France." *World's Work* 33 (March 1917): 505.

———. "Flying for France with the American Escadrille at Verdun." *World's Work* 33 (Nov. 1916).

———. *Flying for France with the American Escadrille at Verdun*. Garden City, N.Y.: Doubleday, Page, 1916.

McCudden, Major James T. B. *Flying Fury: Five Years in the Royal Flying Corps*. Edited by Stanley M. Ulanoff. 1918; Garden City, N.Y.: Doubleday, 1968.

Melville, Herman. "The *Temeraire*." In *Battle Pieces and Aspects of the War*. New York: Harper's, 1866. Reprinted in *Collected Poems*, ed. Howard P. Vincent, vol. 8 of *The Complete Works of Herman Melville*. Chicago: Packard and Co., 1947.

———. "A Utilitarian View of the Monitor's Fight." In *Battle Pieces and Aspects of the War*. New York: Harper's, 1866. Reprinted in *Collected Poems*, ed. Howard P. Vincent, vol. 8 of *The Complete Works of Herman Melville*, 39. Chicago: Packard and Co., 1947.

Middleton, James. "Manhunters of the Air." *World's Work* 34 (Sept. 1917): 513–21.

Miller, H. Crichton. "The Mother Complex." In *Functional Nerve Disease: An Epitome of War Experience for the Practitioner*, ed. H. Crichton Miller, 115–27. London: Henry Frowde, Hodder, and Stoughton, 1920.

Molter, Bennet A. *Knights of the Air*. New York: D. Appleton, 1918.

Morrison, Wilbur H. *Fortress Without a Roof: The Allied Bombing of the Third Reich*. New York: St. Martin's, 1986.

Morrow, John H., Jr. *The Great War in the Air: Military Aviation from 1909 to 1921*. Washington, D.C.: Smithsonian Institution Press, 1993.

Mosse, George L. *Fallen Soldiers: Reshaping the Memory of the World Wars*. New York: Oxford University Press, 1990.

"New Cavalry of the Sky." *Literary Digest* (Aug. 31, 1918): 74–82.

Newbolt, Henry. *The Book of the Happy Warrior*. London: Longmans, Green, 1917.

————. *Tales of the Great War*. London: Longmans, Green, 1916.

Newbolt, Margaret, ed. *The Later Life and Letters of Sir Henry Newbolt*. London: Faber and Faber, 1942.

Nordhoff, Charles, and James Norman Hall. *Falcons of France: A Tale of Youth and the Air*. Boston: Little, Brown, 1929.

Palmer, Frederick D. *Newton D. Baker: America at War*. 2 vols. New York: Dodd, Mead, 1941.

Paret, Peter, Beth Irwin Lewis, and Paul Paret. *Persuasive Images: Poster of War and Revolution from the Hoover Institution Archives*. Princeton, N.J.: Princeton University Press, 1992.

Park, Edwards. *Fighters: The World's Greatest Aces and Their Planes*. Charlottesville, Va: Thomasson-Grant, 1990.

Parry, Richard Lloyd. "A Village Is Destroyed and America Says It Never Happened." *The Independent* (Dec. 4, 2001): 1, 2.

Parson, Edwin C. *The Great Adventure: The Story of the Lafayette Escadrille*. New York: Doubleday, Doran, 1937.

Pelles, George. "Testing Airmen's Nerves." *Illustrated World* 26 (Oct. 1916): 279–82.

Pershing, John J. *My Experiences in the World War*. Vol. 1. New York: Frederick A. Stokes, 1931.

"Personal Glimpses: Quentin Roosevelt Buried Behind the German Lines." *Literary Digest* (Aug. 3, 1918): 52–54.

Peterson, Horace Cornelius. *Propaganda for War: The Campaign against American Neutrality, 1914–1917*. Norman: University of Oklahoma Press, 1939.

Pisano, Dominick A., Thomas J. Dietz, Joanne M. Gernstein, and Karl S. Schneide. *Memory and the Great War in the Air*. Washington, D.C.: National Air and Space Museum, 1992.

"President Ready to Back Up Aircraft Program." *Official Bulletin*, June 23, 1917, 1.

"Program for Building of Government Aircraft Stated." *Official Bulletin*, June 2, 1917, 16.

"'Put the Yankee Punch into the War!' by Airplane Route, Urges Gen. Squier, Director of the Nation's Aviation Service." *Official Bulletin*, June 15, 1917, 2.

"Quentin Roosevelt—An Incident." *The Outlook* (Aug. 28, 1918): 647.

Raleigh, Sir Walter, and H. A. Jones. *War in the Air: Being the Story of the Part Played in the Great War by the Royal Air Force.* 6 vols. Oxford University Press, 1922–37.

Rashid, Ahmed. Taliban: Militant Islam, Oil, and Fundamentalism in Central Asia. New Haven: Yale Nota Bene, 2000.

Read, James Morgan. *Atrocity Propaganda, 1914–1919.* New Haven: Yale University Press, 1941.

Read, William Ronald. Entries for August 1915 to November 1918. In *Complete Diaries.* British Imperial War Museum, Manuscript Archives. Catalogue no. 72/76/3.

Reif, Philip. *Freud: The Mind of the Moralist.* 3d ed. Chicago: University of Chicago Press, 1979.

Remarque, Eric Maria. *All Quiet on the Western Front.* Trans. A. W. Wheen. 1929; New York: Fawcett Crest, 1991.

Renehan, Edward J., Jr. *The Lion's Pride: Theodore Roosevelt and His Family in Peace and War.* New York: Oxford University Press, 1998.

Report of the Committee on Alleged German Outrages (Bryce Report). London: His Majesty's Stationery Office, 1915.

"Reversion to Primitive Emotions as a Result of the War." *Current Opinion* (Aug. 1918): 109–10.

Richthofen, Manfred Freiherr von. *The Red Air Fighter.* With preface and explanatory note by C. G. Grey. London: The "Aeroplane" and General Publishing Co., 1918. Reprint, New York: Arno Press, 1972.

Rickenbacker, Eddie V. *Fighting the Flying Circus.* Edited by Laurence la Tourette Driggs. New York: Lippincott, 1919.

———. *Rickenbacker: His Own Story.* 1967; Greenwich, Conn.: Fawcett Publications, 1969.

Ricks, Thomas E. "Bull's-Eye War: Pinpoint Bombing Shifts Role of GI Joe." *Washington Post,* Dec. 2, 2001, 1.

Robbins, James S. "Humanity of the Air War: Look How Far We Have Come." *National Review* (Oct. 19, 2001).

Robertson, Linda. "Air Wars: Civilized Violence at the Movies and Live from Baghdad." In *Bang Bang, Shoot Shoot: Film Television Guns,* ed. Murray Pomerance and John Sakeris, 133–46. Needham Heights, Mass.: Pearson Education, 2000.

———. "The Strange Case of the Missing Chinese Embassy." In *Closely Watched Brains*, ed. Murray Pomerance and John Sakeris. Boston: Pearson Education, 2001.

Rockwell, Paul Ayres. *War Letters of Kiffin Yates Rockwell: Foreign Legionnaire and Aviator France, 1914–1916*. Garden City, N.Y.: Country Life Press, 1925.

Roosevelt, Theodore. *The Great Adventure* (1918). In *The Works of Theodore Roosevelt*, vol. 21, ed. Hermann Hagedorn. New York: Scribner's, 1925.

———. "Lafayettes of the Air: Young Americans Who Are Flying for France." *Collier's*, July 29, 1916, 16.

———. *Letters*. Selected and edited by Elting E. Morrison. Cambridge: Harvard University Press, 1951–54.

Rossano, Geoffrey L., ed. *The Price of Honor: The World War I Letters of Naval Aviator Kenneth MacLeish*. Annapolis, Md.: Naval Institute Press, 1991.

Sanders, Michael L., and Philip M. Taylor. *British Propaganda of the First World War, 1914–1918*. London: Macmillan, 1982.

Sassoon, Siegfried. *Diaries, 1923–25*. Edited by Rupert Hart-Davis. Boston: Faber and Faber, 1985.

———. "The Poet as Hero." *Cambridge Magazine* 6 (Dec. 2, 1916): 199.

Save the Children Foundation. *State of the World's Mothers 2003: Protecting Women and Children in War and Conflict*. New York: Save the Children Foundation, May 2003.

Scarborough, Rowan. "Size of Force on Ground Key in Plan for Iraq War." *Washington Times*, April 26, 2002. http://washingtontimes.com. Article ID: 200204261019070025.

Schaffer, Ronald. *America in the Great War: The Rise of the War Welfare State*. Oxford: Oxford University Press, 1991.

Schmitt, Eric, and James Dao. "Use of Pinpoint Air Power Comes of Age in New War." *New York Times*, Dec. 24, 2001, 1.

Scott, Alan John Lance. *Sixty Squadron RAF: 1916–1919*. 1920; Novato, Calif.: Presidio Press, 1990.

Seeger, Alan. *Letters and Diaries of Alan Seeger*. New York: Scribner's Sons, 1917.

"Senate Insurgents Block Aviation Bill." *New York Times*, June 19, 1917, 1:1.

"Senator Owen Replies." *New York Times*, July 21, 1917, 3:4.

Shaw, W. B. "America's Young Flying Men." *Review of Reviews* 57 (June 1918): 602–3.

Sherry, Michael S. *The Rise of American Air Power: The Creation of Armageddon.* New Haven: Yale University Press, 1987.

Showalter, Elaine. *The Female Malady: Women, Madness, and English Culture, 1830–1980.* New York: Pantheon Books, 1985.

"$600,000,000 Asked for Huge Air Fleet." *New York Times,* June 16, 1917, 10:8.

Spick, Mike. *The Ace Factor: Air Combat and the Role of Situational Awareness.* Annapolis, Md.: Naval Institute Press, 1988.

Springs, Elliott White. *War Birds: Diary of an Unknown Aviator.* New York: George H. Doran, 1926.

Stokesbury, James L. *A Short History of World War I.* New York: Morrow, 1981.

"Strategic Moves of the War, September 27, 1917." *Scientific American* (October 6, 1917): 245.

Sullivan, Mark. *Our Times: The United States, 1900–1925.* New York: Scribner's Sons, 1926–35.

Tawney, R. H. "Some Reflections of a Soldier." *Nation* 20 (Oct. 21, 1916): 104.

Titler, Dale. *The Day the Red Baron Died.* New York: Ballantine Books, 1970.

Tompkins, Jane. *West of Everything: The Inner Life of Westerns.* Oxford: Oxford University Press, 1992.

Toulmin, H. A. *Air Service, American Expeditionary Force, 1918.* New York: D. Van Nostrand, 1927.

"Transfigured Youth." *The Outlook* (July 31, 1918): 511–12.

Tulasne, Major Joseph. "America's Part in the Allies' Mastery of the Air." *National Geographic* 33 (Jan. 1918): 1–5.

Tye, Lary. *Father of Spin: Edward L. Bernays and the Birth of Public Relations.* New York: Crown, 1998.

Tyson, Ann Scott. "U.S. Is Prevailing with Its Most Finely Tuned War." *Christian Science Monitor,* Nov. 21, 2001, 1.

"U.S. Acquires Aviation Field in France to Train Flyers Graduated in America." "Broad Plans Made to Train Our Airmen." *Official Bulletin,* June 4, 1917, 3.

U.S. News and World Report Staff. *Triumph without Victory: The Unreported History of the Persian Gulf War.* New York: Times Books, 1992.

Vander Meulen, Jacob A. *The Politics of Aircraft: Building an American Military Industry.* Lawrence: University of Kansas Press, 1991.

Vaughn, Stephen. *Holding Fast the Inner Lines: Democracy, Nationalism, and the Committee on Public Information.* Chapel Hill: University of North Carolina Press, 1980.

Walcott, Stuart. "Life Story of an American Airman in France." *National Geographic* (Jan. 1918): 86.

Ward, Larry Wayne. *The Motion Picture Goes to War: The U.S. Government Film Effort during World War I*. Ann Arbor, Mich.: UMI Research, 1985.

Wells, H. G. *The War That Will End War*. London: Frank and Cecil Palmer, 1914.

Wharton, Edith. *The Age of Innocence*. 1920; New York: Collier Books, 1992.

———. *House of Mirth*. New York: Scribner's Sons, 1905.

Whitehouse, Arthur "Arch" George Joseph. *Decisive Air Battles of the First World War*. New York: Duell, Sloan, and Pierce, 1963.

———. *Heroes of the Sunlit Sky*. New York: Curtis Books, 1967.

———. *Legion of the Lafayette*. Garden City, N.Y.: Doubleday, 1962.

"Who Make the Best Aviators?" *Current Opinion* (Aug. 1918): 107, 109, 197.

Wilson, Woodrow. *The Papers of Woodrow Wilson*. Edited by Arthur S. Link et al. Princeton, N.J.: Princeton University Press, 1966–94.

Winter, Jay. *Sites of Memory, Sites of Mourning: The Great War in European Cultural History*. New York: Cambridge University Press, 1995.

Wohl, Robert. *A Passion for Wings: Aviation and the Western Imagination, 1908–1918*. New Haven: Yale University Press, 1994.

Younghusband, Major-General Sir George John. *A Soldier's Memories in Peace and War*. London: H. Jenkins, 1917.

Zieger, Robert H. *America's Great War: World War I and the American Experience*. New York: Rowman and Littlefield, 2002.

Films

Adolphi, John G., dir. *The Woman the Germans Shot*. With Julia Arthur, Creighton Hale, and Paul Panzer. Produced by John L. Plunkitt and Frank J. Carroll. Select Pictures Corp., Dec. 1918. 6 reels.

DeMille, Cecil B., dir. *The Little American*. With Mary Pickford, Jack Holt, Raymond Hatton, Hobart Bosworth, and Ben Alexander. Artcraft Pictures, 1917. 6 reels.

Dintenfass, Mark M., dir. *My Four Years in Germany*. With William Nigh, Halbert Brown, Louis Dean, Earl Schenck, and Karl Dane. Mark M. Dintenfass Productions. My Four Years in Germany Co., March 1918; First National Exhibitors Circuit, April 1918. 10 reels.

Gavin, John. *Martyrdom of Nurse Cavell*. With Vera Pearce. Dominion Exclusives, Ltd., Australia, 1916. 4 reels.

Griffith, D. W., dir. *Hearts of the World*. With Lillian Gish, Robert Harron, and Dorothy Gish. D. W. Griffith Productions, March 1918. 12 reels.

Irving, George, dir. *To Hell with the Kaiser*. With Lawrence Grant, Olive Tell, Earl Schenck, Karl Dane, and May McAvoy. Screen Classics, Inc.–Metro Pictures Corp., 1918. 7 reels.

McKay, Winsor, illustrator. *Sinking of the Lusitania*. Jewel Productions, Inc., 1918.

Perrett, Leonce, with Charles A. Taylor, dir. *Lest We Forget*. With Rita Jolivet and Hamilton Revelle. Metro Pictures Corp., Feb. 1918. 8 reels.

Rupert, Julian, dir. *The Kaiser, the Beast of Berlin*. With Joseph Girard, Lon Chaney, and Elmo Lincoln. Renowned Pictures Corporation-Jewel Productions, Inc., March 1918. 7 reels.

Index

Ace, image of, xii, xv, xvii, xviii, 92,
95, 98, 100–101, 111, 149,
221–22, 227, 230, 247, 262, 264,
280, 301, 317, 331m 363, 368,
372, 386, 388, 400; American
idealization of, 361, 365, 370,
374, 393, 394, 395, 396, 397,
407. *See also* Ace of aces;
Symbolism of WWI: air war
Ace of aces, 231, 233, 234, 235, 240,
392; duel in the sky as epitomizing, 235–37, 240, 247, 253, 398,
400, 406; "free lance" or chivalrous youth, 234, 241–42, 245–
46, 248; "lone wolf" or self-made
man, 234, 249, 254, 258–59,
262, 298, 361, 372. *See also*
Rickenbacker, Eddie
Ace system, 92, 97, 100, 104, 107,
220, 258, 276, 277, 289, 371,
372, 373, 382–83. *See also*
Springs, Elliot White: *War Birds*
Aerial armada: U.S. plan for, vii, ix,
xiii, 18, 23, 29, 31–32, 34, 36,

42, 33–45, 46. *See also* Military
aircraft design and production,
WWI, U.S.
Aircraft design and production, U.S.
See Aircraft Production Board;
Bolling Commission; Military
aircraft design and production,
WWI, U.S.
Aircraft Production Board, 12, 14,
15, 17, 19
Airplane Trust, 33
Air superiority: German, xlvii, 214,
341, 362, 368; U.S. dream of,
xiii, 365
Air supremacy, 8, 9, 32; German,
102; Allied, 226; as semantic
vacuum, 9, 37; *See also* Air
superiority
Al-Qaeda, 418–19, 421
American exceptionalism: air power
an example of, xii, 35, 37, 193;
and conscription, 58, 59. *See also*
Selective Service
Anderson, Graeme H., 316

473